**NOLO** ~~Products & Services~~

 *Books & Software*

Get in-depth information. Nolo publishes hundreds of great books and software programs for consumers and business owners. Order a copy—or download an ebook version instantly—at Nolo.com.

 *Legal Encyclopedia*

Free at Nolo.com. Here are more than 1,400 free articles and answers to common questions about everyday legal issues including wills, bankruptcy, small business formation, divorce, patents, employment and much more.

 *Plain-English Legal Dictionary*

Free at Nolo.com. Stumped by jargon? Look it up in America's most up-to-date source for definitions of legal terms.

 *Online Legal Documents*

Create documents at your computer. Go to Nolo.com to make a will or living trust, form an LLC or corporation or obtain a trademark or provisional patent. For simpler matters, download one of our hundreds of high-quality legal forms, including bills of sale, promissory notes, nondisclosure agreements and many more.

 *Lawyer Directory*

Find an attorney at Nolo.com. Nolo's consumer-friendly lawyer directory provides in-depth profiles of lawyers all over America. From fees and experience to legal philosophy, education and special expertise, you'll find all the information you need to pick the right lawyer. Every lawyer listed has pledged to work diligently and respectfully with clients.

 *Free Legal Updates*

Keep up to date. Check for free updates at Nolo.com. Under "Products," find this book and click "Legal Updates." You can also sign up for our free e-newsletters at Nolo.com/newsletters.

8th edition

The Guardianship Book for California

How to Become a Child's Legal Guardian

Attorneys David Brown & Emily Doskow

Eighth Edition	FEBRUARY 2011
Editor	EMILY DOSKOW
Cover Design	SUSAN PUTNEY
Production	MARGARET LIVINGSTON
Proofreader	ROBERT WELLS
Index	THÉRÈSE SHERE
Printing	DELTA PRINTING SOLUTIONS, INC.

Brown, David Wayne, 1949-
   The guardianship book for California : how to become a child's legal guardian / David Brown and Emily Doskow. -- 8th ed.
      p. cm.
   Includes index.
   Summary: "Provides an overview of legal guardianship of minors, plus includes all of the forms and instructions needed to become a legal guardian in California. All forms and statutes are updated in the 8th edition"--Provided by publisher.
   ISBN-13: 978-1-4133-1360-4 (pbk.)
   ISBN-10: 1-4133-1360-4 (pbk.)
   ISBN-13: 978-1-4133-1339-0 (ebook)
   ISBN-10: 1-4133-1339-6 (ebook)
   1. Guardian and ward--California--Popular works. I. Doskow, Emily. II. Title.
   KFC134.B76 2011
   346.79401'8--dc22
                     2010038388

Please note

We believe accurate, plain-English legal information should help you solve many of your own legal problems. But this text is not a substitute for personalized advice from a knowledgeable lawyer. If you want the help of a trained professional—and we'll always point out situations in which we think that's a good idea—consult an attorney licensed to practice in your state.

Dedications

To my wonderful daughters, Laura and Kate Brown, and to their mother, Nancy Brown.
—DWB

Acknowledgments

The authors extend their thanks to the many people who helped make this book possible:

Phil Campbell, for his careful review and many helpful suggestions for improving the fifth edition. Robert Kosloff, for reviewing and updating the sixth edition.

Paul Muñiz, Deputy County Counsel, Contra Costa County, for his generous gift of time and expertise.

Attorneys Carolyn M. Farren and John P. Kelley (of Greene, Kelley & Tobriner in San Francisco), for sharing their knowledge and experience.

Attorney Virginia Palmer (of Fitzgerald, Abbott & Beardsley in Oakland), for her insightful overview of the guardianship process.

Attorney Gary L. Motsenbocker (of Cone & Motsenbocker in Fresno) and John Boley, Santa Clara County Probate Court Investigator, for reviewing the manuscript and giving excellent suggestions.

Frank Zagone, for his helpful information and for the many resources he suggested.

Legal Services for Children, Inc., and director Christopher Wu, for providing valuable information.

Paralegal Irene M. Zupko (of Paralegal Assistance Unlimited in Fresno), for her suggestions and practical experience.

The many people whose contributions enriched this book, including attorney Michael Surowiec, attorney Jack McElroy, Solano County Superior Court Investigator Michael E. Schmidt, and principal Carol Howell.

Tony Mancuso, for his expertise in providing converted computer software.

Table of Contents

5 Preparing Forms to File for a Guardianship

6 Filing and Serving the Guardianship Papers

7 Temporary Guardianships of a Minor's Person

8 The Guardianship Investigation

9 The Hearing: Preparing, Attending, and What to Do Afterward

10 Guardianship of a Minor's Estate

11 Now That You're a Guardian: Rights and Responsibilities

12 Ending the Guardianship

13 Lawyers and Legal Research

A Appendix A: Glossary of Guardianship Terms

B Appendix B: Forms for Informal Guardianship Situations

Caregiver's Authorization Affidavit

Guardianship Authorization Form

C Appendix C: Forms for Obtaining a Court-Ordered Guardianship

Declaration

Additional Page: Attach to Judicial Council Form or Other Court Paper

Request for Dismissal

Request to Waive Court Fees

Order for Court Fee Waiver

Guardianship Notification Worksheet

Attachment 10 to Petition for Appointment of Guardian of Minor

Consent of Proposed Guardian, Nomination of Guardian, and Consent to
   Appointment of Guardian and Waiver of Notice

Petition for Appointment of Guardian of Minor

Guardianship Petition—Child Information Attachment

Declaration Under Uniform Child Custody Jurisdiction and Enforcement Act
   (UCCJEA)

Notice of Hearing—Guardianship or Conservatorship

Order Dispensing With Notice—Guardianship or Conservatorship

Order Appointing Guardian of Minor

Letters of Guardianship

Confidential Guardian Screening Form

Duties of Guardian and Acknowledgment of Receipt

Index

Introduction:
An Overview of Guardianships

A legal guardianship is created when a court appoints an adult to be responsible for a minor who isn't that adult's child (although they may be related). The adult steps into a parenting role, becoming legally responsible for taking care of the minor's physical needs, managing the minor's assets, or both.

How This Book Can Help You

This book gives helpful information about legal guardianships of minors in California. We provide forms and instructions you can use to obtain a guardianship without a lawyer's help. We also alert you to some situations where a lawyer's help is recommended, and give you tips on finding and dealing with lawyers.

The Guardianship Book for California is specifically directed to the adult who is planning to be the guardian of a minor. However, if you are a minor's parent, or an adult friend or relative who wants to designate someone else as the minor's legal guardian, you can easily modify the instructions in this book to fit your situation. (If you are a minor who is at least 12 years old, you also can petition to have a guardian appointed for you. Minors may also want to contact an organization that gives information, referrals, and legal assistance to children—confidentially and generally free of charge. See "Resources for Minors" in Chapter 13.)

If you're wondering whether to seek a legal guardianship, this book can help you decide. In some situations, a legal guardianship may not be desirable or practical, or there may be easier ways to handle the situation. For example, where a stepparent is taking care of a minor, adoption or a legal guardianship might not be necessary, but some documentation is still advisable.

We discuss alternatives to a legal guardianship, and provide you with forms you'll need and instructions for completing them. We give you practical information on dealing with schools, medical facilities, insurance companies, Social Security, and U.S. passport offices.

In addition, we discuss the legal responsibilities of a guardian and list things you should consider in order to figure out whether you want to accept the responsibilities and duties of a legal guardian.

The actual process of getting a guardianship is not difficult. It will require that the proposed guardian and the minor make at least one appearance in court. In most situations, this is entirely routine, and you will have no difficulty as long as you follow the detailed instructions in this book. The only other equipment you'll need is patience—for completing the required forms and dealing with the legal bureaucracy.

Legal Citations

Throughout the book you will encounter references to California law, called legal "citations." If you are interested in doing legal research, you can look up these citations. (Legal research is discussed in more detail in Chapter 13.)

Abbreviation	Legal Reference
CC	Civil Code
CCP	Code of Civil Procedure
CRC	California Rules of Court
EC	Education Code
FC	Family Code
PC	Probate Code
W&I	Welfare & Institutions Code
USC	United States Code

What This Book Does Not Cover

While this book provides all the help most people will need to obtain a legal guardianship, it does not cover every possible situation. There are some situations where you should consult a lawyer. Some examples are listed here.

- If anyone objects to (contests) the guardianship, or if anyone tries to have you removed after you are named guardian, hire a lawyer. These are unusual occurrences, but sometimes they do happen.

- If you are seeking a guardianship to manage substantial assets inherited by a minor—usually $5,000 or more—a lawyer can help with the special requirements. Although we provide all the information and forms to obtain the guardianship, we do not give step-by-step instructions on how to manage the minor's assets, arrange to have the estate appraised, prepare and file a required Inventory and Appraisal, or prepare and file periodic accountings with the court after the guardianship is established. Normally the help of a legal professional and perhaps an accountant is in order here—and this help can be paid for out of the minor's estate. (See Chapter 10.)

- If you want to become guardian of a minor who lives in California, but you live in another state, you'll need help from a lawyer.

- If there are any unresolved legal proceedings affecting the minor, you'll need to talk to a lawyer. This includes adoption, divorce, custody, juvenile charges against the minor, or other proceedings that have not been finally settled by a court.

- If you want to become guardian of a minor who is physically or emotionally disabled, such as a minor on leave from the California Department of Mental Health or the State Department of Developmental Services, an attorney's help is advisable, to determine whether the minor can be protected by additional means such as establishing a "special needs trust."

- If you want to become guardian of a minor who is "gravely disabled" because of a mental disorder or chronic alcoholism, a special type of mental health conservatorship must be established—and a lawyer will have to help you with that.

- If the minor is a Native American (American Indian), the case will be subject to special federal laws. In this area, you will need the help of an attorney.

What Is a Guardianship?

A guardianship is not a termination of parental rights. It is simply a custody order giving someone other than a parent legal custody of a minor. All minors must have an adult who is responsible for them. This makes sense—after all, you can't expect a six-year-old to register for school, open a checking account, pay bills, or apply for Social Security benefits or public assistance. A court-ordered guardianship is simply legal recognition that an adult has responsibility for taking care of the physical needs of a minor, or for handling the minor's assets.

Guardianships Require Court Proceedings

There are a couple of fairly common mistaken assumptions about guardianships. For example, some people think that a guardianship can be established informally with just an agreement between the child's parent(s) and the person they want to act as guardian. This isn't true—the only way that you can become a legal guardian is through a court order. There are some circumstances where a simple authorization will be enough, though. See "Is a Guardianship Really Necessary?" below.

The other common mistake people make is thinking that when parents name a guardian for their children in a will, that person automatically becomes the guardian if the parent dies. In fact, even if you are named as guardian in a deceased parent's will, you still have to file a request to be named guardian and ask a court to confirm the parent's wishes.

So, don't think that you can rely on a parent's written nomination. You will need a court's approval for a legal guardianship.

When you are appointed guardian of a minor, you must serve as guardian until you're legally released by the court from your duties. This could be when the minor reaches age 18, or earlier if the court ends the guardianship or your role as guardian—for example, if it is determined that you are no longer an appropriate guardian. (See Chapter 12 for information on when and how guardianships are ended.)

While at first it may seem that the biggest burden of becoming a guardian is entering into a long-term relationship with a California court, in reality you typically have little contact with the court after the guardianship is in place. The biggest burden of becoming a guardian, at least when you are guardian only of the minor's person, is the initial appointment process. After that, you have only annual reports to file to keep the court informed of the minor's status.

If you are guardian of a minor's estate (handling the minor's assets), you must have the minor's assets appraised and file a document listing details of what the minor owns, and you must periodically file detailed financial statements. But if you are just going to be guardian of the minor's person (having physical custody of the minor but not managing substantial property the minor owns), you probably will not have any contact with the court after you are appointed guardian.

A guardianship is not necessary for an emancipated minor. In California, this is someone under 18 who has achieved legal adult status by marriage, military service, or court order (FC § 7002). A guardian cannot be appointed for a minor's person if the minor is married or has been divorced, although a guardian could be appointed for such a minor's estate. If a minor's marriage has been annulled, a guardian could be appointed for his person, estate, or both. (See below for more information on the difference between guardianship of a person and an estate.)

Guardianships, Conservatorships, and Adoptions

Guardianships are often confused with conservatorships, which are similar proceedings with the important difference that they involve adults, not minors. If you have a relative or know another adult who needs significant care, a conservatorship, not a guardianship, would be the appropriate procedure. Adoption is a very different type of legal proceeding. The most important difference between a guardianship and an adoption is that an adoption creates a permanent parent-child relationship, while a guardianship does not.

A guardianship is a temporary relationship that ends when a minor reaches adulthood, if not before. It also doesn't change the relationship between the minor and the minor's legal parents, who are still required to support the child. In addition, the child will still inherit from the natural parents. A guardianship can be limited to either the minor's person or the minor's estate, but an adoption creates a parent-child relationship that means the adopting parent is responsible for every aspect of the child's well-being. That relationship is permanent—once a child is adopted, the parent-child relationship can't be ended except in very unusual circumstances.

Two Types of Guardianships

In California there are two types of legal guardianships for minors: guardianship of the person and guardianship of the estate (property such as money, stocks, and real estate). An adult can be named guardian of a minor's person, estate, or both. The general term "guardianship" is commonly used to cover both types.

Guardianship of a Minor's Person

A guardian of the minor's person has legal custody of the minor and is responsible for taking care of the child's well-being. The guardian would provide food, shelter, and health care and take charge of the minor's growth and development. Generally, the guardian has the same right as the parent to consent to or require medical treatment for the minor. In most instances, the minor is or will be living with the proposed guardian, who must have an established permanent residence for the minor in California. A guardianship is not affected if the minor attends and lives at a boarding school or camp for a substantial part of the year.

> **TIP**
>
> **A guardian of the minor's person usually may handle relatively small financial matters on behalf of the minor.** For example, a guardian may handle income of no more than $300 per month, plus public assistance benefits, without having to also become guardian of the minor's estate. The guardian of a minor's person can receive benefits for which the minor qualifies, like welfare or Social Security, unless the agency dispensing benefits specifically requires a guardianship of the minor's estate. Letters of Guardianship of the Person, discussed later, often will specifically say that the guardian does not have the authority to take possession of property.

Guardianship of a Minor's Estate

A guardianship of the minor's estate is necessary if the minor has substantial assets, such as through an inheritance.

Generally, you need a guardianship of the minor's estate to handle an inheritance even if you are the minor's parent. However, a minor's parent may hold the child's property without obtaining a guardianship of the estate if the minor's property is worth less than $5,000 (PC §§ 3400–3402), or if the Uniform Transfers to Minors Act (UTMA) or a trust is used.

If you are going to be handling relatively complicated or extensive financial matters for a minor, you will probably need to become the guardian of the minor's estate. A guardianship of a minor's estate may be needed in the following circumstances:

- The minor has, or is going to receive through a gift or inheritance, assets worth over $5,000. (There are ways to avoid this type of situation, such as by using the Uniform Transfers to Minors Act (UTMA). See below.)

- The minor is the named beneficiary of insurance money or other assets, and estate planning measures were not taken.

- The minor is entitled to receive financial benefits, and the agency dispensing benefits specifically requires guardianship of the minor's estate.

- You were named guardian of the minor's estate in a will, and the person who wrote the will dies.

- A court determines that a guardianship of the minor's estate is necessary.

If the minor is living with you and you plan to apply for welfare or other public assistance benefits, you will need to become guardian of the minor's person only unless the agency requires otherwise.

If either or both of the minor's parents is alive, the minor's money may not be used to support the child—the parents are still responsible for support unless a court orders otherwise. If the parents are deceased or unable to support the child, though, the guardian is required by law to use the estate money and other assets to provide "comfortable and suitable support, maintenance, and education" for the minor as

well as for "those legally entitled to support, maintenance, or education" from the minor (PC § 2420). The guardian must preserve the assets of the estate for the minor (PC § 2401). This means that the court wants to ensure that the guardian handles the minor's assets wisely, and doesn't steal any money.

> **! CAUTION**
> **Once you've established a guardianship of a minor's estate, you'll need to get professional help to maintain the guardianship.** This book instructs you on how to become the guardian of a minor's estate. However, once you are appointed guardian, you may need to be bonded by a surety company, and to have the minor's property appraised by a probate referee. You will need to file a document with the court itemizing the estate's property and appraisal values, file periodic detailed accountings with the court, and possibly attend several court hearings. You will need to hire a legal professional if you become the guardian of a minor's estate, as the details are beyond the scope of this book. (Chapter 10 has more about what's required for guardianship of a minor's estate. And Chapter 13 has information about finding and dealing with lawyers.)

Choosing the Type of Guardianship You Need

Depending on your situation, you may need a guardianship of the minor's person, estate, or both. To help you determine which, refer to the accompanying box, and consider the following examples.

EXAMPLE 1:

When Fred is five years old, his mother is unable to take care of him because of personal problems, and Fred's father is dead. Fred's Aunt Ethel wants to take care of him but she is financially strapped. Aunt

Seeking Guardianship of a Minor's Person, Estate, or Both

You will need a guardianship of the minor's person if:

- The minor is or will be living with you for an extended time period and you believe it is best that you (rather than a parent) have legal custody.

- You will be receiving benefits on behalf of the minor, and the agency giving the benefits requires guardianship of the minor's person, but does not require you to be guardian of the estate.

- Your health insurance plan requires a legal guardianship before it will cover the minor.

- You were named guardian of a minor's person in a deceased person's will, and you intend to have the minor live with you or to care for her needs.

You will need a guardianship of the minor's estate if:

- You were named guardian of a minor's estate in a deceased person's will, there were significant assets left to the minor, and you intend to administer those assets for the minor.

- You are the person responsible for managing a minor's business affairs, and will receive insurance benefits or an inheritance on behalf of the minor (if the agency or company giving the benefits requires guardianship of the minor's estate).

- The minor is entitled to receive benefits, and the agency giving them requires guardianship of the minor's estate.

- The minor is entitled to receive property for which title is required (such as real estate or a vehicle).

- You will be managing major assets or property for a minor.

You will need a guardianship of both the minor's person and estate if:

- You were named guardian of a minor's person and estate in a deceased person's will, substantial assets were left to the minor, and you are willing to accept the responsibility of being a guardian.

- Any of the circumstances listed above require a guardianship of the person and any of the above requirements also require a guardianship of the estate.

Ethel applies for welfare, but is told that in her county she must become Fred's legal guardian before benefits will be paid. As the welfare agency in her county does not require guardianship of the estate, Aunt Ethel obtains a guardianship of Fred's person, which enables her to receive Fred's benefits. The county requires that she keep records of how money is spent on Fred's behalf, but the record-keeping requirement is minimal.

EXAMPLE 2:

Jaime is 15 when his mother, Ellen, decides to go into the military. She discovers that they will not accept her if she has custody of her son. Jaime's father is in jail and has never supported or visited his son. Ellen asks her parents to take care of Jaime while she is in the service, which will probably be at least three years. To deal with the military's "no custody" rule and because it's a good idea anyway, she asks her parents to become Jaime's legal guardians. They obtain guardianship of Jaime's person. (In some cases, the caregivers' affidavit will be accepted by the military instead of a court guardianship. Check with your local JAG officer.)

EXAMPLE 3:

Alice is four years old when her father dies, leaving her as the beneficiary of his life insurance policy. The insurance company refuses to turn the benefits over to her mother, with whom Alice continues to live, because the minor, not the mother, was named as the beneficiary. Alice's mother obtains a guardianship of her daughter's estate only—as a parent she is already legally responsible for Alice's physical well-being. (This problem could have been avoided if Alice's father had filled out the insurance policy differently or if Alice's parents had prepared proper estate planning documents before his death.)

EXAMPLE 4:

Bob's parents both die suddenly when he is eight, leaving a request in their will that Bob's maternal grandparents be appointed guardians of both his person and estate. They also leave Bob all their property, which includes equity in a house, securities, a car, and other personal property. The grandparents obtain guardianship of both Bob's person and estate so they can manage his finances and have legal custody of him. It also enables them to add Bob to their health insurance policy and to avoid hassles when they travel out of the country. (See the discussion of traveling with a minor in Chapter 2.)

Is a Guardianship Really Necessary?

Before you jump to the conclusion that a guardianship is a must for your situation, read this section carefully. Many times, formal guardianships are necessary, but in other situations, there are alternatives.

Do You Need a Guardianship of a Minor's Person?

It is common for an agency "official" to insist that a guardianship of a minor's person is needed. However, it's quite possible that a signed authorization form will do just fine. If someone says you must obtain a guardianship of a minor's person, consider these three rules:

Rule 1. If the minor will be in danger unless you get a legal guardianship, take immediate action to protect the minor. For example, a parent who previously neglected a child might threaten to remove that child from your care and put the child in a dangerous situation.

> **TIP**
> **If you don't have a guardianship, you still can take action.** If you aren't sure whether the minor would be in danger if you don't get a legal guardianship, you can call a local agency for more information and possible intervention. Check the phone book under your county's agencies for "Children's Emergency Services," "Children's Protective Services," "Social Services," or a similar heading. This book does not cover situations in which a minor is in danger of abuse, neglect, or other harm, which would require immediate action.

Rule 2. If you plan to take care of a minor for an extended (perhaps indefinite) time, it makes good sense to get a guardianship of the minor's person—even if you are not absolutely required to do so.

Rule 3. If you were named guardian of a minor's person in his deceased parent's will, the minor has no surviving parent, and you plan to take care of him, you will need to obtain a formal legal guardianship.

You probably won't need a guardianship of the minor's person if:

- You only plan to take care of a minor for a short time—up to three months.
- You live in a community where you are well known and there is general support for informal solutions to problems, instead of official court-ordered resolutions.
- You don't anticipate having contact with agencies and institutions other than schools on behalf of the minor. For example, you might temporarily be caring for a minor who is already enrolled in school, has a doctor, is covered by medical insurance, and whose parents are sending money to support their child.

Read Chapter 2 carefully before proceeding with a legal guardianship. Chapter 2 discusses alternatives to getting a legal guardianship of a minor's person.

Do You Need a Guardianship of a Minor's Estate?

A guardianship of a minor's estate involves a lot of extra work for the guardian, such as having property appraised, maintaining financial records, and preparing periodic accountings for the court. Unfortunately, if a guardianship of a minor's estate is required—for example, by an insurance company, court, or a deceased person's will—there probably isn't a way around it.

Just to make sure that you really need a guardianship of a minor's estate, consider these rules:

Rule 1. A parent can receive money or property on behalf of his child as long as the child's assets will not exceed $5,000.

To receive the assets, the parent must sign a document swearing that the minor's total estate does not exceed $5,000—including the money or property that is to be received. Once the parent provides this document to the person delivering the money or property, the funds can be released to be held in trust until the minor reaches age 18 (PC § 3401). This book does not tell you how to handle this procedure.

Rule 2. An adult can transfer money or property to a minor without court approval using the Uniform Transfers to Minors Act, as long as the value of the minor's property is less than $10,000 (PC §§ 3900–3925).

A simple document can be prepared and signed to transfer the property. We do not cover that procedure in this book.

Rule 3. If the minor is in the position of acquiring substantial assets not covered in Rule 1 or Rule 2 above, you will need a legal guardianship of the minor's estate. If the minor's assets consist solely of money and the amount is under $20,000, the court has discretion to terminate the guardianship of the estate with specific conditions about how the money is to be held, such as a blocked account (PC § 3412). Note that "substantial assets" here does not include public assistance benefits or other relatively small sums of money—in these instances only a guardianship of a minor's person is required.

Using Estate Planning to Avoid Guardianship of a Minor's Estate

Death is a difficult topic in our culture. Many people shut down when the subject of death is raised, preferring the head-in-the-sand technique of avoidance to facing the reality of their own or others' mortality. We bring up the subject because many times, guardianships of a minor's estate could be avoided or simplified with just a little bit of advance planning. "Estate planning" is the term for designating to whom and how property is to be transferred before and after death. Estate planning covers many methods of dealing with assets, including wills, trusts, and gifts. Estate planning helps eliminate the guesswork in distributing property, allows things to be much simpler and less stressful for the survivors, and may also allow for huge savings in taxes and legal costs. There are a variety of estate planning devices that allow an adult to leave assets to minors with little or no use of the probate courts.

RESOURCE

You can find valuable information and step-by-step instructions on estate planning in *Plan Your Estate,* by Denis Clifford (Nolo). To make a will, you can use *Quicken WillMaker Plus* Software (Nolo) or *Nolo's Simple Will Book,* by Denis Clifford. All these resources also give guidance and information on minors and guardians.

When a Minor's Parents Need Guardianship of Their Child's Estate

It may seem strange that parents would need to obtain a guardianship of their own child's estate when their child lives with them. This situation usually arises when a minor inherits money or other property without adequate estate planning. Unfortunately, in these instances, the parents generally don't have any alternative to going to court to obtain a legal guardianship of their child's estate.

EXAMPLE 1:

Karen White and Jeff Black are not married, and they live together with their three young children. Karen dies suddenly, leaving the proceeds of her life insurance policy and all of her assets—which are substantial—to their three children. Jeff has not worked for many years, because he has been staying home taking care of the children, and he has very few assets of his own. Jeff goes to court and becomes guardian of his children's estates, so that he may manage the life insurance proceeds and assets for them. He does not need to obtain guardianship of their persons, since he is a parent and they already live with him.

Jeff needs some job training to go back to work, but he wants to spend a few months at home before starting the training, taking care of the kids following their mother's death. With the help of a lawyer, Jeff makes a motion asking for use of the estate for the support of his children. The judge allows Jeff to use funds from his children's estates to fully support his three children for six months, when he plans to return to the work force. After the six months, Jeff will continue to manage the assets of his children's estates, but he will financially support his children.

EXAMPLE 2:

The Stones live next door to an elderly widower who is extremely fond of their small daughter. When the widower dies, he leaves his house to five-year-old Alice Stone. Alice's parents, Jill and Mike, go to court and obtain guardianship of their daughter's estate so that the asset can be transferred to Alice (via the guardianship of Alice's estate). Both Jill and Mike work full-time and have no problem supporting their daughter. They plan to sell the house Alice inherited and invest the money for Alice's use when she reaches age 18. If Jill and Mike were to make a motion in court asking to use the money for the support of their child, this request would not be granted because they are already able to support her financially.

Should You Be the Guardian?

A guardianship is an ongoing legal responsibility that can last until the minor reaches age 18. You should thoroughly consider all the consequences of being a guardian before you decide to become one. Chapters 10 and 11 give more details about the guardian's responsibilities, but here is the gist of it.

As guardian of a minor's person, you basically assume the role of the minor's parent. This is a responsibility that is never easy, even in the best of times. Often the guardian will be stepping into a family situation that is already laden with problems—perhaps taking on a child who is difficult to handle. While being a guardian can be rewarding, it can be a real source of stress. It can also be a time-consuming job.

As guardian of a minor's estate, you must commit yourself to the time and planning necessary to handle the minor's assets wisely. You must have a noncash estate appraised by a probate referee, file documents with the court itemizing the estate and its appraised value, and complete periodic written financial accountings for the court. You must be "bondable"—able to get surety insurance. You must have good credit and assets of your own in order to qualify for this type of insurance. You must also go to court to get permission for any but the most conservative financial transactions.

Do You Want to Be the Guardian?

An obvious but extremely important question to ask yourself before you take any steps to establish a guardianship is: Do you want to be the guardian?

Of course, your feelings about your potential role as a guardian relate to the circumstances. In a real emergency where everyone involved agrees, such as when a close relative dies or can't take care of her children, it may be easy to agree to be a guardian. On the other hand, if there are bad feelings between family members or the minor has not been cared for properly (for example, perhaps the child has been abandoned or abused) and is hostile, uncommunicative, or emotionally disturbed, you may think twice before going ahead. And you will definitely want to do some additional soul-searching if someone else (perhaps even a natural parent) seems determined to go to court to challenge your petition to be named guardian.

It is sensible to consider your options carefully before going through with the guardianship procedure.

Are You an Appropriate Choice for Guardian of a Minor's Person?

There are no hard and fast rules on who is appropriate to be a guardian. It is up to the discretion of the judge or court commissioner, who will weigh many factors in making a decision. While there is an order of preference for appointing a guardian of a minor's person (see the box below), this system is very flexible, especially if neither parent is responsible for caring for the minor—a common situation in which a guardianship is needed. Usually, there's no debate about who will be the guardian, as there is usually only one person willing and able to assume the role.

The most important consideration in naming a guardian is what is in the child's interest. A judge will consider the love and emotional ties between you and the minor and your ability to "parent" the minor. The judge will also look at practical considerations such as your health and your ability to provide the minor with food, shelter, clothing, and medical care. Any established school, community, and religious ties also will be considered. If you have already taken care of the child for some time,

Deciding Whether You Want to Be a Guardian

- Do you want the ongoing responsibilities of a legal guardianship—including potential liability for the minor's actions? Chapter 11 gives a thorough explanation of these responsibilities. If you don't want these obligations, look into some of the alternatives to guardianships. (Informal alternatives to guardianship of a minor's person are discussed in Chapter 2.)

- For guardianships of the estate, are you willing to continuously manage the minor's assets, provide the court with a required inventory and periodic accountings, and return to court if you need permission to handle certain financial matters? (See Chapter 10 for a discussion of the ongoing responsibilities of a guardianship of a minor's estate.)

- What kind of personal relationship do you have with the minor? Given the nature of this relationship, do you want to act as the legal parent of the minor for the duration of the guardianship?

- Would the guardianship adversely affect you or your family because of your own children, health situation, job, age, or other factors?

- Can you handle the work involved? Do you have the time and energy to take care of the minor and any assets in the estate? Will you be able to make the annual reports to the court?

- What is the financial situation? If the child will receive income from Social Security, welfare, a parent, or the estate of a deceased parent, is this adequate to allow you to provide a decent level of support? If not, are you willing and able to spend some of your own money on the minor?

- Do you anticipate problems with the minor's relatives—including a parent who "abandoned" a minor, and who might suddenly reappear and contest the guardianship? This is rare, but it can happen. If you expect objections, be aware that issues concerning your own background could be used in an attempt to disqualify you from obtaining a guardianship, or later may even be used to have you removed as guardian.

- What kind of relationship do you have with the minor's parents? Are they likely to support the guardianship, or might they be hostile, antagonistic, and interfering?

---

this should be a factor in your favor. Finally, the judge might consider your ability and desire to foster healthy communication and contact between the minor and the minor's parent, if that is relevant. If the guardianship is not contested, the judge only needs to agree that it is "necessary and convenient" in order to grant it. (If it's contested, the judge will look at "the best interests of the child"—a tougher standard.)

A judge typically will consider the minor's wishes (especially for older children), the parents' and other close relatives' wishes (if they are expressed), the proposed guardian's ability and desire to take care of the child, whether the child will be harmed if a guardianship isn't granted, and possibly other alternatives to a guardianship such as foster care placement through the county. While many judges will try to keep families together as much as possible by appointing one guardian for siblings, this is not required by law.

> ### Order of Preference for Appointing Guardian of the Person
>
> Judges have flexibility in choosing who to appoint as guardian. There are, however, some guidelines provided by law (FC §§ 3040, 3041). The law recognizes that other factors enter into every decision, but gives preference:
>
> 1. to one or both parents (either sole or joint custody); then
> 2. to the person with whom the minor has been living in a wholesome and stable environment; then
> 3. to any person determined suitable and able to provide adequate and proper care and guidance for the minor (PC § 1514).

Are You an Appropriate Choice for Guardian of a Minor's Estate?

In deciding whether to appoint you guardian of a minor's estate, a judge should consider your ability to manage and preserve the estate's assets, as well as your concern for the minor. A judge may consider your own financial situation and your ability to manage or hire people to handle relatively large sums of money. The court may also require that you be bonded by a surety insurance company. (See Chapter 10 for more details on the ongoing responsibilities of guardianship of a minor's estate.)

Are There Reasons That You Shouldn't Be Named Guardian?

A judge decides whether to grant a guardianship on the basis of what will best meet the minor's needs. This is sensible; the judge must focus on what is best for the child, not what's best for you. Obviously, however, your lifestyle and your background may well influence a decision about what is best for the minor.

The proposed guardian and minor often are interviewed by a court investigator who then makes a report to the judge. In some counties, the proposed guardian must be fingerprinted, and the investigator will check into whether the proposed guardian has a criminal record. In addition, a routine screening of whether the proposed guardian of a minor's person has ever been reported for child abuse or neglect is always made. Chapter 8 has more about guardianship investigations.

There are several obvious reasons why you might not be appointed guardian, or why you later could be removed as guardian. Bear in mind that conduct that falls in one or more of these categories won't automatically disqualify you—it's up to the judge. But a court might consider you to be an improper guardian in any of the following circumstances:

- If you have been charged with neglecting or abusing a minor, the court would consider you an inappropriate choice for guardianship of a minor's person.

- If you have been convicted of a felony, it could prevent you from being named guardian, or it could be grounds for removal (PC § 2650).

- If you have had other run-ins with the law, your appropriateness as a guardian would probably depend on the crime, how long ago it was committed, and what your lifestyle is like now. For example, if you were "wild" when you were 19, but now at 50 you've been consistently employed for decades, raised your family, own your home, and need to take care of your grandchild, the court won't be interested in the wild oats of your youth.

It's All Relative

Here are some fairly common questions that come up in families about guardianships.

Q: I don't think my sister is a good parent, so can I become her child's guardian?

A: Maybe. The court won't grant a guardianship just because you don't approve of your sister's parenting. Instead, you'd have to prove that it would harm the child to stay with your sister. If the child isn't being abused or neglected, and your sister is caring for the child, your best bet is probably to try first to work it out within the family. But if the child is at risk because of abuse or neglect, you can notify your local social services agency, and petition for guardianship. If your sister would contest the guardianship, you'll need a lawyer's help.

Q: I don't want my unreliable ex-husband to have custody of our small child if something happens to me. Can I choose someone else to be my daughter's guardian?

A: You may execute a will that names someone other than your ex-husband as guardian of your child when you die, but there's no guarantee that the court will follow your wishes. If your ex-husband can parent, and if he objects to whomever you named being appointed guardian, the court probably won't approve your nomination, but will let your husband take the child. If your ex-husband is abusive or neglectful, though, the court might consider appointing someone else. If that's the case, you can note in your will, or in a letter that you attach, the reasons why your ex having custody would be detrimental to your child.

In the event you are terminally ill, you can ask a court to appoint you and someone else jointly as guardians. After your death, the surviving joint guardian will take sole custody of the child. But before approving a joint guardianship like this, the court must find that giving custody to the other parent would be detrimental to the child.

Q: My ex-husband died, leaving all of his money to his children, but he nominated his obnoxious brother as guardian. Can I be named guardian of the estate instead?

A: You could petition the court to be named guardian of the estate. However, the person leaving the money has a right to nominate the guardian of the estate, and the court is obligated to follow that nomination unless the person is unwilling to serve, or isn't an appropriate choice to be guardian of the estate—for example, if he has fraud convictions, bankruptcies, or a poor credit history.

- For guardianships of a minor's estate, if information about your finances or ability to manage money (such as bankruptcy or financial problems) indicates that you would be an inappropriate choice, the court may question you, put restrictions on your powers, or reject you outright.

- If there is any well-known undesirable information about your personal life—for example, alcohol, drug, or gambling problems—these could influence the judge's decision.

If you are in any of these situations, you may be better off not petitioning to be the minor's guardian, especially if anyone is likely to challenge your qualifications in court. However, if the minor has no one to provide proper care, you still might opt to petition for the guardianship, and argue that the negative factor has been eliminated or isn't important.

Do You Need an Attorney or Other Legal Professional to Help You Petition for Guardianship?

If the minor's parents can't care for their child, you have the approval of the minor's close relatives, you are the natural person to take over, and you have the patience to handle the court process, there's normally no reason why you can't do the guardianship petition process on your own, without a lawyer's help. If you need some help with the forms, you might find a document preparer to assist you for a much lower fee than an attorney would charge. Document preparers can't give legal advice, but you can save the money you would have spent for a lawyer for the immediate needs of the child. (See Chapter 13 for information on document preparers.) Many counties have assistance at the court, called Guardianship Clinics, if you are seeking only a guardianship of the minor's person. These clinics are usually run by volunteer members of the local county bar association. Ask your court clerk whether your county offers help like this.

What if you're not sure whether you'll have the support of the minor's relatives, or the natural parents are not completely out of the picture and might contest the guardianship? You may still choose to start the process of obtaining a guardianship on your own. If you run into problems later, you can involve a lawyer then.

If you anticipate problems from the start, such as relatives contesting the guardianship or a parent who you think is unfit insisting on trying to keep or get custody, you will probably want to consult a lawyer first. Then, if someone takes legal action that requires an immediate response, you will not need to hunt for a lawyer in the midst of a crisis.

Even if you do use an attorney for the entire process, this book will help you understand the guardianship procedure and help you make sure that the attorney is doing the job right.

TIP

If you are a foster parent or other adult seeking a guardianship where the minor is a dependent child of the court, the local social services agency and county counsel should handle the guardianship for you. There is a simplified procedure for appointing guardians for minors who were adjudged dependents of the Juvenile Court on or after January 1, 1989 (W&I 366.26). Contact the social worker in charge of the minor's case for more information.

Special Concerns of Stepparents and Coparents

If both of the minor's parents are living, it may not make sense for you to file for a legal guardianship. Even if you are living with and parenting the minor as a stepparent or coparent (in other words, you are parenting with one of the minor's parents but you are not related to the minor), filing guardianship papers could start a custody battle with the other parent. You may decide not to put everyone involved through such a court battle, unless it would be detrimental to the minor for the other parent to have legal custody.

 RESOURCE

- For lesbian and gay couples, an important source of information is *A Legal Guide for Lesbian & Gay Couples*, by Denis Clifford, Frederick Hertz, and Emily Doskow (Nolo).
- For unmarried couples, legal and practical information is available in *Living Together: A Legal Guide for Unmarried Couples*, by Ralph Warner, Toni Ihara, and Frederick Hertz (Nolo).

If you are seeking guardianship of a minor's estate or person and estate, you will probably need the help of a legal professional after you are appointed guardian. (Chapter 13 contains information and tips on how to find and hire attorneys and other legal professionals.)

Using This Book

Here are some tips about how to use this book effectively.

- If you want to avoid going to court for a guardianship of a minor's person, turn to Chapter 2. There you'll find informal alternatives to a legal court-ordered guardianship and suggestions for how to use these informal guardianship authorization documents.

- If you will be seeking public benefits for the minor, or if you will be dealing with agencies and institutions (such as schools, medical facilities, and insurers), read "Dealing With Agencies and Institutions" in Chapter 2. The information is useful for those who are not seeking a legal guardianship, and may also be helpful for those who want a legal guardianship.

- If you have decided to obtain a legal guardianship, read Chapter 3 for an overview of how to prepare and file your papers with a California court. Then read and follow the instructions in Chapters 4, 5, and 6. If you will be seeking guardianship of a minor's estate, you also will be directed to Chapter 10 to help you understand and prepare papers needed to initiate a guardianship of a minor's estate.

- If you need a legal guardianship of a minor's person right away, read and follow the instructions in Chapter 7 in addition to following the instructions for a regular guardianship (Chapters 4, 5, and 6).

- After filing and having your guardianship papers served, read Chapter 8, which gives valuable information about a court investigation that may take place. Then, before the court-appointed hearing date, read Chapter 9 and talk to the minor about the hearing.

- Once you've become a guardian, Chapter 11 gives you an overview of your responsibilities. Guardians of the estate also need to read Chapter 10.
- If a guardianship is no longer needed, you'll find information about how to end it in Chapter 12.
- If you think you need an attorney, you'll find information on how to find a lawyer or legal document preparer, and on how to do some of your own legal research, in Chapter 13.

The Vocabulary of Guardianships

We'll define important terms as we go. And Appendix A, at the back of this book, provides a glossary of terms you are likely to come across in the guardianship process.

Guardianship Forms

Appendixes B and C, at the back of this book, contain the forms you'll need to obtain a legal guardianship or to handle alternatives to a legal guardianship. The entire book explains the step-by-step details of how to fill out and use all of the forms.

Alternatives to a Court-Ordered Guardianship

You are probably reading this chapter because you want to explore the possibility of caring for a minor without getting a formal legal guardianship. Most likely, you either already have or anticipate having a minor living with you. An agency or institution may have informed you that you must get a legal guardianship, but perhaps you still wonder whether there might be a simpler alternative. Fortunately, there often are easy, efficient ways to take responsibility for a minor without bringing the court system into play.

This chapter covers alternatives to guardianship of a minor's person, but not alternatives to guardianship of a minor's estate. This is because when guardianship of a minor's estate is needed (such as to disburse insurance proceeds or to manage a minor's inheritance), there generally is no informal alternative.

At the risk of oversimplifying, you can probably avoid going through the formal court process of getting a legal guardianship of a minor's person if:

1. You conclude after reading Chapter 1 and this chapter that the minor will not suffer negative consequences if you don't get a legal guardianship.

2. You will be taking care of a minor for a relatively short time, or you are a stepparent or coparent and are not in a position to get a guardianship—usually because the other parent is a suitable parent and would contest the guardianship.

3. You want a guardianship primarily to enroll the minor in school or to authorize medical care. (A special form available for this purpose is provided in this chapter—see "Alternatives to Guardianship of a Minor's Person," below.)

4. You are willing to deal with the possible inconvenience and potential problems of using less formal substitute procedures.

Several examples illustrate when alternatives to a legal guardianship might (and might not) be appropriate.

EXAMPLE 1:

Fourteen-year-old Alex has been living with his natural mother and stepfather for several years. His father lives in another state and sees Alex in the summers. Alex's mother frequently goes on business trips, leaving Alex in his stepfather's care. They are concerned that a school or medical situation will arise that requires a parent's consent when neither of Alex's natural parents will be around. Alex's stepfather uses the Caregiver's Authorization Affidavit found below, for situations that might require parental consent.

EXAMPLE 2:

Katrina stays with her uncle for about a month each year, when her parents' work takes them out of the country. There is no need for a legal guardianship because Katrina lives with her uncle for relatively short periods of time. Katrina's parents and uncle can use the informal Guardianship Authorization form below, to cover any situation that might need parental consent while the parents are out of town. Of course, if authorization is needed for a situation that the uncle isn't sure about, he can probably contact Katrina's parents to ask their advice.

EXAMPLE 3:

Cindy's grandparents are taking care of her because her mother is unstable, moves constantly, and has problems with substance abuse. Cindy's grandparents believe that unless they have legal custody of Cindy, the mother is likely to show up at any time and take Cindy away. They can't live with this possibility, so they gently but firmly insist on a legal court guardianship. After thinking about it, Cindy's mother agrees that a legal guardianship would be better for Cindy. Cindy doesn't have any assets, so her grandparents obtain a guardianship of her person only, using the instructions in this book.

Personal Reasons for Avoiding Formal Guardianships

An adult who has care and physical custody of a minor may also have strong personal reasons not to become a legal guardian of the minor's person.

- Dynamics between family members may be such that filing for a guardianship could precipitate a fight for full legal custody. This would be especially likely where a natural parent cares for a minor along with a stepparent or coparent.

- You expect that the minor's parents probably will not consent to a legal guardianship, and will immediately try to remove their child from your custody if you start the process.

- You don't want your personal life scrutinized in court or by a court-appointed investigator. (See Chapter 8 for more information about court investigations of proposed guardians.)

How to Use This Chapter

Everyone should read the section called "Alternatives to Guardianship of a Minor's Person," which contains forms that authorize a nonparent to enroll a minor in school and make other important decisions on the minor's behalf. These forms can be used whether you will be

taking care of a minor for a limited time (a few weeks or months while the parents are out of the area) or for an extended time.

If you will have contact with agencies or institutions and do not plan to obtain a legal guardianship of a minor's person, read "Dealing With Agencies and Institutions." This section gives you information and tips, and alerts you to situations where a legal guardianship may be mandatory.

Alternatives to Guardianship of a Minor's Person

Throughout this chapter we refer to informal custody arrangements as informal "guardianship" situations, even though the use of the term "guardianship" is not technically correct for an informal arrangement. A legal guardianship can only be obtained through a court proceeding. But we have used the word here to describe noncourt procedures in order to encourage you to do the same. This is because using that term may make it more likely that those documents will be accepted by agencies and organizations.

There are two documents that will allow nonparents to enroll children in school and make other decisions for them. Nonparents caring for a minor who lives with them may sign a Caregiver's Authorization Affidavit. By law, schools and medical care providers must accept this form if it is completed correctly (FC § 6550). This form is signed only by the caregiver.

In addition, we recommend that, if possible, at least one parent fill out and sign a Guardianship Authorization form and have it notarized. The Guardianship Authorization form gives the nonparent a broad range of responsibility for the minor, such as allowing the nonparent to obtain benefits and apply for health insurance on behalf of the child.

Bear in mind that these forms should never be used to attempt to resolve custody issues, meaning disputes about who has the legal right to care for a child. If your situation involves a custody problem, you should consult an attorney. (See Chapter 13.)

Caregiver's Authorization Affidavit

If you are caring for a minor who is living with you, you can use a Caregiver's Authorization Affidavit as an informal way to get some limited decision-making authority. A Caregiver's Authorization Affidavit is an official form based on California's recognition that adults who have minors living with them are "caregivers" who often want and need to take some responsibility for the minor's education and other care. A caregiver who has signed a Caregiver's Authorization Affidavit may enroll a child in public school and make school-related medical decisions. In some circumstances, a caregiver may be allowed to authorize other kinds of medical care as well.

To become a legally recognized caregiver, you must sign, under penalty of perjury, a Caregiver's Authorization Affidavit. A sample copy of the form is shown below, and a tear-out copy is in Appendix B at the back of the book. You also may be able to pick up a form at the child's school or medical facility. Instructions for filling out the form are below.

How to Complete the Form

Items 1 through 4: In the appropriate blanks, list the minor's name and date of birth, your name (the adult serving as the caregiver), and your home address.

Items 5 through 8: Only complete these items if you wish to make general medical care decisions on behalf of the minor, and you are a "qualifying relative"—the minor's spouse, parent, stepparent, brother, sister, stepbrother, stepsister, half-brother, half-sister, uncle, aunt, niece, nephew, first cousin, or any person denoted by the prefix "grand" or "great," or the spouse of any of the people specified in this definition (even if the marriage was terminated by death or divorce).

Check Item 5 if you are a qualified relative living with the child. If you're not, you can't fill out this section.

In Item 6, check one or both boxes to indicate that (1) the parent(s) or other person having legal custody of the minor does not object to your plans to authorize medical care, and/or (2) you are unable to contact the parent(s) or other person having custody to notify them of your intention in that regard.

In Items 7 and 8, fill in your date of birth and California driver's license number.

Signature: Signing the affidavit is the equivalent of swearing under penalty of perjury that the child lives with you. As noted in the instructions on the back of the form (shown in Appendix B), the public school in the district in which you (and thus the child) live and medical facilities must rely on your affidavit. The minor's parents do not need to sign.

You may wish to make several "duplicate originals" of the filled out form by photocopying the form before you sign it, then signing each copy. You can then give a signed affidavit to your local school district when enrolling the child, or to a health care provider when authorizing medical care.

Back of the form: Read the back of the Caregiver's Authorization Affidavit form for additional information. You don't need to complete anything on this side of the form. You will find the entire form in Appendix B.

Caregiver's Authorization Affidavit

Use of this affidavit is authorized by Part 1.5 (commencing with Section 6550) of Division 11 of the California Family Code.

Instructions: Completion of items 1-4 and the signing of the affidavit is sufficient to authorize enrollment of a minor in school and authorize school-related medical care. Completion of items 5-8 is additionally required to authorize any other medical care. Print clearly.

The minor named below lives in my home and I am 18 years of age or older.

1. Name of minor: _____.

2. Minor's birth date: _____.

3. My name (adult giving authorization): _____.

4. My home address: _____

   _____.

_____

5. [ ] I am a grandparent, aunt, uncle, or other qualified relative of the minor (see back of this form for a definition of "qualified relative").

6. Check one or both (for example, if one parent was advised and the other cannot be located):

   [ ] I have advised the parent(s) or other person(s) having legal custody of the minor of my intent to authorize medical care, and have received no objection.

   [ ] I am unable to contact the parent(s) or other person(s) having legal custody of the minor at this time, to notify them of my intended authorization.

7. My date of birth: _____.

8. My California driver's license or identification card number: _____.

Warning: Do not sign this form if any of the statements above are incorrect, or you will be committing a crime punishable by a fine, imprisonment, or both.

I declare under penalty of perjury under the laws of the State of California that the foregoing is true and correct.

Dated: _____   Signed: _____

Guardianship Authorization Form

If you're taking care of a minor who has one or two living parents, it's a good idea to have a parent sign a form that will allow you to act in an urgent situation when a parent can't be reached. Appendix B contains a Guardianship Authorization form, in which at least one parent gives a nonparent authority to care for a child. You may use this form instead of or in conjunction with the Caregiver's Authorization Affidavit provided above. The Guardianship Authorization form should cover situations where the Caregiver's Authorization Affidavit does not apply—for example, if you need to apply for benefits or health insurance on the minor's behalf.

The Guardianship Authorization form provided in Appendix B should be signed by you and, if possible, by both parents or the parent who has legal custody of the child. It is important that you and the minor's parents sign this form in the presence of a notary public. Obviously, if you know that the parent(s) will be leaving the area, it would be best to have the form signed beforehand. If the parents have already left, mail the form to them so they can have their section of the form notarized wherever they are.

Single Parent Note: If the minor has only one parent, that parent can sign the Guardianship Authorization form alone. But if there is another living natural parent—for example, an ex-spouse—the Guardianship Authorization form will probably not be sufficient if that other parent wants to claim physical custody of the minor. The Guardianship Authorization form is not intended to be used to resolve custody issues. If your situation involves a custody problem, consult an attorney. (See Chapter 13 for more about attorneys.)

How to Complete the Guardianship Authorization Form

If you will be taking care of more than one minor, complete a separate form for each one.

Information About Minor: Fill in the minor's name, birthdate, age, and year in school (if applicable).

Information About Parents: Fill in the names of whichever of the minor's parents will be signing the form. If you can conveniently get signatures from both parents, fill in the information requested for both parents. If you can only get a signature from one parent, only fill in information about that parent. Fill in the addresses and telephone numbers of each parent who will be signing the form. If the parents will be out of the area, fill in the address and phone numbers where they can most likely be reached.

Information About Proposed Guardian: It's usually preferable to have only one person take on this responsibility, to avoid conflicts between the two caretakers. Fill in your own name, address, and phone number. Also fill in your relationship to the minor.

Emergency Contact: Fill in the name of a person who can be contacted in case of an emergency if you cannot be reached. This might be a friend, relative, or neighbor who lives nearby. If possible, it's best to give the name of someone who has a car or ready access to transportation.

Items 1 through 5: Leave these items blank, but make sure you read them.

Item 6: Fill in the period of time during which the informal guardianship arrangement will be valid. For example, if the parents will be overseas from September 4, 2011, through November 18, 2011, you would fill in those dates.

Item 7: By law, parents are required to support their children, regardless of where the children are living (FC §§ 3900, 3901, 4000). But in the real world, people sometimes make other arrangements. Maybe you are helping out your son, who is going through a difficult emotional and financial time, and you are willing and able to pay expenses of his minor child's upkeep. But on the other hand, maybe you can't afford to take on the financial responsibility. The blank space in this item is the place for you to state how costs of taking care of the minor will be paid.

For example, if you are willing to pay the expenses of taking care of the minor during the informal "guardianship," you might fill in: "The proposed guardian will pay all costs of the minor's upkeep, medical, dental, and living expenses." If a parent will give you money to take care of her child, you might fill in: "The minor's mother will pay all costs of the minor's upkeep, living expenses, medical, and dental expenses." If you agree to provide food and cover school expenses for the minor, but her parents promise to pay for medical and dental expenses, you might fill in: "The proposed guardian will pay all costs of the minor's upkeep, living expenses, and school expenses. The minor's parents will pay all medical and dental expenses."

You have now completed the form. Do not sign it yet, or have the parents sign it. It should be signed by both you and the parents in front of a notary public. We tell you how to do that next.

Copy, Sign, and Notarize the Guardianship Authorization Form

You're now ready to make several copies of the Guardianship Authorization form. We suggest you make at least four copies of the completed but still unsigned form for each minor. That way you will be able to provide an original form for each agency or institution that requires one.

Next, you will need to locate a notary public. It is important to have this document notarized, because the notary's signature and seal confirm that the signatures are legitimate. Banks and real estate offices are good places to find notaries, and private mailbox locations often employ notaries. Or you can look in the yellow pages of the phone book under "Notary Public" or a similar heading. Notaries may charge up to $20 per signature. If you look around, you may be able to find a notary for free, or for a very low price. For example, a local bank may offer notary services free as a service to its customers.

Naturally, if you have to pay a lot for the notary (the cost might get up there if two parents and you are signing multiple originals) you may opt to obtain only one original notarized Guardianship Authorization form. Make sure you get at least one notarized copy, and preferably two. Don't hesitate to call around to find a notary who will help you out for less money.

If possible, go to the notary public together with the parents who will be signing the Guardianship Authorization form. The notary will have each of you produce some kind of identification (such as a driver's license or passport) and will watch each of you sign the document. The notary will then fill out the "Notarization" parts of the form and imprint it with an official notary seal. You will need to sign your name in the notary's book, stating that you signed the document in front of the notary.

If you can't go to a notary with the parents—for example, one of them lives in another state—each form will have to be notarized twice. Send the parents several unsigned copies of the document to sign and have notarized and return to you. Then go to a notary yourself along with the Guardianship Authorization forms that the parents signed and had notarized. There you should sign and have your portion of the document notarized.

Guardianship Authorization, page 1

Guardianship Authorization

Minor

Name: _____

Birthdate: _____ Age: _____ Year in School: _____

Parent 1

Name: _____

Street Address: _____

City: _____ State: _____ Zip Code: _____

Home Phone: _____ Work Phone: _____

Cell Phone: _____

Parent 2

Name: _____

Street Address: _____

City: _____ State: _____ Zip Code: _____

Home Phone: _____ Work Phone: _____

Cell Phone: _____

Proposed Guardian

Name: _____

Street Address: _____

City: _____ State: _____ Zip Code: _____

Home Phone: _____ Work Phone: _____

Cell Phone: _____

Relationship to Minor: _____

In case of emergency, if proposed guardian cannot be reached, please contact: _____

Name: _____ Phone: _____

Cell Phone: _____

Authorization & Consent of Parent(s)

1. I affirm that the minor indicated above is my child and that I have legal custody of her/him. I give my full authorization and consent for my child to live with the proposed guardian, or for the proposed guardian to set a place of residence for my child.

2. I give the proposed guardian permission to act in my place and make decisions pertaining to my child's educational and religious activities including but not limited to enrollment, permission to participate in activities, and consent for medical treatment at school.

3. I give the proposed guardian permission to authorize medical and dental care for my child, including but not limited to medical examinations, X-rays, tests, anesthetic, surgical operations, hospital care, or other treatments that in the proposed guardian's sole opinion are needed or useful for my child. Such medical treatment shall only be provided upon the advice of and supervision by a physician, surgeon, dentist, or other medical practitioner licensed to practice in the United States.

4. I give the proposed guardian permission to apply for benefits on my child's behalf including but not limited to Social Security, public assistance, health insurance, and Veterans Administration benefits.

Guardianship Authorization, page 2

5. I give the proposed guardian permission to apply and obtain for my child any or all of the following: Social Security number, Social Security card, and U.S. passport.

6. This authorization shall cover the period from _____, 20____, to _____, 20____.

7. During the period when the proposed guardian cares for my child, the costs of my child's upkeep, living expenses, medical and dental expenses shall be paid as follows: _____ _____

I declare under penalty of perjury under the laws of the State of California that the foregoing is true and correct.

Parent's Signature: _____   Date: _____, 20____

Parent's Signature: _____   Date: _____, 20____

Notarization

State of California

County of _____

On this _____ day of _____, 20____, before me, a notary public of the State of California, personally appeared _____, personally known to me (or proved to me on the basis of satisfactory evidence) to be the person(s) whose name(s) is/are subscribed to this instrument, and acknowledged that she/he/they executed the same, in his/her/their authorized capacity(ies) and that by his/her/their signature(s) on the instrument the person(s), or the entity upon behalf of which the person(s) acted, executed the instrument.

I certify under PENALTY OF PERJURY under the laws of the State of California that the foregoing paragraph is true and correct.

WITNESS my hand and official seal.

Notary Public: _____   [Seal]

Consent of Proposed Guardian

I solemnly affirm that I will assume full responsibility for the minor who will live with me during the period designated above. I agree to make necessary decisions and to provide consent for the minor as set forth in the above Authorization & Consent by Parent(s). I also agree to the terms of the costs of the minor's upkeep, living expenses, medical and/or dental expenses set forth in the above Authorization & Consent of Parent(s).

I declare under penalty of perjury under the laws of the State of California that the foregoing is true and correct.

Proposed Guardian's Signature: _____   Date: _____, 20_____

Notarization

State of California

County of _____

On this _____ day of _____, 20____, before me, a notary public of the State of California, personally appeared ___ _____, personally known to me (or proved to me on the basis of satisfactory evidence) to be the person(s) whose name(s) is/are subscribed to this instrument, and acknowledged that she/he/they executed the same, in his/her/their authorized capacity(ies) and that by his/her/their signature(s) on the instrument the person(s), or the entity upon behalf of which the person(s) acted, executed the instrument.

I certify under PENALTY OF PERJURY under the laws of the State of California that the foregoing paragraph is true and correct.

WITNESS my hand and official seal.

Notary Public: _____   [Seal]

Now that you have an informal "guardianship" document, you can provide a copy of it to agencies and institutions that require some proof of your authority to care for a minor. Make sure you keep one original of the Guardianship Authorization form in a safe, convenient place. When an agency asks for the form, be sure you hand over a copy or one of several originals. Don't give away your only signed and notarized original.

Dealing With Agencies and Institutions

If you care for a minor who isn't your child, agencies and institutions may give you some unexpected hassles. Agencies—especially those that are distributing benefits—are often cautious when dealing with an adult who claims to be taking care of a minor. They generally want to make sure the benefits will be used to help out the minor.

Unfortunately, in informal "guardianship" situations, it can be very confusing to deal with agencies and institutions that require proof of your authority to act on behalf of a minor. Policies vary so greatly that there are no rules to help you through all situations. The policy of one agency might be quite different from that of a similar agency a few miles away. And, unfortunately, even the requirements of a given agency can sometimes depend more on the opinions of the person with whom you're dealing than on any agency policy.

Public schools are required to accept a Caregiver's Authorization Affidavit to establish that the child lives in the school district, unless they have proof that the child does not live with the caregiver (EC § 48204(a)(4), FC § 6550(a)). In addition, health care providers may legally rely on the Caregiver's Authorization Affidavit (FC § 6550(d)).

In general, most other agencies will be more willing to accept informal "guardianship" authorization as proof if a relative, rather than an unrelated adult, is taking care of a minor. If you are a close relative (grandparent, uncle or aunt, sister or brother), you might not be asked to provide any documentation showing that you are acting as the minor's guardian. However, if you are not a close relative or if you move to a new area where you and the minor aren't known and you need agency support, you will likely be asked to produce documentation showing authorization from a parent or even a court. If you do not plan to get a legal guardianship, here are some suggestions for dealing with agencies and institutions:

- Find out the agency's policies for written authorization before you address your specific situation. If you call for information, you don't have to give your name, and you should be able to get valuable information. For example, an agency may have preprinted authorization forms it prefers you to use. Or it may be more willing to accept an informal "guardianship" arrangement if a natural parent contacts someone there first.

- Be as cooperative as possible, but don't volunteer more information about your custody situation than you are asked for. Often you will be able to simply sign the agency's forms or a Caregiver's Authorization Affidavit, and no one will ask any questions.

- If possible, prepare a Caregiver's Authorization Affidavit as well as a signed and notarized Guardianship Authorization form following the instructions in this chapter. Carry this with you when you go to the agency in person. Then, if written authorization is required, you can provide it on the spot.

- If an agency uses its own preprinted authorization forms, obtain copies and, if possible, have the minor's natural parents complete and sign them. You may need to meet with a representative of the agency to get the forms, and return later once you've obtained the parents' signatures.

- Don't be intimidated by bureaucracy. One agency employee may insist that only a formal guardianship will be accepted, but, as noted, others may be more lenient—especially if you produce legal-looking documents such as the Caregiver's Authorization Affidavit and the Guardianship Authorization form. If you meet resistance, keep trying. Ask to see another agent, or a supervisor if need be. You might even be better off coming back another day instead of trying to cope with one obstinate person.

- If you will receive money or benefits on behalf of the minor from an agency that requires periodic accountings to show how the money has been spent, you must comply with that requirement. For example, the Veterans Administration is almost certain to require these accountings. Social Security and other agencies may also require them.

Here we provide information on the typical policies of a variety of agencies and institutions, and wherever possible, give you the inside scoop on how to approach them. You should be able to get most of them to accept the informal short-term Guardianship Authorization form without hassle.

Schools

Education Code § 48204(a)(4) states that a signed Caregiver's Authorization Affidavit is proof enough that the child lives in the school district, unless the district has evidence to the contrary.

Although some school districts may prefer a formal court-ordered guardianship of the minor's person when a nonparent cares for a minor, they may not insist on this. The school district must accept your Caregiver's Authorization Affidavit as proof the minor lives with you. If a school insists on a formal guardianship, they are in violation of the law. Point out that under EC § 48204(a)(4), you have a right to enroll the minor in school.

Strict Enrollment Policies of Some School Districts

School districts in some of California's larger cities tend to have more rigid enrollment policies than other districts in the state. In addition, enrollment policies tend to be much stricter in school districts that have a history of nondistrict residents trying to enroll children there. This is common when a crowded, poorly funded school district is geographically close to a school district with better-funded facilities. Parents who live outside of the district often try to sneak their kids into the better school district by providing a mailing address of a relative or friend within the school district.

If you live in one of these districts, chances are that you'll be faced with more stringent enrollment paperwork. For example, the school district may require that you produce a signed authorization form from the minor's parent(s) in addition to the Caregiver's Authorization Affidavit.

Medical and Dental Care

The need to have an adult available to consent to a minor's medical treatment may seem at first like one of the most important reasons to get a guardianship. Perhaps you have visions of a child being hit by a car and no doctor being willing to treat her. Fortunately, this is not a realistic worry, as consent by an adult is not required to treat a minor in an emergency.

Formal legal guardianship may be a good idea if you anticipate that the minor will need ongoing health care for serious medical problems. For example, a guardianship may be in order if the minor has a chronic illness that requires periodic hospitalization, surgery, prescription drugs, or other treatments. If you are closely related to the minor, a formal guardianship may not be necessary. You need only sign a Caregiver's Authorization Affidavit (FC § 6550(d)).

In general, a legal guardian or relative caregiver has the same right as the parent to consent to medical treatment for the minor. But you are not automatically entitled to authorize all of the minor's medical, dental, and mental health treatment. Here are some exceptions:

- Nonemergency surgical procedures generally require the consent of a minor age 14 or older, as well as that of the guardian or caretaker.

- A guardian or caregiver cannot involuntarily place a minor in a mental health treatment facility unless the minor is a danger to himself or others, or is gravely disabled (PC § 2356(a), W&I § 5150).

- A guardian or caregiver cannot authorize a minor to be treated with experimental drugs, to be given convulsive treatment, or to be sterilized.

Medical Emergencies (Hospitals)

As mentioned, treating a minor in a medical emergency does not require authorization by a parent, caregiver, or guardian. If a minor is taken to a hospital in an emergency, the doctor providing care can, in any case, sign a document authorizing emergency medical treatment (sometimes called a "treating permit"). Assessing the emergency and the treatment needed is up to the doctor. The doctor's willingness to sign a treating permit would probably depend on the severity of the situation and the medical procedure required.

Routine Medical and Dental Care

Physicians, dentists, and hospitals must allow a relative who has signed a Caregiver's Authorization Affidavit to give consent for a medical procedure for a minor. In addition, the notarized Guardianship Authorization form set out above may be helpful in persuading the medical care provider to treat the minor without the parent's consent.

Some medical professionals might require that a nonrelative caregiver get a formal court guardianship before they will treat the minor. Whether a legal guardianship will be required often depends partly on the needed medical treatment. The more serious the medical problem—short of an acute medical emergency—and the more time there is before action must be taken, the more likely you are to deal with the question of a formal guardianship.

Medical and Dental Insurance Coverage

You and your family may be covered by health insurance, perhaps under an insurance policy at a job. If so, you will probably want to include coverage for any minor for whom you are caring. Although signing the Caregiver's Authorization Affidavit will allow you to consent to a related minor's medical treatment, it will not necessarily qualify the minor for your insurance policy.

Some insurance companies are strict about requiring papers showing a court-appointed guardianship before they will extend coverage to minors who live with you. Others will accept alternative documentation, usually if you suggest it. If your insurance company requires a court-ordered legal guardianship, you will either need to comply with the company's rules, or find alternative coverage.

Check with your insurance carrier to find out:

- whether the minor will be eligible for coverage if you obtain a guardianship and, if so, whether a formal, court-ordered guardianship is required for the minor to be covered; or

- whether the insurance carrier will accept alternate documentation to a court-ordered guardianship for children who live with you. This might be a signed letter from the minor's parent, a document such as the Caregiver's Authorization Affidavit or a Guardianship Authorization form, or some other document the insurance company provides.

Get a firm commitment from the insurance company that the minor will be covered by your insurance if this is the only reason you are seeking a formal guardianship. You might want to get a written statement from the insurance agent, or check the policy regarding coverage in guardianship situations.

If the minor is covered by health insurance through a parent, that coverage stays in place even if a guardianship is granted.

RESOURCE

If neither you nor the child's parents can provide insurance, the minor might be able to get insurance through the state. California has a program called "Healthy Families" that seeks to provide low-cost health, dental, and vision insurance for children and teens. You must meet income guidelines to qualify for the insurance. For more information, look at the program website at www.healthyfamilies.ca.gov, or call 800-880-5305.

Public Assistance

Depending on your income, you and the minor may be eligible for a variety of public assistance benefits. This might include Medi-Cal, TANF (Temporary Assistance to Needy Families, formerly called Aid to Families with Dependent Children (AFDC)) for relatives of a minor, or Boarding Home and Institution (BHI)—also called foster care payments in some counties—for people caring for an unrelated minor. Public assistance funding comes from three sources: the federal government, the state of California, and individual counties.

You are likely to qualify for public assistance without a legal guardianship if you are a close relative of the minor. How closely you must be related (grandmother, uncle, etc.) depends on the policies of the county in which you live. The Guardianship Authorization form above will work instead of a legal guardianship in some counties. But others may require a formal guardianship.

If you are not related to the child you are caring for, you will probably need a formal guardianship. Also, if you already have a legal guardianship and you move to a different county, the new county could require you, as a condition of receiving benefits, to have the case transferred to the court in that county. (See Chapter 11.)

Note: To handle the small amounts of money involved in public assistance programs, remember that unless the agency specifies otherwise, you only need to get a guardianship of the minor's person, not of the estate. You will need to follow the accounting or investigation requirements of the public assistance programs.

Checklist for Applying for Welfare

Here is an overview of the documentation you'll need when applying for public assistance. Check with your local welfare agency for exact requirements in your county.

- minor's birth certificate
- minor's Social Security card
- birth certificate of minor's mother
- your birth certificate, and
- your photo ID.

For help with getting copies of birth certificates, see "How to Get a Copy of a Birth Certificate" in Chapter 3.

Temporary Assistance to Needy Families (TANF)

TANF is a program that provides money to help low-income families with children. If you are a grandparent taking care of your grandchild, you probably can qualify for TANF without obtaining a formal guardianship, if you meet the program's income and need requirements. Some welfare departments will allow other close relatives (brother, sister, uncle, or aunt) to obtain TANF without a guardianship. Others require an aunt or even a sister of a minor to get a formal court guardianship first.

Boarding Home and Institution (BHI) or Foster Care

BHI, called foster care in some counties, is similar to TANF, but it is available to adults with minors living with them who either aren't related or aren't closely related. You can only get BHI payments when there is a formal court guardianship. BHI is also available to licensed foster homes, which qualify for this type of assistance when they obtain licensing. BHI benefits tend to be slightly higher than TANF, and include a back-to-school clothing allowance.

Medi-Cal

Medi-Cal is a program that provides certain low-income people with free or shared costs of medical and some dental care, depending on need. This assistance is available to people who are under age 21, blind, pregnant, or permanently disabled. The minor may be eligible for Medi-Cal depending on income level. To obtain Medi-Cal for a minor living with you, you must be related to the minor (usually grandparent, aunt or uncle, sister or brother, or possibly first cousin), or you must have a formal legal guardianship. Check with your local welfare office.

Custody Problems After Applying for Public Assistance

When a relative applies for public assistance to take care of a child, the family situation is reviewed by the welfare agency and an effort is made to collect support from the natural parents. Occasionally this prompts a natural parent who has been out of the picture for some time to show up and demand physical custody of the child. Where the natural parent is stable and able to care for the child, the appearance may be for the best. But often it isn't, if the motive of the parent demanding custody is to avoid paying child support.

EXAMPLE:

Alfred's grandmother has been taking care of him for several years because her daughter is unable to do so. She does not know the whereabouts of Alfred's father, who abandoned Alfred when he was a baby. After she applies for TANF benefits and supplies the welfare department with the father's Social Security number, he is located and suddenly reappears. He says he would rather take Alfred than make the support payments to the District Attorney's office that located him. Alfred's grandmother wants to keep the child, and doesn't trust the father's motives. She decides to petition for a legal guardianship, with the help of a lawyer, to fight the father's right to have custody of Alfred. She plans to base her case on the fact that Alfred's father had abandoned him, and that Alfred's needs will be better served by continuing to live with her as the person who has cared for him since birth and to whom he is very close. (In a contested case such as this, a lawyer's help would be needed. Information on finding and working with lawyers is in Chapter 13.)

Subsidized (Section 8) Housing

Section 8 (housing covered in Section 8 of the federal United States Housing Act (42 USC § 1437f)) is a housing program for low-income people subsidized by the government. Eligibility requirements for Section 8 housing vary from place to place, because the funding for the housing comes from each city or county. The number of bedrooms for which you qualify might increase if you are taking care of a minor. For example, in some cities there must be a separate bedroom for boys and girls, so if you take in your nephew and already have a daughter and no extra bedroom, in those cities you should qualify for another bedroom.

The policies for Section 8 housing vary depending on the location, so you will need to call the local housing authority for information on what documentation is required. Usually some proof of your authority to care for a minor will be sufficient, and you will not need a formal guardianship. In some counties, the only documentation you will need is proof that you are receiving TANF on behalf of a minor who is living with you. If you are not receiving TANF, in many counties the Guardianship Authorization form in this chapter should be sufficient to qualify you for benefits. However, if the minor's parent is not available to sign such a form, some offices will accept a notarized statement from you instead. On the next page is an example that you can modify to fit your situation and the requirements of your local Housing Authority office.

**SAMPLE NOTARIZED STATEMENT REGARDING PHYSICAL CUSTODY
OF ELIZABETH JONES (FOR SECTION 8 HOUSING)**

I, Lily Jones Kerr, declare that I am Elizabeth Jones's aunt (her father's sister), that I have had physical custody of Elizabeth Jones since July 3, 2010, and that Elizabeth Jones lives with me at 9 Wild Way, Calcity, California 99999. Elizabeth Jones was born on April 12, 2002.

I declare under penalty of perjury under the laws of the State of California that the foregoing is true and correct.

_____ Date:_____

(Signature) Lily Jones Kerr

NOTARIZATION

State of California

County of _____) **ss.**

On this _____ day of _____, 20_____, before me, a notary public of the State of California, personally appeared _____, personally known to me (or proved to me on the basis of satisfactory evidence) to be the person(s) whose name(s) is/are subscribed to this instrument, and acknowledged that she/he/they executed the same, in his/her/their authorized capacity(ies) and that by his/her/their signature(s) on the instrument the person(s), or the entity upon behalf of which the person(s) acted, executed the instrument.

I declare under PENALTY OF PERJURY under the laws of the State of California that the foregoing paragraph is true and correct.

WITNESS my hand and official seal.

Notary Public:_____

[Seal]

Social Security

Social Security is made up of three different but related benefit programs for retired or disabled people and their dependents or survivors. Social Security benefits are not distributed entirely by need, but are paid to the retired or disabled worker or the worker's dependent family largely based on how much the covered person earned on jobs covered by Social Security.

You will likely deal with Social Security if:

- you need a Social Security number or card for the minor, or
- the minor is eligible for Social Security benefits because a covered parent is deceased or disabled.

Social Security Number or Card

The policies of Social Security offices vary slightly. In most circumstances, you won't need a legal guardianship to apply for a Social Security number for a minor who is not your child. The application for a Social Security number has a signature line for either the parent or other specified adult. When you sign the application, indicate your relationship with the minor, such as uncle, aunt, or grandmother. A signed copy of the Guardianship Authorization form probably will be sufficient documentation for your local Social Security office. (Note that in Item 5 of the Guardianship Authorization form, the parents specifically authorize you to apply for a Social Security number or card on behalf of their child.)

It should be no problem to obtain a duplicate card once the minor has been assigned a Social Security number. Minors over the age of 12 can apply for a duplicate Social Security card on their own.

Social Security Benefits

If the minor is entitled to benefits from the Social Security Administration (such as death or disability benefits) and already has a Social Security number, you may not need a legal guardianship. The Social Security Administration (SSA) does not require a guardianship for an adult to receive benefits on behalf of a minor. The person who receives benefits for someone else is called the "representative payee."

To become a representative payee, you must contact the SSA and complete an application form. The application, which is about four pages long, asks a variety of questions about you and the minor, such as whether you are the legal guardian (although it isn't required that you be), whether the minor is living with you, and the names and locations of the minor's relatives. Once you complete the application, the SSA will process it and determine whether you are eligible to become the representative payee.

If a minor who is eligible for benefits lives with you, a legal guardianship will not be required by the SSA. However, if the SSA is apprehensive about turning benefits over to you, getting a legal guardianship of the minor's estate may help, because it would mean that you would be required to account to the court as to how you spend the money.

Veterans Administration Benefits

A minor who is a child of a veteran (whether living or deceased) may be eligible for financial benefits through the Veterans Administration (VA). The type and amount of these benefits depend on the veteran's history of service, and whether the veteran served in a war or during peacetime. Legal guardianship is not required by the VA, and in fact the existence of a legal guardianship does not automatically qualify a guardian to receive benefits on behalf of a minor. The VA's term for the person who receives benefits on someone else's behalf is "fiduciary." To become a fiduciary, you must complete forms that the VA provides. The VA will arrange a personal interview, check into your references, and possibly require periodic accountings. To start the process, contact the VA to find out whether the minor qualifies for benefits, and if so, how to proceed.

Traveling With a Minor Outside the United States

Traveling outside the United States with a minor who is not your child could be a problem if you don't have documentation showing your legal relationship. Immigration officials could detain you either when entering or leaving the country. And if the unexpected arises—such as a medical emergency or a problem with customs—the last thing you'll want to have to do is explain the relationship between you and a minor who is not your child.

It's best to have the minor's parents sign a Guardianship Authorization form, and take an original signed and notarized copy of this document with you on your trip. That way, if any problems arise, such as the need for authorization for medical treatment, you will be prepared.

You'll also need a signed and notarized letter from the minor's parents stating that they know about and approve of your specific travel plans. (See below.)

> **Travel for Noncitizens of the United States**
>
> In this section, we assume that you and the minor who is not your child both are citizens of the United States. If you or the minor are not U.S. citizens, check with the U.S. immigration office or consult with an immigration attorney before attempting to leave the country. (See Chapter 13 on how to find and deal with an attorney.)

U.S. Passports

Most countries require passports for everyone traveling there from the United States, including all minors. Passport applications are available at U.S. Passport offices, some courts, and authorized post offices. A minor under 13 years of age must appear in person when applying for a passport.

If you aren't the minor's legal guardian, you will need to carry a notarized statement from a parent when you travel, stating that you are authorized to obtain a passport for the minor. The Guardianship Authorization form provided above should be sufficient documentation for your local passport office. (Note that Item 5 of the form specifically authorizes you to apply for a passport on behalf of the minor.)

Letter Authorizing Minor to Travel Outside the United States

If you complete a formal guardianship, a certified copy of the Letters of Guardianship and the court order that you get at the end of the process should be enough to allow you to travel outside of the United States with the minor. However, travel authorities are extremely concerned about the kidnapping of children, and are quite strict about having the proper documentation for travel. If you can get one, the best thing you can have is an authorization for foreign travel, signed by the minor's parent or parents. If you don't have a formal guardianship, you absolutely will need an authorization form signed by the parents, or you won't be allowed out of the country with the minor.

The form shown below (and the documentation it recommends you bring along) will provide the necessary proof that everyone who is a parent or has custodial rights has given the appropriate consent to the foreign travel. It also provides information about the child's travel plans and contact information for the child's parents, if necessary.

If there is more than one child who will be traveling outside the country, you should prepare a separate authorization form for each child.

This form has two different options for authorizing language, depending on whether you have one or both parents available to sign the form. You will choose the option that fits your situation, fill in the blanks for that part of the form, and then delete or cross out the option you are not using.

Use Option 1 if you only will get the signature of one parent. The form calls for you to attach a certified copy of the child's birth certificate, so that you can prove that there is only one parent and the signature of the other is not needed. If the other parent is deceased, then you'll need to bring the other parent's death certificate with you. It seems macabre, but if you don't have this documentation, you may not be allowed to travel with the minor.

Avoid this by planning ahead and having your forms and other documents in order.

Use Option 2 if both parents will sign the authorization to allow you travel with the minor. (If the other parent can't be located or refuses to sign the form, then you'll have to get a court order allowing you to travel without that parent's consent.)

Important note about medical care. This form does not permit you to authorize medical care for the child. If you have a formal guardianship, that won't be a problem—but if you don't, make sure you also have a Guardianship Authorization as described in Chapter 1, to ensure that you can authorize necessary medical treatment for the minor.

This authorization for travel form should be signed in front of a notary public. You should keep one of the signed and notarized documents for travel. Give the other to the parents for safekeeping.

Insurance Coverage

If the minor who lives with you is old enough to drive, you'll need to add the minor to your automobile insurance coverage. You should be able to do this without a formal legal guardianship. Most automobile insurers will add nonrelatives if you're willing to pay the premium. Policies differ, so check with your insurance agent for information on how to do this.

If you want other types of insurance coverage for the minor (life, accident, or property), you should also check with your insurance agent for details. (Information on medical and dental insurance coverage is covered above, in "Dealing With Agencies and Institutions.")

Authorization for Foreign Travel With Minor

To Whom It May Concern:

This letter authorizes my child, _____ [name of child], a United States citizen and a minor born on _____ [child's birth date], who carries a United States passport with the number _____ [child's passport number], to travel outside the United States.

[Option 1]

I affirm that I have legal custody of my child, and that I am the child's only legal parent. [Attach copy of birth certificate showing that you are the only legal parent or, if the child's other parent is deceased, copy of child's birth certificate and death certificate of other parent.] I give my full authorization and consent for my child to travel outside of the United States with _____ [name of person who is traveling with child], who is the child's _____ [relationship between child and adult traveling with child].

[Option 2]

We affirm that we are the parents of _____ [child's name] and that we share legal custody. We give our full authorization and consent for our child to travel outside of the United States with _____ [name of person who is traveling with child], who is the child's _____ [relationship between child and adult traveling with child].

The purpose of the travel is _____ [specify vacation, touring, to visit relatives, or other reason].

I/we have approved the following travel plans:

Dates of travel: Destination/Accommodations:

_____   _____

_____   _____

Furthermore, I/we hereby authorize _____ [name of person with whom child will be traveling] to modify the travel plans specified above as he/she deems necessary.

I/we declare under penalty of perjury under the laws of the State of California that the foregoing is true and correct.

Mother's signature: _____ Date: _____
Print name: _____
Home phone: _____ Work phone: _____ Cell phone: _____

Father's signature: _____ Date: _____
Print name: _____
Home phone: _____ Work phone: _____ Cell phone: _____

Certificate of Acknowledgment of Notary Public

State of California
County of _____

On _____, before me, _____, a notary public in and for said state, personally appeared _____, known to me (or proved to me on the basis of satisfactory evidence) to be the person(s) whose name(s) is/are subscribed to the within instrument, and acknowledged to me that he/she/they executed the same in his/her/their authorized capacity and that by his/her/their signature on the instrument, the person(s), or the entity upon behalf of which the person(s) acted, executed the instrument.

I declare under PENALTY OF PERJURY under the laws of the State of California that the foregoing paragraph is true and correct.

WITNESS my hand and official seal.   _____

Notary Public for the State of California   My commission expires_____

Getting Started

Documents and Information You Need

Before you start filling in the forms for a legal guardianship, collect the following information and documents:

- Names and addresses of all of these living relatives of the minor:

    - parents

    - grandparents (parents of both the minor's mother and father)

    - sisters and brothers (if they are under 18 and have one different parent from the minor, you need the name and address of that parent as well)

    - spouse (this is unlikely, and if the minor is married or divorced you may only petition for guardianship of the estate)

    - children (this is unlikely, but if the minor has any children you will need their names and addresses)

    - any legal guardian of the minor, or anyone who has been nominated as legal guardian, and

    - the adult with whom the minor is living (other than you or anyone else in this list).

- Copies of death certificates of the minor's parents if either of them has died. If you don't have copies of the death certificates, you can obtain them by writing to the vital records office of the state where the parent died. The process is the same as that for getting a copy of a birth certificate, described below.

- If you're seeking guardianship because you were named guardian in the will of someone who died, a copy of the will. The law requires anyone holding an original will of someone who died to deposit it with the county clerk in the county in which the deceased person lived. If this has been done, you can get a certified copy from the court for a small fee. If a probate has been opened, get copies of all court-filed documents.

- Copies of any documents relating to property the minor owns or is subject to inherit (such as bank accounts, life insurance policies, real estate, or vehicles).

- Copies of court documents involving the minor. This includes any marriage dissolution, pending custody, adoption, or juvenile court proceedings that affect the minor (for example, copies of the minor's parents' divorce papers or copies of any court papers that anyone has filed to adopt the minor, even if the adoption was not completed).

- The birth certificate of the minor for whom you are seeking a guardianship. This is especially important if you are claiming that the natural father is unknown. See "How to Get a Copy of a Birth Certificate," below.

By the time you've finished your guardianship, you will have accumulated a good many papers and file-endorsed copies of court documents. Make sure that you establish a system to keep all of these documents in a safe place. There are few things more frustrating than losing an important document and having to replace it. File folders or large manila envelopes are particularly helpful for getting and keeping your guardianship case organized. Even better is a cardboard accordion file with a top flap that can be tied securely. You might want to keep several file folders in the accordion file that are separated by category (such as court guardianship papers, birth certificates, other legal proceedings affecting the minor, searches for missing relatives, and correspondence). Then, when you start a new procedure (such as searching for missing relatives), you can open a new file folder with a new label.

How to Get a Copy of a Birth Certificate

If you need a birth certificate for a minor who was born in California, contact the state Office of Vital Records by telephone, in writing, or in person:

Street address: Office of Vital Records, Department of Public Health, 1501 Capital Avenue, Suite 2101, Sacramento.

Mailing address: Office of Vital Records, MS 5103, P.O. Box 997410, Sacramento, CA 94244-7410.

Phone number: 916-445-2684.

Website: www.cdph.ca.gov. You can order a copy of the Birth Certificate Request Form online at the website and then submit it by mail.

If you need a birth certificate for a minor who was born outside of California, you'll have to check with the state where the minor was born. It's becoming more and more difficult to get copies of birth certificates, but with some perseverance—and certainly with the help of the minor's parents, if you have it—you should be able to succeed. You can find addresses for state offices of vital records on the Internet at the National Center for Health Statistics website, at www.cdc.gov/nchs.

The Courts

Different types of courts handle different types of legal matters. In California, guardianships are handled in the probate division of the superior court, unless the minor is a dependent of a juvenile court, in which case the guardianship proceeding is handled in juvenile court.

All California probate courts follow the same basic procedures for guardianships, but courts in different counties (especially those with large populations) commonly have several special procedural rules of their own, usually called "local rules." Many counties have these court rules printed in small pamphlets called local probate rules, probate policy manuals, or memoranda. You can check with the probate court clerk in your county to get a copy. If you cannot get a probate policy manual through the court, you can find it at the county law library. (See Chapter 13 for more information on probate policy manuals and legal research.) Whenever possible in this book, we refer to individual county's rules, but we cannot possibly identify every one used in all counties.

Where to File the Guardianship

You usually will file your guardianship in the county where the minor lives. If the guardianship is only for the estate of the minor, the guardianship petition may be filed in any county in California where the minor has property. "Property" includes real estate as well as personal property, such as vehicles, jewelry, bank accounts, and other assets. If you need to, you can later transfer the case from one county to another. For example, a case might be transferred if it would be more convenient for you to have it in a different court or if you move. (See Chapter 11 for instructions on transferring cases.)

In many counties, the courthouse you deal with will be located in the "county seat," often the largest city in the county. Several of the bigger counties have branch courts in cities other than the county seat. For example, the Contra Costa County Superior Court has a branch in Walnut Creek, in addition to the main court in Martinez. Los Angeles County has a main branch in Los Angeles, and 12 district branches. If there is a branch court close to where the minor lives, local court rules probably will require you to file your guardianship there. To find the superior court in your county, check the telephone directory in the county government listings section. If you find several listings for the superior court, which is likely in larger counties, the one you want is the probate division of the superior court.

Many Courts Have Special Clerks to Answer Procedural Questions

In most of the larger courts, special court clerks give information about guardianship procedures. These clerks are well-versed in the court's specific rules and in guardianship law. The clerks cannot give legal advice, but they will answer questions about the court's procedural requirements. Many courts have designated times of the day when you may call these clerks.

Using the checklist below, phone the probate court and ask the filing clerk for some basic information you'll need to complete your guardianship forms.

How to Use the Forms

Here are some tips on how to use the forms provided in this book. If you follow these suggestions, you can save yourself a lot of time and trouble.

General Tips for Using Forms

There are two types of forms in this book: Judicial Council forms that are issued by the state, and Nolo forms that we have developed to help you with your guardianship petition.

The Judicial Council forms are standard forms that are designed and approved by a group called the California Judicial Council. These forms are used in all the California courts, and most of them are mandatory, meaning that you can't use any alternative forms but must use these for the purpose for which they are designed. There's more about the Judicial Council forms below.

The Nolo forms are designed by us, to help with parts of the process that either don't require a Judicial Council form, like keeping track of tasks you've completed, or that need a supplement to a Judicial Council form.

Blank versions of all the forms, of both types, are in Appendixes B and C. Judicial Council forms are also available on the Internet—there's more information about that below. Before you fill out any of the tear-out forms in the appendixes, make several photocopies of each of them. This will save you many worried moments if you make a mistake or misplace a form. Also, note that many forms have printing on both sides. If the form is two-sided, make sure you copy both sides, but make your copies single-sided. The courts want printing on only one side of each page.

All forms should be completed carefully and neatly, preferably using a computer or typewriter. If you're using a typewriter, it is best to use the larger type size (called "pica" or "10-pitch" type). Some courts may refuse to accept forms with smaller type (called "elite" or "12-pitch" type). If you do not have access to a typewriter, there are document preparation services that can prepare forms for you at a reasonable cost. (See Chapter 13.) Depending on the court's policies, handwritten forms may be accepted if you print clearly and neatly, generally in black ink. If you want to submit handwritten forms, call the court beforehand to make sure they'll be accepted.

Carefully follow the instructions in this book for completing the forms. Also look at any samples provided to make sure you fill in the forms correctly.

Whenever you send a completed form to the court, always keep copies for yourself. When you file papers with the court clerk, take along an extra copy for the clerk to stamp and return to you. Documents can be lost in the mail, misplaced by a clerk, or otherwise sent off into the twilight zone.

Checklist of Information to Obtain From Court Clerk

☐ The proper branch of the court for filing your guardianship papers (you'll need to tell the clerk in what city or town the minor lives)

☐ the mailing address of the court

☐ the street address of the court—if it is different from the mailing address

☐ the fee for filing a petition for a guardianship (if you cannot afford the fees, you may be able to get them waived)

☐ whether there are any special forms or procedures the court requires for guardianships, and

☐ whether the court requires an investigation. This is generally required only when you are seeking guardianship of a minor's person. Who investigates the guardianship will depend on whether you are a blood relative of the minor. Tell the clerk your relationship to the minor, and ask for the name, title, and phone number of the investigator, as well as their office address. Copies of all documents filed need to be submitted to the probate investigator's office. (The investigation is routine, and not a scary process. Chapter 8 tells you all about it.)

Judicial Council Forms

Most of the forms you'll use are Judicial Council forms. Each of these forms has a title in bold print at the bottom of the page, and has information in the lower left-hand corner that will help you identify the form and determine whether it is current. (The form number is also printed in the upper right-hand corner for quick reference.) The number in the lower left-hand corner is the Judicial Council's own identification number. In the sample on the next page, the form name is Petition for Appointment of Guardian of Minor, and the form number is GC-210. Some forms also have citations to California law. For instance, this form has a citation in the lower right-hand corner that reads "Probate Code, § 1510," meaning that the form was designed according to that section of the probate laws.

Near the form number is the date the form was last revised. The forms were current when this book was published. However, Judicial Council forms are subject to change. Many of them stay current for years, but they are reviewed twice each year and can be changed at any time. To be safe, check and make sure the form is current. There are two ways to check. One is to call the court clerk and ask. You'll need to have the form name and number for the clerk to be able to answer your question. The other way is to check on the Internet, at www.courtinfo.ca.gov. Click on the "forms" link, and then use the drop-down list to find the category for "Probate—Guardianships and Conservatorships." Click on "See forms" and check the date next to the form you are using. If it's later than the date on the form in this book, download the form from the computer and use that one instead.

Sample Bottom of Judicial Council Form

Form Adopted for Mandatory and Alternative Mandatory Use Instead of Form GC-210(P) Judicial Council of California GC-210 [Rev. January 1, 2009]	**PETITION FOR APPOINTMENT OF GUARDIAN OF MINOR** (Probate—Guardianships and Conservatorships)	Probate Code, § 1510; Cal. Rules of Court, rule 7.101 www.courtinfo.ca.gov

Local Court Forms

Some courts have their own forms that must be used in addition to the forms in this book. Later on in the book, we discuss when and how to check with the court clerk to see if additional local court forms are required.

Forms to Fill the Gaps

In some instances, a form is desirable but the Judicial Council does not provide one. We have provided forms that are specially designed to fill this gap. These forms show Nolo's copyright in the lower left-hand corner.

General Rules on Completing Forms

As you fill in the guardianship forms, you'll find they follow a standardized, check-the-boxes, fill-in-the-blanks format. Throughout the book, there is specific information about each item on every form. Here is an overview.

If you are using the tear-out forms in the back of the book, make a copy before completing the form—and don't make the copy back to back or two-sided. The form you file should consist of single pages. If you download the forms from the Judicial Council website, they'll be on single pages.

The Caption

Most forms have a heading of several boxes with blank spaces, which is referred to as a "caption." There's a sample caption below. The caption is filled out the same way on almost every form. Here is how to do it.

Attorney or Party Without Attorney: You are a "Party Without Attorney." In capital letters, fill in your full first, middle, and last names, followed by your telephone number and mailing address.

Attorney for (Name): Here the court is asking for the name of the person you are representing. Fill in the words "In Pro Per." This means that you are representing yourself in the proceeding.

Superior Court of California, County of _____: In capital letters, fill in the county in which you are filing the guardianship.

Court Address: Fill in the court's street address, mailing address, and city and zip code. Also fill in the branch name, if there is one. You will get all of this information from the court clerk.

Guardianship of (Name): In capital letters, fill in the full first, middle, and last names of the minor or minors. Make sure that the names are complete and correctly spelled. Do not use nicknames.

Depending on the form, this part of the caption may vary a little bit. You will need to check any boxes that apply.

Minor: Check this box if the guardianship is for only one minor.

Minors: Check this box if the guardianship is for more than one minor. The minors must be full or half sisters or brothers; if they are not, you'll need a separate petition for each minor.

Person: Check this box if the guardianship is for the minor's person. (See Chapter 1.)

Sample Caption

		GC-210

ATTORNEY OR PARTY WITHOUT ATTORNEY *(Name, State Bar number, and address):*
ALICE JANE SMITH
100 Any Street
Fresno, CA 93717

TELEPHONE NO.: 209-555-1212   FAX NO. *(Optional):*

E-MAIL ADDRESS *(Optional):*
ATTORNEY FOR *(Name):* In Pro Per

FOR COURT USE ONLY

SUPERIOR COURT OF CALIFORNIA, COUNTY OF   FRESNO
STREET ADDRESS: 1100 Van Ness Avenue
MAILING ADDRESS: P.O. Box 1628
CITY AND ZIP CODE: Fresno, CA 93717
BRANCH NAME:

GUARDIANSHIP OF *(Name):*
MARK DONALD JONES   MINOR

CASE NUMBER:
12345

PETITION FOR APPOINTMENT OF GUARDIAN OF [X] **MINOR** [ ] **MINORS**
[X] **Person*** [ ] **Estate***

HEARING DATE AND TIME: DEPT.:

Estate: Check this box if the guardianship is for the minor's estate. (See Chapter 1.)

Plaintiff/Petitioner: Sometimes a form calls for this information instead of saying "Guardianship of (Name)." You are the "Plaintiff/Petitioner." Fill in your full name.

Case Number: When you file your first court papers, leave this space blank, as you don't have a case number yet. You will be assigned a case number that will be stamped or written in on the initial guardianship papers you file with the court. From that time on, always fill in that case number here. Copy the number carefully from your filed papers.

Declarations (Oaths)

Some of the forms used in the guardianship process ask you to sign under penalty of perjury. The declaration under penalty of perjury has the same effect as an oath or sworn statement, which means that you could be prosecuted under California law if you lie in it. The word "executed" means signed. To complete the declaration, fill in the date and the city and state (which should be in California) where you

signed the document. Then type or print your name and sign the declaration.

If you sign a document outside of the state of California, you will either need to have it notarized, or sign a declaration that says that it is signed "under penalty of perjury under the laws of the state of California." Some, but not all, forms already use this language, which is valid for declarations signed either inside or outside of California.

Appendix C has a blank Declaration form. If at any time you need to submit an additional Declaration either by itself or attached to another form, you can use this form.

Attachment (Additional) Pages

If you ever need more room to complete any item on any form, you can use a blank piece of typing paper, lined legal paper, or a copy of the Judicial Council Additional Page form in Appendix C. If you use the Judicial Council Additional Page form, make several blank copies of the form before you use it. Save the original form in case you need to add continuation pages to other forms later on. Samples of

Sample Declaration Under Penalty of Perjury

I declare under penalty of perjury under the laws of the State of California that the foregoing is true and correct.

Date:

· ▶ _____
                (TYPE OR PRINT NAME)   (SIGNATURE OF PETITIONER)

---

completed attachments for several items of the Petition for Appointment of Guardian of Minor are contained in Chapter 5.

To complete attachment pages, fill in the title of the guardianship at the top of the page with the full name of the minor and the case number, once it has been assigned.

Next, indicate what form and which items you are continuing. For example, a continuation sheet expanding on the information you supplied in Paragraph 8 of the Petition for Appointment of Guardian of Minor would be called "ATTACHMENT 8 TO PETITION FOR APPOINTMENT OF GUARDIAN OF MINOR." Use a new attachment page for each new item number you continue.

At the bottom right-hand corner, number the pages you're adding to the form. Show which page each one is out of the total, such as page "2 of 4." Obviously, you will need to number these pages after you finish the document, when you know how many total pages you are attaching.

Special Local Rules on Filing Papers

Certain courts have special local rules that tell how papers must be filed. Some of these rules don't seem logical or even sensible, but if you use a court that has them, you have no choice but to comply.

You can find your county's local rules at the Judicial Council website at www.courtinfo. ca.gov/rules/localrules.htm.

How to File Papers With the Court

What happens when you take or send your papers to the court might be a mystery to you, especially if you've never gone to court before. Fortunately, it's really quite simple. Each time you deliver a paper to the court, the court clerk will make it part of the official court record of your case.

How Many Copies Do You Need?

The court usually keeps the original version of all your completed forms, and some courts, especially branch courts, require one additional copy to keep—you'll need to call the court clerk and check. You should always take or send at least one extra copy (over and above the number of copies the court will keep) of the form to the court to be file-stamped and returned to you for your records. Whether you mail or personally take papers to the court, make sure that you also keep one copy at home in case the papers are lost. Depending on the document, you may need to make more copies so that they can be served on a number of people or agencies. You can make all the copies of completed forms before you file them with the court, and have each copy file-stamped, or you can file your papers with the court and then make copies. When in doubt, make extra photocopies. You're better off having too many copies than not having enough.

Take or Mail Papers to the Court

You file a document with the court simply by mailing or handing the document across the counter at the court clerk's office. When you file a document, give the court clerk the original and photocopies. The clerk will keep the original, which goes in your guardianship case file, and may also keep one photocopy, depending on the county policy. The clerk will stamp and return to you any extra copies. In the upper right-hand corner, the copies will have rubber-stamped information showing the date that the original was filed, and indicating that the copy is a file-stamped (or "file-endorsed") copy.

You may choose to go to the court in person to file your papers, in case you've made a mistake or want more information from the clerk. But if going to the courthouse is inconvenient, you can mail your documents to the court. To do this, send your papers to the court along with a self-addressed, stamped envelope with the correct amount of postage to have your file-stamped copies returned to you. If you send your papers by mail, remember to keep an extra photocopy at home, in case your papers are lost in the mail. In a letter, ask the clerk to file the original documents and have extra copies stamped and sent back to you; keep a copy of the letter, too. Below is a sample letter to the clerk.

Getting a Case Number

When you first file your papers with the court, the clerk assigns you a case number. This will either be written or stamped in the caption part of the form. Once the case number has been assigned, put that number on all court papers you later complete. The case number is the court's system of keeping track of cases, and it will be printed on a file folder in which all your court guardianship papers are kept. If you ever need to get information about your case over the telephone, you'll have to know your case number so that the clerk can locate your file.

Some Papers Are Not Returned Right Away

Some forms that you prepare will not be file-stamped and returned to you right away. Instead, the clerk will keep them in the court file. In this book, these papers are flagged by the word "(proposed)," indicating that you won't get them back from the court until a judge has reviewed and approved their contents. These are:

(Proposed) Orders

An order is a document signed by a judge allowing you to do something. For example, after you prepare your proposed Order Appointing Guardian of Minor, it must be signed by a judge to go into effect. Until the judge signs the order, you are not allowed to serve as the minor's legal guardian. In general, after preparing a proposed order (and after Letters of Guardianship are issued— see below), you take or send the original and copies to court. File-stamped copies are returned to you only after the judge signs the original order (which goes into the court's file). In general, guardianship orders are signed only after a court appearance.

(Proposed) Letters of Guardianship

The document verifying that you are authorized to act as guardian is called Letters of Guardianship. If you are appointed guardian

Sample Letter to the Clerk

June 14, 20xx

County Clerk
Superior Court of California
Probate Department
County of San Diego
P.O. Box 128
San Diego, CA 92112-4104

Re: Guardianship of: Kee Wong
        Case No. (Not Assigned Yet)

Dear Clerk:

Enclosed please find:

1. Original and five (5) copies of:

    PETITION FOR APPOINTMENT OF GUARDIAN OF MINOR;
    CONSENT OF PROPOSED GUARDIAN, NOMINATION OF GUARDIAN,
    AND CONSENT TO APPOINTMENT OF GUARDIAN, AND WAIVER OF NOTICE; and
    NOTICE OF HEARING (GUARDIANSHIP).

2. Original and two (2) copies of:

    CONFIDENTIAL GUARDIAN SCREENING FORM;
    DUTIES OF GUARDIAN; UCCJEA DECLARATION;
    (PROPOSED) ORDER APPOINTING GUARDIAN; and
    ACKNOWLEDGMENT OF RECEIPT.

3. Check in the amount of $355; and

4. Self-addressed, stamped envelope.

Please return copies to me after you file them. Also please provide me with a guardianship hearing date at least six weeks away from the date of this letter.

Sincerely,

David Wong

David Wong
1 Main Street
San Diego, CA 92101
Phone: 619-555-1212

for a limited time, you will obtain Letters of Temporary Guardianship. This form has a seal on it, meaning it was "issued" by the court. Letters can only be obtained after a judge signs an order appointing you guardian or temporary guardian.

Amending Filed Documents

If, after you file the papers for the guardianship but before you are appointed guardian, you find a serious error or want to change some wording on the documents, you can file an "amended" document to take the place of the incorrect document. Use the same title as the original document, but print or type the word "AMENDED" before the name of the form. If you are using a preprinted form, print or type the word "AMENDED" both before the form's printed name in the caption and on the bottom of the page. Then complete and file the original and copies of the amended form with the court, and have copies served on all of the people or agencies who were served with notice of the guardianship. You might need to amend a document if:

- the facts or situation stated change substantially after you file the document with the court

- you discover a serious error on the document after it is filed, or

- after filing a Petition for Appointment of Guardian of Minor, you become aware of any proceedings that affect the minor and weren't included in the initial petition—in this situation, you *must* amend the petition within ten days of the time you find out about them. This includes adoptions, juvenile court matters, marriage dissolution, custody, or other similar proceedings affecting the minor. This is discussed in more detail in Chapter 6.

Stopping the Court Procedure

What happens if you have filed your initial guardianship documents, and you change your mind about becoming a guardian, or the situation changes so that a guardianship is no longer needed? In most cases, as long as you have not yet been appointed guardian, you can stop the process simply by filing a document called a Request for Dismissal with the court clerk. The court may, however, be reluctant to dismiss a case if there were allegations in the petition of parental abuse. Here is how to do it.

Prepare and File a Request for Dismissal

Use the Request for Dismissal form in Appendix C. Make at least one copy of the form, in case you make a mistake or later need to change or amend it.

How to Complete the Form

Caption: Request for Dismissal

In the first box fill in your name, address, telephone number, and the words "In Pro Per," following the general instructions in the section above, "General Rules on Completing Forms."

In the next box, insert the county in which your guardianship proceeding is taking place and the court's address. If your case is in a certain branch of the court, insert the branch on the last line of that box.

Just below the court and county information box, insert your name after the words, "Plaintiff/Petitioner." Leave the "Defendant/ Respondent" line blank.

In the box titled "Request for Dismissal," check the box next to the word "Other" and type in "Guardianship of the Person" or "Estate" or "Person and Estate" (whichever one applies) next to the word "Other." Fill in the case number at the far right.

Item 1a: Check box (2), entitled "Without prejudice." This means that if you change your mind, you can file another guardianship action.

Item 1b: Check box (5), entitled "Entire action of all parties and all causes of action."

Skip down to the first place where it says "Date," and fill in the date. Below the date, type or print your name on the line provided and check the box in front of the words, "Party Without Attorney." Below your signature, check the box that says "Party Without Attorney." Sign your name on the signature line at the right and below that, check the box before the words "Plaintiff/Petitioner."

You don't need to fill in the rest of the boxes on the first page. On the second page, put your name in the box at the top where it says "Petitioner," and leave the line for "Respondent" blank. Put your case number in the box on the right. You only need to complete the second page if you have received a waiver of your court fees and costs. If you have, then you will need to put your name in item 1, and check box 2.a, indicating that you are not recovering anything of value from the guardianship petition.

Fill in the date you are signing the form, print your name to the left of the signature page, and sign your name where indicated.

Make at least two copies of the completed document, and take or send the original and one copy to the clerk, using the instructions given above.

Note: If you already have a hearing date for the guardianship, call the court and have the hearing date canceled as soon as possible. In legal slang, this is called being "taken off calendar." You will probably also need to send a confirming letter to the court stating that you wish to cancel the hearing date.

This dismissal procedure covers guardianships which have not yet been granted. If you have already been named guardian of a minor, you must get the court's permission to resign as guardian or end the guardianship altogether. (See Chapter 12.) If you don't wish to stop the process, but simply need more time before the hearing on the guardianship petition, you may be able to obtain a new hearing date. (See Chapter 6.)

Filing Fees and Court Costs

When you first file your guardianship documents, you will be required to pay a filing fee—currently $355 in most counties, but be sure you check. In addition, if your county requires an investigation, those costs run anywhere from $200 for an estate-only investigation to $800 for a complete investigation in some counties. A routine investigation is almost always required for nonrelatives petitioning to be guardians of a minor's person, and it may be required for relatives of the minor as well, depending on the individual court's policy. (There is more information about investigations in Chapter 8.)

Waiving Court Fees and Costs

If you have a very low income or can't afford the court fees, the court may order that you do not have to pay court fees and costs. You don't have to be absolutely destitute, but you really must be unable to pay. If you are petitioning for guardianship of a minor's estate and you have a very low income, you can apply for a waiver of court fees and costs in order to proceed with the guardianship. Once you are appointed guardian of the minor's estate, you will reimburse the court using money from the estate.

To have your fees waived, you need to fill out two forms that give information about

Sample Request for Dismissal, page 1

CIV-110

ATTORNEY OR PARTY WITHOUT ATTORNEY *(Name, State Bar number, and address):*
Daniel Eric Hong
120 Any Street
Madera, CA 93637

TELEPHONE NO.: 209-555-1212   FAX NO. *(Optional):*

E-MAIL ADDRESS *(Optional):*

ATTORNEY FOR *(Name):* In Pro Per

FOR COURT USE ONLY

SUPERIOR COURT OF CALIFORNIA, COUNTY OF Madera
STREET ADDRESS: 209 West Yosemite Street
MAILING ADDRESS:
CITY AND ZIP CODE: Madera, CA
BRANCH NAME:

PLAINTIFF/PETITIONER: Daniel Eric Hong

DEFENDANT/RESPONDENT:

REQUEST FOR DISMISSAL
[ ] **Personal Injury, Property Damage, or Wrongful Death**
    [ ] **Motor Vehicle** [ ] **Other**
[ ] **Family Law** [ ] **Eminent Domain**
[✓] **Other** *(specify)* : Guardianship of the Person

CASE NUMBER:
123456

- A conformed copy will not be returned by the clerk unless a method of return is provided with the document. -

1. TO THE CLERK: Please **dismiss** this action as follows:
  a. (1) [ ] With prejudice (2) [✓] Without prejudice
  b. (1) [ ] Complaint (2) [ ] Petition
    (3) [ ] Cross-complaint filed by *(name):*   on *(date):*
    (4) [ ] Cross-complaint filed by *(name):*   on *(date):*
    (5) [✓] Entire action of all parties and all causes of action
    (6) [ ] Other *(specify):**

2. *(Complete in all cases except family law cases.)*
  [ ] Court fees and costs were waived for a party in this case. *(This information may be obtained from the clerk. If this box is checked, the declaration on the back of this form must be completed).*

Date: May 1, 20xx

Daniel Eric Hong .... ▶ _____
(TYPE OR PRINT NAME OF [ ] ATTORNEY [✓] PARTY WITHOUT ATTORNEY)   (SIGNATURE)

*If dismissal requested is of specified parties only of specified causes of action only, or of specified cross-complaints only, so state and identify the parties, causes of action, or cross-complaints to be dismissed.

Attorney or party without attorney for:
[✓] Plaintiff/Petitioner   [ ] Defendant/Respondent
[ ] Cross–Complainant

3. **TO THE CLERK:** Consent to the above dismissal is hereby given.**
  Date:

▶ _____
(TYPE OR PRINT NAME OF [ ] ATTORNEY [ ] PARTY WITHOUT ATTORNEY)   (SIGNATURE)

** If a cross-complaint – or Response (Family Law) seeking affirmative relief – is on file, the attorney for cross-complainant (respondent) must sign this consent if required by Code of Civil Procedure section 581 (i) or (j).

Attorney or party without attorney for:
[ ] Plaintiff/Petitioner   [ ] Defendant/Respondent
[ ] Cross–Complainant

(To be completed by clerk)
4. [ ] Dismissal entered as requested on *(date):*
5. [ ] Dismissal entered on *(date):*   as to only *(name):*
6. [ ] Dismissal **not entered** as requested for the following reasons *(specify):*

7. a. [ ] Attorney or party without attorney notified on *(date):*
  b. [ ] Attorney or party without attorney not notified. Filing party failed to provide
    [ ] a copy to be conformed [ ] means to return conformed copy

Date: _____   Clerk, by _____ , Deputy

Page 1 of 2

Form Adopted for Mandatory Use
Judicial Council of California
CIV-110 [Rev. July 1, 2009]

REQUEST FOR DISMISSAL

Code of Civil Procedure, § 581 et seq.;
Gov. Code, § 68637(c); Cal. Rules of Court, rule 3.1390
www.courtinfo.ca.gov

Sample Request for Dismissal, page 2

CIV-110

PLAINTIFF/PETITIONER: Daniel Eric Hong	CASE NUMBER:
DEFENDANT/RESPONDENT:	123456

Declaration Concerning Waived Court Fees

> The court has a statutory lien for waived fees and costs on any recovery of $10,000 or more in value by settlement, compromise, arbitration award, mediation settlement, or other recovery. The court's lien must be paid before the court will dismiss the case.

1. The court waived fees and costs in this action for *(name):*

2. The person in item 1 *(check one):*
   a. ☐ is not recovering anything of value by this action.
   b. ☐ is recovering less than $10,000 in value by this action.
   c. ☐ is recovering $10,000 or more in value by this action. *(If item 2c is checked, item 3 must be completed.)*

3. ☐ All court fees and costs that were waived in this action have been paid to the court *(check one):* ☐ Yes ☐ No

I declare under penalty of perjury under the laws of the State of California that the information above is true and correct.

Date: _____

_____
(TYPE OR PRINT NAME OF ☐ ATTORNEY ☐ PARTY MAKING DECLARATION)

▶ _____
(SIGNATURE)

CIV-110 [Rev. July 1, 2009]	**REQUEST FOR DISMISSAL**	Page 2 of 2

your income and expenses. If you are currently receiving public assistance such as CalWORKs or TANF (formerly AFDC), food stamps, county relief, general relief, General Assistance, SSI, or SSP, you should have no problem qualifying for the fee waiver. You should also qualify for a waiver of court fees and costs if your gross monthly income (your monthly income before taxes or deductions are taken out) is equal to or less than the amounts shown in the chart below. These figures were taken from the fee waiver application form and were current when this book went to press. Check with the clerk to make sure the form is up to date; if it is, the amounts listed are too.

Qualifying Income for Waiver of Court Fees and Costs	
Number in Family	Monthly Family Income
1	$1,128.13
2	$1,517.71
3	$1,907.30
4	$2,296.88
5	$2,686.46
6	$3,076.05
Each additional	$ 389.59

If you don't automatically qualify for a fee waiver, or you earn more than the amounts shown on the chart, then you'll have to show the court that you can't pay the court fees. You'll submit information about your income and expenses, and a judge will review the information and decide whether to waive some or all of the expenses.

If you qualify to have court fees and costs waived, and your financial situation later changes, you must immediately notify the court if you become able to pay. By law, the court could order you to appear anytime within three years after you file for a fee waiver to answer questions about your ability to pay.

It's easy to apply for a waiver of court fees and costs. You complete two forms:

- Request to Waive Court Fees; and
- Order on Court Fee Waiver.

Make copies of these forms, and file them along with the rest of your guardianship papers. Here are instructions on how to complete the fee waiver forms.

Request to Waive Court Fees (Superior Court)

In this form, you tell why you cannot pay court expenses, and request that they be waived.

CAPTION: Request to Waive Court Fees

Fill in the court information in the box on the right, and insert your name.

Leave the case number blank for now, as it hasn't been assigned yet.

Item 2: Fill in your employer information if you have one, or type "unemployed."

Item 3: Type in "In Pro Per."

Item 4: This item is already completed for you.

Item 5. You will check one of the three boxes under item 5.

Item 5a. If you are receiving one of the types of public assistance listed under item 5a, check the main box and the box for the type(s) of assistance you receive, then skip items 5b and 5c. If you check this box, you won't need to complete any part of the second page of the form. You can skip to item 6 then sign the form.

Item 5b. If your family income is less than the amounts listed under this item, check the box for this item. You'll need to fill out items 7, 8, and 9 on the second page of the form.

Item 5c. If you don't qualify for a fee waiver under either of the other criteria, but you don't have enough money to pay all of your court fees and still pay your household expenses, you can submit your income and expense information and ask the court to waive your fees on that basis. Check box c and then check one of the other boxes, depending on whether you want the court to waive all court fees, waive some court fees, or allow you to make payments over time. On the line that says "Explain," insert the words "see page 2," and then complete all of the items on page 2 (instructions below).

Item 6. It's unlikely you will need to check this box, but if you have filed a previous fee waiver request in the past six months, check the box and, if you have a copy of that previous request, check the second box and attach it.

Date and signature. Fill in the date and your name and sign the form.

CAPTION: Page Two of the Request to Waive Court Fees

Fill in your name on the line at the top of the page. Leave the Case Number blank for now, as the number hasn't been assigned yet.

Item 7: Check this box if the amount of your earnings changes a great deal each month, such as if you are self-employed and make a fair amount of money one month but very little another month.

Item 8: In this Item you provide information about your monthly income. If you checked Item 7, you will need to use averages for each of the figures required. For example, to get a monthly average of your income for the last year, add up your total earnings for the last 12 months and divide that amount by 12.

Item 8a: Fill in the amount of your gross monthly pay. This is the income you receive each month before any taxes or deductions are taken out.

Items 8a(1)–(4): Fill in the type and amount of each of your payroll deductions in the spaces provided. Then add together all of the amounts you filled in for Items 9b(1)–(4) and fill in the total payroll deduction amount.

Item 8b: Total the payroll deductions. Fill in this amount.

Item 8c: Subtract 8b from 8a to get your total monthly take-home pay.

Item 8d: Fill in any other amounts of money you get each month, and tell where you get them from (Items 8d(1)–(4)).

Item 8e: Add together Items 8c and 8d(1)-(4) and enter the total.

Item 9a: List the people who live in your household and the requested information about each of them.

Item 9b: Total the income of everyone else living in your household, and enter the total. Just below that, enter the total of Items 8e and 9b.

Items 10a–e: Fill in the value of any property you own, including money, vehicles, real estate, and personal property.

Items 11a–m: In these items you tell how much you pay each month in living expenses. Make sure you list all of your expenses.

Total Monthly Expenses: Fill in the total of all your monthly expenses by adding together all of the amounts you filled in for Items 11a–11m and entering this amount.

If there is any reason why you can't pay court fees and costs other than that you just don't make enough money, check the box inside the box on the bottom left side of the page, and attach an explanation as instructed in that box. This might include unusual medical expenses, money spent for recent family emergencies, or other unusual expenses. You will need to attach an additional page to the Request to Waive Court Fees to provide this information. Follow the instructions for preparing attachment pages in this chapter, and label the page "Attachment

Sample Request to Waive Court Fees, page 1

FW-001	**Request to Waive Court Fees**	**CONFIDENTIAL**

Clerk stamps date here when form is filed.

If you are getting public benefits, are a low-income person, or do not have enough income to pay for household's basic needs and your court fees, you may use this form to ask the court to waive all or part of your court fees. The court may order you to answer questions about your finances. If the court waives the fees, you may still have to pay later if:
- You cannot give the court proof of your eligibility,
- Your financial situation improves during this case, or
- You settle your civil case for **$10,000** or more. The trial court that waives your fees will have a lien on any such settlement in the amount of the waived fees and costs. The court may also charge you any collection costs.

Fill in court name and street address:

Alameda County Superior Court
1225 Fallon Street
Oakland, CA 94612

(1) Your Information (person asking the court to waive the fees):
Name: Marcia J. Jones

Street or mailing address: 2001 City Street
City: Oakland   State: CA   Zip: 94619
Phone number: 510-555-1212

Fill in case number and name:

Case Number:

Case Name:
Guardianship of Jeffrey Jones

(2) Your Job, if you have one (job title): unemployed
Name of employer: _____
Employer's address: _____

(3) Your lawyer, if you have one (name, firm or affiliation, address, phone number, and State Bar number):
In Pro Per
_____

a. The lawyer has agreed to advance all or a portion of your fees or costs (check one):   Yes ☐   No ☐
b. (If yes, your lawyer must sign here) Lawyer's signature: _____
   If your lawyer is not providing legal-aid type services based on your low income, you may have to go to a hearing to explain why you are asking the court to waive the fees.

(4) What court's fees or costs are you asking to be waived?
☑ Superior Court (See Information Sheet on Waiver of Superior Court Fees and Costs (form FW-001-INFO).)
☐ Supreme Court, Court of Appeal, or Appellate Division of Superior Court (See Information Sheet on Waiver of Appellate Court Fees and Costs (form APP-015/FW-015-INFO).)

(5) Why are you asking the court to waive your court fees?
a. ☑ I receive (check all that apply): ☐ Medi-Cal ☑ Food Stamps ☐ SSI ☐ SSP ☐ County Relief/General Assistance ☐ IHSS (In-Home Supportive Services) ☑ CalWORKS or Tribal TANF (Tribal Temporary Assistance for Needy Families) ☐ CAPI (Cash Assistance Program for Aged, Blind and Disabled)
b. ☐ My gross monthly household income (before deductions for taxes) is less than the amount listed below. (If you check 5b you must fill out 7, 8 and 9 on page 2 of this form.)

Family Size	Family Income	Family Size	Family Income	Family Size	Family Income	
1	$1,128.13	3	$1,907.30	5	$2,686.46	If more than 6 people at home, add $389.59
2	$1,517.71	4	$2,296.88	6	$3,076.05	for each extra person.

c. ☐ I do not have enough income to pay for my household's basic needs *and* the court fees. I ask the court to (check one): ☐ waive all court fees ☐ waive some of the court fees ☐ let me make payments over time (Explain): _____ (If you check 5c, you must fill out page 2.)

(6) ☐ Check here if you asked the court to waive your court fees for this case in the last six months. (If your previous request is reasonably available, please attach it to this form and check here: ☐)

I declare under penalty of perjury under the laws of the State of California that the information I have provided on this form and all attachments is true and correct.

Date: 6/12/20xx

Marcia J. Jones   ▶ _____
Print your name here   *Sign here*

Judicial Council of California, www.courtinfo.ca.gov
Revised July 2, 2009, Mandatory Form
Government Code, § 68633
Cal. Rules of Court, rules 3.51, 8.26, and 8.818

Request to Waive Court Fees

FW-001, Page 1 of 2

Sample Request to Waive Court Fees, page 2

	Case Number:

Your name: Marcia J. Jones

If you checked 5a on page 1, do not fill out below. If you checked 5b, fill out questions 7, 8, and 9 only. If you checked 5c, you must fill out this entire page. If you need more space, attach form MC-025 or attach a sheet of paper and write Financial Information and your name and case number at the top.

(7) ☐ Check here if your income changes a lot from month to month. Fill out below based on your average income for the past 12 months.

(8) **Your Monthly Income**
a. Gross monthly income *(before deductions):* $ _____
   List each payroll deduction and amount below:
   (1) _____ $ _____
   (2) _____ $ _____
   (3) _____ $ _____
   (4) _____ $ _____
b. Total deductions *(add 8a (1)-(4) above):* $ _____
c. Total monthly take-home pay *(8a minus 8b):* $ _____
d. List the source and amount of *any* other income you get each month, including: spousal/child support, retirement, social security, disability, unemployment, military basic allowance for quarters (BAQ), veterans payments, dividends, interest, trust income, annuities, net business or rental income, reimbursement for job-related expenses, gambling or lottery winnings, etc.
   (1) _____ $ _____
   (2) _____ $ _____
   (3) _____ $ _____
   (4) _____ $ _____
e. Your total monthly income is *(8c plus 8d):* $ _____

(9) **Household Income**
a. List all other persons living in your home and their income; include only your spouse and all individuals who depend in whole or in part on you for support, or on whom you depend in whole or in part for support.

Name	Age	Relationship	Gross Monthly Income
(1)			$
(2)			$
(3)			$
(4)			$

b. Total monthly income of persons above: $ _____

Total monthly income *and* household income *(8e plus 9b):* $ _____

To list any other facts you want the court to know, such as unusual medical expenses, family emergencies, etc., attach form MC-025. Or attach a sheet of paper, and write Financial Information and your name and case number at the top. Check here if you attach another page. ☐

***Important!* If your financial situation or ability to pay court fees improves, you must notify the court within five days on form FW-010.**

(10) **Your Money and Property**
a. Cash ------------------------- $ _____
b. All financial accounts *(List bank name and amount):*
   (1) _____ $ _____
   (2) _____ $ _____
   (3) _____ $ _____
   (4) _____ $ _____

c. Cars, boats, and other vehicles

Make / Year	Fair Market Value	How Much You Still Owe
(1)	$	$
(2)	$	$
(3)	$	$

d. Real estate

Address	Fair Market Value	How Much You Still Owe
(1)	$	$
(2)	$	$
(3)	$	$

e. Other personal property (jewelry, furniture, furs, stocks, bonds, etc.):

Describe	Fair Market Value	How Much You Still Owe
(1)	$	$
(2)	$	$
(3)	$	$

(11) **Your Monthly Expenses**
(Do not include payroll deductions you already listed in 8b.)

a.	Rent or house payment & maintenance	$
b.	Food and household supplies	$
c.	Utilities and telephone	$
d.	Clothing	$
e.	Laundry and cleaning	$
f.	Medical and dental expenses	$
g.	Insurance (life, health, accident, etc.)	$
h.	School, child care	$
i.	Child, spousal support (another marriage)	$
j.	Transportation, gas, auto repair and insurance	$
k.	Installment payments (list each below): Paid to:	
	(1)	$
	(2)	$
	(3)	$
l.	Wages/earnings withheld by court order	$
m.	Any other monthly expenses (list each below): Paid to:	How Much?
	(1)	$
	(2)	$
	(3)	$

Total monthly expenses *(add 11a –11m above):* $ _____

Request to Waive Court Fees

FW-001, Page 2 of 2

12 to Request to Waive Court Fees." Then, in your own words, explain why you cannot pay the court fees and costs.

Important: If you have not already dated and signed the form on the first page, make sure you do this now.

Order on Court Fee Waiver

This form is for the judge to use to tell you whether your court fees and costs are waived and you do not have to pay them, or whether you only have to pay some of them, or whether you must take additional steps.

CAPTION: Order on Court Fee Waiver

Fill in the court name and address in the box on the right.

Item 1. Fill in your present name and your address.

Item 2. Fill in the words "In Pro Per" on the first line and leave the rest of the item blank.

Item 3. If you haven't filed a previous request for a fee waiver, fill in the date that you are filing this request on the first line. If there was a previous order, check the second box and fill in the date you filed that request.

Item 4. Leave the rest of the first page blank.

Caption on Page 2. At the top of the page, fill in your present name and the name(s) of any other Petitioners. Leave the case number blank, as you don't have a case number yet.

Leave the rest of the second page blank for the judge to complete.

Put these two completed forms in a safe, convenient place. When you come to Chapter 6, you will find specific instructions on applying for a fee waiver. For now, you are ready to turn to Chapter 4.

Sample Order on Court Fee Waiver,
(In Forma Pauperis), page 1

FW-003 | **Order on Court Fee Waiver (Superior Court)**

Clerk stamps date here when form is filed.

(1) Person who asked the court to waive court fees:

Name: Marcia J. Jones

Street or mailing address: 2001 City Street

City: Oakland   State: CA   Zip: 94619

(2) Lawyer, if person in (1) has one *(name, address, phone number, e-mail, and State Bar number):* In Pro Per

Fill in court name and street address:

Superior Court of California, County of
Alameda
1225 Fallon Street
Oakland, CA 94612

(3) A request to waive court fees was filed on *(date):* 6/12/20xx

☐ The court made a previous fee waiver order in this case on *(date):*

Fill in case number and case name:

Case Number:

Case Name:
Guardianship of Jeffrey Jones

Read this form carefully. All checked boxes ☑ are court orders.

Notice: The court may order you to answer questions about your finances and later order you to pay back the waived fees. If this happens and you do not pay, the court can make you pay the fees and also charge you collection fees. If there is a change in your financial circumstances during this case that increases your ability to pay fees and costs, you must notify the trial court within five days. (Use form FW-010.) If you win your case, the trial court may order the other side to pay the fees. If you settle your civil case for **$10,000** or more, the trial court will have a lien on the settlement in the amount of the waived fees. The trial court may not dismiss the case until the lien is paid.

(4) After reviewing your *(check one):*   ☑ *Request to Waive Court Fees*   ☐ *Request to Waive Additional Court Fees* **the court makes the following orders:**

a. ☐ The court **grants** your request, as follows:

(1) ☐ **Fee Waiver.** The court grants your request and waives your court fees and costs listed below. *(Cal. Rules of Court, rule 3.55.)* You do not have to pay the court fees for the following:

- Filing papers in Superior Court
- Making copies and certifying copies
- Sheriff's fee to give notice
- Reporter's daily fee *(for up to 60 days following the fee waiver order at the court-approved daily rate)*
- Preparing and certifying the clerk's transcript on appeal
- Giving notice and certificates
- Sending papers to another court department
- Court-appointed interpreter in small claims court
- Court fees for phone hearings

(2) ☐ **Additional Fee Waiver.** The court grants your request and waives your additional superior court fees and costs that are checked below. *(Cal. Rules of Court, rule 3.56.)* You do not have to pay for the checked items.

☐ Jury fees and expenses
☐ Fees for court-appointed experts
☐ Reporter's daily fees *(beyond the 60-day period following the fee waiver order)*
☐ Other *(specify):*
☐ Fees for a peace officer to testify in court
☐ Court-appointed interpreter fees for a witness

(3) ☐ **Fee Waiver for Appeal.** The court grants your request and waives the fees and costs checked below, for your appeal. *(Cal. Rules of Court, rules 3.55, 3.56, 8.26, and 8.818.)* You do not have to pay for the checked items.

☐ Preparing and certifying clerk's transcript for appeal
☐ Other *(specify):*

Judicial Council of California, www.courtinfo.ca.gov
Revised July 1, 2009, Mandatory Form
Government Code, § 68634(e)
California Rules of Court, rule 3.52

Order on Court Fee Waiver (Superior Court)

FW-003, Page 1 of 2

**Sample Order on Court Fee Waiver,
(In Forma Pauperis), page 2**

Your name: Marcia J. Jones _____

Case Number: _____

b. ☐ The court **denies** your request, as follows:

> **Warning!** If you miss the deadline below, the court cannot process your request for hearing or the court papers you filed with your original request. If the papers were a notice of appeal, the appeal may be dismissed.

(1) ☐ The court **denies** your request because it is incomplete. You have **10 days** after the clerk gives notice of this order (see date below) to:
- Pay your fees and costs, or
- File a new revised request that includes the items listed below *(specify incomplete items):*

_____

(2) ☐ The court **denies** your request because the information you provided on the request shows that you are not eligible for the fee waiver you requested *(specify reasons):* _____

_____

The court has enclosed a blank *Request for Hearing About Court Fee Waiver Order (Superior Court)*, form FW-006. You have **10 days** after the clerk gives notice of this order (see date below) to:
- Pay your fees and costs, or
- Ask for a hearing in order to show the court more information. *(Use form FW-006 to request hearing.)*

c. ☐ The court needs more information to decide whether to grant your request. You must go to court on the date below. The hearing will be about *(specify questions regarding eligibility):* _____

_____

☐ Bring the following proof to support your request if reasonably available:_____

Hearing Date →

Date: _____ Time: _____ Name and address of court if different from page 1:
_____

Dept.: _____ Rm.: _____
_____

> **Warning!** If item c is checked, and you do not go to court on your hearing date, the judge will deny your request to waive court fees, and you will have 10 days to pay your fees. If you miss that deadline, the court cannot process the court papers you filed with your request. If the papers were a notice of appeal, the appeal may be dismissed.

Date: _____   _____
                                   Signature of (check one): ☐ *Judicial Officer*   ☐ *Clerk, Deputy*

Request for Accommodations. Assistive listening systems, computer-assisted real-time captioning, or sign language interpreter services are available if you ask at least 5 days before your hearing. Contact the clerk's office for *Request for Accommodation,* Form MC-410. (Civil Code, § 54.8.)

Clerk's Certificate of Service

I certify that I am not involved in this case and *(check one):*   ☐ A certificate of mailing is attached.

☐ I handed a copy of this order to the party and attorney, if any, listed in ① and ②, at the court, on the date below.

☐ This order was mailed first class, postage paid, to the party and attorney, if any, at the addresses listed in ① and ②, from *(city):* _____, California on the date below.

Date: _____   Clerk, by _____, Deputy

Revised July 1, 2009

This is a Court Order.

FW-003, Page 2 of 2

Order on Court Fee Waiver (Superior Court)

Notifying Minor's Relatives and Obtaining Their Consent

Although many guardianships are not contested, certain relatives of the minor are entitled by law to know in advance about the guardianship proceeding. Frequently, notification is a formality, because everyone agrees with the guardianship. Formality or not, all those entitled to notice must receive copies of guardianship documents (by mail or personal delivery) at least 20 days before the hearing date, unless they sign a document stating that they waive notification. These relatives have a legal right to contest the guardianship in court, and you have a legal obligation to give them notice.

TIP

How do you know when your hearing date is? You will get a hearing date when you file your initial guardianship papers with the court. The hearing date usually is about 45 days after you file your papers. If you need a guardianship order sooner, you may file for a temporary guardianship as well. (See Chapter 7.)

When we refer to notifying relatives in the rest of this chapter, it also includes anyone who is the minor's legal guardian, has been nominated legal guardian, or has physical custody of the minor (other than you).

SEE AN EXPERT

When more than one adult wants to be guardian, the guardianship probably will be contested. If this is your situation, you should consult a lawyer. (See Chapter 13.)

Notifying the required people about the proceeding is one of the most important factors in obtaining a guardianship. It is essential that you read this chapter very carefully and follow the instructions. We cover notification procedures here—before you complete and file the guardianship papers with the court—because figuring out who to notify and how to notify them will affect what comes later.

By law, close relatives of the minor must be notified about the guardianship proceeding, unless they waive this right. Documents must be given or mailed by a certain procedure called "service of process." (This is covered in detail in Chapter 6.) The minor's parents, a minor who is over 12, and anyone who is either the minor's legal guardian or has been nominated as legal guardian must personally be given copies of the guardianship documents. The minor's grandparents, siblings, spouse, and any adult with whom the minor is living can be sent copies of the guardianship documents by regular U.S. mail. You will probably need to have several agencies served in addition to the minor's relatives who are entitled to notice. There are instructions for how to do this later on in the book.

If any of the relatives entitled to notice are deceased, you will simply list them on a form and indicate that they are deceased. But maybe you don't know or can't locate some of the relatives. For example, maybe the minor's father is not known by name, is not listed on the minor's birth certificate, and you don't know how to find out who or where he is. If you don't know the whereabouts of all those who must be notified, you must go through a special procedure to attempt to locate them. This chapter will give you instructions on how to search for relatives.

Overview of How to Notify Relatives

In the rest of this chapter, you will find out how to notify the minor's relatives and possibly get their written consents to the guardianship, which means that you won't need to have them served with guardianship papers. If you haven't discussed the guardianship with the minor's relatives yet, that's fine for now. Here is an overview of the steps you will be taking as you proceed through this chapter:

Step 1: In the section below called "Guardianship Notification Worksheet," you will begin to complete the Guardianship Notification Worksheet form. You'll list the names and addresses of relatives who are entitled to notice of the guardianship, and whether you need to locate them.

Step 2: If you don't know the names or whereabouts of some relatives, you will try to locate them, using the methods described in "Try to Find the Minor's Unknown or Missing Relatives," below. If you know the names and addresses of all relatives, skip that section.

Step 3: If you can't locate all of the relatives, you will complete a form called Attachment 10 to Petition for Appointment of Guardian of Minor that explains your attempts and what happened, following the instructions in "After You've Searched for Missing Relatives," below.

Step 4: You will complete the Consent of Proposed Guardian, Nomination of Guardian, and Consent to Appointment of Guardian and Waiver of Notice form following the instructions in the section called "Consent of Proposed Guardian, Nomination of Guardian, and Consent to Appointment of Guardian and Waiver of Notice Form," below.

Step 5: Read "Discussing the Guardianship With the Minor's Relatives," below, which discusses bringing up the subject of the possible guardianship with relatives who don't know about it yet and with the minor's parents.

Step 6: Obtain signatures of the minor's parents, if they are willing, on both the Nomination of Guardian and the Waiver of Notice and Consent forms.

Step 7: Contact those relatives you think will be willing to sign the Waiver of Notice and Consent form, which states that they know about the guardianship, agree to it, and don't need to receive any legal documentation about it. Obtain signatures of relatives who agree to sign the form.

Step 8: Continue filling in the Guardianship Notification Worksheet as instructed at the end of this chapter. You are then ready to go on to Chapter 5, where you will find out how to complete the rest of the required forms needed to petition for a guardianship.

Guardianship Notification Worksheet

In Appendix C at the back of this book, you'll find a Guardianship Notification Worksheet. Before you get started, make at least one photocopy of the worksheet. You'll use the Guardianship Notification Worksheet to determine who is required to know about the guardianship and how best to handle the notification. As you go through this chapter, it may be helpful to look at the completed sample of the worksheet provided here.

You're ready to start filling in the Guardianship Notification Worksheet. This is just the start—you'll be completing more of the worksheet as you go through the chapter. Don't worry about being able to completely fill in or even understand it all at once. By the end of this chapter, you'll have completed most of the worksheet.

First, complete Items 1 and 2 in Part 1 of the Guardianship Notification Worksheet.

Item 1: In the blanks in the first column, fill in the names and addresses of each of the minor's relatives and legal guardians or nominees (other than you). If any relatives are unknown or deceased, fill in their names followed by the word "unknown" or "deceased." Here are the people you will list:

- **Minor:** The person for whom you are seeking the guardianship.

- **Minor's mother:** The minor's natural mother (related by blood). (If the minor was adopted, you'll probably need to see a lawyer. See Chapter 13.)

- **Minor's father:** The minor's natural father (related by blood).

- **Minor's maternal grandparents:** The parents of the minor's mother.

- **Minor's paternal grandparents:** The parents of the minor's father.

- **Minor's spouse:** This only applies if you are seeking guardianship of a minor's estate. You cannot seek guardianship of a minor's person if the minor has married, unless that marriage was annulled.

- **Minor's sisters and brothers:** The brothers and sisters of the minor who have the same two parents as the minor. In addition, if the minor has any half-sisters and half-brothers, include them. If any of the minor's half-sisters or half-brothers are under age 18, also fill in the name and address of the different parent if they're not listed elsewhere on the worksheet. You do not need to list stepsisters or stepbrothers who are not blood relatives.

- **Minor's children:** If the minor has any children, list their names and addresses. Also find out and fill in the name and address of the other parent of the minor's children, if it's not listed elsewhere on the worksheet.

- **Anyone currently having legal custody of minor:** It's unlikely, but possible, that the minor already has a legal guardian, or someone other than the minor's parents

have legal custody. If so, list that person's name and address. Remember that this does not include you.

- **Anyone nominated as minor's legal guardian:** It's unlikely, but possible, that someone other than you has also been nominated legal guardian of the minor. If so, list the guardian's name and address. Remember that this does not include you.

- **Anyone having physical custody of the minor:** If the minor is living with someone other than you, and that person is not listed elsewhere on this worksheet, list that name and address here.

Item 2: Indicate whether each of the relatives listed must be located. If you know the name and address of a relative, or if a relative is deceased, fill in the word "No," meaning that you don't need to locate that relative. If you don't know the relative's name or address, fill in the word "Yes," meaning that you'll need to locate the person.

For now, leave the rest of the form blank. You'll be using this worksheet several times later on, so keep it in a convenient place.

Try to Find Minor's Unknown or Missing Relatives

If you have the names and addresses of all living relatives listed on the Guardianship Notification Worksheet, you may skip this section. But you may not know the names or addresses of all of the minor's relatives who are entitled to notice of the guardianship proceeding. Unfortunately, this means you will need to put in some time and effort trying to track down these relatives.

If you don't need a guardianship immediately (within two months of the time you complete a search for any missing relatives), follow the steps set out in this section. However, if you

Guardianship Notification Worksheet
Part 1. Relatives

(1) Names and addresses of minor's relatives and other people entitled to notice	(2) Need to locate?	(3) Date located	(4) Will sign Waiver of Notice & Consent?	(5) Need to have served?	(6) Service type, if need to have served (see Chapter 6 for instructions)	(7) Date served or Order Dispensing Notice	(8) Date filed Proof of Service
Minor Molly Denise Schwartz 60 W. West Street Oakland, CA 94612	No	—	**Cannot sign since under 18**	**Only if 12 or over, or if minor has a child** No	Personal		
Minor's mother Angela Natalie Schwartz 100 N. North Street Byron, CA 94514	No	—	Yes	No	Personal or Notice and Acknowledgment of Receipt		
Minor's father Jerry Schwartz	Yes	—	—	—	Personal or Notice and Acknowledgment of Receipt		
Minor's maternal grandparents (mother's parents) Betty Brower Nate Brower 9 Bright Street Boston, MA 02131	No No	— —	No No	Yes Yes	Mail		
Minor's paternal grandparents (father's parents) Penny Schwartz, Deceased Brian Schwartz	 Yes	—	—	—	Mail		
Minor's spouse—can only petition for guardianship of the estate _____	—	—	—	**Can sign only if 18 or over**	Mail		

Guardianship Notification Worksheet
Part 1. Relatives (continued)

(1) Names and addresses of minor's relatives and other people entitled to notice	(2) Need to locate?	(3) Date located	(4) Will sign Waiver of Notice & Consent?	(5) Need to have served?	(6) Service type, if need to have served (see Chapter 6 for instructions)	(7) Date served or Order Dispensing Notice	(8) Date filed Proof of Service
Minor's sisters and brothers (include their ages; if parents not listed elsewhere on worksheet, list their names and addresses)			**Cannot sign since under 18**	**Only if 12 or over, or if minor has a child**	**Mail, if over 12. Serve parents, if under 18**		
Dana Schwartz (Age 20) 167 E. East Ave. New York, NY 10003	No	—	Yes	No			
Mick Schwartz (Age 4) 100 N. North St. Byron, CA 94514	No	—	No	No (serving parents)			
Minor's children (if child's other parent not listed elsewhere on worksheet, list name and address) _____	—	—	**Cannot sign since under 18**	—	**Not required, but must serve both of child's parents**		
Anyone presently having legal custody of minor (not including you) _____	—	—	—	—	**Personal or Notice and Acknowledgment of Receipt**		
Anyone nominated minor's legal guardian (not including you) _____	—	—	—	—	**Personal or Notice and Acknowledgment of Receipt**		
Anyone who has physical custody of minor (not including you)	—	—	—	—	**Mail**		

need a guardianship right away, you may be able to get a temporary guardianship quickly, even before your search is complete. (See Chapter 7 for instructions.)

You must try with "due diligence" to locate any relative who is entitled to notice. This means that you must do your very best to find and give that person notice. One judge explained "doing your best" by saying that you should look for the person as if they owed you $25,000. If, after doing everything reasonably within your power, you still can't locate the relative, Chapter 5 gives you instructions on seeking an order from a judge allowing for that relative not to be served. The judge has the right to decide what is reasonable, however, and may require that you try harder than you already have. There are no hard and fast rules about what an individual judge will require, but in general, courts tend to be very reluctant to dispense with notice to the parents of a minor, and are somewhat more lenient in dispensing with notice to other relatives.

EXAMPLE 1:

You know that the minor's father went to Alaska several years ago, but you don't know where he lives and you don't want to go to the library to look in the telephone book for all fairly populous cities in Alaska to try to locate him. This would not be considered adequate reason not to give notice. However, if you had checked all of the phone books and other resources reasonably available to you (set out in this section) and still couldn't locate the minor's father, a judge probably would determine that you couldn't reasonably be expected to give him notice.

EXAMPLE 2:

You are seeking guardianship of your daughter's child. The child's father has never seen his daughter. Your daughter does not know where the father is. She knows only that his name is John Jones, and that he lived with his wife in Los Angeles five years ago. You would prepare documents asking for a judge to waive notice requirements for the minor's father and paternal grandparents. A judge probably would determine that you couldn't reasonably be expected to give the child's father or paternal grandparents notice.

How to Locate Relatives

This section gives a summary of some of the most stringent requirements in California for searching for relatives who must get notice of a guardianship. Your county may be more lenient, depending on which relatives cannot be located and on the attitude of the particular judge. Some judges expect you to spend at least three hours in the search for a relative, particularly a parent. We recommend that you follow all suggestions in this section when attempting to find the minor's parents. To find any other missing relatives, you may want to follow all the suggestions in this section as well.

Keep an accurate written record of your efforts when you attempt to locate the missing relative. Enter the date of each attempt, and a simple explanation of what happened. For example, "On September 1, 20xx, I called directory assistance in Sacramento, California, and requested the telephone numbers and addresses for John Xerox, and there were no listings."

If you seek information by mail, keep copies of the letter and returned correspondence. If someone else conducts the search for missing relatives for you, have that person keep accurate records of the attempts. Follow up any leads you get.

When checking with friends or employers who may know the missing relative, be discreet. Simply say that you are trying to contact the person, but don't volunteer information about the guardianship or say that the person may have something to do with a court proceeding.

Check With the Telephone Company

To find the missing relative, begin with the obvious. Check telephone directories and directory assistance in cities where the relative has lived recently. Most public libraries carry copies of telephone directories for many cities, including phone books for areas outside of California. Local telephone company offices also may have copies of phone books for many areas.

Check With Friends and Relatives

Contact the minor's other relatives to see whether they know how to locate the missing relative. They may be able to give you leads such as a former address, telephone number, or the name of someone else who might know how to locate the relative. Remember to be discreet when you contact friends and relatives. Make sure you keep a written record of the dates and results of your inquiries.

Check the Internet

Start with a search engine like Google, Yahoo!, or Bing. Put in the person's name and, if you know it, their last known address. If the name is fairly common, you're likely to come up with a lot more names than you can handle, and this might not be the best option for you. But if it's unusual enough that you don't get too many names, you may find useful information. Often, you'll get an offer from a site that's in the business of locating people to find the person you're looking for, for a fee. There may be times when this is worth it, especially if the name is somewhat unusual and the general location

seems right. Going ahead and paying the small fee to find out whether it's the person you're looking for will impress the judge with your commitment to actually finding the person.

Check With Former Employers

If you know where the missing relative used to work, contact former employers to find out whether they have an address, telephone number, or the name of someone else who might know how to locate the relative. Again, do not volunteer information about why you are trying to find the person. Keep a written record of the dates and results of your inquiries.

Check Last Known Address

Talk to the people living at the relative's last known address, if you know it. If the people living there don't know the whereabouts of the missing relative, check with the neighbors on both sides either by letter, by phone, or in person.

If the last known address is a mental or penal institution, contact the person in charge of the institution and ask for the relative's current address from the institution's records. Remember to be discreet about why you are trying to find the person. The institution's records may be confidential, but they may forward mail, and if so, you can write to the relative in care of the institution.

If the missing relative has moved and left a forwarding address, you can obtain it from the U.S. Post Office. Simply send a postcard or envelope to the last known address with the words "Address Correction Requested" printed next to the old address. The post office will return it to you with the correct address. Or, if you want to send a letter to the missing relative, next to the last known address print the words "Address Correction and Forwarding Requested." The post office will forward the letter and return a postcard to you with the new address and postage due.

Check Voter Registration Records

In California, you can find a listing for registered voters that includes their name, address, phone number, birthdate, party affiliation if any, and date of registration. To look at these records, contact the registrar of voters for the county where you believe the relative lives. You may be able to get this information over the phone. If the person has moved within the same county, the registrar may have the new address.

Military Services

If you're looking for a missing service member, you have a challenge ahead of you. Especially since September 11, it's difficult to find military personnel. If you know the person's Social Security number, you're one step ahead of the game. A copy of a military identification card will also be very helpful. Without either one, you're really going to have an uphill battle.

If you do have a Social Security number, you can try a number of ways to locate the missing relative. First, if you're not sure whether the person is still in the military, you can find out using a new Web link. Go to www.dmdc.osd.mil/scra/owa/home. Once you know that, you can move on to finding the relative.

Ways you can look for your spouse include:

Military locators. Each branch of the service has a Worldwide Military Locator Service. Not all of them are online yet. If you write or call, you'll need to explain who you are and why you are searching, and provide all the information you have about the missing relative.

Base commander. You can try contacting the base commander at the last known military base, to see whether the commanding officer has information about the person's new assignment.

Military Locators

Army: http://armycomrel.custhelp.com and enter "locator" into the search box.

> Commander
> U.S. Army Enlisted Records & Evaluation Center
> ATTN: Locator
> 8899 East 56th Street
> Fort Benjamin Harrison, IN 46249-5301

Marines:

> Marine Corps Commandant
> USMC Headquarters
> Code MMSB-10
> Quantico, VA 22134-5030
> Telephone: 703-650-3942

Navy:

> Navy World Wide Locator
> Naval Personnel Command
> Pers-312F
> 5720 Integrity Drive
> Millington, TN 38055-3120

Air Force:

> HQ AFMPC/RMIQL
> 550 C Street West, Suite 50
> Randolph AFB
> TX 78150-4752
> 210-652-5774

Federal Parent Locator. If the missing relative is a parent, you might be able to make use of the Federal Parent Locator Service at www.acf.hhs.gov/programs/cse/newhire.

Other Internet sources. The "Globemaster U.S. Military Aviation Database" is a private website that contains links to all branches of the U.S. armed forces, and provides extensive information, including a locator for U.S. military personnel. www.globemaster.de.

After You've Searched for Missing Relatives

Once you've found the names and addresses of any missing relatives, fill in the information in Item 1 of the Guardianship Notification Worksheet for each relative. Fill in the date each relative was located in Item 3.

If, after carefully following the instructions in this chapter, you still can't find the names and addresses of all the minor's relatives, you must prepare a document that tells how you searched for the relatives.

Attachment 10 to Petition for Appointment of Guardian of Minor (Due Diligence Declaration)

If you have located all of the minor's living relatives listed on the Guardianship Notification Worksheet, you may skip this section and go on to the next one.

However, if any relatives are missing, you must complete a form called "Attachment 10 to Petition for Appointment of Guardian of Minor" (also known as a Due Diligence Declaration), which tells how you searched for the relatives. A blank copy is in Appendix C, and a sample is shown below. Before you begin filling in this form, you will need to make some photocopies. This form must be filled out for each missing relative, so for each missing relative, make one photocopy. If anyone other than you helped search, make one photocopy for each relative that person tried to find.

How to Complete the Form

CAPTION: Attachment 10 to Petition for Appointment of Guardian of Minor

Fill in the caption following the general instructions in Chapter 3.

Leave the case number blank, since it hasn't been assigned yet.

After the word "I," fill in either your name or the name of the person who conducted the search.

In the next blank, after the word "I am," fill in the word "petitioner," if you are the person who searched for the relative. If someone else searched for the relative, fill in the words "not a party," which means they are not petitioning to be the minor's guardian.

In the blank following the words "I have made the following attempts to locate," fill in the name of the missing relative.

In the blank following the words "who is related to the minor in this action as," fill in how the missing relative is related to the minor. For example, this might be "maternal uncle," if the relative is a brother of the minor's mother, or "paternal grandmother," if the relative is the mother of the minor's father.

In Items 1 through 8, you will give a detailed description of each attempt made to locate the missing relative. If you need additional space, fill in the words "This item continued on attachment," and complete an attachment following the instructions in Chapter 3. If you or the person conducting the search wrote letters to anyone during the course of the search, add the words "copies of correspondence attached" for that item—and then make sure you remember to attach copies.

Item 1: Check this item if the person conducting the search looked in telephone directories. Then list the date each attempt was made, the city of the telephone directory, and the results of the search (such as no one was listed under that name, or you called and it was the wrong person).

Item 2: Check this item if the person conducting the search contacted directory assistance. Then list the date each attempt was made, the city or area code that was called, and the results of the search (such as no one was listed under that name, or you called and it was the wrong person).

Item 3: Check this item if the person conducting the search contacted the missing relative's friends and relatives. Then list the date each attempt was made, the name and relationship to the missing relative of each person who was contacted, and the results of the search (such as a friend didn't know the whereabouts of the missing relative, or a sister gave a telephone number for the missing relative that had been disconnected). Be specific and detailed about each attempt.

Item 4: Check this item if the person conducting the search contacted the missing relative's former employers. Then list the date each attempt was made, the name of each former employer who was contacted, and the results of the search (such as the former employer had fired the missing relative and didn't know where he'd gone, or the former employer had the forwarding address of a business that went bankrupt two years ago).

Item 5: Check this item if the person conducting the search looked into the missing relative's last known address (which you always should). Then list the date each attempt was made and the results of the search (such as you went to the house and the missing relative was no longer living there and the tenant didn't know where the relative had moved, or the post office did not have a forwarding address on file).

Item 6: Check this item if the person conducting the search consulted voter registration records. Then list the date each attempt was made, the county and state of each registry of voters that was contacted, and the results of the search (such as the missing relative was not registered to vote, or was no longer at the address listed with the registry of voters).

Item 7: Check this item if the person conducting the search consulted the department of motor vehicles. Then list the date each attempt was made, the state in which the motor vehicles department was contacted, and the results of the search (such as the missing relative was not registered with the motor vehicles department, there was no current address listed, or the motor vehicles department wouldn't give out information, which will be the case in many states).

Item 8: Check this item if the person conducting the search contacted any other source not listed in Items 1 through 7. Then list the date each attempt was made and a detailed description of the results of the search (such as you checked with the army and there was no forwarding address on file, or you checked with the court where the missing relative had filed a divorce and there was no current address listed in the court's files).

Finally, fill in the date, print the name of the person who conducted the search, and either sign the form or have it signed, depending on whether you or someone else conducted the search.

For now, you can put this form aside. You will come back to it later—in Chapter 5.

Consent of Proposed Guardian, Nomination of Guardian, and Consent to Appointment of Guardian and Waiver of Notice Form

You're now ready to prepare a form called the "Consent of Proposed Guardian, Nomination of Guardian, and Consent to Appointment of Guardian and Waiver of Notice." Completing this form will help you understand the process

**Sample Attachment 10 to Petition for
Appointment of Guardian of Minor, page 1**

GUARDIANSHIP OF (Name):	Case Number:
BRIAN TIMOTHY MICHAELS	123456

ATTACHMENT 10
to Petition for Appointment of Guardian of Minor

I _____SUSAN STEVENSON_____, declare that I am ___THE PROPOSED GUARDIAN___ in this guardianship case, that I have made the following attempts to locate _____FRED MICHAELS_____, who is related to the minor in this action as _____NATURAL FATHER_____. To date my efforts have been unsuccessful.

1. ☒ I checked in telephone directories for listings. The details of my attempts are:

    9/2/10   I WENT TO THE PUBLIC LIBRARY AND CHECKED IN THE ANCHORAGE TELEPHONE BOOKS. THERE WAS ONE LISTING FOR F.M. MICHAELS, AND NO OTHER LISTINGS FOR EITHER F. OR FRED MICHAELS.

    9/2/10   I CALLED THE NUMBER LISTED FOR F.M. MICHAELS, 907-999-9999. A MAN WHO IDENTIFIED HIMSELF AS FRANK MICHAELS ANSWERED. HE HAD NEVER HEARD OF FRED MICHAELS.

2. ☒ I checked with directory assistance. The details of my attempts are:

    I CALLED DIRECTORY ASSISTANCE ON 9/1/10. THERE WERE NO LISTINGS FOR FRED MICHAELS OR F. MICHAELS IN ANCHORAGE OR THE SURROUNDING AREA.

3. ☒ I checked with friends and relatives. The details of my attempts are:

    9/12/10   I CALLED FRED MICHAELS'S SISTER, KAREN BRADFORD. SHE HAS NOT TALKED TO FRED IN SIX YEARS AND DOES NOT KNOW WHERE HE IS.

    9/14/10   I WROTE A LETTER TO FRED MICHAELS'S BROTHER, MICHAEL MICHAELS. THE LETTER WAS RETURNED FROM THE POST OFFICE MARKED "MOVED, LEFT NO FORWARDING ADDRESS."

    I DO NOT KNOW ANY OTHER FRIENDS OR RELATIVES OF FRED MICHAELS.

4. ☒ I checked with former employers. The details of my attempts are:

    I CALLED BOSSCO ON 9/6/10 AT 907-999-8888. THE RECEPTIONIST, KATHLEEN SMITH, SAID FRED MICHAELS QUIT THREE YEARS AGO. THE LAST SHE HEARD, HE WAS PLANNING TO MOVE TO SPAIN. SHE DID NOT HAVE A FORWARDING ADDRESS FOR FRED MICHAELS.

**ATTACHMENT 10 TO PETITION FOR
APPOINTMENT OF GUARDIAN OF MINOR**

Sample Attachment 10 to Petition for
Appointment of Guardian of Minor, page 2

GUARDIANSHIP OF (Name):	Case Number:
BRIAN TIMOTHY MICHAELS	123456

5.   X I checked the last known residence address. The details of my attempts are:

I SENT A LETTER TO FRED MICHAELS AT 1 COLD STREET, ANCHORAGE, ALASKA, ON 4/1/09. IT WAS RETURNED ON 9/11/10 FROM THE POST OFFICE, MARKED "ADDRESSEE UNKNOWN, NOT DELIVERABLE." I DO NOT HAVE ANY OTHER ADDRESS FOR FRED MICHAELS.

6.   X I checked with voter registration records. The details of my attempts are:

I SENT A LETTER TO THE REGISTRAR OF VOTERS IN ANCHORAGE, ALASKA, ON 9/1/10. THEY WROTE BACK SAYING FRED MICHAELS WAS NOT REGISTERED TO VOTE THERE. COPIES OF CORRESPONDENCE ARE ATTACHED.

7.   X I checked with the motor vehicles department. The details of my attempts are:

I SENT A LETTER TO THE ALASKA MOTOR VEHICLES DEPARTMENT ON 9/1/10, REQUESTING INFORMATION ON FRED MICHAELS AND F. MICHAELS. THERE IS NO ONE REGISTERED UNDER EITHER NAME IN ALASKA. COPIES OF CORRESPONDENCE ARE ATTACHED.

8.   X Other (specify):

I WROTE TO THE U.S. NAVY ON 9/4/10. FRED MICHAELS WAS NOT A MEMBER OF THE NAVY AT ANY TIME. COPIES OF CORRESPONDENCE ARE ATTACHED.

I ENTERED "FRED MICHAELS" INTO SEARCH ENGINES AT WWW.GOOGLE.COM AND WWW.YAHOO.COM. I ALSO SEARCHED ON WWW.FACEBOOK.COM AND WWW.LINKEDIN.COM. NONE OF THE INFORMATION RETRIEVED LED TO ANY CONTACT INFORMATION FOR THE FRED MICHAELS I AM SEEKING.

I declare under penalty of perjury under the laws of the state of California that the foregoing is true and correct.

Date: 9/29/10

SUSAN STEVENSON   *Susan Stevenson*
   (TYPE OR PRINT NAME)   (SIGNATURE)

ATTACHMENT 10 TO PETITION FOR
APPOINTMENT OF GUARDIAN OF MINOR

of notifying relatives and getting their written consents to the guardianship. This form is actually three forms put together on one page. Despite three forms being compressed into one, it is very easy to prepare and understand. There are separate instructions for each part. Because the form has such a long name, we may sometimes refer to it only by the particular part that our instructions relate to.

How to Complete the Form

CAPTION: Consent of Proposed Guardian, Nomination of Guardian, and Consent to Appointment of Guardian and Waiver of Notice

Fill in the caption following the general instructions in Chapter 3.

Where you seek guardianship of more than one minor, use one form for each child, listing the name of each minor on a separate form.

There are three boxes entitled "Consent of Proposed Guardian," "Nomination of Guardian," and "Consent to Appointment of Guardian and Waiver of Notice." After you finish filling in the form, check the boxes applying to each part of the form you completed.

1. Consent of Proposed Guardian

In the first part of the form, you—the proposed guardian—sign a simple statement in which you agree to be guardian. Obviously, this is implied if you're the one petitioning for the guardianship. But the form is designed to include the possibility that someone such as a parent or adult relative is asking the court to appoint another adult who agrees to be guardian. You need to complete this part even though you are asking to have yourself appointed guardian.

Check the box next to the words "Consent of Proposed Guardian" located in the caption.

Next check the box next to the word "person," "estate," or both, depending on the type of guardianship you are seeking. Then fill in the date and your full name, and sign just above the words "Signature of proposed guardian." You have now completed the Consent of Proposed Guardian part of the form.

2. Nomination of Guardian

In the second part of the form, the minor's parents may nominate the guardian. Whether you'll fill in the Nomination of Guardian depends on your situation. Although it isn't mandatory that a parent nominate a proposed guardian, it is desirable. A judge will be more likely to grant the guardianship if the minor's parents approve of it, so your nomination as guardian is an extremely important part of the guardianship process. Filling out the Nomination of Guardian portion of the form is very easy. What should be done carefully is obtaining signatures of the minor's parents. In the rare situation where someone is donating a gift to the minor and you are seeking guardianship of the minor's estate, the adult who gives the gift would make the nomination.

Whenever a parent agrees with the guardianship and is willing to nominate you as guardian, this part of the form should be used. If both parents will nominate you as guardian, fill out a separate Nomination of Guardian for each of them. You can use as many forms as you need to.

If you haven't discussed the guardianship with the minor's parents, but think they might go along with it, complete this part of the form. If you are certain that the minor's parents won't approve of the guardianship, you do not need to complete this part of the form. But bear in mind that if the parents are likely to contest the guardianship, you will need to see an attorney. See "Discussing the Guardianship With the Minor's Relatives," below.

If a deceased parent has nominated you to be guardian in a will, you do not need to fill out this part of the form, unless the other parent is alive and willing to sign the nomination.

To complete this part of the form, first check the "Nomination of Guardian" box in the caption.

If a parent will be nominating you as guardian, check the box next to the words "a parent of the minor." In the rare situation where you are seeking guardianship of the estate because an adult is donating a gift to a minor, check the box next to the words "donor of a gift to the minor."

After the words "I nominate (name and address)," fill in your name and residence address. Then check the boxes next to the words "person," "estate," or both, depending on the type of guardianship you are seeking. Below this, you will again find a sentence that begins "I nominate (name and address)." The form has this language twice for the unusual situation in which a parent nominates one person as guardian of the minor's person and another as guardian of the minor's estate. Ignore the second nomination unless you and someone else are being nominated for these two different types of guardian of the same minor. If that's your situation, fill in the requested information for the other proposed guardian.

Print or type the date and the name of the person making the nomination at the left of this part of the form. You will later have the person making the nomination sign above the word "Signature" on the right. For now, this part of the form is complete.

3. Consent to Appointment of Guardian and Waiver of Notice

In the third and last part of the form, any or all of the minor's relatives may indicate that they consent to the proposed guardianship and agree to give up the right to be notified at all stages of the proceeding, which will make things easier for you. The minor isn't allowed to sign this form. Again, as discussed, although it isn't necessary to have this form signed, doing so will save you the trouble of having legal notices served on the minor's relatives, including the parents if they are making the nomination.

The final portion of the form begins about two-thirds down the page. First, check the box just before the words "Consent to Appointment of Guardian and Waiver of Notice" located in the caption. Next, in the bottom section, fill in each name to the left of the signature line, and each person's relationship to the minor to the right side of each signature line. If applicable, list the parent making the nomination first, then the other living parent willing to agree and waive notice. Then, using the Guardianship Notification Worksheet as a guide, list the names of all adult relatives whose signatures can be obtained. Signatures may also be obtained for anyone currently having legal custody of the minor, anyone nominated the minor's legal guardian, and anyone who has physical custody of the minor (not including you).

If you need more space to list all the relatives, check the box next to the words "Continued on Attachment 4" at the bottom left of the form. Then prepare a continuation of the form on an Additional Page Judicial Council form provided in Appendix C or on a plain piece of typing paper. (See Chapter 3 for instructions on how to prepare attachment pages.) Label the additional page "Attachment to Consent to Appointment of Guardian and Waiver of Notice" at the top. On the attachment, continue listing the minor's relatives, following the same format as the original Consent to Appointment of Guardian and Waiver of Notice.

Sample Consent of Proposed Guardian, Nomination of Guardian, and Consent to Appointment of Guardian and Waiver of Notice

GC-211

ATTORNEY OR PARTY WITHOUT ATTORNEY *(Name, State Bar number, and address):*	FOR COURT USE ONLY
NEIL DAVID ELLIS 2863 MY STREET MARTINEZ, CA 94553 TELEPHONE NO.: 925-555-1212 FAX NO. *(Optional):* E-MAIL ADDRESS *(Optional):* ATTORNEY FOR *(Name):* IN PRO PER	

SUPERIOR COURT OF CALIFORNIA, COUNTY OF ALAMEDA
STREET ADDRESS: 1225 FALLON STREET
MAILING ADDRESS:
CITY AND ZIP CODE: OAKLAND, CA 94612
BRANCH NAME:

GUARDIANSHIP OF THE [X] PERSON [X] ESTATE OF *(Name):*

[X] CONSENT OF PROPOSED GUARDIAN [X] NOMINATION OF GUARDIAN [X] CONSENT TO APPOINTMENT OF GUARDIAN AND WAIVER OF NOTICE	CASE NUMBER: 123456

CONSENT OF PROPOSED GUARDIAN

1. I consent to serve as guardian of the [X] person [X] estate of the minor.

Date: 3/31/20xx

NEIL DAVID ELLIS ▸ *Neil David Ellis*
(TYPE OR PRINT NAME)   (SIGNATURE OF PROPOSED GUARDIAN)

NOMINATION OF GUARDIAN

2. I am [X] a parent of the minor [ ] a donor of a gift to the minor. I nominate *(name and address):*
   NEIL DAVID ELLIS, 4565 MAIN STREET, OAKLAND, CA 94606

   as guardian of the [X] person [X] estate of the minor.

3. I am [ ] a parent of the minor [ ] a donor of a gift to the minor. I nominate *(name and address):*

   as guardian of the [ ] person [ ] estate of the minor.

Date: 3/31/20xx

ANDREW ELLIS ▸ *Andrew Ellis*
(TYPE OR PRINT NAME)   (SIGNATURE)

> **NOTICE:** The guardian of the person of a minor child has full legal and physical custody until the child becomes an adult or is adopted, the court changes guardians, or the court terminates the guardianship. Parents or other interested persons must petition the court to terminate the guardianship. The court will not do so unless the judge decides that termination would be in the child's best interest.

CONSENT TO APPOINTMENT OF GUARDIAN AND WAIVER OF NOTICE

4. I consent to appointment of the guardian as requested in the *Petition for Appointment of Guardian of Minor*, filed on *(date):* 3/31/20xx . I am entitled to notice in this proceeding, but I waive notice of hearing of the petition, including notice of any request for independent powers contained in it. I waive timely receipt of a copy of the petition.

3/31/20xx	ANDREW ELLIS	▸		FATHER
DATE	(TYPE OR PRINT NAME)		(SIGNATURE)	RELATIONSHIP TO MINOR
3/31/20xx	SARAH ELLIS-SMITH	▸		SISTER
DATE	(TYPE OR PRINT NAME)		(SIGNATURE)	RELATIONSHIP TO MINOR
3/29/20xx	HELEN PETERSON	▸		MATERNAL GRANDMOTHER
DATE	(TYPE OR PRINT NAME)		(SIGNATURE)	RELATIONSHIP TO MINOR

[ ] Continued on Attachment 4.

Page 1 of 1

Form Adopted for Mandatory Use
Judicial Council of California
GC-211 [Rev. January 1, 2004]

CONSENT OF PROPOSED GUARDIAN, NOMINATION OF GUARDIAN, AND CONSENT TO APPOINTMENT OF GUARDIAN AND WAIVER OF NOTICE

Probate Code, §§ 1204, 1500–1502

You're now ready to go back to the caption at the top of the page and make sure you have checked the boxes for the parts of the form you've completed. Set this form aside for now. You will come back to it later, when you're ready to obtain signatures from the minor's relatives.

Discussing the Guardianship With the Minor's Relatives

If you haven't already told the minor's relatives about the guardianship, it's now time to think about doing this. This section gives you an overview of why you'll be talking to the relatives, and what you'll be saying.

You aren't required to discuss the guardianship with any of the minor's relatives, but it's generally a good idea for two reasons:

1. If any relatives agree with the guardianship, you may be able to get their signatures on the Consent to Appointment of Guardian and Waiver of Notice form. If they sign this form, you won't need to have them served with legal papers.

2. If a relative isn't in favor of the guardianship, you'll have more time to prepare yourself for a possible challenge to your appointment as guardian. (If a relative objects to the guardianship by filing papers with the court or showing up at the hearing, you will need to consult a lawyer—see Chapter 13.)

How you approach the minor's relatives is extremely important. You might want to call them on the telephone or get together with them in person. You might choose to write a letter, especially if they don't live nearby. No matter what method you choose for bringing up the guardianship, make sure you do it in a friendly and open way. You are seeking a guardianship because you believe it's best for the minor, so be sure you communicate these intentions. If you get the idea that the minor's relatives aren't going to cooperate, don't push the matter. You aren't required to get any signatures on the Consent to Appointment of Guardian and Waiver of Notice, and it isn't even essential that both parents sign the Nomination part of the form. It just makes things a little easier for you if you can obtain the signatures.

EXAMPLE:

Susan wants to become the guardian of her sister's only child, Annie, who is five years old. Susan's sister is in favor of the guardianship, because she is going through personal problems and cannot care for her daughter. She is willing to sign legal documents nominating Susan as guardian and waiving her right to notice of the guardianship. Susan's parents also agree with the guardianship and are willing to waive their right to legal notification, which Susan knows because they have discussed the guardianship at great length. Susan decides not to ask Annie's father if he'll sign documents consenting to the guardianship, because she has never gotten along well with him. Susan plans to have him served with the guardianship papers instead. Susan contacts Annie's paternal grandparents, but they are unwilling to sign legal documents, so she must have them served as well.

Talking With the Minor's Relatives

Here are some things to keep in mind when you tell the minor's relatives that you're going to seek a legal guardianship:

- Be prepared. Know what a legal guardianship is, and how you get one. If they ask questions, answer them as best you can. It might help to show them this book, as it may address their questions or concerns.

- Carefully and respectfully explain why the guardianship would be best for the minor. It helps to be diplomatic. For example, it would not be a good idea to say: "Your daughter is a terrible mother, and I bet she had a lousy childhood." On the other hand, it might be helpful to say: "She's found that taking care of her child is too much of a responsibility right now, and I'm happy to help out by taking the child in and being his legal guardian."

- Talk over any concerns the relatives have, such as whether you'll be willing to let them visit the minor.

- Let them know that you'd like their signature on the Consent to Appointment of Guardian and Waiver of Notice part of the form. Tell them that by signing the form they're saying that they agree with the guardianship, and don't need to be formally notified of any legal proceedings.

- Never try to pressure a relative into signing a Consent to Appointment of Guardian and Waiver of Notice form. Remember that if you can't get a relative's signature, it simply means that you'll have to arrange to have the person served with guardianship papers.

- Be prepared for the judge to instruct you that you should not be talking to the minor about the legal proceedings.

Special Considerations for Talking With the Minor's Parents

When you talk to the minor's parents, find out whether they are willing to nominate you as guardian and to waive their right to formal notice of the guardianship proceeding. Getting the parents' support may not be a problem, as the minor's parents may have suggested the guardianship or at least be in favor of it.

But what if you fear for the welfare of the child, or the minor's parents don't know of your plans and may be hostile when they find out? In these situations you should be very careful in how you bring up the guardianship. After all, if a parent gets nervous and leaves the area with her child, your plans to obtain a legal guardianship will amount to nothing. In addition to the tips for talking to relatives listed above, here are some suggestions for dealing with the minor's parents:

- Reassure the minor's parents that you are not taking their child away from them. In the case of a guardianship of a minor's person, explain that you are seeking legal custody of the minor, but you are *not* attempting to adopt the minor. If the parents later want to have the guardianship ended, they (or even you) can petition the court to do so.

- Be reasonable. Explain why the guardianship would be best for everyone concerned, without blaming, insulting, or implying that the parents have done something wrong.

- Remind the minor's parents that you want to do what's best for their child. Let them know that you want to help out, and you believe a guardianship will be best for their child.

Remember that if the minor is in danger of abuse or neglect, you will need to take immediate action. If you aren't sure whether the minor would be in danger if you don't get a legal guardianship, you can call a local agency for more information and possible intervention. Check the phone book under your county's agencies for "Children's Emergency Services," "Children's Protective Services," "Child Abuse Reporting," or a similar heading.

Obtain Signatures From Relatives on the Nomination and Waiver of Notice Forms

You are now ready to make photocopies and obtain signatures on the last two parts of the three-part Consent of Proposed Guardian, Nomination, Consent and Waiver of Notice form. You'll need:

- Two copies of the form for each parent who will be signing the Nomination of Guardian or the Consent to Appointment of Guardian and Waiver of Notice; and

- Two copies for each relative who will be signing a Consent to Appointment of Guardian and Waiver of Notice.

Obtain Signatures From the Minor's Parents

If possible, you should get the minor's living parents to sign the Nomination of Guardian form. Using the suggestions for approaching the minor's parents listed above, ask them to sign both the Nomination of Guardian and the Consent to Appointment of Guardian and Waiver of Notice form. If both parents are willing to sign, you will need to have them each sign a photocopy of the form.

Once you have these signatures, don't let the signed original forms out of your hands until you file them with the court. For example, if you're going to be obtaining Consent to Appointment of Guardian and Waiver of Notice signatures from the minor's relatives, make sure you send out photocopies of the form, not the originals.

If you do not know where one or both of the minor's parents are, you need not obtain their signatures. However, you will need to make reasonable efforts to locate the parents to notify them of the guardianship proceedings

following the guidelines in this chapter. In the rare situation where the guardianship is for the minor's estate, and a donor of a gift is making the nomination, you should have the donor sign the Nomination of Guardian.

Obtain Signatures From the Minor's Other Relatives

Each and every one of the people listed in Part 1 of the Guardianship Notification Worksheet must be served with formal legal papers unless they sign a Consent to Appointment of Guardian and Waiver of Notice form or can't be found. If any relatives voluntarily sign a Consent and Waiver of Notice form, you will be free of the requirement to send them documents about the guardianship proceeding. So, as you can see, obtaining these signatures can save you a good deal of time and trouble. Here is how to do it.

Make two photocopies of the unsigned form for *each* of the minor's relatives you listed on the form. Contact each relative and tell her about the guardianship, following the suggestions in this chapter. If a relative supports the guardianship, ask her to sign a copy of the Consent to Appointment of Guardian and Waiver of Notice. Do this in person if possible, and by mail if that's not possible. If she wants a copy of the form, give one to her.

It is not necessary that every relative entitled to notice sign the same Consent to Appointment of Guardian and Waiver of Notice form. For example, if you are going to mail the form to out-of-state relatives for their signatures, send an unsigned form. That way, if they don't return it to you, you won't risk losing the signatures you already obtained. Naturally, if you are going in person to obtain signatures from more than one person, they can sign the same form.

Once you have obtained all the signatures you can get, you have completed this form. For now, put all original signed copies of the form in a safe, convenient place.

Continue Filling In the Worksheet

As you've gone through the process of talking to the minor's relatives and getting their signatures on the Consent to Appointment of Guardian and Waiver of Notice, you may have filled in more of the Guardianship Notification Worksheet. If not, here is the time to catch up. You can now fill in Items 4 and 5. (You'll complete the Guardianship Notification Worksheet fully by the end of Chapter 6.)

Item 4: In this item, answer whether each relative is willing to consent to the guardianship and waive notice. This applies to the third section of the Consent of Proposed Guardian, Nomination, and Consent and Waiver of Notice form. For each relative, indicate whether they will sign—or already have signed—a Consent to Appointment of Guardian and Waiver of Notice. When you obtain a signature, also jot down the date it was signed. In the form, we remind you that certain relatives may not sign because they are under age 18.

Item 5: As you've learned, all relatives must be served, except those who consented and waived notice and those who can't be located. For each relative, write down "yes" if they need to be served, and "no" if they do not need to be served because they either can't be found or have signed a Consent to Appointment of Guardian and Waiver of Notice. Note that the form already contains information about serving the minor and the minor's siblings. Underneath this information, fill in whether they need to be served.

You may now put the Guardianship Notification Worksheet aside and go on to Chapter 5. Again, keep this worksheet handy, as you will find it useful when you fill out other forms. ●

Preparing Forms to File for a Guardianship

I f you haven't already read Chapter 3 ("Getting Started"), do so now. That chapter contains basic information on how to get organized, how to prepare legal forms, and how to apply to have court fees waived. We also tell you how to find out in which court to file your guardianship papers, and what information you'll need to obtain from that court. At this point we assume that you are familiar with the material in Chapter 3. Of course, remember that you can always refer back to Chapter 3 for a review—there's no reason to memorize everything.

In Chapter 4 ("Notifying Minor's Relatives and Obtaining Their Consent"), you began filling out documents required for the legal guardianship. You're now about to complete the rest of the forms required to file for a guardianship. But first, here are a few words of encouragement. You'll need to complete several legal forms to obtain a guardianship, but you can usually complete the process by yourself. The step-by-step instructions here will take you through each form and help you complete each procedure. As long as you're patient—and willing to spend a little time preparing and double-checking your work—you shouldn't have any trouble.

Here's an overview of the steps you'll take:

Step 1: If you skipped Chapter 1 or Chapter 3, go back and read them before filling in the forms in this chapter.

Step 2: Read the instructions and complete the forms in Chapter 4.

Step 3: Complete the rest of the documents you'll need to file for a legal guardianship (instructions for all forms are in this chapter):

- **Petition for Appointment of Guardian of Minor(s).** This form must be completed following the instructions below. If you are seeking guardianship of a minor's estate or person and estate, you will also periodically refer to Chapter 10 to complete the petition.

- **Child Information Attachment.** For each child involved in the guardianship action, you must complete an attachment and submit it with the petition.

- **Declaration Under Uniform Child Custody Jurisdiction and Enforcement Act.** This form is completed if you are seeking guardianship of a minor's person. You don't need it if you are seeking only guardianship of the estate.

- **Notice of Hearing.** This form, which lists information about when and where the guardianship hearing will take place, must be completed following the instructions below.

- **(Proposed) Order Dispensing With Notice.** You only complete this form if you could not locate some relatives, or if you obtained their signatures on a Consent and Waiver of Notice form.

- **(Proposed) Order Appointing Guardian of Minor.** This form must be completed following the instructions below.

- **(Proposed) Letters of Guardianship.** This form must be completed following the instructions below.

- **Confidential Guardian Screening Form.** This form must be completed following the instructions below.

- **Duties of Guardian and Acknowledgment of Receipt.** This five-page information sheet summarizes your responsibilities as a guardian. You should read it, then fill out and sign the Acknowledgment of Receipt portion at the end. This tells the court you have read the form.

- **Supplemental documents** may be required by your local court. A list and samples of some of these documents are below.

Step 4: If you need a guardianship of a minor's person right away (within six weeks), turn to Chapter 7, where you will find instructions on completing temporary guardianship documents.

Step 5: Once you have completed the forms in this chapter, turn to Chapter 6, which tells you how to file and serve your papers.

Petition for Appointment of Guardian of Minor(s) and Child Information Attachment

To begin guardianship proceedings, you must file a "petition" with the court. The Petition for Appointment of Guardian of Minor is the document in which you summarize why you should be appointed the minor's guardian. Because you are the person filing the Petition for Appointment of Guardian of Minor, you are referred to as the "petitioner" in the proceedings.

The following instructions are complete if you are seeking guardianship of a minor's person only. If, however, you are seeking guardianship of a minor's estate or guardianship of both a minor's person and estate, you will occasionally need to turn to Chapter 10 for additional instructions as noted.

CAUTION

Don't get confused about what forms to use. There are two different forms that you can use if you are seeking guardianship of the person only (not the estate or person and estate). There is one form that you can **only** use if you are seeking guardianship of the person **only**, and its form number is GC-210(P). We have left that form out of this book, because it's less versatile than the form that we have included, which is form GC-210. The form that we include can be used for guardianship of the person

only, of the estate only, or of both the person and the estate. Don't let a clerk tell you that because you're only seeking guardianship of the minor's person you have to use form GC-210(P). That's not true, and the form says so itself—check the bottom of the first page.

Before you begin, have handy the Guardianship Notification Worksheet you began completing in Chapter 4. You will need to refer to this worksheet periodically.

How to Complete the Petition Form

CAPTION: Petition for Appointment of Guardian of Minor(s)

Fill in the caption following the general instructions in Chapter 3.

At the bottom of the caption, check the boxes to indicate whether you are seeking guardianship of one minor or more than one, and whether you are seeking guardianship of the person, estate, or both. Make sure you know exactly what type of guardianship you are seeking. This is discussed in detail in Chapter 1.

Leave the case number blank. You will be assigned a case number when you file your documents with the court. Also, leave the boxes for the hearing date and location blank. The clerk will fill these in as well.

Item 1: After the words "Petitioner (name each)" fill in your full first, middle, and last names. This means that you are the person who is filing for the guardianship. If you are seeking to be guardian jointly with someone else (such as a spouse), fill in the names of all petitioners.

Item 1a: Skip this item if you are only seeking guardianship of the minor's estate. If you are seeking guardianship of the minor's person or person and estate, fill in your full first, middle, and last names, followed by your address and telephone number. This indicates that you are the proposed guardian of the minor's person.

Item 1b: Skip this item if you are only seeking guardianship of the minor's person. If you are seeking guardianship of the minor's estate or person and estate, fill in your full first, middle, and last names, followed by your address and telephone number. This indicates that you are the proposed guardian of the minor's estate.

Item 1c: If you are seeking guardianship of a minor's estate or person and estate, turn to the section called "Completing Estate Items in the Petition" in Chapter 10 for instructions on how to complete this item.

If you are seeking guardianship of a minor's person only, check the box before the words "bond not be required" and check the box before the words "because the petition is for guardian of the person only." In the extremely rare case where the court would require bond for the guardian of a minor's person only, the judge would make the order at your court hearing. This petition would not have to be amended. Leave the rest of this item blank.

Item 1d: If you are seeking guardianship of a minor's person only, skip this item. If you are seeking guardianship of a minor's estate or person and estate, turn to "Completing Estate Items in the Petition" in Chapter 10 for instructions on how to complete this item.

Item 1e: If you are seeking guardianship of a minor's estate only, skip this item. This item only applies to guardianships of the minor's person or person and estate, but normally this box is not checked. It is used where a guardian intends to either move the minor out of California or to insist that a minor 14 years or older receive nonemergency medical treatment against the minor's wishes. A guardian cannot do either of these without a specific court order, which will require the help of an attorney. (See Chapter 13.)

Item 1f: A number of people must get written notice of the guardianship proceeding unless they signed the Consent and Waiver of Notice, or you are unable to locate them. Look at the Guardianship Notification Worksheet for information needed to complete this item. Then check this box if you could not locate one or more relatives entitled to notice, after you searched for them following the guidelines in Chapter 4. More information about having notice waived will be given in the instructions for Item 10, where you will complete an Attachment 10.

Item 1g: Leave this item blank unless the minor is 12 years of age or older and will be at the guardianship hearing, or all of the following are true:

- You are seeking guardianship of a minor's estate, and the only money you'll be receiving on behalf of the minor are public benefit payments such as Temporary Assistance to Needy Families (TANF), General Assistance from a county, or Supplemental Security Income and State Supplemental Program (SSI/SSP) benefits paid through the Social Security Administration; *and*

- the minor does not receive more than $300 per month in addition to these benefits; *and*

- the entire amount of assets belonging to the minor does not exceed $5,000 (excluding clothes and ordinary household items); *and*

- any money you receive on behalf of the minor will be spent for her benefit.

If you complete this item, you will request that you not be required to file periodic accountings with the court, which will make your job as guardian of a minor's estate much easier.

If you are in either of these situations, complete an Attachment 1g following the general instructions for completing forms in Chapter 3, using as a guide the sample that follows the sample petition, below.

Item 2: List the names and birth dates of each minor as to whom you are seeking to establish a guardianship. If there are more than four minors, check the box after Item 2d and prepare an attachment listing their names and birth dates. Then, for each minor you will need to fill out an additional form. Use the form provided in Appendix C entitled "Guardianship Petition—Child Information Attachment." Instructions and a sample form are provided below.

Item 3: Check only one box, whichever applies:

Check box 3a if you are related to the minor. You'll explain the relationship when you fill out the attachment.

Leave box 3b blank. This is intended to be checked only by a minor over age 12 who is the petitioner in the guardianship. This book does not cover situations where the minor is the one seeking the guardianship. See Chapter 13 for how to do your own research, or how to find and deal with attorneys.

Check box 3c if you're not related to the minor by blood or marriage. You'll use the Child Information Attachment to describe your relationship with the minor.

Item 4: Note that you may need to check more than one box in this item.

Check box 4a if either or both of the minor's parents nominated you in writing to be the minor's guardian, or if someone who's giving property to the minor nominated you in writing to be the guardian of that part of the minor's estate. You will have to attach a copy of the written nomination as "Attachment 4." This could be a copy of a letter from a parent asking you to care for the minor, or a copy of a will that nominates you as guardian. If the parent or, for guardianship of a minor's estate only, the person who gave the minor a gift, is available and willing to sign a nomination form, the better practice is to file a separate

Nomination of Guardian. (See Chapter 4.) If you have signatures of one or both of the minor's parents on the Nomination of Guardian section of the three-part Consent of Proposed Guardian, Nomination, and Consent to Appointment of Guardian and Waiver of Notice form (Chapter 4), you don't need to attach a copy as long as you file the signed Nomination of Guardian form with the court.

Check box 4b if you are a relative of the minor. You'll use the Child Information Attachment to explain your relationship.

Check box 4c if you're not a relative of the minor and you haven't been nominated in writing by the minor's parents. Again, the Child Information Attachment will tell the court who you are.

Box 4d doesn't apply to you, as you are not a professional fiduciary (a person whose job it is to take charge of someone else's property).

Item 5: Check this item only if you eventually hope to adopt the minor, even if you haven't yet filed a petition for adoption. When you check this item, it guides the court investigator or social services department in conducting the investigation. If you do file a petition to adopt the minor, the guardianship proceeding should be consolidated with the adoption proceeding and transferred to the court's adoption or family law division.

Item 6: Except for very rare situations, you will leave this item blank. It asks whether anyone besides you has been nominated guardian. For example, a parent may nominate a guardian of the minor's person or estate, and a donor of a gift may nominate a guardian in a will or other document. If a person *other than you* has been nominated for a guardianship either of the minor's person or estate but you want to be the guardian instead, contact an attorney. (See Chapter 13.) The law requires that the first person nominated

Sample Petition for Appointment of Guardian of Minor, page 1

GC-210

ATTORNEY OR PARTY WITHOUT ATTORNEY *(Name, State Bar number, and address)*:	FOR COURT USE ONLY
Patricia Ann Lee 2 West Street Santa Ana, CA 92702 TELEPHONE NO.: 714-555-1212　　FAX NO. *(Optional)*: E-MAIL ADDRESS *(Optional)*: ATTORNEY FOR *(Name)*: In Pro Per	

SUPERIOR COURT OF CALIFORNIA, COUNTY OF Orange
STREET ADDRESS: 700 Civic Center Drive West
MAILING ADDRESS: P.O. Box 838
CITY AND ZIP CODE: Santa Ana, CA 92702
BRANCH NAME:

GUARDIANSHIP OF *(Name)*: Daniel Frank Lee and Sara Winters Lee 　　　　　MINOR	CASE NUMBER:
PETITION FOR APPOINTMENT OF GUARDIAN OF ☐ MINOR ☑ MINORS 　　　　☑ Person*　☐ Estate*	HEARING DATE AND TIME: 　　DEPT.:

1. **Petitioner** *(name each)*: Patricia Ann Lee

   requests that

   a. ☑ *(Name)*: Patricia Ann Lee
   　　(Address 2 West Street, Santa Ana, CA 92702
   　　and telephone): 714-555-1212

   　　be appointed guardian of the PERSON of the minor or minors named in item 2 and Letters issue upon qualification.

   b. ☐ *(Name)*:
   　　(Address
   　　and telephone):

   　　be appointed guardian of the ESTATE of the minor or minors named in item 2 and Letters issue upon qualification.

   c. (1) ☑ bond not be required ☑ because the petition is for guardian of the person only ☐ because the proposed
   　　　guardian is a corporate fiduciary or an exempt government agency ☐ for the reasons stated in Attachment 1c.

   　　(2) ☐ $　　　　　bond be fixed. It will be furnished by an authorized surety company or as otherwise provided by law.
   　　　(Specify reasons in Attachment 1c if the amount is different from the minimum required by Prob. Code, § 8482.)

   　　(3) ☐ $　　　　　in deposits in a blocked account be allowed. Receipts will be filed.
   　　　(Specify institution and location):

   d. ☐ authorization be granted under Probate Code section 2590 to exercise the powers specified in Attachment 9.
   e. ☐ orders relating to the powers and duties of the proposed guardian of the person under Probate Code sections 2351–2358
   　　be granted *(specify orders, facts, and reasons in Attachment 1e)*.
   f. ☐ an order dispensing with notice to the persons named in Attachment 10 be granted.
   g. ☑ other orders be granted *(specify in Attachment 1g)*.

2. Attached is a copy of *Guardianship Petition—Child Information Attachment* (form GC-210(CA)) for **each** minor for whom this
   petition requests the appointment of a guardian. The full legal name and date of birth of each minor is :

   a. Name: Daniel Frank Lee 　　　　　Date of Birth *(month/day/year)*: 11/1/1998
   b. Name: Sara Winters Lee 　　　　　Date of Birth *(month/day/year)*: 5/15/2003
   c. Name: 　　　　　Date of Birth *(month/day/year)*:
   d. Name: 　　　　　Date of Birth *(month/day/year)*:

   ☐ The names and dates of birth of additional minors are specified on Attachment 2 to this petition.

* You MAY use this form or form GC-210(P) for a guardianship of the person. You MUST use this form for a guardianship
of the estate or the person and estate. Do NOT use this form for a temporary guardianship.

Page 1 of 3

Form Adopted for Mandatory and Alternative Mandatory Use Instead of Form GC-210(P) Judicial Council of California GC-210 [Rev. July 1, 2009]	**PETITION FOR APPOINTMENT OF GUARDIAN OF MINOR** (Probate—Guardianships and Conservatorships)	Probate Code, § 1510; Cal. Rules of Court, rule 7.101 *www.courtinfo.ca.gov*

Sample Petition for Appointment of Guardian of Minor, page 2

GC-210

GUARDIANSHIP OF *(Name):*	CASE NUMBER:
☐ Daniel Frank Lee and Sara Winters Lee MINOR	

3. Petitioner is

  a. ☑ related to the minor or minors named in item 2, as shown in item 7 of each minor's attached form GC-210(CA).

  b. ☐ the minor named in item 2, who is 12 years of age or older.

  c. ☐ other person on behalf of minor or minors named in item 2, as shown in item 7 of each minor's attached form GC-210(CA).

4. The proposed guardian is *(check all that apply):*

  a. ☐ a nominee *(affix a copy of nomination as Attachment 4a or file* Nomination of Guardian *(form GC-211, items 2 and 3) with this petition.*

  b. ☑ related to the minor or minors named in item 2, as shown in item 3 of each minor's attached form GC-210(CA).

  c. ☐ other, as shown in item 3 of each minor's attached form GC-210(CA).

  d. ☐ a professional fiduciary within the meaning of the Professional Fiduciaries Act. The proposed guardian's license status is shown in item 1 on page 1 of the attached Professional Fiduciary Attachment. *(Use form GC-210(A-PF)/GC-310(A-PF) for this attachment.)*

5. ☐ Petitioner, with intent to adopt, has accepted or intends to accept physical care or custody of the minor.

6. ☐ A person other than the proposed guardian has been nominated as the guardian of the minor by ☐ will ☐ other writing. A copy of the nomination is affixed as Attachment 6. *(Specify name and address of nominee in item 2 of minor's attached form GC-210(CA).)*

7. ☐ **Character and estimated value of property of the estate** *(complete if petition requests appointment of a guardian of the estate or the person and estate):*

  a. Personal property: $

  b. Annual gross income from all sources, including real and personal property, wages, pensions, and public benefits: $ _____

  c. **Total:** $ _____

  d. Real property: $

8. Appointment of a guardian of the ☑ person ☐ estate of the minor or minors named in item 2 is necessary or convenient for the following reasons:

The minors' mother died on January 5, 2011. Their father lives in San Francisco in a residential hotel, and does not have the means to support the minors. The minors have had very little contact with their father, and he is in favor of this guardianship. I am the minors' paternal grandmother, and have helped their mother to care for them since they were infants. I cared for her and for the children when she was ill and have been taking care of the minors in my home since their mother died. We have a close relationship and I will continue to care for them like they are my own children.

  ☐ Continued in Attachment 8.   ☐ Parental custody would be detrimental to the minor or minors named in item 2.

9. ☐ Granting the proposed guardian of the estate powers to be exercised independently under Probate Code section 2590 would be to the advantage and benefit and in the best interest of the guardianship estate. Reasons for this request and the powers requested are specified in Attachment 9.

10. ☐ Notice to the persons named in Attachment 10 should be dispensed with under Probate Code section 1511 because

  ☐ they cannot with reasonable diligence be given notice *(specify names and efforts to locate in Attachment 10).*

  ☐ giving notice to them would be contrary to the interest of justice *(specify names and reasons in Attachment 10).*

GC-210 [Rev. July 1, 2009]   **PETITION FOR APPOINTMENT OF GUARDIAN OF MINOR**   Page 2 of 3
(Probate—Guardianships and Conservatorships)

Sample Petition for Appointment of Guardian of Minor, page 3

GC-210

GUARDIANSHIP OF (Name):	CASE NUMBER:
— Daniel Frank Lee and Sara Winters Lee	
MINOR	

11. ☐ (Complete this item if this petition is filed by a person who is not related to a minor named in item 2 and is not a petition for appointment of a guardian of the estate only.)

    a. ☐ Petitioner is the proposed guardian and will promptly furnish all information requested by any agency referred to in Probate Code section 1543.

    b. ☐ Petitioner is not the proposed guardian. A statement by the proposed guardian that he or she will promptly furnish all information requested by any agency referred to in Probate Code section 1543 is affixed as Attachment 11b.

    c. The proposed guardian's home ☐ is ☐ is not a licensed foster family home.

    d. ☐ The proposed guardian has never filed a petition for adoption of the minor ☐ except as specified in Attachment 11d.

12. ☑ Attached to this petition is a *Declaration Under Uniform Child Custody Jurisdiction and Enforcement Act (UCCJEA)* (form FL-105/GC-120) concerning all children listed in item 2. *(Guardianship of the person or the person and estate.)*

13. Filed with this petition are the following *(check all that apply)*:

    ☑ *Consent of Proposed Guardian* (form GC-211, item 1)
    ☐ *Nomination of Guardian* (form GC-211, items 2 and 3)
    ☑ *Consent to Appointment of Guardian and Waiver* of Notice (form GC-211, item 4)
    ☐ *Petition for Appointment of Temporary Guardian* (form GC-110)
    ☐ *Petition for Appointment of Temporary Guardian of the Person* (form GC-110(P))
    ☑ *Confidential Guardianship Screening Form* (form GC-212)

    Other *(specify):*

14. All attachments to this form are incorporated by this reference as though placed here in this form. There are _____ pages attached to this form.

Date: _____

▶ _____
(SIGNATURE OF ATTORNEY*)

* (All petitioners must also sign (Prob. Code, § 1020).)

I declare under penalty of perjury under the laws of the State of California that the foregoing is true and correct.

Date: February 15, 2011

Patricia Ann Lee
_____
(TYPE OR PRINT NAME)

▶ _____
(SIGNATURE OF PETITIONER)

_____
(TYPE OR PRINT NAME)

▶ _____
(SIGNATURE OF PETITIONER)

_____
(TYPE OR PRINT NAME)

▶ _____
(SIGNATURE OF PETITIONER)

| GC-210 [Rev. July 1, 2009] | **PETITION FOR APPOINTMENT OF GUARDIAN OF MINOR** (Probate—Guardianships and Conservatorships) | Page 3 of 3 |

**Sample Attachment 1g to Petition for Appointment of Guardian of Minor:
Request for Additional Orders, page 1**

1 GUARDIANSHIP OF (Name): ___Daniel Frank Lee___ Case Number: _____

2

3   ATTACHMENT 1g

4   to Petition for Appointment of Guardian of Minor:
                    Request for Additional Orders

5

6 [X] REQUEST FOR ORDER WAIVING SERVICE BY MAIL OF ORDER APPOINTING GUARDIAN

7   OF MINOR

8   1. The minor who is the subject of this guardianship proceeding is at

9 least 12 years of age, and will attend the hearing on this petition.

10   2. The minor has received notice of the guardianship proceeding. The

11 original proof of service is or will be filed with the court by the time of

12 the guardianship hearing.

13   3. An extra copy of the Order Appointing Guardian of Minor will be

14 available to the minor at the hearing.

15   4. It would be an unnecessary inconvenience to mail the minor a copy of

16 the Order Appointing Guardian of Minor before Letters of Guardianship issue.

17

18 [ ] REQUEST FOR ORDER WAIVING ACCOUNTINGS (Probate Code §2628)

19   1.[ ] This petition is for the guardianship of the [ ] estate or

20 [ ] person and estate of_____.

21   2.[ ] Petitioner is or will be receiving the following public benefit

22 payments on behalf of the minor:

23   [ ] Temporary Assistance to Needy Families (TANF);

24   [ ] General Assistance from _____

25   County; or

26   [ ] Supplemental Security Income and State Supplemental Program

27   (SSI/SSP) benefits paid through the Social Security Admini-

28   stration.

**Sample Attachment 1g to Petition for Appointment of Guardian of Minor:
Request for Additional Orders, page 2**

```
1    3.[ ] The minor receives:

2         [ ]  less than $300 per month in addition to these benefits; or

3         [ ]  no additional money per month in addition to these benefits.

4    4. The entire assets belonging to the minor do not exceed $5,000

5    (excluding clothes and ordinary household items).

6    5. Any money petitioner will receive on behalf of the minor will be

7    spent for the benefit of the minor.

8    6. It would be an unnecessary inconvenience to complete accountings for

9    the minor's estate, and such accountings should be waived pursuant to Probate

10   Code §2628.

11

12

13

14

15

16

17

18

19

20

21

22

23

24

25

26

27

28
```

be given preference for guardianship unless that person is found to be unsuitable. If this is your situation, check the first box, and either the box next to the word "will" or "other nomination." You'll provide the name and address of the other person nominated on the Child Information Attachment. You also would have to attach a copy of the nomination as Attachment 6.

It is possible that one person would be nominated guardian of a minor's person, and another person nominated guardian of the estate of the same minor. In this case, there might not be a conflict between the two guardianships. This is, however, beyond the scope of this book—if that's your situation, see a lawyer.

Item 7: If you are seeking guardianship of a minor's person only, skip this item. If you are seeking guardianship of a minor's estate, or person and estate, turn to Chapter 10 to complete this item.

Item 8: Check one or both boxes next to the words "person" and "estate" on the first line, whichever applies. Then explain why you are asking to become the guardian. If you need more room, check the box that says "Continued in Attachment 8," and prepare an attachment.

Do not check the box on the second line before the words "Parental custody of the minor would be detrimental to the minor or minors named in item 2." This box is for situations where the parent or parents are contesting the guardianship, which is beyond the scope of this book. If that is your situation, see a lawyer.

Item 9: If you are seeking guardianship of a minor's person only, skip this item. If you are seeking guardianship of a minor's estate, or person and estate, turn to the section called "Completing Estate Items in the Petition" in Chapter 10 to complete this item.

Item 10: If you checked Item 1f of this form, you will need to complete this item. If you did not check Item 1f, skip to Item 11.

To complete this item, you again will need to look at the Guardianship Notification Worksheet. If you were unable to locate one or more relatives, check the first box next to the words "they cannot with reasonable diligence be given notice." You will then have to add an Attachment 10 explaining your efforts to locate each person. Fortunately, you should have already completed a Due Diligence Declaration for each relative you couldn't locate, following the instructions in Chapter 4. If for some reason you didn't complete Due Diligence Declarations for all missing relatives for whom you searched, turn to Chapter 4 and do it now. A blank form is in Appendix C.

Do not check the second box next to the words "the giving of notice would be contrary to the interest of justice," which refers to situations in which you want to avoid notifying a person whose whereabouts are known. If there is a relative you can locate but don't want to notify for what you think are very good reasons, you will need to consult a lawyer. (See Chapter 13.)

EXAMPLE:

Baby Judy's grandmother is planning to seek a guardianship of Judy's person. Judy's unmarried mother (the grandmother's daughter) is 15 years old, and agrees with the guardianship. Judy's father (who is not listed on her birth certificate) is also 15 years old. Both he and his parents have made it clear that they want nothing to do with Judy or her family. They have sent a letter to Judy's grandmother requesting that she never contact them, and tell no one who the father is since it only causes pain and hard feelings. In their letter they also suggest that she put the baby up for adoption. With the help of a lawyer, Judy's grandmother obtains permission from a judge that allows her not to list Judy's father or his parents in the guardianship documents and not to serve them with the papers.

Item 11: As the instructions on the form indicate, you only need to complete this item (11a–c) if all three of the following are true:

1. You are only seeking guardianship of the minor's person, *and*

2. You are not related to the minor, *and*

3. You were not nominated guardian by one or both parents of the minor.

Skip this item if:

- You are only seeking guardianship of the minor's estate, *or*

- You are related to the minor, *or*

- You were nominated in writing by a parent of the minor to be the minor's guardian.

Item 11a: If this item applies to you, check the first box. It says that you, the petitioner, are the proposed guardian, and that you'll give information to agencies—such as local social services agencies—that might request it. If such information is ever requested, which is unlikely unless you seek to adopt the minor, it would probably be similar to the information an investigator would request. (See Chapter 8.)

Item 11b: Do not check Item 11b unless you, the petitioner, are not also the proposed guardian.

This book assumes that you, the petitioner, are also the proposed guardian. However, if you are not also the proposed guardian, you must prepare an Attachment 11b following the instructions in Chapter 3. On the attachment type in the words "I am the proposed guardian and will promptly furnish all information

requested by any agency referred to in Section 1543 of the Probate Code." Then put a signature line for the proposed guardian to sign, and obtain the proposed guardian's signature.

Item 11c: Check the first box next to the word "is" only if your home is a licensed foster care home. If you do not contract with government agencies such as counties to take children into your home temporarily, and are not licensed for this, check the second box next to the words "is not."

Item 11d: Check the first box. If you have never filed a petition for the minor's adoption, go on to Item 12. If you have filed a petition for the minor's adoption, also check the box next to the words "except as specified in Attachment 11d." You then also need to prepare an attachment, following the instructions for preparing attachments in Chapter 3. Label the top of the attachment "Attachment 11d to Petition for Appointment of Guardian of Minor: Information on Petition for Adoption of Minor." In Attachment 11d, you must include information about the adoption proceeding. If your adoption petition was denied, see a lawyer, who will help you explain to the judge why you still should be appointed the child's guardian.

Item 12: Check this box if you are petitioning for guardianship of the person (or the person and estate) of a minor or minors. You must attach the UCCJEA declaration as described a little bit later in this chapter. If you are only petitioning for guardianship of an estate, skip this item.

Item 13: This item tells the court what other separate legal documents you are filing at the same time as the Petition for Appointment of Guardian of Minor. If you are filing the three-part Consent of Proposed Guardian, Nomination, and Consent to Appointment of Guardian and Waiver of Notice form discussed in Chapter 4, check any of the three boxes that follow, as they apply. The first three boxes all refer to the three-part Consent of Proposed Guardian, Nomination, and Consent to Appointment of Guardian and Waiver of Notice form. Check the first box next to "Consent of Proposed Guardian." Make sure you have completed and signed this portion of that form following the instructions in Chapter 4.

Check the second box next to "Nomination of Guardian" if you have completed this section of the form and you have the signatures of one or both of the minor's parents.

Check the third box next to "Consent to Appointment of Guardian and Waiver of Notice" if you have completed this section of the form and you have the signatures of some or all of the minor's relatives.

Check the fourth box only if you will be filing a Petition for Appointment of Temporary Guardian. (See Chapter 7 for information and instructions on how to petition for a temporary guardianship.) Ignore the fifth box, as it relates to a form that we've chosen not to use in this book. You can use either form GC-110 or GC-110(P) if you are only petitioning for temporary guardianship of a minor's person, and this book explains how to use GC-110. So leave the fifth box blank even if you're petitioning for temporary guardianship.

Check the sixth box, next to "Confidential Guardianship Screening Form." The form is described later in this chapter.

Item 14: If you are not attaching any additional pages, fill in the word "None." Otherwise, count up and enter the number of total pages to be attached. If you include any pages that are double-sided photocopies, count each side as a separate page. A checklist of possible attachments follows. The attachments all should be stapled (in numerical order) to the Petition for Appointment of Guardian of Minor before you file it with the court. If you are seeking guardianship of a minor's person or person and estate, leave this item blank until you complete the Child Information Attachment form or forms and the Declaration Under Uniform Child Custody Jurisdiction and Enforcement Act (UCCJEA), following the instructions below.

Date and Signature: Skip the first space for the date and the first line for a signature (under which it says "signature of attorney"). Fill in the signing date in the next space provided. Directly underneath, to the left of the second signature line (under which it says "type or print name"), type or clearly print your name in capital letters. Then sign your name on the line provided (under which it says "signature of petitioner"). If there is more than one person petitioning to be the guardian, each of you must sign here. You're now ready to prepare the next form.

Checklist of Possible Attachments to Petition for Appointment of Guardian of Minor

☐ Child Information Attachment. (Instructions are below; the form is provided in Appendix C.)

☐ Attachment 1c: Information on bond requirements.

☐ *Attachment 1e: Information on special orders for guardianship of a minor's person. (This material is beyond the scope of this book.)*

☐ Attachment 1g: Request for additional orders waiving service of Order Appointing Guardian of Minor and Waiving Accounting.

☐ Attachment 4: Copy of nomination of proposed guardian.

☐ Attachment 8: Statement of reasons why guardianship should be approved. *(A statement of reasons why parental custody is detrimental may also be included, but is beyond the scope of this book.)*

☐ *Attachment 9: Information on additional powers for guardianship of a minor's estate. (This material is beyond the scope of this book.)*

☐ Attachment 10: Efforts to locate relatives. (See Item 10, above.)

☐ *Attachment 11: Copy of nomination of a person other than the proposed guardian. (This material is beyond the scope of this book.)*

☐ Attachment 11a: Information pursuant to Probate Code Section 1543. (See Item 11b, above.)

☐ Attachment 11b: Statement by proposed guardian other than petitioner regarding willingness to furnish information to agencies.

☐ Attachment 11d: Information on Petition for Adoption of Minor. (See Item 11d, above.)

☐ Attachment 12: Declaration Under Uniform Child Custody Jurisdiction and Enforcement Act (UCCJEA). (Instructions and a completed sample are provided in this chapter. A form is provided in Appendix C.)

How to Complete the Child Information Attachment Form

For each of the minors who are named in your petition, you must fill out a separate Child Information Attachment.

CAPTION: Guardianship Petition—Child Information Attachment

At the top of the form, first fill in the names of all of the minors of whom you are seeking guardianship where it says "Guardianship of (all children's names)," and then fill in the name of the child whose information will be included on this form where it says "This child's name." If there's only one child, these lines will say the same thing. Leave the case number blank for now.

Just above Item 1, there are two unnumbered items to fill out. Where it says "This form is attached to," check the first box (you're using form GC-210, not GC-210(P)). On the next line, check the appropriate box for this child and indicate whether you're petitioning for guardianship of the person, estate, or both.

Next, you'll provide information about the child.

Item 1a: Enter the minor's full legal name, spelling out the middle name, and date of birth.

Item 1b: Enter the minor's current address and telephone number.

Items 1c(1) and 1c(2): If you know that the minor does not have Native American ancestry and is not a member of or eligible for membership in an Indian tribe, check the "No" box in both Items 1c(1) and 1c(2), and move on to Item 1d.

If you know that the minor is a member of, or is eligible for membership in, an Indian tribe, or you're not sure but you think it's possible, check either the "Yes" or the "Not sure" box in item 1c(1), and check the "Yes" box in item 1c(2). In either event, you will need to provide some additional information, and you'll need a lawyer's help to make sure that you're doing what the law requires.

Item 1d: If the minor is married or divorced, you won't be able to seek a guardianship of the person, only the estate. Check the appropriate box, most likely "Never married." If the child has been married or is divorced, check the appropriate box to answer the question that follows.

Item 1e: This item asks whether the minor is receiving public assistance benefits of any kind. Public assistance payments that support minors are not made directly to the minors, but to a parent or other adult. A portion of the benefits belong to the child even though someone else receives them. (See Chapter 2 for more information on public benefits.)

Check the first box next to the word "Yes" if you know that the minor receives public benefits. Check the second box next to the word "No" if you know that the minor does not receive public benefits, and check the third box next to the word "Unknown" if you're not sure. If you check the "Yes" box, proceed to the chart below and check the box for the type of benefits the minor receives and the amount of the benefit, if you know it. If you don't, just check the box and put "unknown" in the box with the dollar sign. If the minor receives benefits other than TANF, Social Security, or Veterans benefits, check the "Other" box and list the type of benefit.

Item 1f: Check this box if any living person has legal custody of the minor. This would be both of the minor's parents if they are still alive—unless a court decree of divorce or legal separation has given "legal custody" to one parent and the other has no rights of custody—or the surviving parent if one is deceased. (Many California courts award joint legal custody in a divorce even if one parent has physical custody, so if you aren't sure who has legal custody, get copies of the court decree of divorce or legal separation.)

If you aren't sure who has legal custody, list the names and addresses of anyone who might have legal custody of the minor. Even if the minor is living with you, you do not have legal custody unless you have been granted that right by the court. However, when you become the minor's guardian, you will have legal custody.

CAPTION: Guardianship Petition—Child Information Attachment (page 2)

Fill in the information at the top of the page as you did in the caption on the first page.

Item 1g: If the minor lives with you or with someone else who doesn't have legal custody of the minor, check this box and fill in the name and address of the person the minor lives with.

Item 1h: This item asks for information about any adoption, juvenile court, divorce, or custody proceedings relating to the minor. These might include any of the following:

Divorce: You must list any divorce case between the minor's parents, whether it's currently happening or whether it was completed many years ago.

Custody: If there's any pending custody fight between the minor's parents or any other people, you must list it.

Adoption: If the minor is involved in any pending adoption proceeding, you must list it. For example, if you are seeking a guardianship

Sample Child Information Attachment, page 1

GC-210(CA)	**Guardianship Petition—Child Information Attachment**	**Case Number:**

Guardianship of *(all children's names):* Daniel Frank Lee and Sara Winters Lee

This child's name: Daniel Frank Lee

Fill out a separate copy of this form for **each** child for whom you want the court to appoint a guardian.

This form is attached to the Petition, ☑ **item 2 of form GC-210,** or ☐ **item 8 of form GC-210(P).**

The Petition asks for the appointment of a guardian of this child's *(specify):* ☑ person ☐ estate ☐ person and estate

① Tell the court about this child

   a. Child's full legal name: Daniel   Frank   Lee   Date of birth: 11/1/1998
                  First   *Middle*   *Last*   *Month/Day/Year*

   b. Child's current address: 2 West Street, Santa Ana, CA 92702
      telephone: 714-555-1212

   c. *(Answer the questions in item c only if the Petition to which this form is attached asks for the appointment of a guardian of this child's person or this child's person and estate.)*

     (1) Is this child a member of, or eligible for membership in, an Indian tribe recognized by the federal government? ☑ No ☐ Not sure ☐ Yes, *(specify tribe):* _____
        (If you checked "Yes" to item (1), this guardianship case is subject to the Indian Child Welfare Act *("ICWA") (25 U.S.C. § 1901, et seq.). If you checked "Not sure" or "No" to item 1, answer item (2)).*

     (2) Do you know or have reason to know (within the meaning of Prob. Code, § 1460.2, Welf. & Inst. Code, § 224.3, and rule 7.1015 of the Cal. Rules of Court), that this child may be an Indian child?
        ☑ No ☐ Yes *(If you checked "Yes" to either item (1) or item (2), you must fill out a* Notice of Child Custody Proceeding for Indian Child *(Form ICWA-030) ("Notice"). Your attorney must serve copies of the* Notice, *together with copies of your petition and all attachments, including this form, on the child's parents; any Indian custodian (as defined in ICWA, at 25 U.S.C. § 1903, and Probate Code section 1449); any Indian tribe that may have a connection to the child; the Bureau of Indian Affairs; and possibly the U. S. Secretary of the Interior, by certified or registered U. S. Mail, return receipt requested. If you are not represented by an attorney in this case, the court will serve copies of these papers, but you must first fill out the original* Notice *and deliver it to the court. After service, the original* Notice *and all return receipts must be filed with the court. Service of the* Notice *is in addition to service of any other notices required in this case.)*

   d. Is this child married? ☐ Yes ☐ No ☑ Never married   If you checked "No," was this child formerly married but the marriage was dissolved or ended in divorce? ☐ Yes ☐ No
      (The court cannot appoint a guardian of the person for a minor child who is married or whose marriage was dissolved or ended in divorce.)

   e. Is this child receiving public assistance? ☑ Yes ☐ No ☐ Unknown *(If you checked "Yes," fill out below.)*

Type of Aid	Monthly Benefit	Type of Aid	Monthly Benefit
☑ TANF (Temporary Asst. for Needy Families)	$ 345.00	☐ Other *(explain):*	$
☐ Social Security	$	☐ Other *(explain):*	$
☐ Dept. Veterans Affairs Benefits	$		

   f. Name and address of the person with *legal* custody of this child: Martin Lee, 2501 Hyde Street, San Francisco, CA (father)

Judicial Council of California
www.courtinfo.ca.gov
Revised January 1, 2008, Mandatory Form
Probate Code, §§ 1449, 1459.5, 1510,
Cal Rules of Court, rule 7.1015

Guardianship Petition—Child Information Attachment
(Probate—Guardianships and Conservatorships)

GC-210(CA), Page 1 of 4
→

American LegalNet, Inc.
www.FormsWorkflow.com

Sample Child Information Attachment, page 2

Guardianship of *(all children's names):* Daniel Frank Lee and Sara Winters Lee

Case Number:

This child's name: Daniel Frank Lee

(1) **Tell the court about this child (continued)**

g. ☑ *(Check this box and fill out below if the person the child lives with is not the person with legal custody.)*
Name and address of the person this child lives with (has the care of the child): _____
Petitioner, Patricia Ann Lee, 2 West Street, Santa Ana, CA 92702 (telephone 714-555-1212)

h. ☑ *(Check this box if this child has been involved in an adoption, juvenile court, marriage dissolution (divorce), domestic relations, custody, or other similar court case.)* Describe the court case below:

Type of Case	Court District or County and State	Case Number (if known)
Juvenile Court	Orange County, CA	08-3579
Divorce (custody)	Santa Clara County	12457

i. ☐ *(Check this box if this child is in or on leave from an institution supervised by the California Department of Developmental Services or the California Department of Mental Health.)* Write the name of the institution here: _____

(2) **List the names and addresses of this child's relatives and other persons shown below:**

Relationship	Name	Home Address (Street, City, State, Zip)
Father	Martin Lee	2501 Hyde Street, San Francisco, CA 94109
Mother	Sarita Winters	deceased
Grandfather (Father's father)	George Lee	deceased
Grandmother (Father's mother)	Patricia Ann Lee (petitioner)	2 West Street, Santa Ana, CA 92702
Grandfather (Mother's father)	Bart Winters	45 Madrone Drive, San Jose, CA
Grandmother (Mother's mother)	Margaret Winters	45 Madrone Drive, San Jose, CA
Brother/Sister	Sara Winters Lee	2 West Street, Santa Ana, CA 92702
Brother/Sister		
Brother/Sister		

Guardianship Petition—Child Information Attachment
(Probate—Guardianships and Conservatorships)

GC-210(CA), Page 2 of 4
→

Sample Child Information Attachment, page 3

Guardianship of *(all children's names):* Daniel Frank Lee and Sara Winters Lee

Case Number:

This child's name: Daniel Frank Lee

② Names and addresses of this child's relatives and other persons (continued):

Relationship	Name	Home Address (Street, City, State, Zip)
Brother/Sister		
Brother/Sister		

☐ *Check here if this child has additional brothers or sisters, including half-brothers and half-sisters, and list their names and addresses on a separate sheet of paper. Write "Form GC-210(CA)," the name of this child, and "Item 2:—Other Siblings" at the top of the paper and attach it to this form.*

Spouse
(Guardianship of the estate only)

Person nominated as guardian of this child
(Other than a proposed guardian listed in ③)

③ Information about the proposed guardian:

a. Name *(name all proposed guardians if more than one):* Patricia Ann Lee

b. Relationship(s) to the child named in ① *(check all that apply):*

☑ Relative *(specify relationships of all proposed guardians to the child):* paternal grandmother

☐ Not a relative *(explain interest in or connection to this child):*

④ *Explain why appointing the person in ③ guardian would be best for this child:* The minor's mother died on February 1, 2009. His father (my son) cannot take care of him or his sister, and he supports my petition for guardianship. I have helped Frank's mother take care of him and his sister since they were born, and I will continue to care for them like they are my own children.

☐ *Check here if you need more space. Continue your explanation on a separate sheet of paper. Write "Form GC-210(CA)," the name of this child, and "Attachment 4:—Best Interest of Child" at the top of the paper and attach it to this form.*

Sample Child Information Attachment, page 4

Guardianship of *(all children's names):* Daniel Frank Lee and Sara Winters Lee

Case Number:

This child's name: Daniel Frank Lee

(5) Do one or both of this child's parents agree that the person in **(3)** can be the child's guardian?

a. Father: ☑ Yes ☐ No ☐ Not known at this time.

b. Mother: ☐ Yes ☐ No ☐ Not known at this time.

(You may file a filled-out Consent to Appointment of Guardian and Waiver of Notice (form GC-211, item 4) signed by the child's parent or parents (or any adult relative listed in (2)) who agree. The court may excuse you from having to give notice of the court hearing on your request for appointment of a guardian to a parent or other relative who signs that form.)

(6) **Suitability for guardianship of this child**

a. Does this child live with the person in **(3)** now?   ☑ Yes ☐ No

b. If the court approves the guardianship, will this child live with the person in **(3)**?   ☑ Yes ☐ No

c. Does the person in **(3)** plan to adopt this child now?   ☐ Yes ☑ No

(7) ☐ **Check this box if you (the petitioner) are *not* the person in (3), and fill in below.**

Your relationship to this child:

☐ Relative *(specify):* _____

☐ Not a relative *(explain your interest in or connection to this child):* _____

_____

_____

_____

(8) Except as otherwise stated in this form, the statements made in the Petition to which this form is attached fully apply to this child.

in order to prevent a minor from being placed in a foster home or adopted, you must tell the court that these proceedings exist.

Juvenile court actions: List all juvenile court actions involving the minor, including pending cases and any cases that are final, and including any case that made the minor a "dependent" or "ward" of the juvenile court, and any criminal case involving the minor.

If any of these proceedings exist, list them on the form in the columns provided for the type of case, location of the court, and the case number. You can expect to be asked for paperwork relating to these cases, so you should begin the process of collecting it.

SEE AN EXPERT

See a lawyer if there are pending cases. If you know of any case of the type listed above that has been filed but not finally decided by the court, see a lawyer for advice about how it might affect your guardianship petition. In some instances, such as a pending adoption, the cases may be consolidated. You probably shouldn't do your own guardianship if there are open cases of any kind that affect the minor's legal status, unless both parents consent to the guardianship by nominating you as guardian.

Item 1i: This item asks whether the minor is either a patient in or on leave from an institution operated by the State Department of Mental Health or the State Department of Developmental Services. If the minor is a patient or on leave and you must check this box, you should see an attorney for help with the guardianship. Otherwise, leave the box blank and move on to the next item.

Item 2: Look at the Guardianship Notification Worksheet from Chapter 4 to complete this item. Using the worksheet, list the name and address of each of the minor's close relatives as listed on this page. If you do not know a

name or address for a particular relative, fill in the word "unknown." If a relative has died, fill in the word "deceased." If both the minor's mother and father are listed on the minor's birth certificate, make sure you list them even if you do not know where they are.

CAUTION

Don't skip anyone. It is essential that you list all known names and addresses. If you know the name or address of a parent or spouse but do not list them, that person may later claim you didn't properly get the guardianship, and may ask a court to end it.

This item moves over onto the third page. Before moving on to finish it, make sure you've filled in the information at the top of the third page: the names of all minors involved in the guardianship proceeding, and the name of the particular minor that this attachment applies to. Leave the case number blank.

If the minor has more relatives than will fit into the spaces provided, check the box at the bottom of the list and prepare an attachment according to the instructions on the form. If the minor has a spouse, or if someone else has been nominated as the minor's guardian, fill in the names and addresses of those people at the end of the list—but if either of these things is true, you'll need to talk to a lawyer before proceeding with your guardianship petition.

Item 3a: List your name and, if someone else is petitioning with you, the other person's name as well.

Item 3b: Check the appropriate box stating whether you are related to the minor or not. If you are a relative, note your relationship—for example, "maternal grandmother" or "paternal aunt." If you're not a relative, explain how you are connected to the child. For example, you might say "The minor's mother was my best friend since childhood, and I have been involved in his life since he was born, and have lived with him for the last three years."

Item 4: In this item, you can give more explanation about why appointing you guardian is appropriate. You might include the same language you put in the Petition for Appointment of Guardian, Item 8, or you could keep it even more brief by saying "The minor has a close relationship with the proposed guardian and the proposed guardian cares about the minor and her best interests and is willing to support the minor and care for the minor indefinitely, just as a parent would." If you don't have enough space for all that you want to say, prepare an attachment on a separate sheet of paper, labeling it "Attachment to Form GC-210(A), Child Information Attachment."

Before moving on to Item 5, make sure you've filled in the information at the top of the fourth page: the names of all minors involved in the guardianship proceeding, and the name of the particular minor that this attachment applies to. Leave the case number blank.

Item 5: If one or both of the minor's parents have consented to the guardianship, check the appropriate box or boxes in Item 5. If this is the case, you should have already filled out the Consent to Appointment of Guardian and Waiver of Notice form. See Chapter 4.

Item 6a: If the minor lives with you already, check "Yes." Otherwise, check "No."

Item 6b: If the minor will begin or continue living with you when the guardianship is approved, check "Yes." If you're in the unusual situation of becoming guardian for a child who does not and will not live with you, check "No."

Item 6c: If the guardianship is one step on the way to an adoption that you hope to complete right away, check "Yes." If you intend to adopt the minor, but think it will be some time in the future, check "No."

Item 7: In this book, we're assuming that you are both the petitioner and the person who wants to be the guardian. If that's the case, you don't need to answer this question. If you're petitioning for guardianship on behalf of someone else, fill in your relationship to the child and, if you're not a relative, explain your connection to the minor.

Item 8: There's nothing you need to do with this item, except make sure that it's true—each of the statements you made in the Petition for Appointment of Guardian apply to the child that you're referring to in this attachment.

If you're petitioning for guardianship of more than one child, go back and fill out another Child Information Attachment for each minor who is named in your petition.

Declaration Under Uniform Child Custody Jurisdiction and Enforcement Act (UCCJEA) (Guardianship of a Minor's Person Only)

Skip this entire section if you are only seeking guardianship of a minor's estate. But if you are seeking guardianship of a minor's person, or person and estate, you must complete a two-page form called a Declaration Under Uniform Child Custody Jurisdiction and Enforcement Act (UCCJEA). This form—which we refer to as the UCCJEA Declaration—will be attached to the petition as Attachment 17.

The UCCJEA Declaration gives information about you, the minor, and the minor's custody situation. You may recall that you listed information about divorce, adoption, juvenile court, and other custody proceedings involving the minor in Item 1h of the Child Information Attachment. But even though some of the information on the UCCJEA Declaration is repetitious, you must complete it if you want to be appointed guardian of a minor's person.

How to Complete the Form

CAPTION: Declaration Under Uniform Child Custody Jurisdiction and Enforcement Act

Fill in the caption following the general instructions in Chapter 3.

Leave the case number blank. You will be assigned a case number when you file your documents with the court.

Item 1: This item states that you are involved in a legal action to determine custody of the minor.

Item 2: This item applies if the minor has allegedly been abused. If so, the minor's address and the address of the person alleging the abuse may remain confidential in all court documents.

Item 3: List the number of minors for whom you are seeking guardianship. You are given room in this item to fill in information for up to two minors. If you are seeking guardianship of more than two minors, you must add attachment pages. (This is covered below in Item 3c.)

Item 3a: In the spaces provided, fill in the minor's complete first, middle, and last names, place and date of birth, and sex. If the address is to remain confidential (see Item 2, above), check the box that says "Confidential."

Next are boxes for you to list all the places where the minor has lived for the past five years—unless, of course, the minor is under five years of age. If you don't know the exact dates, give the closest approximation. Start with the place the minor is now living, and then continue listing the rest in reverse chronological order.

For each time period, indicate the months and years on each side of the word "to" and make sure that the second date you fill in is the same as the first date in the box above. For example, if the minor now lives with you and has been since June 2006, the left-hand box in the first row would read "6/06 to present." In this example, "6/06" is when the child moved, so the information on the line below that should read "5/05 to 6/06" if the child lived at the previous address between May 2005 and June 2006.

- *Period of residence:* In the first column, list the month and year the minor began living at each address, and the month and year the minor moved from that address.

- *Address:* For each period of residence, fill in the street address, city, and state where the minor is or was living.

- *Person child lived with:* For each period of residence, fill in the names of the adults with whom the minor is or was living, along with their current address. Of course, if the minor is living with you, list your address again in this column.

- *Relationship:* For each period of residence, fill in the relationship of the person with whom the minor lived. For example, this might be "mother and father," "maternal uncle," or "stepmother."

Item 3b: If you are only seeking guardianship of one minor, skip this item. Otherwise, fill in the name, place and date of birth, and sex of the additional minor. If this minor has lived at the same address as the minor listed in Item 3a, check the box next to the words "Residence information is the same as given above for the minor listed in 3a." Otherwise, provide the information requested following the instructions for Item 3a.

Item 3c: If the child or children have lived in more than four locations over the previous five years, check this box and prepare an attachment 3c that lists the same information requested on this form, for each previous residence within the last five years.

Item 3d: If you are seeking guardianship of one or two minors, skip this item. If you are seeking guardianship of three or more minors, check this box. You must prepare an attachment to the form following the instructions in Chapter 3. Label the document "Attachment 3d to Declaration Under Uniform Child Custody Jurisdiction and Enforcement Act" at the top. Then give the same information for each additional minor that is asked for in Items 3a and 3b.

CAPTION: Page Two of the Declaration Under Uniform Child Custody Jurisdiction and Enforcement Act

In capital letters fill in the minor's first, middle, and last names after the words "Guardianship of."

Leave the case number blank.

Item 4: This item requires information on any other legal proceeding involving the minor that you know about or in which you have participated, such as litigation, divorce, adoption, guardianship, or juvenile court. Your involvement may have been either as a party (such as petitioner, respondent, plaintiff, or defendant), or as a witness. You must include proceedings in other states. If you have not been involved in any such proceeding as a party or witness, and you don't have any information about such a case, simply check the "No" box and skip to Item 5.

If you have knowledge of or have participated in other such proceedings, check the "Yes" box. You must then fill in the requested information in Items 4a–e:

Item 4a: If the case you're aware of or participated in was in family court (generally, a divorce case), check box 4a and put in all

the information that you know relating to the case. If you know there was a case but you don't know the case number, court, or date of any court order, you can try asking the minor's parents or checking with the local court. Put in as much information as you have. Include the name of every child involved in the proceeding, and state your connection to the case, which will be either "party," "witness," or, if you weren't involved but just know about it, "none." Finally, in the column for "case status," tell the court whatever you know about where things stand. For example, you might put in "dismissed" or "concluded" if you know the case is over. If it's not over, fill in the word "pending." However, if the family court case involves custody of the minor and it isn't concluded, you should talk to a lawyer before proceeding with your guardianship.

If you have a copy of court orders that involve the minor, attach them. If you don't, you aren't required to get one, but it will probably speed things up if you do. You can go to the court where the matter was filed and get a copy for a small fee. The court website will probably have instructions about how to get copies of filed paperwork, and you can find the link to the website at www.courtinfo.ca.gov/courts/find.htm.

Item 4b: If the case was a guardianship matter, follow the same instructions as above to complete the information requested.

Item 4c: If the case wasn't a divorce case or a guardianship, and also wasn't an adoption or juvenile delinquency case (which are dealt with just below), check "other" and complete the requested information. This might be a personal injury lawsuit or some other type of case that doesn't deal with the minor's family status.

Items 4d and 4e: If the case you're aware of or were involved in is a juvenile delinquency or dependency matter or an adoption, check the appropriate box. In this situation, all you need to provide is the case number and the name and location of the court.

Item 5: This item applies to situations where there is domestic violence and a court has issued a restraining order or protective order against the batterer. If there's no domestic violence restraining order against the minor, either of the minor's parents, or anyone who is a legal guardian of the minor, skip this item.

If the minor or the minor's parents are involved in any type of court proceeding in which a domestic violence restraining order exists, check the box next to Item 5. Then check one of the boxes in Items 5a–5d depending on what type of court case is involved, and list the county and state where the proceeding is pending, and the case number if you know it. Enter the date that the orders expire in the last column.

Item 6: If anyone other than you has physical custody of the minor, has visitation rights under a divorce or other decree, or merely claims to have the right to custody or visitation of the minor, you must check the "Yes" box and provide specific information regarding this item. Normally, this would be one or both of the minor's parents, even if the parents are not insisting on their right to visit or care for the child. If none of these situations applies, check the "No" box, and skip the instructions for the rest of this item.

If you checked the "Yes" box, complete Items 7a–c. As discussed many times earlier, you should not attempt to do a guardianship proceeding yourself if you are aware of a parent or other person who opposes it or who insists on getting legal custody of the minor. If the guardianship is contested, consult a lawyer. (See Chapter 13.)

Items 7a–c: In these boxes (a, b, and c), list information on up to three people who claim or have the right to custody or visitation. List the names and addresses of any individuals in the spaces provided and check whether that person "Has physical custody," "Claims custody rights," or "Claims visitation rights." In the space below that, list the name of the minor.

Now fill in the date and your name in the spaces provided, and sign your name.

Item 7: Check the box. If you are not attaching any additional pages, fill in the word "None." Otherwise, count up and enter the number of total pages to be attached.

Finally, attach this document to the Petition for Appointment of Guardian of Minor as Attachment 12. Make sure you have listed the correct number of total attachment pages in Item 14 of the petition.

Notice of Hearing

The Notice of Hearing form tells everyone entitled to notice when and where the guardianship petition will be heard in court. When you file your papers with the court, the clerk will give you a hearing date and place. The clerk will write or stamp this information on the Notice of Hearing form.

How to Complete the Form

CAPTION: Notice of Hearing

Fill in the caption following the general instructions in Chapter 3.

Check the box next to the word "Guardianship" and the box next to "person," "estate," or both. Then check the box next to the word "Minor." Type in the name of the minor after "(Name)."

Leave the case number blank.

Sample Declaration Under Uniform Child Custody Jurisdiction and Enforcement Act (UCCJEA), page 1

FL-105/GC-120

ATTORNEY OR PARTY WITHOUT ATTORNEY *(Name, State Bar number, and address)*:	FOR COURT USE ONLY
Patricia Ann Lee 2 West Street Santa Ana, CA 92702 TELEPHONE NO.: 714-555-1212 FAX NO. *(Optional)*: E-MAIL ADDRESS *(Optional)*: ATTORNEY FOR *(Name)*: In Pro Per	

SUPERIOR COURT OF CALIFORNIA, COUNTY OF Orange
STREET ADDRESS: 700 Civic Center Drive West
MAILING ADDRESS: P.O. Box 838
CITY AND ZIP CODE: Santa Ana, CA 92702
BRANCH NAME:

(This section applies only to family law cases.)
PETITIONER:
RESPONDENT:
OTHER PARTY:

(This section apples only to guardianship cases.)
GUARDIANSHIP OF *(Name)*: Daniel F. Lee and Sara W. Lee   Minor

CASE NUMBER:

DECLARATION UNDER UNIFORM CHILD CUSTODY JURISDICTION AND ENFORCEMENT ACT (UCCJEA)

1. **I am a party** to this proceeding to determine custody of a child.

2. ☐ My present address and the present address of each child residing with me is confidential under Family Code section 3429 as I have indicated in item 3.

3. There are *(specify number):* _____ minor children who are subject to this proceeding, as follows:
   (Insert the information requested below. The residence information must be given for the last FIVE years.)

a. Child's name	Place of birth	Date of birth	Sex
Daniel Frank Lee	San Jose, CA	11/1/1998	M

Period of residence	Address 2 West Street, Santa Ana	Person child lived with *(name and complete current address)*	Relationship
2/15/10 to present	☐ Confidential	Patricia Ann Lee ☐ Confidential	grandmother
8/2001 to 2/15/10	Child's residence *(City, State)* 2001 Carver Drive, Orange, CA	Person child lived with *(name and complete current address)* Sarita Winters, deceased	mother
11/1/98 to 8/2001	Child's residence *(City, State)* 225 N. First Street San Jose, CA	Person child lived with *(name and complete current address)* Sarita Winters, deceased Martin Lee, San Francisco, CA	parents
to	Child's residence *(City, State)*	Person child lived with *(name and complete current address)*	

b. Child's name	Place of birth	Date of birth	Sex
Sara Winters Lee ☑ Residence information is the same as given above for child a. *(If NOT the same, provide the information below.)*	Orange, CA	5/15/2003	F

Period of residence	Address	Person child lived with *(name and complete current address)*	Relationship
to present	☐ Confidential	☐ Confidential	
to	Child's residence *(City, State)*	Person child lived with *(name and complete current address)*	
to	Child's residence *(City, State)*	Person child lived with *(name and complete current address)*	
to	Child's residence *(City, State)*	Person child lived with *(name and complete current address)*	

c. ☐ Additional residence information for a child listed in item a or b is continued on attachment 3c.

d. ☐ Additional children are listed on form *FL-105(A)/GC-120(A)*. *(Provide all requested information for additional children.)*

Page 1 of 2

Form Adopted for Mandatory Use Judicial Council of California FL-105/GC-120 [Rev. January 1, 2009]	**DECLARATION UNDER UNIFORM CHILD CUSTODY JURISDICTION AND ENFORCEMENT ACT (UCCJEA)**	Family Code, § 3400 et seq.; Probate Code, §§ 1510(f), 1512 *www.courtinfo.ca.gov*

Sample Declaration Under Uniform Child Custody Jurisdiction and Enforcement Act (UCCJEA), page 2

FL-105/GC-120

SHORT TITLE: Petition for guardianship of Daniel F. Lee and Sara W. Lee	CASE NUMBER:

4. Do you have information about, or have you participated as a party or as a witness or in some other capacity in, another court case or custody or visitation proceeding, in California or elsewhere, concerning a child subject to this proceeding?

   ☑ Yes ☐ No *(If yes, attach a copy of the orders (if you have one) and provide the following information):*

Proceeding	Case number	Court *(name, state, location)*	Court order or judgment *(date)*	Name of each child	Your connection to the case	Case status
a. ☑ Family	FL-18753	Santa Clara County Superior Court	2002	Daniel / Sara Lee	None	Divorced
b. ☐ Guardianship						
c. ☐ Other						

Proceeding	Case Number	Court *(name, state, location)*
d. ☐ Juvenile Delinquency/ Juvenile Dependency		
e. ☐ Adoption		

5. ☐ One or more domestic violence restraining/protective orders are now in effect. *(Attach a copy of the orders if you have one and provide the following information):*

Court	County	State	Case number *(if known)*	Orders expire *(date)*
a. ☐ Criminal				
b. ☐ Family				
c. ☐ Juvenile Delinquency/ Juvenile Dependency				
d. ☐ Other				

6. Do you know of any person who is not a party to this proceeding who has physical custody or claims to have custody of or visitation rights with any child in this case? ☑ Yes ☐ No *(If yes, provide the following information):*

a. Name and address of person Martin Lee 2501 Hyde Street San Francisco, CA ☐ Has physical custody ☐ Claims custody rights ☑ Claims visitation rights Name of each child Daniel and Sara Lee	b. Name and address of person ☐ Has physical custody ☐ Claims custody rights ☐ Claims visitation rights Name of each child	c. Name and address of person ☐ Has physical custody ☐ Claims custody rights ☐ Claims visitation rights Name of each child

I declare under penalty of perjury under the laws of the State of California that the foregoing is true and correct.

Date:

Patricia Ann Lee ▶

_____   _____
(TYPE OR PRINT NAME)   (SIGNATURE OF DECLARANT)

7. ☐ Number of pages attached:_____

NOTICE TO DECLARANT: You have a continuing duty to inform this court if you obtain any information about a custody proceeding in a California court or any other court concerning a child subject to this proceeding.

FL-105/GC-120 [Rev. January 1, 2009]   **DECLARATION UNDER UNIFORM CHILD CUSTODY JURISDICTION AND ENFORCEMENT ACT (UCCJEA)**   Page 2 of 2

Sample Notice of Hearing, page 1

GC-020

ATTORNEY OR PARTY WITHOUT ATTORNEY *(Name, State Bar number, and address):*

John Bruce Rivera
100 Pine Road
Napa, CA 94559

TELEPHONE NO.: 707-555-1212   FAX NO. *(Optional):*

E-MAIL ADDRESS *(Optional):*

ATTORNEY FOR *(Name):*   In Pro Per

FOR COURT USE ONLY

SUPERIOR COURT OF CALIFORNIA, COUNTY OF Napa

STREET ADDRESS: Courthouse, Room 3
MAILING ADDRESS: P.O. Box 880
CITY AND ZIP CODE: Napa, CA 94559
BRANCH NAME:

[X] GUARDIANSHIP   [ ] CONSERVATORSHIP   OF THE   [X] PERSON   [ ] ESTATE
OF *(Name):*   Sharon Mead

[X] MINOR   [ ] (PROPOSED) CONSERVATEE

NOTICE OF HEARING—GUARDIANSHIP OR CONSERVATORSHIP

CASE NUMBER:

This notice is required by law.
This notice does not require you to appear in court, but you may attend the hearing if you wish.

---

1. NOTICE is given that *(name):*   John B. Rivera
   (representative capacity, if any): proposed guardian of the person of Sharon Mead
   has filed *(specify):*
   Petition for Appointment of Guardian of Minor - Person

2. You may refer to documents on file in this proceeding for more information. *(Some documents filed with the court are confidential. Under some circumstances you or your attorney may be able to see or receive copies of confidential documents if you file papers in the proceeding or apply to the court.)*

3. [ ] The petition includes an application for the independent exercise of powers by a guardian or conservator under
   [ ] Probate Code section 2108   [ ] Probate Code section 2590.
   Powers requested are   [ ] specified below   [ ] specified in Attachment 3.

4. A HEARING on the matter will be held as follows:

   a. Date: Time: [ ] Dept.:   [ ] Room:

   b. Address of court   [X] same as noted above   [ ] is *(specify):*

Assistive listening systems, computer-assisted real-time captioning, or sign language interpreter services are available upon request if at least 5 days notice is provided. Contact the clerk's office for *Request for Accommodations by Persons with Disabilities and Order* (form MC-410). (Civil Code section 54.8.)

Page 1 of 2

Form Adopted for Mandatory Use
Judicial Council of California
GC-020 [Rev. July 1, 2005]

NOTICE OF HEARING—GUARDIANSHIP OR CONSERVATORSHIP
(Probate—Guardianships and Conservatorships)

Probate Code, §§ 1264,
1460–1469, 1511, 1822
www.courtinfo.ca.gov

Sample Notice of Hearing, page 2

[X] GUARDIANSHIP	[ ] CONSERVATORSHIP OF THE	[X] PERSON	[ ] ESTATE	CASE NUMBER:

OF *(Name)*: Sharon Mead

[X] MINOR   [ ] (PROPOSED) CONSERVATEE

NOTE: *

A copy of this *Notice of Hearing—Guardianship or Conservatorship* ("Notice") must be "served" on—delivered to—each person who has the right under the law to be notified of the date, time, place, and purpose of a court hearing in a guardianship or conservatorship. Copies of this Notice may be served by mail in most situations. In a guardianship, however, copies of this Notice must sometimes be personally served on certain persons; and copies of this Notice may be personally served instead of served by mail in both guardianships and conservatorships. The petitioner (the person who requested the court hearing) **may not personally perform either service by mail or personal service**, but must show the court that copies of this Notice have been served in a way the law allows. The petitioner does this by arranging for someone else to perform the service and complete and sign a proof of service, which the petitioner then files with the original Notice.

This page contains a proof of service that may be used only to show service by mail. To show personal service, each person who performs the service must complete and sign a proof of personal service, and each signed copy of that proof of service must be attached to this Notice when it is filed with the court.. You may use form GC-020(P) to show personal service of this Notice.

* *(This Note replaces the clerk's certificate of posting on prior versions of this form. If notice by posting is desired, attach a copy of form GC-020(C), Clerk's Certificate of Posting Notice of Hearing—Guardianship or Conservatorship. (See Prob. Code, § 2543(c).)*

PROOF OF SERVICE BY MAIL

1. I am over the age of 18 and not a party to this cause. I am a resident of or employed in the county where the mailing occurred.
2. My residence or business address is *(specify)*:

3. I served the foregoing *Notice of Hearing—Guardianship or Conservatorship* on each person named below by enclosing a copy in an envelope addressed as shown below AND
   a. [ ] **depositing** the sealed envelope with the United States Postal Service on the date and at the place shown in item 4 with the postage fully prepaid.
   b. [ ] **placing** the envelope for collection and mailing on the date and at the place shown in item 4 following our ordinary business practices. I am readily familiar with this business's practice for collecting and processing correspondence for mailing. On the same day that correspondence is placed for collection and mailing, it is deposited in the ordinary course of business with the United States Postal Service in a sealed envelope with postage fully prepaid.

4. a. Date mailed: b. Place mailed *(city, state)*:

5. [ ] I served with the *Notice of Hearing—Guardianship or Conservatorship* a copy of the petition or other document referred to in the Notice.

I declare under penalty of perjury under the laws of the State of California that the foregoing is true and correct.

Date:

▶

_____   _____
(TYPE OR PRINT NAME OF PERSON COMPLETING THIS FORM)   (SIGNATURE OF PERSON COMPLETING THIS FORM)

NAME AND ADDRESS OF EACH PERSON TO WHOM NOTICE WAS MAILED

	Name of person served	Address *(number, street, city, state, and zip code)*
1.		
2.		
3.		
4.		

[ ] Continued on an attachment. *(You may use form DE-120(MA)/GC-020(MA) to show additional persons served.)*

GC-020 [Rev. July 1, 2005]   **NOTICE OF HEARING—GUARDIANSHIP OR CONSERVATORSHIP**   Page 2 of 2
(Probate—Guardianships and Conservatorships)

Item 1: After the words "NOTICE is given that (name)," in capital letters fill in your full first, middle, and last names exactly as you entered them on the Petition for Appointment of Guardian of Minor. Just below, after the words "(representative capacity, if any)," enter the words that apply: "proposed guardian of the person," "proposed guardian of the estate," or "proposed guardian of the person and estate." Just below this, after the words "has filed (specify)," enter the words "Petition for Appointment of Guardian of Minor—" followed by the words "person," "estate," or "person and estate" as appropriate.

Item 2: Read this item. You do not have to do anything, however. It simply states that others may check all the papers on file with the court.

Item 3: Skip this item if you are only seeking guardianship of a minor's person. This item is only relevant to the guardian of a minor's estate or person and estate, but normally, it is left blank. It is used only when you ask for permission to take unusual or speculative action with the minor's assets, for which you will need assistance from an attorney.

Item 4a: Leave this blank for now. The clerk will fill it in when you file the form.

Item 4b: Check the box before the words "same as noted above."

Leave the back of the form—the clerk's certificate of posting and proof of service by mail—blank for now. You will complete the proof of service later, after you file your papers with the court. Make sure to photocopy the back of the form when you make copies.

(Proposed) Order Dispensing With Notice

As discussed, it is not necessary to notify the minor's relatives of the guardianship proceeding if:

- they have signed a Waiver of Notice and Consent form, or

- their whereabouts are unknown although you've diligently tried, without success, to locate them. Remember that you must genuinely be unable to find out the name or location of the person, rather than not wanting to try.

You don't need to do this form and you may skip this entire section if no relatives signed a Consent and Waiver of Notice form *and* you have the names and addresses of all of the minor's living relatives listed on the Guardianship Notification Worksheet. In that case, skip ahead to "(Proposed) Order Appointing Guardian," below.

To get permission from a judge to waive notice for relatives, you must prepare an Order Dispensing With Notice. Before you begin filling out this form, have handy the Guardianship Notification Worksheet and all completed copies of the Due Diligence Declaration (Attachment 10 to Petition for Appointment of Guardian of Minor). You will need to refer to these forms.

How to Complete the Form

CAPTION: Order Dispensing With Notice

Fill in the caption following the general instructions in Chapter 3.

Do not check the box next to the word "CONSERVATORSHIP," as this box is used only in conservatorship proceedings.

Leave the case number blank.

Sample Order Dispensing With Notice

GC-021

ATTORNEY OR PARTY WITHOUT ATTORNEY *(Name, state bar number, and address)*:	TELEPHONE AND FAX NOS.:	FOR COURT USE ONLY
Sandra Elizabeth Freeman 28 Commuter Blvd. Los Angeles, CA 90012	213-555-1212	

ATTORNEY FOR *(Name)*: In Pro Per

SUPERIOR COURT OF CALIFORNIA, COUNTY OF Los Angeles

STREET ADDRESS: 111 North Hill Street
MAILING ADDRESS: P.O. Box 151
CITY AND ZIP CODE: Los Angeles, CA 90053
BRANCH NAME:

[X] GUARDIANSHIP [ ] CONSERVATORSHIP OF *(Name)*:

Jane Melissa Fox   [X] MINOR   [ ] CONSERVATEE

ORDER DISPENSING WITH NOTICE

CASE NUMBER: 123456

1. **THE COURT FINDS** that a petition for *(specify)*:   Guardianship of the estate
   has been filed and

   a. [X] *(for guardianship only)* the following persons cannot with reasonable diligence be given notice *(names)*:

      James Fox (Minor's father)
      Susan Fox (Minor's paternal grandmother)
      Clancy Fox (Minor's paternal grandfather)

   b. [ ] *(for guardianship only)* the giving of notice to the following persons is contrary to the interest of justice *(names)*:

   c. [ ] good cause exists for dispensing with notice to the following persons referred to in Probate Code section 1460(b) *(names)*:

   d. [X] other *(specify)*: The following people who are entitled to notice have waived
      notice and consented to the appointment of the proposed guardian:
      Jennifer Freeman (Minor's mother)
      Alexander Freeman (Minor's maternal grandfather)
      Henry Fox (Minor's brother)

2. **THE COURT ORDERS** that notice of hearing on the petition for *(specify)*: Guardianship of the Estate

   a. [ ] is not required except to persons requesting special notice under Probate Code section 2700.
   b. [X] is dispensed with to the following persons *(names)*:

      James Fox, Susan Fox, Clancy Fox, Jennifer Freeman,
      Alexander Freeman, and Henry Fox

Date: _____   _____
                                JUDGE OF THE SUPERIOR COURT

Form Approved by the
Judicial Council of California
GC-021 [Rev. January 1, 1998]
Mandatory Form [1/1/2000]

**ORDER DISPENSING WITH NOTICE
GUARDIANSHIP OR CONSERVATORSHIP**

WEST GROUP
Official Publisher

Probate Code, § 1460

Item 1: After the words "THE COURT FINDS that a petition for (specify)," fill in the words "Guardianship of the person," "Guardianship of the estate," or "Guardianship of the person and estate" depending on the type of guardianship you are seeking.

Item 1a: This item only applies if there are relatives of the minor who could not be located. If this does not apply to you, skip this item. In Chapter 4, you completed a Due Diligence Declaration for each of the minor's relatives who could not be located despite your diligent efforts. (These declarations are attached to the petition as Attachment 10.) Check the box next to "a." and list each of the missing relatives' names and relationships to the minor in the blank space provided.

Item 1b: This item only applies to the rare situation where you propose not giving notice to a relative for some reason other than being unable to locate her. If this is your situation, see a lawyer, because it is very difficult to get a judge to waive notice to relatives. (See Chapter 13 for information on finding and dealing with lawyers.)

Item 1c: Skip this item.

Item 1d: This item only applies if you have been able to get some, but not all, of the minor's living relatives who are entitled to notice to sign a Consent to Appointment of Guardian and Waiver of Notice form described in Chapter 4. Look at the Guardianship Notification Worksheet for a listing of everyone entitled to notice. If only certain relatives signed the Consent to Appointment of Guardian and Waiver of Notice forms, check the box next to "d." and fill in the words: "The following people who are entitled to notice have waived notice and consented to the appointment of the proposed guardian:" and then list their names and relationships to the minor.

Item 2: After the words "THE COURT ORDERS that notice of hearing on the petition for (specify)," again fill in the kind of petition you have filed: "Guardianship of the person," "Guardianship of the estate," or "Guardianship of the person and estate."

Item 2a: Leave this item blank.

Item 2b: Check the box. Then in the space provided list the names of:

- all of the minor's relatives who signed a Consent to Appointment of Guardian and Waiver of Notice form, and

- all of the minor's relatives you cannot locate.

The form is now complete. Leave the date and signature line blank. The judge will fill these in if and when the order is approved. The judge should do away with required notice for all relatives who signed a Consent to Appointment of Guardian and Waiver of Notice. As discussed in Chapter 4, depending on your thoroughness in searching for missing relatives, and how close they are to the minor, a judge may or may not sign the Order Dispensing With Notice for those relatives. The judge will learn that information from your petition and attachments, including your declaration regarding your search for missing relatives.

(Proposed) Order Appointing Guardian of Minor

In order for you to become the minor's guardian, the judge must sign an order appointing you.

How to Complete the Form

CAPTION: Order Appointing Guardian of Minor

Fill in the caption following the general instructions in Chapter 3.

Check the boxes to indicate whether you are seeking guardianship of the person, estate, or both.

Leave the case number blank. You will be assigned a case number when you file your documents with the court.

Item 1: In this item you give information about when the hearing will be held and who will attend. If there are any changes or additions, they may be filled in at the hearing by the judge or clerk.

Item 1a: Leave this item blank, unless you know the name of the judge or commissioner who will be hearing the guardianship case. If you do, fill in the name.

Item 1b: This item may be left blank. It will be completed at the hearing.

Item 1c: Check this box. Then fill in your full first, middle, and last names.

Item 1d: Check this box. Then after the words "Attorney for petitioner (name)," fill in your full first, middle, and last names, followed by the words "appearing In Pro Per."

Item 1e: Ordinarily this item is left blank, except for the rare situation where the minor for whom you are seeking the guardianship has an attorney. If that's the case, fill in the attorney's name. If the minor is being represented separately by an attorney, there's a good likelihood that the guardianship will be contested and you'll also need the help of a lawyer. (See Chapter 13.)

Item 2a: If no relatives signed a Consent and Waiver of Notice form *and* you have the names and addresses of all of the minor's living relatives listed on the Guardianship Notification Worksheet, check the first box before the words "All notices required by law have been given." This means you expect to

have all of the relatives served with notice of the guardianship. Don't worry that the form says you've already given notice when you actually haven't. This is a proposed order. By the time you actually ask the judge to sign it, you will have served the relatives and given the court proof that you've done so, and the statement will have to be true. If it's not, the judge won't grant the guardianship.

Item 2b: If you completed an Order Dispensing With Notice following the instructions in this chapter, check the second box next to the words "Notice of hearing to the following persons." Skip the next box, before the words "has been." Check the box next to the words "should be dispensed with (names)." In the space provided, list the names of each person listed in Item 2b of the Order Dispensing With Notice.

Item 3: Depending on the type of guardianship you are seeking, check the boxes before the words "person," "estate," or both.

Item 4: Leave this item blank. It corresponds to Item 1e of the Petition for Appointment of Guardian of Minor, which was also left blank.

Item 5: Ordinarily this item is left blank, except for the rare situation when an attorney has been appointed to represent the minor— not you, the petitioner. If an attorney is representing the minor, check the box and fill in the attorney's name and the amount the attorney is charging. If the minor is being represented by an attorney, the guardianship will likely be contested, and you also should consult an attorney. (See Chapter 13.)

Item 6: In Chapter 3, you called the clerk and obtained information about the guardianship investigator. Complete this item only if a court-appointed investigator will be conducting an investigation. Investigation policies vary depending on the court, but often an investigator is appointed by the court if you are seeking guardianship of the minor's person and are related to the minor by blood. If so, check the box and then fill in the investigator's name, title, address, and telephone number. If you don't have this information, call the probate court clerk, say what kind of guardianship you are seeking (person, estate, or both), and what your relationship is to the minor. If a court investigation will be required, get the name, title, address, and telephone number of the court investigator, and enter the information on the form.

Item 7a: If you are only seeking guardianship of a minor's estate, skip this item. If you are seeking guardianship of a minor's person or person and estate, fill in your full name, address, and telephone number in the spaces provided. After the words "is appointed guardian of the PERSON of (name)," fill in the minor's full first, middle, and last names.

CAPTION: Page Two of the Order Appointing Guardian of Minor

After the words "GUARDIANSHIP OF (NAME)," in capital letters fill in the minor's full first, middle, and last names.

Leave the case number blank.

Item 7b: If you are only seeking guardianship of a minor's person, skip this item. If you are seeking guardianship of a minor's estate or person and estate, fill in your full name, address, and telephone number in the spaces provided. After the words "is appointed guardian of the ESTATE of (name)," fill in the minor's full first, middle, and last names.

Item 8c: Check the box in this item only if you checked the box in Item 2b of this form, and listed relatives of the minor you could not locate.

Items 9a, 9b, and 9c: To complete these items, look at Item 1c of the Petition for Appointment of Guardian of Minor.

Check Item 9a if you checked Item 1c(1) of the petition.

Check Item 9b if you checked Item 1c(2) of the petition. Then fill in the amount of bond requested in Item 1c(1) of the petition.

Check Item 9c if you checked Item 1c(3) of the petition. Then fill in the name of the financial institution and amount to be deposited, as indicated in Item 1c(3) of the petition.

If you want to use the interest or dividends to support the minor, check the box before the words "Additional orders in Attachment 9c." Prepare an Attachment 9c asking that withdrawal of "interest" or "dividends" (depending on the type of assets being placed in a blocked account) not require a court order.

Item 9d: Check this box if you are only seeking guardianship of the person.

Item 10: Skip this item unless the minor is being represented separately by an attorney. If this is the situation, check the first box if the minor's parents will be paying the minor's legal fees. Or check the second box if the minor's estate will be paying the minor's legal fees. Then after the words "to (name)," fill in the name of the lawyer who is representing the minor, and the amount of legal fees in the blank provided. If legal fees are to be paid as soon as the guardianship is granted, check the first box before the word "forthwith." If any other payment arrangements have been made, check the second box before the words "as follows," and list the arrangements in the space provided.

Item 11: Skip this item. It corresponds to Item 1d of the Petition for Appointment of Guardian of Minor, which was also left blank.

Item 12: Skip this item. It corresponds to Item 1e of the Petition for Appointment of Guardian of Minor, which was also left blank.

Item 13: Skip this item.

Sample Order Appointing Guardian of Minor, page 1

GC-240

ATTORNEY OR PARTY WITHOUT ATTORNEY *(Name, state bar number, and address):*	TELEPHONE AND FAX NOS.:	FOR COURT USE ONLY
Patricia Ann Lee 2 West Street Santa Ana, CA 92702	714-555-1212	

ATTORNEY FOR *(Name):*   In Pro Per

SUPERIOR COURT OF CALIFORNIA, COUNTY OF Orange
STREET ADDRESS: 700 Civic Center Drive West
MAILING ADDRESS: P.O. Box 838
CITY AND ZIP CODE: Santa Ana, CA 92702
BRANCH NAME:

GUARDIANSHIP OF THE [X] PERSON [ ] ESTATE OF *(Name):*

Daniel Frank Lee   MINOR

ORDER APPOINTING GUARDIAN OF [X] MINOR [ ] MINORS	CASE NUMBER:

WARNING: THIS APPOINTMENT IS NOT EFFECTIVE UNTIL LETTERS HAVE ISSUED.

1. The petition for appointment of guardian came on for hearing as follows *(check boxes c, d, and e to indicate personal presence):*

   a. Judge *(name):*
   b. Hearing date: Time: [ ] Dept.:   [ ] Room:

   c. [X] Petitioner *(name):* Patricia Ann Lee
   d. [X] Attorney for Petitioner *(name):* Patricia Ann Lee appearing In Pro Per
   e. [ ] Attorney for minor *(name, address, and telephone):*

THE COURT FINDS

2. a. [ ] All notices required by law have been given.
   b. [X] Notice of hearing to the following persons [ ] has been [X] should be   dispensed with *(names):*
   Martin Lee
3. [X] Appointment of a guardian of the [X] person [ ] estate   of the minor is necessary and convenient.

4. [ ] Granting the guardian powers to be exercised independently under Probate Code section 2590 is to the advantage and benefit and is in the best interest of the guardianship estate.

5. [ ] Attorney *(name):*   has been appointed by the court as legal counsel to represent the minor in these proceedings. The cost for representation is: $

6. [X] The appointed court investigator, probation officer, or domestic relations investigator is *(name, title, address, and telephone):*
   Ira Investigator, 700 Civic Center Drive West, Santa Ana, CA 92702
   714-999-9999

THE COURT ORDERS

7. a. *(Name):* Patricia Ann Lee
   (Address): 2 West Street   *(Telephone):* 714-555-1212
   Santa Ana, CA 92702

   is appointed guardian of the PERSON of *(name):* Daniel Frank Lee
   and *Letters* shall issue upon qualification.

Do NOT use this form for a temporary guardianship.   (Continued on reverse)

| Form Approved by the
Judicial Council of California
GC-240 [Rev. January 1, 1998]
Mandatory Form [1/1/2000] | **ORDER APPOINTING GUARDIAN OF MINOR** | WEST GROUP
Official Publisher | Probate Code, §§ 1514,
2310 |

Sample Order Appointing Guardian of Minor, page 2

GUARDIANSHIP OF *(Name)*: Daniel Frank Lee	CASE NUMBER:
MINOR	

7. b. *(Name)*:
     (Address):   *(Telephone)*:

     is appointed guardian of the ESTATE of *(name)*:
     and *Letters* shall issue upon qualification.

8. [X] Notice of hearing to the persons named in item 2b is dispensed with.

9. a. [X] Bond is not required.
    b. [ ] Bond is fixed at: $ to be furnished by an authorized surety company or as otherwise
        provided by law.
    c. [ ] Deposits of: $ are ordered to be placed in a blocked account at *(specify institution and*
        location):

        and receipts shall be filed. No withdrawals shall be made without a court order. [ ] Additional orders in Attachment 9c.
    d. [X] The guardian is not authorized to take possession of money or any other property without a specific court order.

10. [ ] For legal services rendered on behalf of the minor, [ ] parents of the minor [ ] minor's estate shall pay to
     (name):   the sum of: $
      [ ] forthwith [ ] as follows *(specify terms, including any combination of payors)*:

11. [ ] The guardian of the estate is granted authorization under Probate Code section 2590 to exercise independently the powers
      specified in Attachment 11 [ ] subject to the conditions provided.

12. [ ] Orders are granted relating to the powers and duties of the guardian of the person under Probate Code sections 2351-2358
      as specified in Attachment 12.

13. [ ] Orders are granted relating to the conditions imposed under Probate Code section 2402 upon the guardian of the estate as
      specified in Attachment 13.

14. [X] Other orders as specified in Attachment 14 are granted.

15. [ ] The probate referee appointed is *(name and address)*:

16. Number of boxes checked in items 8-15: 3

17. Number of pages attached: 1

Date:

                                            JUDGE OF THE SUPERIOR COURT
                          [ ] SIGNATURE FOLLOWS LAST ATTACHMENT

GC-240 [Rev. January, 1 1998]   **ORDER APPOINTING GUARDIAN OF MINOR**   **WEST GROUP**   Page two
                                                       Official Publisher

Sample Attachment 14 to Order Appointing Guardian of Minor: Additional Orders

GUARDIANSHIP OF (Name): Daniel Frank Lee _____ Case Number:_____

ATTACHMENT 14
to Order Appointing Guardian of Minor: Additional Orders

☒ ORDER WAIVING SERVICE BY MAIL OF ORDER APPOINTING GUARDIAN OF MINOR

☒ Service by mail of the Order Appointing Guardian of Minor on ____ Daniel Frank Lee _____, a minor over the age of 12 who is the subject of this guardianship proceeding, is waived, because the minor personally appeared at the hearing and was advised of the nature of the Order Appointing Guardian of Minor.

☐ ORDER WAIVING ACCOUNTINGS (Probate Code § 2628)

☐ Accountings for the estate of _____ are waived, since the income of the estate consists of public assistance benefits of the type stated in Probate Code § 2628. Pursuant to Probate Code § 2628, the minor's estate does not exceed $5,000 (excluding clothes and ordinary household items), and the minor receives no more than $750 per month in addition to public assistance benefits.

Item 14: If the minor is over age 12 and you completed an Attachment 1g for your Petition, then check this box and include Attachment 14 with the Order (a sample is below).

Item 15: Leave this item blank.

Item 16: Count up the number of boxes you checked on this page and insert the number here.

Item 17: Fill in the number of pages attached. If you are not attaching any additional pages, fill in the word "None."

Leave the date and signature line blank. These will be completed at the hearing by the judge or the clerk.

(Proposed) Letters of Guardianship

The Letters of Guardianship form is the document that states that you have the court's authority to act as guardian. Although it is an extremely important document, you'll find it very easy to prepare.

How to Complete the Form

CAPTION: Letters of Guardianship

Fill in the caption following the general instructions in Chapter 3. Where you seek guardianship of more than one minor, use one form for each child, listing the name of each minor on a separate form.

Leave the case number blank. You will be assigned a case number when you file your documents with the court.

Item 1: In capital letters, after the word "(Name)," fill in your full first, middle, and last names. Check the box or boxes next to the words "person," "estate," or both, depending on the type of guardianship you are seeking. After the words "of (name)," in capital letters fill in the minor's full first, middle, and last names.

Items 2a–2d: Leave these items blank. They apply to situations where you are seeking powers beyond those ordinarily granted, for which you need an attorney's assistance.

Item 3: Check this box if you are seeking only guardianship of the person.

Item 4: If you are not attaching any additional pages, fill in the word "None." Otherwise, count up and enter the number of total pages to be attached.

Leave the rest of the form blank, including the date. The clerk will fill it in, and will also deal with the Affirmation and Certification sections on the second page.

Sample Letters of Guardianship, page 1

GC-250

ATTORNEY OR PARTY WITHOUT ATTORNEY (Name, State Bar number, and address):	FOR COURT USE ONLY

Barbara Faith Johnson
10 Some Street
Redding, CA 96001
TELEPHONE NO.: 916-555-1212   FAX NO. (Optional):
E-MAIL ADDRESS (Optional):
ATTORNEY FOR (Name): In Pro Per

SUPERIOR COURT OF CALIFORNIA, COUNTY OF Shasta
STREET ADDRESS: 1500 Court Street
MAILING ADDRESS: P.O. Box 880
CITY AND ZIP CODE: Redding, CA 96099
BRANCH NAME:

GUARDIANSHIP OF
(Name): Susan Beth Simpson

MINOR

LETTERS OF GUARDIANSHIP ☑ Person ☑ Estate	CASE NUMBER: 123456

LETTERS

1. (Name): Barbara Faith Johnson   is appointed guardian of the ☑ person ☑ estate
   of (name):

2. ☐ Other powers have been granted and conditions have been imposed as follows:

   a. ☐ Powers to be exercised independently under Probate Code section 2590 are specified in attachment 2a
       (specify powers, restrictions, conditions, and limitations).

   b. ☐ Conditions relating to the care and custody of the property under Probate Code section 2402 are specified in
       attachment 2b.

   c. ☐ Conditions relating to the care, treatment, education, and welfare of the minor under Probate Code section 2358
       are specified in attachment 2c.

   d. ☐ Other powers granted or conditions imposed are ☐ specified on attachment 2d. ☐ specified below.

3. ☐ The guardian is not authorized to take possession of money or any other property without a specific court order.

4. Number of pages attached: __0__

WITNESS, clerk of the court, with seal of the court affixed.

(SEAL)	Date:
	Clerk, by _____ , Deputy

Page 1 of 2

Form Adopted for Mandatory Use Judicial Council of California GC-250 [Rev. January 1, 2009]	**LETTERS OF GUARDIANSHIP** **(Probate—Guardianships and Conservatorships)**	Probate Code, §§ 2310, 2311, 2890–2893 www.courtinfo.ca.gov

Sample Letters of Guardianship, page 2

GC-250

GUARDIANSHIP OF	CASE NUMBER:
(Name): Susan Beth Simpson	123456

MINOR

NOTICE TO INSTITUTIONS AND FINANCIAL INSTITUTIONS
(Probate Code sections 2890–2893)

When these *Letters of Guardianship* (Letters) are delivered to you as an employee or other representative of an *institution* or *financial institution* (described below) in order for the guardian of the estate (1) to take possession or control of an asset of the minor named above held by your institution (including changing title, withdrawing all or any portion of the asset, or transferring all or any portion of the asset) or (2) to open or change the name of an account or a safe-deposit box in your financial institution to reflect the guardianship, you must fill out Judicial Council form GC-050 (for an institution) or form GC-051 (for a financial institution). An officer authorized by your institution or financial institution must date and sign the form, and you must file the completed form with the court.

There is no filing fee for filing the form. You may either arrange for personal delivery of the form or mail it to the court for filing at the address given for the court on page 1 of these Letters.

The guardian should deliver a blank copy of the appropriate form to you with these Letters, but it is your institution's or financial institution's responsibility to complete the correct form, have an authorized officer sign it, and file the completed form with the court. If the correct form is not delivered with these Letters or is unavailable for any other reason, blank copies of the forms may be obtained from the court. The forms may also be accessed from the judicial branch's public Web site free of charge. The Internet address (URL) is *www.courtinfo.ca.gov/forms/*. Select the form group *Probate—Guardianships and Conservatorships* and scroll down to form GC-050 for an institution or form GC-051 for a financial institution. The forms may be printed out as blank forms and filled in by typewriter (nonfillable form) or may be filled out online and printed out ready for signature and filing (fillable form).

An *institution* under California Probate Code section 2890(c) is an insurance company, insurance broker, insurance agent, investment company, investment bank, securities broker-dealer, investment advisor, financial planner, financial advisor, or any other person who takes, holds, or controls an asset subject to a conservatorship or guardianship other than a financial institution. Institutions must file a *Notice of Taking Possession or Control of an Asset of Minor or Conservatee* (form GC-050) for an asset of the minor or conservatee held by the institution. A single form may be filed for all affected assets held by the institution.

A *financial institution* under California Probate Code section 2892(b) is a bank, trust (including a Totten trust account but excluding other trust arrangements described in Probate Code section 82(b)), savings and loan association, savings bank, industrial bank, or credit union. Financial institutions must file a *Notice of Opening or Changing a Guardianship or Conservatorship Account or Safe-Deposit Box* (form GC-051) for an account or a safe-deposit box held by the financial institution. A single form may be filed for all affected accounts or safe-deposit boxes held by the financial institution.

LETTERS OF GUARDIANSHIP
AFFIRMATION

I solemnly affirm that I will perform according to law the duties of guardian.

Executed on *(date)*: _____ , at *(place)*: _____

Barbara Faith Johnson
_____   ▶ _____
(TYPE OR PRINT NAME)   (SIGNATURE OF APPOINTEE)

CERTIFICATION

I certify that this document, including any attachments, is a correct copy of the original on file in my office, and that the Letters issued to the person appointed above have not been revoked, annulled, or set aside, and are still in full force and effect.

(SEAL)	
	Date:
	Clerk, by _____ , Deputy

GC-250 [Rev. January 1, 2009]

LETTERS OF GUARDIANSHIP
(Probate—Guardianships and Conservatorships)

Page 2 of 2

Confidential Guardian Screening Form

You must complete this form, which requests personal information about you, for the use of the local social services agency that will conduct an investigation. (Although the form can be accessed by such agencies, it will not be made a part of the court's public file.)

How to Complete the Form

CAPTION: Confidential Guardian Screening Form

Fill in the caption following the general instructions in Chapter 3. Each proposed guardian must fill out one of these forms.

Leave the case number blank.

Item 1: List your name, date of birth, Social Security number, driver's license number, and home, work, and cell phone numbers.

Items 2-5: Check the boxes next to "I am not" or "I have not," or, if applicable, "I am" or "I have," to answer questions pertaining to possible sex offender status, arrests or convictions for felonies or misdemeanors (minor traffic infractions don't count), protective orders, or psychiatric or other therapy.

Items 6-9: Check the boxes next to "No," or "Yes" if applicable, to answer questions regarding persons living in your home in Items 6 and 7, and 9. Check "I am" or "I am not" as appropriate, under Item 8.

CAPTION: Page two of the Confidential Guardian Screening Form

In capital letters, fill in the minor's first, middle, and last names after the words "GUARDIANSHIP OF:"

Leave the case number blank.

Items 10-12. Check the box next to "Yes" or "No" to answer more questions about you and anyone living in your home.

Item 13: Check the box next to "I do not have" or "I have or may have" an adverse interest. This refers to you having a financial interest that might work against the minor's interests. This is usually not the case for a guardianship of a minor's person. In a guardianship of the minor's estate, your ownership of certain property in which the minor had an interest, or vice versa, might constitute such a financial interest.

Items 14-19: Check the boxes next to "I have," "I am," "I have not," or "I am not" to answer questions about previous guardianships or bankruptcies and as to whether you are licensed as a professional fiduciary.

Attachments: If you checked "I am" or "I have" or "Yes" to any of the questions in Items 2 through 16, 18, or 19, or "I am not" in answer to Item 17, you will need to give details on a separate attachment, numbered to correspond with the item. For example, if you checked "I have" on Item 19, indicating that you filed for bankruptcy within the past ten years, your "Attachment 19" might read as follows: "In July 20xx, I filed a Chapter 7 bankruptcy proceeding, Case No. 01-00123-BK, in the U.S. Bankruptcy Court for the Southern District of California, because of tax liabilities my ex-husband incurred, and for which I was legally responsible." Follow the instructions for preparing attachment pages in Chapter 3, and label the page "Attachment [number] to Confidential Guardian Screening Form."

Items 20-22: List the name, home phone number, school, school phone number, and other phone number if applicable, for each minor. If more than three minors are involved, check the box next to the words "information on additional minors is attached," and prepare an attachment with the same information.

Date and Signature: Write the date you are signing the form. Directly above "TYPE OR PRINT NAME," type your name, and sign where indicated.

Sample Confidential Guardian Screening Form, page 1

CONFIDENTIAL (DO NOT ATTACH TO PETITION)

GC-212

ATTORNEY OR PARTY WITHOUT ATTORNEY *(Name, State Bar number, and address):*
Patricia Ann Lee
2 West Street
Santa Ana, CA 92702

FOR COURT USE ONLY

TELEPHONE NO.: 714-555-1212   FAX NO. *(Optional):*

E-MAIL ADDRESS *(Optional):*

ATTORNEY FOR *(Name):* In Pro Per

SUPERIOR COURT OF CALIFORNIA, COUNTY OF Orange
STREET ADDRESS: 700 Civic Center Drive West
MAILING ADDRESS: P.O. Box 838
CITY AND ZIP CODE: Santa Ana, CA 92702
BRANCH NAME:

GUARDIANSHIP OF
(Name): Daniel Frank Lee and Sara Winters Lee

MINOR

CASE NUMBER:

| CONFIDENTIAL GUARDIAN SCREENING FORM
Guardianship of ☑ Person ☐ Estate | HEARING DATE AND TIME: | DEPT.: |

The proposed guardian must complete and sign this form. The person requesting appointment of a guardian must submit the completed and signed form to the court with the guardianship petition.
This form must remain confidential.

How This Form Will Be Used

This form is **confidential** and will not be a part of the public file in this case. Each proposed guardian must complete and sign a separate copy of this form under rule 7.1001 of the California Rules of Court. The information provided will be used by the court and by persons and agencies designated by the court to assist the court in determining whether to appoint the proposed guardian as guardian. The proposed guardian **must** respond to each item.

1. a. **Proposed guardian** *(name):* Patricia Ann Lee
   b. Date of birth: 10/10/1958
   c. Social security number: 111-22-3333 d. Driver's license number: N8567899   State: CA
   e. Telephone numbers: Home: 714-555-1212   Work: 714-555-8989   Other:

2. ☐ I am   ☑ I am not   required to register as a sex offender under California Penal Code section 290.
   (If you checked "I am," explain in Attachment 2.)

3. ☐ I have   ☑ I have not   been charged with, arrested for, or convicted of a crime deemed to be a felony or a misdemeanor. *(If you checked "I have," explain in Attachment 3.)*
   ☐ *(Check here if you have been arrested for drug or alcohol-related offenses.)*

4. ☐ I have   ☑ I have not   had a restraining order or protective order filed against me in the last 10 years.
   (If you checked "I have," explain in Attachment 4.)

5. ☐ I am   ☑ I am not   receiving services from a psychiatrist, psychologist, or therapist for a mental health–related issue.
   (If you checked "I am," explain in Attachment 5.)

6. Do you, or does any other person living in your home, have a social worker or parole or probation officer assigned to him or her?
   ☐ Yes   ☑ No   *(If you checked "Yes," explain in Attachment 6 and provide the name and address of each social worker, parole officer, or probation officer.)*

7. Have you, or has any other person living in your home, been charged with, arrested for, or convicted of any form of child abuse, neglect, or molestation?   ☐ Yes   ☑ No   *(If you checked "Yes," explain in Attachment 7.)*

8. ☐ I am   ☑ I am not   aware of any reports alleging any form of child abuse, neglect, or molestation made to any
   ☐   agency charged with protecting children (e.g., Child Protective Services) or any other law enforcement agency regarding me or any other person living in my home. *(If you checked "I am," explain in Attachment 8 and provide the name and address of each agency.)*

9. Have you, or has any other person living in your home, habitually used any illegal substances or abused alcohol?
   ☐ Yes   ☑ No   *(If you checked "Yes," explain in Attachment 9.)*

Page 1 of 2

Form Adopted for Mandatory Use
Judicial Council of California
GC-212 [Rev. July 1, 2009]

CONFIDENTIAL GUARDIAN SCREENING FORM
(Probate—Guardianships and Conservatorships)

Probate Code, § 1516;
Family Code, § 3011;
Cal. Rules of Court, rule 7.1001
www.courtinfo.ca.gov

Sample Confidential Guardian Screening Form, page 2

CONFIDENTIAL		GC-212
GUARDIANSHIP OF *(Name):* Daniel Frank Lee and Sara Winters Lee	MINOR	CASE NUMBER:

10. Have you, or has any other person living in your home, been charged with, arrested for, or convicted of a crime involving illegal substances or alcohol?
　　☐ Yes　☑ No　　*(If you checked "Yes," explain in Attachment 10.)*

11. Do you or does any other person living in your home suffer from mental illness?
　　☐ Yes　☑ No　　*(If you checked "Yes," explain in Attachment 11.)*

12. Do you suffer from any physical disability that would impair your ability to perform the duties of guardian?
　　☐ Yes　☑ No　　*(If you checked 'Yes," explain in Attachment 12.)*

13. ☐ I have or may have　☑ I do not have　an adverse interest that the court may consider to be a risk to, or to have an effect on, my ability to faithfully perform the duties of guardian.
　　(If you checked "I have or may have," explain in Attachment 13.)

14. ☐ I have　☑ I have not　previously been appointed guardian, conservator, executor, or fiduciary in another proceeding.
　　(If you checked "I have," explain in Attachment 14.)

15. ☐ I have　☑ I have not　been removed as guardian, conservator, executor, or fiduciary in any other proceeding.
　　(If you checked "I have," explain in Attachment 15.)

16. ☐ I am　☑ I am not　a private professional fiduciary, as defined in Business and Professions Code section 6501(f).
　　(If you checked "I am," respond to item 17. If you checked "I am not," go to item 18.)

17. ☐ I am　☑ I am not　currently licensed by the Professional Fiduciaries Bureau of the Department of Consumer Affairs. My license status and information is stated in item 1 on page 1 of the Professional Fiduciary Attachment signed by me and attached to the petition that proposes my appointment as guardian in this matter. *(Complete and sign the Professional Fiduciary Attachment and attach it to the petition, or deliver it to the petitioner for attachment, before the petition is filed. See item 4d of the petition. Use form GC-210(A-PF)/GC-310(A-PF) for this attachment.)*

18. ☐ I am　☑ I am not　a responsible corporate officer authorized to act for *(name of corporation):*

　　a California nonprofit charitable corporation that meets the requirements for appointment as guardian of the proposed ward under Probate Code section 2104. I certify that the corporation's articles of incorporation specifically authorize it to accept appointments as guardian. *(If you checked "I am," explain the circumstances of the corporation's care of, counseling of, or financial assistance to the proposed ward in Attachment 18.)*

19. ☐ I have　☑ I have not　filed for bankruptcy protection within the last 10 years.
　　(If you checked "I have," explain in Attachment 19.)

MINORS' CONTACT INFORMATION

20. Minor's name: Daniel Frank Lee　　School *(name):* Orange Heights Middle School
　　Home telephone: 714-555-1212　　School telephone: 714-555-9876　Other telephone:

21. Minor's name: Sara Winters Lee　　School *(name):* Redwood Elementary School
　　Home telephone: 714-555-1212　　School telephone: 714-555-6789　Other telephone:

22. Minor's name:　　School *(name):*
　　Home telephone:　　School telephone:　　Other telephone:
　　☐ Information on additional minors is attached.

DECLARATION

I declare under penalty of perjury under the laws of the State of California that the foregoing is true and correct.

Date: 2/1/20xx

Patricia Ann Lee
　▶
_____　　_____
(TYPE OR PRINT NAME OF PROPOSED GUARDIAN)　　(SIGNATURE OF PROPOSED GUARDIAN)*

* Each proposed guardian must fill out and file a separate screening form.

GC-212 [Rev. July 1, 2009]　**CONFIDENTIAL GUARDIAN SCREENING FORM**　Page 2 of 2
(Probate—Guardianships and Conservatorships)

Duties of Guardian and Acknowledgment of Receipt

This form is an information sheet summarizing your duties as a guardian. You should fill out the case caption information following the general instructions in Chapter 3. On each of pages 2, 3, 4, and 5, fill in the minor's first, middle, and last name in capital letters after the words "GUARDIAN OF (NAME):" at the top of each page. Again, leave the case number blank. Finally, type your name at the lower left of page 5 in the space provided for that, and sign the form. Of course, you should also read the form to be sure you understand your duties.

Prepare Supplemental Documents If Required

Depending on your situation and the court in which you are filing, you may need to prepare additional local court forms. Copies of local forms are not supplied in this book, so you must contact your court to arrange to get copies. Call or visit the website of your local court to find out its requirements.

Larger Courts May Require Declaration for Filing and Assignment

In some counties, a special form is required if you want your case to be filed in a branch court —which may be closer and more convenient— rather than the main court. Branch courts are discussed in Chapter 3, along with information about where to file your papers. If you will be filing in a branch court, call the court clerk and ask whether there is a local declaration for filing and assignment form, and find out how to obtain a copy. These forms are self-explanatory and easy to complete.

Some Courts Require Additional Forms

You may need to complete a form that gives the current addresses of the proposed guardian and minor. The form in Appendix C in the back of the book entitled Change of Residence Notice contains substantially the same information as any of the local court forms. Chapter 11 gives instructions on how to complete the Change of Residence Notice form, and provides a completed sample. However, many courts require that you use their local forms, so to be on the safe side, check with the court to find out whether one is required.

In fact, you should always check with your local court to find out whether there are any special local requirements. For example, many courts have their own investigation or screening forms in addition to the Confidential Screening Form above. Some courts may ask for a separate declaration from you addressing particular issues. And some courts have specific concerns, like whether the minor is involved in any lawsuits for personal injuries. The court clerk will be able to tell you whether there are any local forms you need to complete, so be sure to ask. You can also look for this information on your court's website. To find the site, go to www.courtinfo.ca.gov/courts/find.html.

When You Need a Guardianship Right Away

If you need a guardianship sooner than six weeks from the date you file your papers with the court, you may be able to obtain a temporary guardianship that goes into effect sooner—usually within five days. In addition to the documents you prepared in this chapter, you will need to prepare papers for a temporary guardianship and file them with the court, following the instructions in Chapter 7.

Sample Duties of Guardian, page 1

<table>
<tr>
<td colspan="2">

GC-248

ATTORNEY OR PARTY WITHOUT ATTORNEY *(Name, state bar number, and address)*:
  PATRICIA ANN LEE
  2 West Street
  Santa Ana, CA 92702
    TELEPHONE NO.: 714-555-1212   FAX NO. *(Optional)*:
E-MAIL ADDRESS *(Optional)*:
ATTORNEY FOR *(Name)*:   In Pro Per

FOR COURT USE ONLY

</td>
</tr>
</table>

SUPERIOR COURT OF CALIFORNIA, COUNTY OF ORANGE
  STREET ADDRESS: 700 Civic Center Drive West
  MAILING ADDRESS: P.O. Box 838
  CITY AND ZIP CODE: Santa Ana, CA 92702
  BRANCH NAME:

GUARDIANSHIP OF THE   [X] PERSON   [ ] ESTATE

OF *(Name)*:   Daniel Frank Lee   MINOR

DUTIES OF GUARDIAN and Acknowledgment of Receipt	CASE NUMBER:

DUTIES OF GUARDIAN

When you are appointed by the court as a guardian of a minor, you become an officer of the court and assume certain duties and obligations. An attorney is best qualified to advise you about these matters. You should clearly understand the information on this form. You will find additional information in the *Guardianship Pamphlet (for Guardianships of Children in the Probate Court)* (Form GC-205), which is available from the court.

1. GUARDIANSHIP OF THE PERSON

If the probate court appoints you as a *guardian of the person* for a child, you will be required to assume important duties and obligations.

a.   **Fundamental responsibilities** - The guardian of the person of a child has the care, custody, and control of the child. As guardian, you are responsible for providing for food, clothing, shelter, education, and all the medical and dental needs of the child. You must provide for the safety, protection, and physical and emotional growth of the child.

b.   **Custody** - As guardian of the person of the child, you have full legal and physical custody of the child and are responsible for **all** decisions relating to the child. The child's parents can no longer make decisions for the child while there is a guardianship. The parents' rights are suspended—not terminated—as long as a guardian is appointed for a minor.

c.   **Education** - As guardian of the person of the child, you are responsible for the child's education. You determine where the child should attend school. As the child's advocate within the school system, you should attend conferences and play an active role in the child's education. For younger children, you may want to consider enrolling the child in Head Start or other similar programs. For older children, you should consider their future educational needs such as college or a specialized school. You must assist the child in obtaining services if the child has special educational needs. You should help the child in setting and attaining his or her educational goals.

d.   **Residence** - As guardian, you have the right to determine where the child lives. The child will normally live with you, but when it is necessary, you are allowed to make other arrangements if it is in the best interest of the child. You should obtain court approval before placing the child back with his or her parents.

As guardian, you **do not** have the right to change the child's residence to a place outside of California unless you first receive the court's permission. If the court grants permission, California law requires that you establish legal guardianship in the state where the child will be living. Individual states have different rules regarding guardianships. You should seek additional information about guardianships in the state where you want the child to live.

(Continued on reverse)

Form Adopted for Mandatory Use
Judicial Council of California
GC-248 [New January 1, 2001]

DUTIES OF GUARDIAN
(Probate)

Page one of five

Sample Duties of Guardian, page 2

GC-248

GUARDIAN OF (Name): DANIEL FRANK LEE	MINOR	CASE NUMBER:

e. **Medical treatment** - As guardian, you are responsible for meeting the medical needs of the child. In most cases, you have the authority to consent to the child's medical treatment. However, if the child is 14 years or older, surgery may not be performed on the child unless either (1) both the child and the guardian consent or (2) a court order is obtained that specifically authorizes the surgery. This holds true except in emergencies. A guardian may not place a child involuntarily in a mental health treatment facility under a probate guardianship. A mental health conservatorship proceeding is required for such an involuntary commitment. However, the guardian may secure counseling and other necessary mental health services for the child. The law also allows older and more mature children to consent to their own treatment in certain situations such as outpatient mental health treatment, medical care related to pregnancy or sexually transmitted diseases, and drug and alcohol treatment.

f. **Community resources** - There are agencies in each county that may be helpful in meeting the specific needs of children who come from conflicted, troubled, or deprived environments. If the child has special needs, you must strive to meet those needs or secure appropriate services.

g. **Financial support** - Even when the child has a guardian, the parents are still obligated to financially support the child. The guardian may take action to obtain child support. The child may also be eligible for Temporary Aid for Needy Families, TANF (formerly known as AFDC), social security benefits, Veterans Administration benefits, Indian child welfare benefits, and other public or private funds.

h. **Visitation** - The court may require that you allow visitation or contact between the child and his or her parents. The child's needs often require that the parent-child relationship be maintained, within reason. However, the court may place restrictions on the visits, such as the requirement of supervision. The court may also impose other conditions in the child's best interest.

i. **Driver's license** - As guardian of the person, you have the authority to consent to the minor's application for a driver's license. If you consent, you will become liable for any civil damages that may result if the minor causes an accident. The law requires that anyone signing the DMV application obtain insurance to cover the minor.

j. **Enlistment in the armed services** - The guardian may consent to a minor's enlistment in the armed services. If the minor enters into active duty with the armed forces, the minor becomes emancipated under California law.

k. **Marriage** - For the minor to marry, the guardian **and the court** must give permission. If the minor enters a valid marriage, the minor becomes emancipated under California law.

l. **Change of address** - A guardian must notify the court in writing of any change in the address of either the child or the guardian. This includes any changes that result from the child's leaving the guardian's home or returning to the parent's home. You **must** always obtain **court permission** before you move the child to another state or country.

m. **Court visitors and status reports** - Some counties have a program in which "court visitors" track and review guardianships. If your county has such a program, you will be expected to cooperate with all requests of the court visitor. As guardian, you may also be required to fill out and file status reports. In all counties, you must cooperate with the court and court investigators.

n. **Misconduct of the child** - A guardian, like a parent, is liable for the harm and damages caused by the willful misconduct of a child. There are special rules concerning harm caused by the use of a firearm. If you are concerned about your possible liability, you should consult an attorney.

o. **Additional responsibilities** - The court may place other conditions on the guardianship or additional duties upon you, as guardian. For example, the court may require the guardian to complete counseling or parenting classes, to obtain specific services for the child, or to follow a scheduled visitation plan between the child and the child's parents or relatives. As guardian, you must follow all court orders.

(Continued on page three)

GC-248 [New January 1, 2001]

DUTIES OF GUARDIAN
(Probate)

Page two of five

Sample Duties of Guardian, page 3

GC-248

GUARDIAN OF (Name):	CASE NUMBER:
DANIEL FRANK LEE MINOR	

p. **Termination of guardianship of the person** - A guardianship of the person automatically ends when the child reaches the age of 18, is adopted, marries, is emancipated by court order, enters into active military duty, or dies. If none of these events has occurred, the child, a parent, or the guardian may petition the court for termination of guardianship. But it must be shown that the guardianship is no longer necessary or that termination of the guardianship is in the child's best interest.

2. GUARDIANSHIP OF THE ESTATE

If the court appoints you as *guardian of the child's estate,* you will have additional duties and obligations. The money and other assets of the child are called the child's "estate."' Appointment as guardian of a child's estate is taken very seriously by the court. The guardian of the estate is required to manage the child's funds, collect and make an inventory of the assets, keep accurate financial records, and regularly file financial accountings with the court.

MANAGING THE ESTATE

a. **Prudent investments** - As guardian of the estate, you must manage the child's assets with the care of a prudent person dealing with someone else's property. This means that you must be cautious and may not make speculative or risky investments.

b. **Keeping estate assets separate** - As guardian of the estate, you must keep the money and property of the child's estate separate from everyone else's, including your own. When you open a bank account for the estate, the account name must indicate that it is a *guardianship* account and not your personal account. You should use the child's social security number when opening estate accounts. You should never deposit estate funds in your personal account or otherwise mix them with your own funds or anyone else's funds, even for brief periods. Securities in the estate must be held in a name that shows that they are estate property and not your personal property.

c. **Interest-bearing accounts and other investments** - Except for checking accounts intended for ordinary expenses, you should place estate funds in interest-bearing accounts. You may deposit estate funds in insured accounts in federally insured financial institutions, but you should not put more than $100,000 in any single institution. You should consult with an attorney before making other kinds of investments.

d. **Blocked accounts** - A *blocked account is* an account with a financial institution in which money is placed. No person may withdraw funds from a blocked account without the court's permission. Depending on the amount and character of the child's property, the guardian may elect **or the court may require** that estate assets be placed in a blocked account. As guardian of the estate, you must follow the directions of the court and the procedures required to deposit funds in this type of account. The use of a blocked account is a safeguard and may save the estate the cost of a bond.

e. **Other restrictions** - As guardian of the estate, you will have many other restrictions on your authority to deal with estate assets. Without prior court order, you **may not** pay fees to yourself or your attorney. You may not make a gift of estate assets to anyone. You may not borrow money from the estate. As guardian, you may not use estate funds to purchase real property without a prior court order. If you do not obtain the court's permission to spend estate funds, you may be compelled to reimburse the estate from your own personal funds and may be removed as guardian. You should consult with an attorney concerning the legal requirements relating to sales, leases, mortgages, and investment of estate property. If the child of whose estate you are the guardian has a living parent or if that child receives assets or is entitled to support from another source, you must obtain court approval before using guardianship assets for the child's support, maintenance, or education. You must file a petition or include a request for approval in the original petition, and set forth which exceptional circumstances justify any use of guardianship assets for the child's support. The court will ordinarily grant such a petition for only a limited period of time, usually not to exceed one year, and only for specific and limited purposes.

INVENTORY OF ESTATE PROPERTY

f. **Locate the estate's property** - As guardian of the estate, you must locate, take possession of, and protect the child's income and assets that will be administered in the estate. You must change the ownership of all assets into the guardianship estate's name. For real estate, you should record a copy of your *Letters of Guardianship* with the county recorder in each county where the child owns real property.

(Continued on reverse)

GC-248 [New January 1, 2001]

DUTIES OF GUARDIAN
(Probate)

Page three of five

Sample Duties of Guardian, page 4

GC-248

| GUARDIAN OF (Name): DANIEL FRANK LEE   MINOR | CASE NUMBER: |

g. **Determine the value of the property** - As guardian of the estate, you must arrange to have a court-appointed referee determine the value of the estate property unless the appointment is waived by the court. You—not the referee—must determine the value of certain "cash items." An attorney can advise you about how to do this.

h. **File an inventory and appraisal** - As guardian of the estate, you must file an inventory and appraisal within 90 days after your appointment. You may be required to return to court 90 days after your appointment as guardian of the estate to ensure that you have properly filed the inventory and appraisal.

INSURANCE

i. **Insurance coverage** - As guardian of the estate, you should make sure that there is appropriate and sufficient insurance covering the assets and risks of the estate. You should maintain the insurance in force throughout the entire period of the guardianship or until the insured asset is sold.

RECORD KEEPING AND ACCOUNTING

j. **Records** - As guardian of the estate, you must keep complete, accurate records of each financial transaction affecting the estate. The checkbook for the guardianship checking account is essential for keeping records of income and expenditures. You should also keep receipts for all purchases. Record keeping is critical because you will have to prepare an accounting of all money and property that you have received, what you have spent, the date of each transaction, and its purpose. You will also have to be able to describe in detail what is left after you have paid the estate's expenses.

k. **Accountings** - As guardian of the estate, you must file a petition requesting that the court review and approve your accounting one year after your appointment and at least every two years after that. The court may ask that you justify some or all expenditures. You should have receipts and other documents available for the court's review, if requested. If you do not file your accounting as required, the court will order you to do so. You may be removed as guardian for failure to file an accounting.

l. **Format** - As guardian of the estate, you must comply with all state and local rules when filing your accounting. A particular format is specified in the Probate Code, which you must follow when you present your account to the court. You should check local rules for any special local requirements.

m. **Legal advice** - An attorney can advise you and help you prepare your inventories, accountings, and petitions to the court. If you have questions, you should consult with an attorney.

3. OTHER GENERAL INFORMATION

a. **Removal of a guardian** - A guardian may be removed for specific reasons or when it is in the child's best interest. A guardian may be removed either on the court's own motion or by a petition filed by the child, a relative of the child, or any other interested person. If necessary, the court may appoint a successor guardian, or the court may return the child to a parent if that is found to be in the child's best interest.

b. **Legal documents** - For your appointment as guardian to be valid, the *Order Appointing Guardian of Minor* must be signed. Once the court signs the order, the guardian **must** go to the clerk's office, where *Letters of Guardianship* will be issued. *Letters of Guardianship* is a legal document that provides proof that you have been appointed and are serving as the guardian of a minor. You should obtain several certified copies of the *Letters* from the clerk. These legal documents will be of assistance to you in the performance of your duties, such as enrolling the child in school, obtaining medical care, and taking care of estate business.

c. **Attorneys and legal resources** - If you have an attorney, the attorney will advise you on your duties and responsibilities, the limits of your authority, the rights of the child, and your dealings with the court. **If you have legal questions, you should consult with your attorney.** Please remember that the court staff cannot give you legal advice.

(Continued on page five)

DUTIES OF GUARDIAN
(Probate)

Sample Duties of Guardian, page 5

GC-248

GUARDIAN OF (Name):		CASE NUMBER:
DANIEL FRANK LEE	MINOR	

If you are not represented by an attorney, you may obtain answers to your questions by contacting community resources, private publications, or your local law library.

NOTICE: This statement of duties is a summary and is not a complete statement of the law. Your conduct as a probate guardian is governed by the law itself and not by this summary.

ACKNOWLEDGMENT OF RECEIPT

1.   I have petitioned the court to be appointed as a guardian.

2.   I acknowledge that I have received a copy of this statement of the duties of the position of guardian.

Date: 2/1/20xx

PATRICIA ANN LEE
_____
(TYPE OR PRINT NAME)

▶ *Patricia Ann Lee*
_____
(SIGNATURE OF PETITIONER)

Date:

_____
(TYPE OR PRINT NAME)

▶
_____
(SIGNATURE OF PETITIONER)

Date:

_____
(TYPE OR PRINT NAME)

▶
_____
(SIGNATURE OF PETITIONER)

GC-248 [New January 1, 2001]

DUTIES OF GUARDIAN
(Probate)

Page five of five

Filing and Serving the Guardianship Papers

Check Your Work

After you have filled out and signed the initial guardianship documents following the instructions in Chapters 4 and 5, review them carefully. Make sure the correct attachments are numbered and fastened to the appropriate documents. Be sure that all the proper boxes are checked, everyone's name is spelled correctly, and any necessary signatures have been obtained.

> **TIP**
>
> **Call the court clerk.** When all your documents are ready for filing, call the clerk in the court's probate department. Tell the clerk that you are filing a guardianship petition, and that you want to verify that you've completed all the required paperwork. Identify the documents you have prepared, and ask whether others are required. If the clerk will not give you this information, check a copy of the court's local probate rules. (See Chapter 13.) If the court's local rules require any additional forms, arrange to get copies. You usually can get forms online, by going to court, or through the mail by sending a letter to the court explaining what forms you want, and enclosing a self-addressed, stamped envelope. Check in advance whether there is a charge for these additional forms—if so, it will be a small fee. Finally, ask how many copies of all guardianship documents are required by the court. Some courts only need the original completed forms, while others keep the original and one or possibly more additional copies.

File Guardianship Documents and Get a Hearing Date

At last you're ready to copy your papers and file them with the court. Chapter 3 gives general rules on how to file your papers with the court. Here is an explanation of some specifics.

Photocopy Documents

The documents you'll file for the guardianship are listed in the following chart. Regardless of whether you take or mail your documents to the court, always keep an extra copy of each document at home, in case something happens to the ones you're filing. Remember that you're better off having too many copies than not enough.

You'll need an extra copy of the Petition for Appointment of Guardian of Minor—including all attachments—and the Notice of Hearing for each person and agency that must be served. "Determine Who Must Be Served," in this chapter, discusses which people and agencies must be served. You may either skip to that section now and figure out how many people and agencies must be served, or estimate the number of copies you'll need by looking at the Guardianship Notification Worksheet, which lists relatives and agencies to be served.

Take or Send Guardianship Documents to Court

Now that you've made photocopies of the completed forms, you are ready to file them with the court clerk. You may either take or mail your documents to the court, following the instructions in Chapter 3. When your documents are filed, the clerk should give you a "Probate Guardian Pamphlet" that briefly summarizes guardianship laws and procedures. You will be assigned a case number. This is the time to request a hearing date, following the instructions below.

Applying for a Waiver of Court Fees and Costs

Skip this section unless you have a very low income and are applying to have court fees and costs waived. If you are applying for a fee waiver, you should have prepared and copied the necessary documents. (See the accompanying list.)

By law, you may file your guardianship papers with the court at the same time as the fee waiver request, without paying a filing fee. Some clerks may tell you that you'll have to wait a few days for a judge to grant the fee waiver before you can file your guardianship papers. If this happens, be polite but firm. Tell the clerk that you are entitled to file your papers under Rule 3.50 of the California Rules of Court. If for some reason the clerk still will not file your papers, ask to speak with a supervisor, and ask the supervisor to file your papers as required under Rule 3.50.

If you file your documents in person, you may have to take the fee waiver documents to be reviewed and filed by a clerk in a different department or courtroom from the probate court's filing desk. To find out the procedure, call or go to the probate department, and ask the clerk where to file your fee waiver documents.

The court has five days to review a Request to Waive Court Fees. If the court doesn't deny your request within that five-day period, your fees and costs are automatically waived (CRC 985(e)). If you don't get any notification from the court within a week after you file your fee waiver documents, call the clerk to find out whether your fees were waived.

Otherwise, when you receive the form back from the court, review it carefully, as your next steps depend on what it says.

- If box 4a is checked, your fee waiver process is complete and you can go ahead with your guardianship.
- If box 4b is checked, pay particular attention to the deadlines in the additional boxes.

- If box 4b(1) is checked, this means the court has denied your request pending receiving more information from you. If you don't have any more information, you might have to go ahead and pay the filing fees. However, if the things that the court specifies in this item are things that you can provide, do so. This may mean filing a revised version of your Request to Waive Court Fees, with additional information included or documents attached. If you have the information requested, ask the court clerk what is the best way to present it to the judge.

- If box 4b(2) is checked, this means the court has denied your request for specific reasons, which will be listed. Your choices at that point are to go ahead and pay the court fees, or to file a Request for Hearing About Court Fee Waiver Order (see instructions below). If you are going to ask for a hearing, you need to file the request within ten days after the date listed in the Clerk's Certificate of Service at the bottom of the order.

- If box 4c is checked, then the judge wants you to come to court and provide more information. The form should state what the judge wants to know and what documentation you should bring. Make sure that you go to court on the date specified.

Request for Hearing About Court Fee Waiver Order (Superior Court)

If the judge has denied your request for a fee waiver and you think the reasons given are incorrect, you can file this form to ask for a hearing in front of the judge.

Guardianship Documents to Be Filed With the Court

Depending on your situation, you may be filing all or just some of these documents:

YOU MUST FILE:	NUMBER OF COPIES NEEDED*
☐ Consent of Proposed Guardian, Nomination of Guardian, and Consent to Appointment of Guardian and Waiver of Notice, three-part form (Chapter 4)**	Original + 2
☐ Petition for Appointment of Guardian of Minor and attachments (Chapter 5)***	Original + 2 + one for each person entitled to notice
☐ Notice of Hearing (Chapter 5)	Original + 2 + one for each person entitled to notice
☐ (Proposed) Order Appointing Guardian of Minor (Chapter 5)	Original + 2 + one for each minor over age 12
☐ (Proposed) Letters of Guardianship (Chapter 5)	Original + 2 + any additional copies needed for agencies (4–5 recommended)
☐ Confidential Guardian Screening Form (Chapter 5)	Original + 2
☐ Duties of Guardian and Acknowledgment of Receipt (Chapter 5)	Original + 2
YOU MAY FILE:	**NUMBER OF COPIES NEEDED***
☐ (Proposed) Order Dispensing With Notice (Chapter 5)	Original + 2
Fee Waiver Documents, if you have a very low income and are applying for a waiver of court fees and costs (Chapters 3 and 6):	
☐ Request to Waive Court Fees	Original + 2
☐ (Proposed) Order on Court Fee Waiver	Original + 2
☐ Request for Hearing About Court Fee Waiver Order (if necessary after receiving Order)	Original + 2
☐ Order on Court Fee Waiver After Hearing (if necessary)	Original + 2
Supplemental documents, if required (Chapter 5):	
☐ Declaration for Filing and Assignment	Original + 2
☐ Notification to Court of Address on Guardianship	Original + 2
☐ Other required local forms	Original + 2
Additional documents for a temporary guardianship, if applicable (Chapter 7):	
☐ Petition for Appointment of Temporary Guardian (if required)	Original + 2 + one for each person entitled to notice
☐ Notice of Hearing (for Temporary Guardianship if required by local rules)	Original + 2 + one for each person entitled to notice (if required)
☐ (Proposed) Order for Appointment of Temporary Guardian	Original + 2
☐ (Proposed) Letters of Temporary Guardian needed by agencies	Original + 2 + any additional copies

* The two copies listed include one that you leave at home when you take or send your papers to the court. You may need at least one additional copy of all documents if the court's local rules require it.

** If you haven't obtained any signatures on the Nomination of Guardian or Waiver of Notice and Consent portions of the form, you must still complete and sign the Consent of Proposed Guardian section.

*** The Declaration Under Uniform Child Custody Jurisdiction and Enforcement Act (UCCJEA) is attached to the petition as Attachment 12. It is required for all petitioners seeking guardianship of a minor's person or person and estate.

FORM

You'll find a blank copy of the Request for Hearing About Court Fee Waiver Order (Superior Court) in Appendix C at the back of the book. You can also download the form at www.courtinfo.ca.gov/forms/fillable/fw006.pdf.

Caption. On the right, fill in the address of the court, your case number, and, in the box for "Case Name," the words "Guardianship Petition of [your name]."

Item 1. Fill in your name, address, and telephone number.

Item 2. Fill in the words "In Pro Per."

Item 3. Fill in the date that is stamped in the upper right corner of the Order on Court Fee Waiver. Check the box below, and attach the Order.

Item 4. You do not need to do anything with this item.

Item 5. If you want to give the judge advance notice of what you're going to argue at the hearing, check this box and type in the statement you want to make about why the judge's decision was wrong. You should try very hard to contain everything you want to say in the space provided, but if it's just not possible, you can attach another page, following the instructions on the form. If there are documents you think the court should see and you didn't attach them to your original request, you can attach them to this form.

Date and signature line. Fill in the date, then print your name on the left and sign on the right.

Take this form to the court and file it just as you did your original petition, along with the Order (see below). The clerk will give you a hearing date. See Chapter 9, "The Hearing," for general information about preparing for the court hearing.

Order on Court Fee Waiver After Hearing

Along with your Request for Hearing, you must submit an Order to the court. The clerk won't file it, but will hold it in the file for the hearing.

FORM

You'll find a blank copy of the Order on Court Fee Waiver After Hearing (Superior Court) in Appendix C at the back of the book. You can also download the form at www.courtinfo.ca.gov/forms/fillable/fw008.pdf.

Caption. On the right, fill in the address of the court, your case number, and, in the box for "Case Name," the words "Guardianship Petition of [your name]."

Item 1. Fill in your name, address, and telephone number.

Item 2. Fill in the words "In Pro Per."

Item 3. Fill in the date that is stamped in the upper right corner of your original request to waive court fees.

Item 4. Fill in the date of the hearing and the department where the hearing will be, if you know this information. If you don't, leave this blank and the clerk or judge will fill it in later. Check the box next to "Person in 1."

Item 5. Don't check any boxes; the judge will fill out this form. Do not date or sign the form.

Caption on Page 2. At the top of the page, fill in your name and the case number.

After the hearing, the judge's clerk will give you a completed Order that will tell you what to do—and whatever it says, that's what you'll have to do. You can't ask again for the judge to reconsider.

If the judge checked box 5a, your fee waiver has been granted and you can proceed with your case. If box 5b is checked, your request has been denied for the reasons stated on the Order.

However, if box 5b(2) is checked, the court will allow you to pay the court fees over time, and will specify how much the payments are to be and what fees the payments apply to.

If the judge checked box 5c, your request has been partially granted and the Order will specify whether you must pay a certain percentage of all the fees, or only pay certain fees.

(Proposed) Orders and Letters Will Not Be Returned

When you give your documents to the court clerk, the clerk will stamp and return most of them—but not all. The clerk will keep any proposed orders—which require a judge's signature—and Letters of Guardianship or Letters of Temporary Guardianship. At the hearing, the judge will decide whether to sign the orders, and whether you will be named guardian. You will get copies of the signed papers then, as long as you submitted extra photocopies. To alert you to these forms, they are referred to as "proposed" documents in the instructions.

Get a Hearing Date

When you file your guardianship papers with the court, you will be assigned a date and time when you and the minor must appear in court before a judge, who will decide whether to grant the guardianship. In some counties, a probate commissioner hears guardianship cases. For purposes of a guardianship, the probate commissioner has the same authority as a judge. This court appearance is called a "hearing." You must appear in court with the minor, even if it seems like a formality because everyone involved is in favor of the guardianship. At the hearing, you will tell the judge why a guardianship is needed, and that you agree to take on the responsibility. The judge will

probably ask you and the minor a few questions before making a decision.

Generally, the court clerk will either assign you a date, or ask you to choose a hearing date when you file your papers. Sometimes clerks automatically assign you a hearing date unless you ask to choose your own. If you make it clear from the start that you want to select a date, you'll probably have better luck getting a date and time convenient for you. Follow the guidelines in this section about the timing of the hearing.

Ask the clerk to fill in Item 3 of the Notice of Hearing with the date, time, and location of the hearing. The clerk also should date and sign the original Notice of Hearing in the space below Item 3. Some clerks stamp in the hearing information or affix printed labels. Sometimes clerks will only complete one Notice of Hearing, and ask you to "conform" the rest of the copies, meaning that you must write in the same information on your additional copies of forms. Some courts may require you to fill out a simple local form to request a hearing date.

The clerk should return the *original* Notice of Hearing to you without filing it.

When Should the Hearing Be?

Be sure to request that your hearing be scheduled at least 45 days after the date you file your guardianship papers. If you can't wait this long, you may need to file for a temporary guardianship in addition to a general guardianship. For example, a school or medical provider might require you to have a guardianship before allowing school enrollment or authorizing a medical treatment. Instructions for preparing and filing forms for a temporary guardianship are in Chapter 7.

Otherwise, getting a hearing date several weeks away allows time to have the guardianship papers served and to make sure your proofs of service are completed and filed with the court. Also, many counties' local court rules require that all guardianship applications be reviewed by an investigator associated with the court, social services department of the county, or probation department. (The guardianship investigation is discussed in Chapter 8.)

Obtaining a Hearing Date Over the Phone

If you mail in your papers to be filed by the court and the clerk inadvertently forgets to give you a hearing date, in most counties you can call the court clerk and get one, rather than having to go back to court to have the date assigned. Tell the clerk the case number, which will be stamped on your papers once you've filed them with the court. Tell the clerk that you have filed a guardianship petition, and would like to get a hearing date. Follow the instructions above for selecting the court date.

Local Rules May Require the Investigation Be Completed Before a Hearing Date Is Assigned

It is possible that you may not get a hearing date when you file your papers, because the court's policy requires an investigation to be completed before the hearing date may be assigned. If this is your court's policy, then obviously you'll need to wait to schedule a hearing date. (See Chapter 8 for more informa-tion on the guardianship investigation.)

Check to See That You Have Original Notice of Hearing

Most courts do not accept the original Notice of Hearing for filing until everyone entitled to notice has been served. When you file your papers, check to see whether you have the original signed document. You can tell which is the original because the clerk's name is signed, rather than stamped as it is on the copies.

If you're not sure, ask the clerk which is the original. If the clerk gives the original Notice of Hearing back to you, make sure you keep it in a safe place. You will need to file it with the court, along with proofs of service, after everyone entitled to notice has been served.

Follow Local Court Procedures

Some courts have special procedures for guardianship cases. If you want to obtain a guardianship, you will have to follow the court's local rules—regardless of your opinion about them. For example, when you file your documents you may be required to:

- be fingerprinted
- have your guardianship documents reviewed by a court investigator or examiner before they're filed, and
- fill out documents pertaining to the guard-ianship investigation. (See Chapter 8 for more information about investigations.)

You can check with the court clerk, check the court's website, or review the local probate policy manual before filing your documents to find what special procedures the court follows.

Continuing (Postponing) the Hearing Date

If you want the hearing date rescheduled—called "continued" in legalese—read this section very carefully. If you don't follow your court's local procedures, you could end up having to file another petition—and pay the expensive filing fees all over again.

Here are several reasons why you might need to postpone the hearing date once it has been set:

- You cannot have the minor's relatives served in time.
- Someone objects to the guardianship, and you need time to find a lawyer.

- The investigation is not completed in time.
- It's impossible for you to appear in court on that date (usually because some urgent matter has come up).

Check Local Procedures

If you need to continue the hearing, call the clerk at the probate court. Explain that you want to continue the guardianship hearing and get a new date. Local procedures vary depending on the court, and this book does not cover them in detail. They should be outlined in the court's probate policy manual and local rules.

Here are some of the ways continuances are handled at different courts:

- The clerk may give you a new date over the telephone and ask for a letter confirming the new date.
- You may be required to complete an amended Notice of Hearing with the new hearing date, and have it served by mail on everyone entitled to notice.
- You may need to get the new date by appearing at the scheduled hearing and requesting it at that time.
- You may be required to submit a formal motion for continuance to the court, which would require additional research or an attorney's help. (See Chapter 13.)

Amending the Petition for Appointment of Guardian of Minor

If, after filing your Petition for Appointment of Guardian of Minor, you become aware of any proceedings that affect the minor that weren't disclosed in the petition you already filed with the court, you must amend it within ten days of the time you find out about the proceedings. This includes adoptions, juvenile court matters, marriage, divorce, or other similar proceedings affecting the minor (PC § 1512). In addition,

if you find that you have made a serious error or if the situation set out in any document has changed, file an amended document right away. ("Amending Filed Documents" in Chapter 3 discusses how to prepare and file amended documents.)

If you file an amended petition, it must contain a full set of attachments, including the UCCJEA Declaration for guardianship of a minor's person. If you originally petition for one type of guardianship and wish to add another, you must also complete a new Consent of Proposed Guardian, Nomination of Guardian, and Consent to Appointment of Guardian and Waiver of Notice form.

Note: Depending on local rules, you may be required to continue the hearing date if the amended documents are not served on everyone entitled to notice well in advance of the hearing date. The amount of time required would depend on the court. Check your court's local policies.

Local Court Forms May Be Required After You File Your Papers

Local court rules sometimes require you to complete additional forms *after* you file the initial guardianship papers. These additional local court forms usually are for those seeking guardianship of a minor's person, and relate to screening or investigating the prospective guardian.

If the clerk gives you more forms to complete when you file your guardianship papers, look at them carefully before leaving the court. The forms probably will be self-explanatory, but if you are confused by something, you might be able to get additional information from the clerk. However, court clerks can't answer every question you might have. By law, they're forbidden to direct you in any way that might be considered giving legal advice—only lawyers can do that. If you do need more help, the court clerk may refer you to a local service that gives free or low-cost legal assistance. (Or see Chapter 13 for information about doing your own research or finding a lawyer.)

Make sure you understand from the start when all forms are due back at the court, and follow those deadlines carefully. For example, if a form must be completed and returned within ten days and you don't get it back for 11 or 12, you may lose your scheduled hearing date. That could mean a lot of extra work, because you'd have to get a new hearing date and have those entitled to notice served again.

Because local rules vary widely, we cannot give you information on all possible forms that may be required. However, here are some of the forms the clerk may give you to fulfill local requirements:

Information for Court Investigation

In some counties, there are special forms for anyone seeking appointment as guardian of a minor's person. For example, the Fresno County Superior Court has a four-page Guardianship Questionnaire that asks for information about the minor, the minor's natural parents, and you and your plans to care for the minor. This questionnaire may seem overwhelming at first, but with a little patience, you shouldn't have trouble completing it.

Special Form for Agencies Entitled to Notice

Some counties have special forms you must send to agencies to notify them of the guardianship petition. For example, the Alameda County Superior Court has a form that must be completed and sent to the county's local social services agency. It is used to screen the potential guardian for reports of prior child abuse or neglect, then returned to the court or court investigator.

Serving Papers

When someone personally delivers or sends legal documents by mail, this formal notice is called "service of process." When someone entitled to notice receives these documents, the person has been "served." Depending on the legal requirements, service can be completed:

- by mail (documents are sent by regular U.S. mail)
- by personal service (documents are either personally handed to or left near the person), or
- by Notice and Acknowledgment of Receipt (documents are mailed to the person along with a special form that the recipient signs and mails back saying that the papers were received).

Having documents properly served is an essential part of the process of obtaining a guardianship. The reason for this is simple: A person who is being affected by the guardianship has a constitutional right to be notified of the proceedings. The person may contest your appointment as guardian by filing papers with the court or appearing before the judge at the hearing. Before you can have a court hearing on the guardianship, the court must be assured that everyone entitled to know about the hearing was given notice, waived the right to notice, or cannot be located.

There are specific rules about how documents must be served for the service to be legally valid. As the person petitioning for the guardianship, you cannot serve papers yourself. The person who serves papers must be over 18 years old and must not be involved in the legal action. If you don't follow service rules to the letter, you will have to start over again—rescheduling your case for a new hearing date and having everyone served all over again—even if only one person was served incorrectly.

What Papers Must Be Served?

Every person and agency entitled to notice of the guardianship proceeding must be served with two documents:

- Petition for Appointment of Guardian of Minor—including all of the attachments, and

- Notice of Hearing.

Make sure you have one copy of each of these documents for every person or agency entitled to service, plus one for yourself and one extra for the court, if required.

When Must Papers Be Served?

The guardianship papers must be served at least 20 days before the date listed in the Notice of Hearing in the box in Item 4. That means that you must mail the documents at least 20 days before the hearing date, or personally serve them at least 20 days before the hearing date. Some courts only require 15 days' notice for service by mail, while others require 20 days' notice. To play it safe, we advise you to give at least 20 days' notice. (Personal service is covered in "Personal Service and Notice and Acknowledgment of Receipt," and service by mail is discussed in detail in "Having

Documents Served by Mail," both in this chapter.)

If you do not comply with these requirements, the guardianship will not be heard on the scheduled hearing date. To be safe, have the papers served immediately after you file them with the court. (If papers are not served properly or on time, see "Continuing (Postponing) the Hearing Date," above, which gives important information about having a hearing continued.)

Who May Serve the Papers?

The law forbids you, the person filing for the guardianship, from serving the papers yourself. Fortunately, service can be made by any other person 18 years of age or older who is not involved in the guardianship proceeding—meaning they're not listed anywhere on the Petition for Appointment of Guardian of Minor. This could be a friend, family member, acquaintance, or employee. Or, for a fee, you can hire a professional process server or marshal or sheriff's deputy to serve the papers.

For mail service, it's fine to ask a friend or relative to drop the papers in the mail for you. The legal assumption is that papers are received when they are properly deposited in the U.S. mail. There's no reason to pay a professional to mail your papers.

However, arranging to have someone personally served can be a little tricky. If you anticipate that there might be problems serving the minor's parents or anyone else entitled to personal service, it's worth the money to hire a professional process server or marshal or sheriff's deputy. If anyone later questions the validity of the service in court, a process server's testimony tends to be much more persuasive than that of a friend or relative who may be biased about the outcome.

Good professional process servers are commonly quick and resourceful at serving evasive people. They are usually a little more expensive than marshals or sheriffs, but the money you'll save in having the papers served faster may justify the extra expense, since you won't have to go back to court for a new hearing date. Some process servers charge a flat fee for service within a particular geographical area, while others charge for each attempted delivery and additional amounts for each mile they travel to attempt service. You can get information about the fees by calling the process servers before you hire them.

To find a good process serving firm in the area where the person requiring service lives or works, get a recommendation from a paralegal or attorney, if you know one. If not, you can check the yellow pages for process servers.

You will need to give the process server copies of the papers to be served, and the date by which service must be completed. The process server won't be familiar with the person you're serving, so you'll need to help out by providing as much detailed information as possible, such as the best hours to find the person at home or work, and a general physical description. It's even better if you can provide a recent photograph.

If you choose to have a marshal or deputy serve the papers, call the marshal's office or civil division of the county sheriff's office to find out who serves court papers in your county. Marshals are the enforcement officers for some counties who serve court papers. Some counties, such as Los Angeles, have marshals' offices separate from sheriffs' offices. But in many other counties, especially in Northern California, the sheriff is designated as the marshal for—among other things—serving papers.

To ask a sheriff or marshal to serve papers, go to their office with copies of the papers to be served, pay a fee (usually in the $25 to $50 range) for each person to be served, and fill out a form giving the information they'll need to complete service.

Some people choose to have a marshal or deputy sheriff serve their papers because it may be less expensive. However, this choice may mean it takes longer to have papers served, because these offices tend to be busy and law enforcement officers only serve papers during regular business hours. If you only have a few weeks before your guardianship hearing date, it's probably best to use a professional process server.

CAUTION

If you think the person you're serving will be upset by getting the papers, have a professional serve them. Although you can have papers served by anyone who's 18 or over and not involved in the guardianship case, don't put your friends or relatives in an uncomfortable position. If you think that someone you're serving might be upset to receive the papers, hire a professional—they're used to it.

Determine Who Must Be Served

In addition to the relatives who must be served, certain agencies also may be entitled to notice of the guardianship. You must serve each of the relatives and agencies entitled to notice at least 20 days before the hearing date. To avoid problems later on, make sure everyone entitled to notice is served correctly. The best way to do this is by using the Guardianship Notification Worksheet to figure out who must be served and how.

Which Relatives Must Be Served?

In Chapter 4, you began to fill in Part 1 of the Guardianship Notification Worksheet. Now you'll use that worksheet to figure out which relatives must be served.

In Item 5, for each relative, you answered the question "Need to have served?" Each of the relatives for whom you answered "Yes" must be served. If you submitted an Order Dispensing Notice, do not serve anyone who's listed on it. At the hearing, the judge will decide whether to grant the order—for now, you will have to assume that service will not be required. Anyone for whom the Order Dispensing Notice is signed does not have to be served, so for them Item 5 should be answered "No."

Item 6 of the Guardianship Notification Worksheet gives a summary of how each person must be served. Here is a more detailed explanation of service requirements for people who have not signed a Consent to Appointment of Guardian and Waiver of Notice or for whom an Order Dispensing Notice is not signed:

- **Minor.** A minor who is 12 years of age or older must be personally served with notice of the guardianship, and cannot sign a document waiving the right to service. A minor who is younger than 12 does not get served with notice of the guardianship, except if she has a child. If the minor must be served, you can explain that, as part of the guardianship procedure, someone other than you will be delivering the legal papers.

- **Minor's mother and father.** The minor's parents may be served either personally or by Notice and Acknowledgment of Receipt. (Documents are mailed to the person along with a special form saying that the papers were received; the recipient signs and mails back the form.)

- **Minor's grandparents.** The minor's maternal and paternal grandparents are served by mail.

- **Minor's spouse.** The minor's spouse is served by mail.

- **Minor's sisters and brothers.** The minor's siblings are served by mail if they are 12 or older. If they are between the ages of 12 and 18, you must also have their parents served by mail. In most instances, you'll already be doing this because they're also the parents of the minor for whom you're seeking guardianship. But occasionally the minor may have a half-brother or half-sister whose other parent must be served. Siblings under 12 years of age do not have to be served.

- **Minor's children.** The minor's children do not need to be served. However, you'll need to serve the minor's child's other parent by mail.

- **Anyone having legal custody of the minor.** If the minor has a legal guardian or someone other than the parents has legal custody, that person must be served either personally or by Notice and Acknowledgment of Receipt.

- **Anyone nominated minor's legal guardian.** Anyone besides you who has been nominated as the minor's legal guardian must be served either personally or by Notice and Acknowledgment of Receipt.

- **Anyone having physical custody of the minor.** Anyone other than you who has physical custody of the minor must be served by mail.

Which Agencies Must Be Served?

You may be required to serve one or more agencies with notice of the guardianship because by law, certain agencies may be required to investigate your appropriateness as guardian.

Other agencies are entitled to notice so they can monitor benefits to which the minor may be entitled. All agencies are served by mail.

As you go through each agency listed in this section, fill in Part 2 of the Guardianship Notification Worksheet. Indicate whether each agency needs to be served, and fill in the names and addresses of those that do. A completed sample is shown at the end of this chapter.

Local Social Services Agency

If you are seeking guardianship of a minor's person, you must serve the local agency that screens every proposed guardian for a history of child abuse or neglect. In some counties this local agency also conducts an investigation. (See Chapter 8 for information about investigations.)

The "government" pages in the front of your local telephone book should list county services. Look for a heading such as "Children's Emergency Services," "Children's Protective Services," "Social Services," "Probation Department," or "Welfare Department." Call the number and explain that you are filing guardianship papers with the court and need the address of the local agency that screens guardianships for the court. You may need to make several calls to track down the correct address. You can also ask the court clerk for this information, but the clerk may not want to give it to you—there are rules about court clerks not giving legal advice and some might think this question crosses the line.

Court Investigator

In some counties, an investigator who works for the superior court in which you file the guardianship will conduct an investigation. This is in addition to the social services screening. If you don't already have the name and address of the court investigator who handles

guardianships, call the court and ask for this information. (See Chapter 8 for information about investigations.)

State Director of Social Services

If you are not a blood relative of the minor and you are seeking guardianship of the minor's person, you must serve the State Director of Social Services. Stepparents are not blood relatives, nor are uncles or aunts who are only related to a minor by marriage. If you're not sure whether you're a blood relative of the minor, go ahead and have the State Director of Social Services served by mail—just in case it's required. Here is the address:

Director of Social Services
ATTN: M.S. 19-31
744 "P" Street
Sacramento, CA 95814
916-657-2598
916-654-6012 (fax)

Directors of Mental Health and Developmental Services

Look at your Petition for Appointment of Guardian of Minor you filed with the court. If you answered "Yes" to Item 7a, you must serve the Director of Mental Health (if the minor is a patient of or on leave from a state mental hospital), or the Director of Developmental Services (if the minor is developmentally disabled) (PC § 1461). Here are their addresses:

Director of Mental Health
State of California
ATTN: Legal Offices
1600 Ninth Street, Room 151
Sacramento, CA 95814
800-896-4042 or 916-654-3890
916-654-3198 (fax)
800-896-2512 (TTY)

Director of Developmental Services
State of California
ATTN: Office of Legal Affairs
1600 Ninth Street, Room 240
Sacramento, CA 95814
916-654-1897
916-654-2167 (fax)

Department of Veterans Affairs

Now look at Item 7b of the Petition for Appointment of Guardian of Minor that you filed with the court. If you answered "Yes" to Item 7b (checked the second box), you must serve the office of the Department of Veterans Affairs (PC § 1461.5). If you happen to know the claim number for the veteran, note it on the outside of the envelope.

In California, there are three regional offices of the Department of Veterans Affairs. Use the office closest to the court in which you are filing the guardianship. If you're not sure which one to use, call the agency.

The main office is in Sacramento:

California Department of Veterans Affairs
1227 O Street
Sacramento, CA 95814
800-952-5626
800-324-5966 (TDD)
800-221-8998 (Outside California)

The Northern California address is:

Department of Veterans Affairs
Regional Office–Northern California
1301 Clay Street, Room 1130 North
Oakland, CA 94612
800-827-1000
510-286-0627

There are two Southern California addresses. Use the Los Angeles address if the court is north of Riverside. Use the San Diego address if the court is located in or south of Riverside.

Department of Veterans Affairs
Regional Office–Los Angeles
11000 Wilshire Blvd.
Los Angeles, CA 90024
800-827-1000
213-620-2755
310-235-7155

   or

Department of Veterans Affairs
Regional Office–San Diego
8810 Rio San Diego Drive
San Diego, CA 92108
800-827-1000
619-400-0070

Personal Service and Notice and Acknowledgment of Receipt

You have used the Guardianship Notification Worksheet to figure out who—if anyone—must be served personally, by mail, or by notice and acknowledgment of receipt. Remember that minors 12 and older must be served personally. (If the minor is under 12, she does not have to be served unless she has a child, in which case she should be served personally.) Bear in mind that you cannot give the documents to the minor yourself, and she cannot sign a document waiving her right to notice.

How to Have Documents Served Personally

For personal service, copies of the Petition for Appointment of Guardian of Minor and Notice of Hearing must be handed to or left for each person by a process server.

If you hire a law enforcement officer or a registered process server, that person will know how to serve someone personally. See "Who May Serve the Papers?" above. But if you use a relative, neighbor, or friend, you need to give careful instructions. Give the server a detailed description of the person to be served (for example, "mid-40s, graying hair, about 5'10", medium build, and wears horn-rimmed glasses"). Provide a photograph if you have one.

The server must give copies of the legal papers to the person being served. This means that the server must actually see and be able to talk to the person, regardless of whether the person is willing to take the papers. Once the server sees and identifies the person, and is close enough to complete the service, it doesn't matter if the person gets angry, tries to run away, refuses to take the papers, or even rips them up. The server can put the papers on the ground as close as possible to the person's feet, saying something like "This is for you" or "You have been served," and leave.

Under no circumstance should the server pick up the papers again once they have been served in this manner. That would invalidate the service and it would have to be done again. And the person serving should never try to force anyone to take the papers—it's unnecessary and may subject the server (or even you) to a lawsuit for assault or battery.

If a nonprofessional is serving the papers for you, it's best to serve the person at home. Service can be made at the person's workplace, but we recommend you use a professional server if that's necessary, unless the person is agreeable about being served. The server shouldn't disturb anyone very early or very late in the day. Your server should understand that personal service is not completed by simply leaving the papers on the person's porch, or in the mailbox (which, incidentally, is illegal under Postal Service regulations).

How to Have Documents Served by Notice and Acknowledgment of Receipt

Anyone over age 18 who is entitled to personal service may be served by mail instead, if the person is willing to sign and immediately return to you a document confirming notice of the guardianship proceeding. This document is called a Notice and Acknowledgment of Receipt.

The problem with this method is that by law, the person being served is allowed 20 days to send the signed form back to you, so you might not have enough time before the hearing date to have service done this way. Also, unless a relative is extremely responsible and cooperative (but for some reason didn't sign a Waiver of Notice and Consent), you should have documents served personally on anyone entitled to personal service. There is no penalty for failing to sign and return the Notice and Acknowledgment of Receipt for guardianship cases. So it's up to the recipient whether to sign and return it to you.

If you're not sure you'll get the signed document back promptly, you could try this method of service but be prepared to have the person served personally if the Notice and Acknowledgment of Receipt doesn't come back to you at least 20 days before the hearing date. If possible, contact the person you are serving to let them know about the guardianship proceeding and to make sure they're willing to sign the Notice and Acknowledgment of Receipt.

Even though you will prepare the documents being served, someone else must put them in the mail and sign a Proof of Service. You will need a separate Notice and Acknowledgment of Receipt for each person to whom you're sending notice of the guardianship.

How to Complete Notice and Acknowledgment of Receipt Form

CAPTION: Notice and Acknowledgment of Receipt

Fill in the caption following the general instructions in Chapter 3.

TO: Just under the caption there is a dotted line after the word "TO."

Fill in the full first and last names of the person being served. If more than one person is being served, you must complete a separate Notice and Acknowledgment of Receipt for each person, even if all of them live at the same address.

Dated: Fill in the date the documents will be mailed. At the right is a signature line and the words "(Signature of sender)." Sign your name on this line.

Item 1: Leave this item blank.

Item 2: Check the box entitled "Other: (Specify)." Then list the full title of each document you are serving, such as the Petition for Appointment of Guardian of Minor and Notice of Hearing.

Leave the rest of the form blank. The person to whom you send the documents must date and sign the form and return it to you to verify receipt.

How to Copy and Have Notice and Acknowledgment of Receipt Sent

Make two copies of the Notice and Acknowledgment of Receipt, and keep one for your records. Then put the following in an envelope, with the correct amount of postage, addressed to the person being served:

- signed original and one copy of the Notice and Acknowledgment of Receipt
- a self-addressed, stamped envelope, and
- one copy of each of the documents you listed in Item 2 of the Notice and Acknowledgment of Receipt.

You might want to prepare a cover letter to the person being served so the procedure will not seem threatening, especially if for some reason you haven't yet discussed the guardianship. Your cover letter might go something like the sample letter that follows.

Sample Letter

August 10, 20xx

Kim Yu

2 Anyplace

Calcity, CA 99999

Re: Guardianship of John Todd Yu
       Case No. 12345

Dear Kim:

I've enclosed documents letting you know that I intend to become John's legal guardian. As you know, I've been taking care of John for almost a year now, and I think it would be best to go to court to make the guardianship official.

I'd appreciate it if you would sign the enclosed original Notice and Acknowledgment of Receipt, showing that you've been given notice of the guardianship proceeding. Then return it to me in the enclosed self-addressed, stamped envelope. I need to get a signed copy of the Notice and Acknowledgment of Receipt to the court right away, so please send it back to me as soon as possible.

I hope everything is going well with you. Please call me if you have any questions.

Sincerely,

Joyce Margaret Yu

Joyce Margaret Yu

Enclosures

Sample Notice and Acknowledgment of Receipt

POS-015

ATTORNEY OR PARTY WITHOUT ATTORNEY *(Name, State Bar number, and address):*	FOR COURT USE ONLY

ATTORNEY OR PARTY WITHOUT ATTORNEY *(Name, State Bar number, and address):*

Joyce Margaret Yu
19 North Avenue
Fairfield, CA 94533

TELEPHONE NO.: 707-555-1212   FAX NO. *(Optional):*

E-MAIL ADDRESS *(Optional):*

ATTORNEY FOR *(Name):*   In Pro Per

SUPERIOR COURT OF CALIFORNIA, COUNTY OF Solano
STREET ADDRESS: 600 Union Avenue, Hall of Justice
MAILING ADDRESS: P.O. Box 1
CITY AND ZIP CODE: Fairfield, CA 94533
BRANCH NAME:

PLAINTIFF/PETITIONER: Guardianship of John Todd Yu, Minor

DEFENDANT/RESPONDENT:

NOTICE AND ACKNOWLEDGMENT OF RECEIPT—CIVIL

CASE NUMBER: 12345

TO *(insert name of party being served):*   Kim Yu

NOTICE

The summons and other documents identified below are being served pursuant to section 415.30 of the California Code of Civil Procedure. Your failure to complete this form and return it within 20 days from the date of mailing shown below may subject you (or the party on whose behalf you are being served) to liability for the payment of any expenses incurred in serving a summons on you in any other manner permitted by law.

If you are being served on behalf of a corporation, an unincorporated association (including a partnership), or other entity, this form must be signed by you in the name of such entity or by a person authorized to receive service of process on behalf of such entity. In all other cases, this form must be signed by you personally or by a person authorized by you to acknowledge receipt of summons. If you return this form to the sender, service of a summons is deemed complete on the day you sign the acknowledgment of receipt below.

Date of mailing: 8/10/20xx

Joyce Margaret Yu
(TYPE OR PRINT NAME)   ►_____
                                        (SIGNATURE OF SENDER—MUST NOT BE A PARTY IN THIS CASE)

ACKNOWLEDGMENT OF RECEIPT

This acknowledges receipt of *(to be completed by sender before mailing):*
1. ☐   A copy of the summons and of the complaint.
2. ☒   Other *(specify):*

Petition for Appointment of Guardian of Minor
Notice of Hearing

(To be completed by recipient):

Date this form is signed:

_____   ►_____
(TYPE OR PRINT YOUR NAME AND NAME OF ENTITY, IF ANY,   (SIGNATURE OF PERSON ACKNOWLEDGING RECEIPT, WITH TITLE IF
ON WHOSE BEHALF THIS FORM IS SIGNED)   ACKNOWLEDGMENT IS MADE ON BEHALF OF ANOTHER PERSON OR ENTITY)

Page 1 of 1

Form Adopted for Mandatory Use
Judicial Council of California
POS-015 [Rev. January 1, 2005]

NOTICE AND ACKNOWLEDGMENT OF RECEIPT — CIVIL

Code of Civil Procedure,
§§ 415.30, 417.10
www.courtinfo.ca.gov

After you have assembled all of the above documents and made sure that you have an extra copy of everything for your files, have someone else mail them. The envelope, with correct postage attached, should simply be put in a U.S. mailbox. The person who mails the papers must be at least 18 years old, must not be involved in the guardianship, and must live or work in the city where the mailing occurs.

> **CAUTION**
>
> **Do not have the papers served by certified or registered mail.** This kind of mail must be signed for before delivery. If the recipient isn't home when the envelope arrives, she must make a special trip to the post office—which can lead to further delays.

Complete Proof of Service for Personal Service or by Notice and Acknowledgment of Receipt Form

Once the papers have been served, you must complete a Proof of Service for Personal Service or by Notice and Acknowledgment of Receipt form. This form is a declaration by someone (other than you) stating how and when the documents were served. After the form is filled in, the person who served the papers must sign it.

You can use this form for people who were served either personally or by Notice and Acknowledgment of Receipt. Complete a separate proof of service form for each person served.

How to Complete the Form

CAPTION: Proof of Service of Summons (This is the correct form to use even though you are not serving a summons.)

Fill in the caption following the general instructions in Chapter 3.

Item 1: Leave this item blank. It simply states that the person who served the documents is at least 18 years old and not involved in the guardianship action.

Item 2: Check box 2f, and list the documents you are serving.

Item 3: Fill in the name of the person served, and the person's relationship to the minor or to the guardianship proceeding.

Item 4: Enter the address of the person served.

Item 5a: Check this box if the person was personally served and fill in the date and time of service. If the person was served by mail along with a Notice and Acknowledgment of Receipt, skip this item and go on to Item 5c.

Item 5b: Check this box if you left the documents at the person's workplace or home without actually putting them into the person's hands, as described above. Skip this item if the person was served directly or by notice and acknowledgment of receipt.

If you check this box, you will also need to fill in the date and time of the substituted service, and the name of the person you left the papers with.

Item 5b(1): Check this box if your process server left the documents at the person's workplace.

Item 5b(2): Check this box if your process server left the documents at the person's home with another responsible adult.

Item 5b(3): Check this box if your process server left the papers with someone at a mailing address other than a home or business—for example, a private mailbox service.

Item 5b(4): Check this box if you had the documents mailed to the person after you substituted service, and fill in the date and location from which the documents were mailed. You should always mail copies of the documents if you end up having to use substituted service. Fill in the city and state

Sample Proof of Service for Personal Service or by Notice and Acknowledgment of Receipt, page 1

POS-010

ATTORNEY OR PARTY WITHOUT ATTORNEY (Name, State Bar number, and address):	FOR COURT USE ONLY
Georgia A. Franklin 100 East Street Berkeley, CA 94703 TELEPHONE NO.: 510-555-1212 FAX NO. (Optional): E-MAIL ADDRESS (Optional): ATTORNEY FOR (Name): In Pro Per	

SUPERIOR COURT OF CALIFORNIA, COUNTY OF Alameda
STREET ADDRESS: 1225 Fallon Street
MAILING ADDRESS:
CITY AND ZIP CODE: Oakland, CA 94612
BRANCH NAME:

PLAINTIFF/PETITIONER: Guardianship of Sharon Danielle Turner, Minor DEFENDANT/RESPONDENT:	CASE NUMBER: 1000
PROOF OF SERVICE OF SUMMONS	Ref. No. or File No.:

(Separate proof of service is required for each party served.)

1. At the time of service I was at least 18 years of age and not a party to this action.
2. I served copies of:
   a. ☐ summons
   b. ☐ complaint
   c. ☐ Alternative Dispute Resolution (ADR) package
   d. ☐ Civil Case Cover Sheet *(served in complex cases only)*
   e. ☐ cross-complaint
   f. ☒ other *(specify documents):* Petition for Appointment of Guardian with Attachment; Notice of Hearing
3. a. Party served *(specify name of party as shown on documents served):*
   Howard Turner

   b. ☐ Person (other than the party in item 3a) served on behalf of an entity or as an authorized agent (and not a person under item 5b on whom substituted service was made) *(specify name and relationship to the party named in item 3a):*

4. Address where the party was served:
   222 Third Street, Alameda, CA 94550
5. I served the party *(check proper box)*
   a. ☒ **by personal service.** I personally delivered the documents listed in item 2 to the party or person authorized to receive service of process for the party (1) on *(date):* 3/16/xx (2) at *(time):* 2:00 p.m.
   b. ☐ **by substituted service.** On *(date):* at *(time):* I left the documents listed in item 2 with or in the presence of *(name and title or relationship to person indicated in item 3):*

      (1) ☐ **(business)** a person at least 18 years of age apparently in charge at the office or usual place of business of the person to be served. I informed him or her of the general nature of the papers.

      (2) ☐ **(home)** a competent member of the household (at least 18 years of age) at the dwelling house or usual place of abode of the party. I informed him or her of the general nature of the papers.

      (3) ☐ **(physical address unknown)** a person at least 18 years of age apparently in charge at the usual mailing address of the person to be served, other than a United States Postal Service post office box. I informed him or her of the general nature of the papers.

      (4) ☐ I thereafter mailed (by first-class, postage prepaid) copies of the documents to the person to be served at the place where the copies were left (Code Civ. Proc., § 415.20). I mailed the documents on *(date):* from *(city):* **or** ☐ a declaration of mailing is attached.

      (5) ☐ I attach a **declaration of diligence** stating actions taken first to attempt personal service.

Page 1 of 2

Form Adopted for Mandatory Use Judicial Council of California POS-010 [Rev. January 1, 2007]	**PROOF OF SERVICE OF SUMMONS**	Code of Civil Procedure, § 417.10

Sample Proof of Service for Personal Service or
by Notice and Acknowledgment of Receipt, page 2

PLAINTIFF/PETITIONER: Guardianship of Sharon Danielle Turner, Minor	CASE NUMBER:
DEFENDANT/RESPONDENT:	1000

5.   c. ☐   **by mail and acknowledgment of receipt of service.** I mailed the documents listed in item 2 to the party, to the address shown in item 4, by first-class mail, postage prepaid,

     (1) on *(date):*   (2) from *(city):*

     (3) ☐ with two copies of the *Notice and Acknowledgment of Receipt* and a postage-paid return envelope addressed to me. *(Attach completed* Notice and Acknowledgement of Receipt.*)* (Code Civ. Proc., § 415.30.)

     (4) ☐ to an address outside California with return receipt requested. (Code Civ. Proc., § 415.40.)

  d. ☐   **by other means** *(specify means of service and authorizing code section):*

     ☐ Additional page describing service is attached.

6.   The "Notice to the Person Served" (on the summons) was completed as follows:
  a. ☒ as an individual defendant.
  b. ☐ as the person sued under the fictitious name of *(specify):*
  c. ☐ as occupant.
  d. ☐ On behalf of *(specify):*
     under the following Code of Civil Procedure section:

☐ 416.10 (corporation)	☐ 415.95 (business organization, form unknown)
☐ 416.20 (defunct corporation)	☐ 416.60 (minor)
☐ 416.30 (joint stock company/association)	☐ 416.70 (ward or conservatee)
☐ 416.40 (association or partnership)	☐ 416.90 (authorized person)
☐ 416.50 (public entity)	☐ 415.46 (occupant)
	☐ other:

7.   **Person who served papers**
  a. Name: Emma Frand
  b. Address: 400 West Way, Alameda, CA 94550
  c. Telephone number: 510-555-1345
  d. **The fee** for service was: $ 0
  e. I am:
     (1) ☒ not a registered California process server.
     (2) ☐ exempt from registration under Business and Professions Code section 22350(b).
     (3) ☐ a registered California process server:
       (i) ☐ owner ☐ employee ☐ independent contractor.
       (ii) Registration No.:
       (iii) County:

8.   ☒   **I declare** under penalty of perjury under the laws of the State of California that the foregoing is true and correct.

     or

9.   ☐   **I am a California sheriff or marshal and** I certify that the foregoing is true and correct.

Date: 3/18/xx

Emma Frand   ▶
_____   _____
(NAME OF PERSON WHO SERVED PAPERS/SHERIFF OR MARSHAL)   (SIGNATURE)

POS-010 [Rev. January 1, 2007]   **PROOF OF SERVICE OF SUMMONS**   Page 2 of 2

where the documents were mailed. This must be the county where the person mailing them either lives or works.

Item 5b(5): You will need to attach a declaration that describes for the judge all the ways you tried to accomplish personal service before you used substituted service. Use the Declaration form described in Chapter 3, and give simple descriptions of each step you took. For example, "I went to Howard Turner's house on July 10 at 10 a.m., July 12 at 8 a.m., and July 13 at 6:30 p.m., and did not find him at home any of those times. Finally on July 16, I went to the house and a woman was there who told me she was the housekeeper who works there twice a week. She accepted the papers from me and said she would give them to Howard Turner."

Item 5c: If you used a Notice and Acknowledgment of Receipt, check this box, and enter the date and place of mailing of the Notice and Acknowledgment form. Check box (3) and attach the Notice and Acknowledgment of Receipt form signed by you as the sender and by the recipient as well.

Having Documents Served by Mail

Using the Guardianship Notification Worksheet as a guide, write or type on envelopes the names and addresses of every person and agency who must be served. If two people are being served at the same address, prepare a separate envelope for each one. Place a copy of the Petition for Appointment of Guardian of Minor and Notice of Hearing in each envelope, and seal the envelopes.

After you have affixed the correct amount of postage to each envelope and made sure that you have an extra copy of everything for your files, have someone mail the envelopes for you. The person who serves the papers must be at least 18 years old, must not be involved in the guardianship proceeding, and must live or work in the city where the mailing occurs. The envelopes should simply be put in a mailbox— do not have them sent by certified or registered mail. It's an unnecessary expense, and can create delays if the recipient isn't home to sign for the mail.

Complete the Proof of Service

Once service has taken place, complete a Proof of Service by Mail form. This form is a declaration by someone (other than you) stating how and when the documents were served. After the form is filled in, the person who serves the papers must sign it.

You may either use the Proof of Service by First-Class Mail form following the instructions just below, or—if you have the original Notice of Hearing—the back of the Notice of Hearing form following the instructions further below. You can call your court to find out whether it requires the back of the Notice of Hearing. You do not need to fill out both forms.

Proof of Service by First-Class Mail Form

There is a Proof of Service by Mail form in the back of this book in Appendix C. This Proof of Service by Mail form may be used whenever you have any document served on someone by mail. You may use just one Proof of Service by Mail form for everyone who was served by mail as long as the envelopes were deposited by one person at the same time. (A different form is used for anyone served by Notice and Acknowledgment of Receipt, even though it is also mailed. Instructions for that form are above.)

How to Complete the Form

CAPTION: Proof of Service by First-Class Mail
Fill in the caption following the general instructions in Chapter 3.

Item 1: Leave this item blank.

Item 2: Fill in the business or residence address of the person who served the documents.

Item 3: Fill in the date the documents were mailed and the city where they were mailed, then list the documents that were in each envelope. You should be able to list all of the documents served without using an attachment.

Item 4: Check box (a) if the person serving the documents put them directly into a mailbox. Check box (b) if the person left the envelope(s) for processing at the server's place of business, assuming they would be mailed the same day.

Item 5: If only one person is being served, fill in their name under item (a) and their address under item (b). However, it's much more likely that multiple people need to be served, and you'll need to use a form called Attachment to Proof of Service by First-Class Mail—Civil (Persons Served). There's a sample shown below just following the proof of service. If you're using this form, check the box in Item 5, and then fill out the attachment with the names and addresses of each person served.

Finally, have the person who served the documents fill in the date, sign the form on the signature line, and neatly type or print the person's name on the line provided. Instructions on how to file the proof of service are covered later in this chapter.

Back of Notice of Hearing

When you prepared the Notice of Hearing, you left the back of the form blank. If you have the original signed Notice of Hearing, you may use the proof of service on the back. If the clerk filed the original signed Notice of Hearing, complete the Proof of Service by Mail following the instructions above.

How to Complete the Form

CAPTION: Page Two of the Notice of Hearing
Check the boxes before the words "GUARD-IANSHIP," "PERSON," and "MINOR," and fill in the minor's name after the words "GUARDIANSHIP OF."

Fill in the case number.

Proof of Service by Mail: Complete this section if an adult other than the court clerk is mailing papers for you.

Item 1: This sentence is a confirmation that the person who served the papers is over 18 and not a party to the guardianship.

Item 2: Fill in the home or business address of the person who served the papers.

Item 3: Check the box in Item 3a if the person who served the papers mailed them by bringing them to a U.S. post office or dropping them into a U.S. Postal Service mailbox. Check the box in Item 3b if the person who served the papers mailed them from a business.

Item 4a: Fill in the date the documents were mailed.

Item 4b: Fill in the city and state where the documents were mailed.

Item 5: Check this box.

Date and Signature Lines: Fill in the date and the name of the person who served the papers in the spaces provided. Do not sign.

Name and Address of Each Person to Whom Notice was Mailed: Fill in the names and addresses of everyone to whom papers were mailed. If you need more room, check the box at the bottom of the page before the words "List of names and addresses continued on attachment." Then prepare an attachment entitled "Attachment to Notice of Hearing," listing the names and addresses of any additional people served. Have the person who served the papers sign on the appropriate line.

Copy and File Proofs of Service and Possibly Notice of Hearing

You're now ready to photocopy the proofs of service and file them with the court. You'll also file the original signed Notice of Hearing, if you have it. (See "Having Documents Served by Mail," above.) These papers should be filed at least five business days before the hearing date (don't include weekends or holidays when you count days).

Make at least two or three copies of each proof of service. If you have the original Notice of Hearing and you completed the proof of service on the back, also make two or three copies of it. If the court already has the original signed Notice of Hearing, file only the proofs of service with the court. Note that you should not use the proof of service on the back of the Notice of Hearing form unless you have the original.

You are now ready to file these documents with the court, following the instructions in Chapter 3. Make sure that you get a date-stamped copy of each paper from the court. If you send the documents by mail, keep an extra copy for your records in case the form is lost in the mail or misplaced at court.

Important: When you file the proofs of service, make sure the original Notice of Hearing is filed with the court. If you don't have the original Notice of Hearing, ask the clerk to check the court file to see whether it was previously filed.

Sample Proof of Service by Mail

<table>
<tr>
<td colspan="2">
ATTORNEY OR PARTY WITHOUT ATTORNEY (Name, State Bar number, and address):
Georgia Anna Franklin
100 East Street
Berkeley, CA 94703

TELEPHONE NO.: 510-555-1212
E-MAIL ADDRESS (Optional):   FAX NO. (Optional):
ATTORNEY FOR (Name):
</td>
<td>
POS-030

FOR COURT USE ONLY
</td>
</tr>
</table>

SUPERIOR COURT OF CALIFORNIA, COUNTY OF Alameda

STREET ADDRESS: 1225 Fallon Street

MAILING ADDRESS:

CITY AND ZIP CODE: Oakland, CA 94612

BRANCH NAME: Northern

PETITIONER/PLAINTIFF:
Guardianship of Sharon Danielle Turner, a minor

RESPONDENT/DEFENDANT:

PROOF OF SERVICE BY FIRST-CLASS MAIL—CIVIL	CASE NUMBER: 1000

(Do not use this Proof of Service to show service of a Summons and Complaint.)

1. I am over 18 years of age and **not a party to this action.** I am a resident of or employed in the county where the mailing took place.

2. My residence or business address is:
   400 West Way, Alameda, CA 94550

3. On *(date):* 6/14/20xx   I mailed from *(city and state):* Alameda, CA
   the following **documents** *(specify):*
   Petition for Appointment of Guardian of Minor
   Notice of Hearing

   ☐ The documents are listed in the *Attachment to Proof of Service by First-Class Mail—Civil (Documents Served)* (form POS-030(D)).

4. I served the documents by enclosing them in an envelope and *(check one):*
   a. ☒ **depositing** the sealed envelope with the United States Postal Service with the postage fully prepaid.
   b. ☐ **placing** the envelope for collection and mailing following our ordinary business practices. I am readily familiar with this business's practice for collecting and processing correspondence for mailing. On the same day that correspondence is placed for collection and mailing, it is deposited in the ordinary course of business with the United States Postal Service in a sealed envelope with postage fully prepaid.

5. The envelope was addressed and mailed as follows:
   a. **Name** of person served:
   b. **Address** of person served:

   ☒ The name and address of each person to whom I mailed the documents is listed in the *Attachment to Proof of Service by First-Class Mail—Civil (Persons Served)* (POS-030(P)).

I declare under penalty of perjury under the laws of the State of California that the foregoing is true and correct.

Date: 6/14/20xx

Emma Frand

▶

(TYPE OR PRINT NAME OF PERSON COMPLETING THIS FORM)	(SIGNATURE OF PERSON COMPLETING THIS FORM)

Form Approved for Optional Use Judicial Council of California POS-030 [New January 1, 2005]	**PROOF OF SERVICE BY FIRST-CLASS MAIL—CIVIL** **(Proof of Service)**	Code of Civil Procedure, §§ 1013, 1013a *www.courtinfo.ca.gov*

Sample Attachment to Proof of Service by Mail

POS-030(P)

SHORT TITLE:	CASE NUMBER:
Guardianship of Sharon Danielle Turner, a minor	1000

ATTACHMENT TO PROOF OF SERVICE BY FIRST-CLASS MAIL—CIVIL (PERSONS SERVED)

(This Attachment is for use with form POS-030)

NAME AND ADDRESS OF EACH PERSON SERVED BY MAIL:

Name of Person Served	Address *(number, street, city, and zip code)*
Ruth Turner	100 Any Street Alameda, CA 94550
Bill Turner	1090 Any Street Alameda, CA 94550
Cynthia Jackson	900 Some Street Berkeley, CA 94701
Elizabeth Smith	6 City Boulevard Oakland, CA 94612
Jan Smith	10 Metropolitan Avenue Oakland, CA 94610

Form Approved for Optional Use
Judicial Council of California
POS-030(P) [New January 1, 2005]

ATTACHMENT TO PROOF OF SERVICE BY FIRST-CLASS MAIL—CIVIL (PERSONS SERVED)
(Proof of Service)

Page 2 of 2

Sample Notice of Hearing—Guardianship or Conservatorship

[X] GUARDIANSHIP [ ] CONSERVATORSHIP OF THE [X] PERSON [ ] ESTATE	CASE NUMBER:
OF *(Name):* Rebecca Diane Stone	
[X] MINOR [ ] (PROPOSED) CONSERVATEE	

NOTE: *

A copy of this *Notice of Hearing—Guardianship or Conservatorship* ("Notice") must be "served" on—delivered to—each person who has the right under the law to be notified of the date, time, place, and purpose of a court hearing in a guardianship or conservatorship. Copies of this Notice may be served by mail in most situations. In a guardianship, however, copies of this Notice must sometimes be personally served on certain persons; and copies of this Notice may be personally served instead of served by mail in both guardianships and conservatorships. The petitioner (the person who requested the court hearing) **may not personally perform either service by mail or personal service**, but must show the court that copies of this Notice have been served in a way the law allows. The petitioner does this by arranging for someone else to perform the service and complete and sign a proof of service, which the petitioner then files with the original Notice.

This page contains a proof of service that may be used only to show service by mail. To show personal service, each person who performs the service must complete and sign a proof of personal service, and each signed copy of that proof of service must be attached to this Notice when it is filed with the court.. You may use form GC-020(P) to show personal service of this Notice.

* *(This Note replaces the clerk's certificate of posting on prior versions of this form. If notice by posting is desired, attach a copy of form GC-020(C), Clerk's Certificate of Posting Notice of Hearing—Guardianship or Conservatorship. (See Prob. Code, § 2543(c).)*

PROOF OF SERVICE BY MAIL

1. I am over the age of 18 and not a party to this cause. I am a resident of or employed in the county where the mailing occurred.
2. My residence or business address is *(specify):*

3. I served the foregoing *Notice of Hearing—Guardianship or Conservatorship* on each person named below by enclosing a copy in an envelope addressed as shown below AND
   a. [X] **depositing** the sealed envelope with the United States Postal Service on the date and at the place shown in item 4 with the postage fully prepaid.
   b. [ ] **placing** the envelope for collection and mailing on the date and at the place shown in item 4 following our ordinary business practices. I am readily familiar with this business's practice for collecting and processing correspondence for mailing. On the same day that correspondence is placed for collection and mailing, it is deposited in the ordinary course of business with the United States Postal Service in a sealed envelope with postage fully prepaid.

4. a. Date mailed: 12/7/xx   b. Place mailed *(city, state):* Antioch, CA
5. [X] I served with the *Notice of Hearing—Guardianship or Conservatorship* a copy of the petition or other document referred to in the Notice.

I declare under penalty of perjury under the laws of the State of California that the foregoing is true and correct.

Date: 12/9/xx

Emma Frand   ▶

_____   _____
(TYPE OR PRINT NAME OF PERSON COMPLETING THIS FORM)   (SIGNATURE OF PERSON COMPLETING THIS FORM)

NAME AND ADDRESS OF EACH PERSON TO WHOM NOTICE WAS MAILED

	Name of person served	Address *(number, street, city, state, and zip code)*
1.	Frederick Stone	1 West Street Anycity, CA 94901
2.	John Stone	1 West Street Anycity, CA 94901
3.	Jane Doe	25 East Avenue Othercity, CA 94998
4.	Nina Smith	22 South Street Anycity, CA 94901

[X] Continued on an attachment. *(You may use form DE-120(MA)/GC-020(MA) to show additional persons served.)*

GC-020 [Rev. July 1, 2005]   **NOTICE OF HEARING—GUARDIANSHIP OR CONSERVATORSHIP**   Page 2 of 2
(Probate—Guardianships and Conservatorships)

Complete the Guardianship Notification Worksheet

Once you receive your proofs of service back from the court, you may complete the Guardianship Notification Worksheet.

Worksheet—Part 1: Relatives

Item 7: If you haven't already filled in the date each person was served, put in this information. If you've submitted an Order Dispensing Notice, either because you couldn't locate someone or because the person signed a Consent and Waiver of Notice, leave this item blank for that person.

Item 8: Fill in the date the proof of service was filed with the court. You'll find this stamped in the upper right-hand corner of each filed proof of service.

Worksheet—Part 2: Agencies

If you haven't already filled in the date each agency was served, fill in this information. Then fill in the date the proof of service was filed with the court. You'll find this stamped in the upper right-hand corner of each filed proof of service.

Guardianship Notification Worksheet
Part 1. Relatives

(1) Names and addresses of minor's relatives and other people entitled to notice	(2) Need to locate?	(3) Date located	(4) Will sign Waiver of Notice & Consent?	(5) Need to have served?	(6) Service type, if need to have served (see Chapter 6 for instructions)	(7) Date served or Order Dispensing Notice	(8) Date file Proof of Service
Minor Molly Denise Schwartz 60 W. West Street Oakland, CA 94612	No	—	**Cannot sign since under 18**	**Only if 12 or over, or if minor has a child** No	Personal		
Minor's mother Angela Natalie Schwartz 100 N. North Street Byron, CA 94514	No	—	Yes	No	**Personal or Notice and Acknowledgment of Receipt**	9/6/xx order signed	
Minor's father Jerry Schwartz 800 S. South Street San Diego, CA 92138	Yes	—	—	—	**Personal or Notice and Acknowledgment of Receipt**	9/6/xx order signed	
Minor's maternal grandparents (mother's parents) Betty Brower Nate Brower 9 Bright Street Boston, MA 02131	No No	— —	No No	Yes Yes	**Mail**	8/8/xx 8/8/xx	8/18/xx 8/18/xx
Minor's paternal grandparents (father's parents) Penny Schwartz, Deceased Brian Schwartz 200 E. West Way Pittsburg, PA	Yes	5/22/00	No	— Yes	**Mail**	— 8/24/xx	8/26/xx
Minor's spouse—can only petition for guardianship of the estate	—	—	**Can sign only if 18 or over**	—	**Mail**		

Page 1 of 3

Guardianship Notification Worksheet
Part 1. Relatives (continued)

(1) Names and addresses of minor's relatives and other people entitled to notice	(2) Need to locate?	(3) Date located	(4) Will sign Waiver of Notice & Consent?	(5) Need to have served?	(6) Service type, if need to have served (see Chapter 6 for instructions)	(7) Date served or Order Dispensing Notice	(8) Date file Proof of Service
Minor's sisters and brothers (include their ages; if parents not listed elsewhere on worksheet, list their names and addresses)			**Cannot sign since under 18**	**Only if 12 or over, or if minor has a child**	**Mail, if over 12. Serve parents, if under 18**		
Dana Schwartz (Age 20) 167 E. East Ave. New York, NY 10003	No	—	Yes	No		9/6/xx order signed	
Mick Schwartz (Age 4) 100 N. North St. Byron, CA 94514	No	—	No	No (serving parents)			
Minor's children (if child's other parent not listed elsewhere on worksheet, list name and address) _____	—	—	**Cannot sign since under 18**	—	**Not required, but must served both of child's parents**		
Anyone presently having legal custody of minor (not including you) _____	—	—	—	—	**Personal or Notice and Acknowledgment of Receipt**		
Anyone nominated minor's legal guardian (not including you) _____	—	—	—	—	**Personal or Notice and Acknowledgment of Receipt**		
Anyone who has physical custody of minor (not including you) _____	—	—	—	—	**Mail**		

Guardianship Notification Worksheet
Part 2. Agencies

(1) Name and address of agencies entitled to notice (See Chapter 6)	(2) Need to have served?	(3) Service type, if need to have served	(7) Date Served	(8) Date file Proof of Service
Local Social Service Agency				
Child Protective Services Sylvia Smith -J000 401 Broadway Oakland, CA 94607	Yes	Mail	6/8/xx	6/18/xx
Court investigator				
Judith Schindler, Court Investigator Administration Building 1221 Oak Street, Room 20 Oakland, CA 94612	Yes	Mail	6/8/xx	6/18/xx
State Director of Social Services				
Attn: M.S. 19-31 744 "P" Street Sacramento, CA 95814	Yes	Mail	6/8/xx	6/18/xx
Director of Mental Health _____	No	Mail	—	—
Director of Developmental Services _____	No	Mail	—	—
Veterans Administration				
Regional Office - Northern California Office of the Veterans Administration 211 Main Street San Francisco, CA 94105	Yes	Mail	6/8/xx	6/18/xx

Temporary Guardianships of a Minor's Person

You won't have the right to act as a minor's legal guardian until you are appointed by the court. The fact that you've filed and had the necessary guardianship papers served does not give you any legal status as the minor's guardian until the court approves the guardianship, which happens when you attend a hearing and are formally appointed.

However, in urgent situations you can get a temporary guardianship before the regular guardianship is completed. It usually takes less than five days from the date papers are filed in court to obtain the temporary guardianship. A temporary guardian is not a substitute for a regular guardian, but is someone who serves for a short period of time, often until the regular guardian is appointed. The regular guardian and the temporary guardian are usually, although not necessarily, the same person.

A temporary guardian generally has only the duties and responsibilities that are "necessary to provide for the temporary care, maintenance, and support" of the minor (PC § 2252). A temporary guardian has the same responsibilities as a regular guardian to make decisions about medical treatment for a minor. (See Chapter 11.) A temporary guardian may be given additional powers with the court's permission, but such additional powers are beyond the scope of this book. A temporary guardian should not move the minor out of California without prior permission from the court.

In this chapter, we cover only temporary guardianships of a minor's person or person and estate, not temporary guardianships of a minor's estate only. A judge will probably not allow a proposed temporary guardian to manage a minor's financial affairs unless there is an extraordinary reason. If you want a temporary guardianship of a minor's estate only, see a lawyer. (See Chapter 13 for information on how to find and hire a lawyer.)

When to Seek a Temporary Guardianship

There are some situations in which you need guardianship powers right away, before the hearing date for the regular guardianship, which is usually about six weeks from the date you file your petition. For example:

- The minor may require nonemergency medical treatment before the hearing. (A child does not need a guardian to obtain emergency medical care.)
- You need a temporary guardianship to qualify to receive public assistance on behalf of the minor.
- The minor's school will not allow her to enroll without a formal guardianship, and the minor would miss school while the hearing is pending.
- The minor's mother wants to go into the armed services, which require that the child must be in someone else's legal custody while she is in the service.
- Both parents have deserted the minor, and no one has legal authority to make decisions on the minor's behalf.
- The court calendar is congested, and you cannot get a hearing date before you need to make an important decision about the minor's care or schooling.

In any of these, and other urgent situations, you may apply to the court for a temporary guardianship. The temporary guardianship gives you guardianship powers for a limited time—usually 30 days or up until the time of the hearing, whichever is earlier. A temporary guardianship of a minor's person can usually be completed within about five days of filing your papers with the court.

If a Temporary Guardianship Is Granted at the Regular Guardianship Hearing

Occasionally, at a regular guardianship hearing the court grants only a temporary guardianship. Usually, this is on the recommendation of the investigator, who feels something should be taken care of before the regular guardianship is granted. For example, the minor might first need to get counseling, or a change in the living arrangements might be required—such as giving the minor a separate bedroom. Or possibly the guardianship hearing must be continued because the judge wants someone who couldn't be located to be served, and a temporary guardianship is desirable in the meantime.

If only a temporary guardianship is granted at the regular guardianship hearing and the hearing is continued to another date, you will need to prepare and submit to the judge an Order Appointing Temporary Guardian, and obtain Letters of Temporary Guardianship following the instructions in this chapter.

Note: If the judge does not actually grant the temporary guardianship, but simply recommends that you file papers for a temporary guardianship, you will also need to complete the Petition for Appointment of Temporary Guardian and follow all the steps in this chapter for obtaining a temporary guardianship.

Overview of the Temporary Guardianship Process

This chapter takes you through the steps of obtaining a temporary guardianship of a minor's person. Here is a brief overview:

Step 1: Call the court and find out specific local procedures for obtaining a temporary guardianship.

Step 2: Complete all of the forms needed to obtain a regular guardianship as described in Chapters 4 and 5. Temporary guardianship papers can only be filed if the regular guardianship papers have already been filed, or are being filed at the same time.

Step 3: Following the instructions in this chapter, complete three additional forms: Petition for Appointment of Temporary Guardian, Order Appointing Temporary Guardian, and Letters of Temporary Guardianship. You may also need to complete a Notice of Hearing, depending on your court's procedures.

Step 4: If the minor's parents are available and willing, have them sign an attachment to the Petition for Appointment of Temporary Guardian nominating you as temporary guardian and waiving their right to notice.

Step 5: Make copies and then file both the regular guardianship and temporary guardianship papers with the court.

Step 6: Serve notice of the temporary guardianship on the minor's living parents, the minor, if 12 or over, and anyone with a valid court order allowing visitation rights (such as a stepparent or grandparent who got these rights in a divorce proceeding). If the temporary guardianship is heard "ex parte" (without notice) or the court excuses you from this requirement at least five days before the hearing date (ten days if service is by mail), you don't need to do this.

Step 7: Attend a hearing, if it is required. Often temporary guardianships are granted without a hearing. In some counties, temporary guardianship documents are taken to the judge and signed right away.

Step 8: Ask the clerk to issue Letters of Temporary Guardianship.

Step 9: If you need to extend the temporary guardianship, follow the instructions for obtaining an ex parte order to extend the temporary guardianship.

Call the Court

Before you get started filling in the temporary guardianship documents, you will need to call the court. Each court has its own special procedures for obtaining a temporary guardianship, and you will need to understand your court's procedures.

There is usually a special probate court clerk who handles procedural questions. You may be required to call that clerk during certain hours of the day. If the court clerk cannot give you the information, consult the local probate policy manual. Or you can ask for the name and number of the clerk of the probate judge or commissioner who handles guardianships, if that clerk is different from the one you've already talked to.

Explain that you are filing a temporary guardianship pending the hearing on a regular guardianship petition. Then find out:

- **Are temporary guardianship petitions heard ex parte?** If a petition is heard ex parte (pronounced "ex-partay"), you won't have a full hearing in front of a judge. Often the "hearing" consists only of a judge reviewing your documents and then signing your order. Court policies vary, so you will need to find out the local rules.

Note: If the court grants your petition ex parte—without notice to parents and others—*and* the hearing on the regular guardianship petition is more than 30 days off, the judge is required by law to set a hearing on the temporary guardianship, with notice to all parties, within 30 days of the ex parte order. In that case, the judge will limit the temporary guardianship order to last only until that hearing. If the judge sets such a hearing, you will have to provide written notice of it with a Notice of Hearing, which must be served on the same individuals you had served with the regular guardianship petition and Notice of Hearing. (See Chapter 5 on preparing a Notice of Hearing, and Chapter 6 for instructions on serving your papers.)

- **Do the minor's parent(s), the minor, or anyone else need to be served?** Normally, even a petition for temporary guardianship must be served on the minor's parents, the minor if age 12 or older, and anyone else who has court-ordered visitation rights with the minor (such as a stepparent or grandparent who got those rights in a divorce between parents). If the temporary guardianship is granted, any parent or other person who has court-ordered visitation rights with the child may still continue visitation unless the court orders otherwise (PC § 2250(g)).

The parents, the minor (if 12 or over), and anyone with court-ordered visitation rights, all must be served with the ex parte petition. A court can waive this service requirement when there is a showing that giving notice to these parties would be detrimental to the child. The court also has the right to order that other people be served if that would be in the minor's best interests. Also, if you think it is likely that the guardianship will be contested, the judge probably will think so too, and may require service. (If either the temporary guardianship or the regular guardianship is contested, consult an attorney.) If service is required, you'll have to serve your petition for temporary guardianship and the Notice of Hearing personally at least five days before the scheduled temporary guardianship hearing. Some courts don't require personal service, but instead require that notice be given by telephone a day or two before the hearing.

- **When and how are temporary guardianship petitions heard?** Find out the days and times guardianship petitions are heard, the location, the judge or commissioner who will hear and decide them, and how you may schedule your petition. If you need to have the minor and the minor's parents served, you'll need to allow enough time to accomplish that. In some areas, you simply bring your papers to the judge when they are complete. Others want to put the temporary guardianship matter on the court calendar to be heard by a judge later.

- **Where are temporary guardianship documents filed?** Some courts require that you file your temporary guardianship documents along with your regular guardianship papers. Others have you bring them to a special room after you've already filed your regular guardianship papers. Very often, temporary guardianship papers are left with the judge's clerk to be reviewed.

- **How long will it take for the judge to rule on the temporary guardianship?** Some courts take several days to decide on temporary guardianships, while others decide immediately. If the minor or the minor's parents must be served, it will probably take a little longer.

Complete the Regular Guardianship Documents

As we have emphasized, temporary guardianship papers can be filed only if the regular guardianship papers have either already been filed, or are being filed at the same time. Complete the regular guardianship documents following the instructions in Chapters 4 and 5.

Complete Temporary Guardianship Documents

You will need to fill in three or four forms in addition to the regular guardianship papers. These documents are similar to those you completed in Chapter 5, so you should find them easy to complete.

Petition for Appointment of Temporary Guardian

The Petition for Appointment of Temporary Guardian is the document in which you summarize reasons why you urgently need to be appointed temporary guardian. This form is similar to the Petition for Appointment of Guardian of Minor you completed in Chapter 5. However, it is simpler because it requires mostly specific information about why you need to be appointed temporary guardian before the date of the regular guardianship hearing.

Important: Before you begin filling in this form, you will need to complete the Petition for Appointment of Guardian of Minor following the instructions in Chapter 5. Refer to that completed form to fill in this document.

> **CAUTION**
>
> **Don't get confused about what forms to use.** There are two different forms that you can use if you are seeking temporary guardianship of the person only (not the estate or person and estate). There is one form that you can only use if you are seeking temporary guardianship of the person only, and its form number is GC-110(P). We have left that form out of this book, because it's less versatile than the form that we have included, which is form GC-110. The form that we include can be used for temporary guardianship of the person only, of the estate only, or of the person and the estate. Don't let a clerk tell you that because you're only seeking temporary guardianship of the minor's person you

have to use form GC-110(P). That's not true, and the form says so itself—check the bottom of the first page.

How to Complete the Form

CAPTION: Petition for Appointment of Temporary Guardian

Fill in the caption following the general instructions in Chapter 3.

Where you seek guardianship of more than one minor, use one form for each child, listing the name of each minor on a separate form.

Check the box next to the word "Person" to indicate you are seeking temporary guardianship of the minor's person, or next to "Person and Estate" if you're seeking both.

Leave the case number blank, unless a case number has been assigned because you have already filed regular guardianship documents with the court.

Item 1: After the word "Petitioner (name)," fill in your full first, middle, and last names. This means that you are the person who is filing for the temporary guardianship.

Item 1a: Fill in your full first, middle, and last names again, followed by your address. Then check the boxes before the words "guardian" and "minor."

Item 1b: If you're seeking guardianship of the minor's person and estate, fill in your name and address again.

Item 1c: If you're only asking for temporary guardianship of the minor's person, check box (1) before "bond not be required because petition is for a temporary guardianship of the person only." If you're seeking guardianship of both the minor's person and estate, you'll check the same box you checked when you filled out the regular guardianship documents and figured out whether you would need to post bond or not (this is also explained in "Completing Estate Items in the Petition" in Chapter 10).

Item 1d: Skip this item if the minor is under 12 years of age.

Item 1e: Normally this box should not be checked. It is used where a temporary guardian intends to exercise powers beyond those a guardian is ordinarily allowed to exercise, such as moving the minor out of state or insisting on providing nonemergency medical treatment against the minor's will. These sorts of powers are almost never granted as part of a temporary guardianship. Contact an attorney if you think you may need these extraordinary powers.

If the minor is 12 or older, and it is essential that you obtain the temporary guardianship within five days, check this item and then explain why you need the temporary guardianship so urgently on an Attachment 1e. Follow the instructions for preparing an attachment set out in Chapter 3 and label it "Attachment 1e to the Petition for Appointment of Temporary Guardian."

If you can't locate one or both of the minor's parents (or another person who has visitation orders) within five days, or the parents or person with visitation orders knows of the proposed guardianship and will sign a document authorizing you to serve as temporary guardian, ask the judge to waive notice requirements for the parents or person with visitation order. Check this item, then state the circumstances in your own words on an Attachment 1e.

If the parents or person with visitation orders approves of the temporary guardianship and will sign a document saying so, type or write the following on a piece of paper: "I, *[person's name]*, am a parent of/have a visitation order with *[minor's name]*, the subject of this temporary guardianship. I nominate *[your name]* as temporary guardian of the person of *[minor's name]*, and request that no bond be required. I also waive notice of the hearing of

Sample Petition for Appointment of Temporary Guardian or Conservator, page 1

GC-110

ATTORNEY OR PARTY WITHOUT ATTORNEY *(Name, State Bar number, and address):*	FOR COURT USE ONLY
Patricia Ann Lee 2 West Street Santa Ana, CA 92702 TELEPHONE NO.: 714-555-1212 FAX NO. *(Optional):* E-MAIL ADDRESS *(Optional):* ATTORNEY FOR *(Name):* In Pro Per	

SUPERIOR COURT OF CALIFORNIA, COUNTY OF Orange
STREET ADDRESS: 700 Civic Center Drive West
MAILING ADDRESS: P.O. Box 838
CITY AND ZIP CODE: Santa Ana, CA 92702
BRANCH NAME:

TEMPORARY GUARDIANSHIP OF *(Name):* Daniel Frank Lee MINOR	CASE NUMBER:

PETITION FOR APPOINTMENT OF TEMPORARY GUARDIAN ☑ Person* ☐ Estate* ☐ Person and Estate*	HEARING DATE:
	DEPT.: TIME:

1. **Petitioner** *(name each):*
   Patricia Ann Lee   **requests that**
   a. *(Name):* Patricia Ann Lee
      (Address and telephone number): 2 West Street, Santa Ana, CA 92702, 714-555-1212

      be appointed temporary guardian of the PERSON of the minor and Letters issue upon qualification.
   b. *(Name):*
      (Address and telephone number):

      be appointed temporary guardian of the ESTATE of the minor and Letters issue upon qualification.
   c. (1) ☑ bond not be required because petition is for a temporary guardianship of the person only.
      (2) ☐ bond not be required for the reasons stated in attachment 1c.
      (3) ☐ $ _____ bond be fixed. It will be furnished by an admitted surety insurer or as otherwise provided by law.
         (Specify reasons in Attachment 1c if the amount is different from maximum required by Probate Code section 2320 and Cal. Rules of Court, rule 7.207(c).)
      (4) ☐ $ _____ in deposits in a blocked account be allowed. Receipts will be filed.
         (Specify institution and location):

   d. ☐ a request for an exception to notice of the hearing on this petition for good cause is filed with this petition.
   e. ☐ the powers specified in attachment 1e be granted in addition to the powers provided by law.
   f. ☐ other orders be granted *(specify in attachment 1f).*

2. **The minor is** *(name):* Daniel Frank Lee

   Current address: Current telephone no.:
   2 West Street, Santa Ana, CA 92702   714-555-1212
3. **The minor requires a temporary guardian to** ☑ provide for temporary care, maintenance, and support
   ☐ protect property from loss or injury   because *(facts are* ☐ *specified in attachment 3* ☑ *as follows):*

   The petitioner is the minor's paternal grandmother and has been caring for him since before his mother's death on February 1. The minor needs to be enrolled in summer school and the school requires guardianship papers.

You MAY use this form or form GC-110(P) for a temporary guardianship of the person. You MUST use this form for a temporary guardianship of the estate or the person and estate.   Page 1 of 2

Form Adopted for Mandatory and Alternative Mandatory Use Instead of Form GC-110(P) Judicial Council of California GC-110 [Rev. July 1, 2008]	**PETITION FOR APPOINTMENT OF TEMPORARY GUARDIAN** **(Probate—Guardianships and Conservatorships)**	Probate Code, § 2250; Cal. Rules of Court, rules 7.101, 7.1012 www.courtinfo.ca.gov

Sample Petition for Appointment of Temporary Guardian or Conservator, page 2

<table>
<tr><td>TEMPORARY GUARDIANSHIP OF
(Name): Daniel Frank Lee</td><td></td><td>CASE NUMBER:</td></tr>
<tr><td></td><td>MINOR</td><td></td></tr>
</table>

GC-110

3. ☐ *(Facts supporting appointment of a temporary guardian (continued)):*

4. **Temporary guardianship is required**
   a. ☑ pending the hearing on the petition for appointment of a general guardian.
   b. ☐ pending the appeal under Probate Code section 1301.
   c. ☐ during the suspension of powers of the guardian.

5. ☐ **Character and estimated value of the property of the estate** *(complete if a temporary guardianship of the estate or person and estate is requested):*
   a. Personal property: $
   b. Annual gross income from all sources, including real and personal property, wages, pensions, and public benefits: $
   c. Additional amount for cost of recovery on the bond, calculated as required under Cal. Rules of Court, rule 7.207(c): $ _____
   d. **Total:** $ _____

6. Petitioner believes the minor ☐ will ☑ will not attend the hearing.

7. All attachments to this form are incorporated by this reference as though placed here in this form. There are ___0___ pages attached to this form.

Date:

▶ _____
(SIGNATURE OF ATTORNEY*)

* **(Signature of all petitioners also required (Prob. Code, § 1020).)**

I declare under penalty of perjury under the laws of the State of California that the foregoing is true and correct.

Date: 4/4/20xx

Patricia Ann Lee
_____
(TYPE OR PRINT NAME)

▶ _____
(SIGNATURE OF PETITIONER)

_____
(TYPE OR PRINT NAME)

▶ _____
(SIGNATURE OF PETITIONER)

GC-110 [Rev. July 1, 2008]

PETITION FOR APPOINTMENT OF TEMPORARY GUARDIAN
(Probate—Guardianships and Conservatorships)

Page 2 of 2

the Petition for Appointment of Temporary Guardian." Have the person sign and date the document, and attach it to the petition as Attachment 1e.

Item 1f: Skip this item.

Item 2: In the spaces provided, fill in the minor's full name, address, and telephone number.

Item 3: This item is the most important part of the Petition for Appointment of Temporary Guardian. Check the box before the words "provide for temporary care, maintenance, and support." If you're petitioning for temporary guardianship of the minor's person and estate, check the box next to the words "protect property from loss or injury."

Finally, unless you need more room than the blank space provided, check the box before the words "as follows." If you need more room, check the box before the words "specified in attachment 3," and add an additional page following the instructions in Chapter 3. In the blank space or on Attachment 3, explain why a temporary guardianship is necessary now, and why you cannot wait until the hearing date several weeks away. Be as detailed and specific as possible, and list dates, times, and places where appropriate. State facts, rather than mere conclusions. Here are a few examples:

EXAMPLE 1:

"I am the sister of the minor's mother. I am taking care of Jacques, who has been living with me in Stockton, California, for the past three months. Jacques' natural father is deceased, and his mother lives in Harrisburg, Pennsylvania. I have discussed both the guardianship and the temporary guardianship with Jacques' mother over the phone, and she approves of both. Jacques has severe food allergies (to wheat, eggs, dairy products, and sugar) and has just begun undergoing treatments. His doctor is unwilling to continue the treatments without the approval of a legal guardian. I need a temporary guardianship so that I can authorize those medical treatments."

EXAMPLE 2:

"I am Jill's father's brother, and have taken care of and lived with Jill for the past two months. Jill's parents are both on a one-year sabbatical in New Zealand. I live in a school district different from that in which Jill's parents live, and wish to enroll her for school here. Classes in Morescience High School in our district resume on September 10th, only two weeks away. I have just been informed that to enroll Jill there, I must be her legal guardian. There is insufficient time to have the Petition for Appointment of Guardian of Minor heard within that period. I have spoken to Jill, who is 16 years old, and she wants me to obtain a temporary guardianship as soon as possible. In addition, her parents will be signing and returning a Nomination of Guardian and Waiver of Notice and Consent of the legal guardianship within the next two weeks."

CAPTION: Page Two of the Petition for Appointment of Temporary Guardian

In the caption at the top of the page, fill in the minor's full first, middle, and last names.

Leave the case number blank, unless a case number has been assigned because you already filed regular guardianship documents with the court.

Item 3 (continued): If you began on the first page to state facts in support of your petition, you can check this box and use the additional space.

Item 4a: Check the box before the words "pending the hearing on the petition..."

This indicates you are seeking a temporary guardianship only while you're waiting for your hearing date for the regular guardianship.

Items 4b and 4c: Skip these items.

Item 5: If you're petitioning only for temporary guardianship of the minor's person, skip this item. If you're petitioning for temporary guardianship of the minor's person and estate, you'll need to fill in this information. You may already know it, if bond isn't waived and you were required to calculate the amount of bond for the regular guardianship documents. But if you didn't, you'll need to list the required amounts and total them under item 5d. Chapter 10 explains how.

Item 6: Earlier in this chapter, you called the court clerk to find out whether temporary guardianships could proceed ex parte, meaning a hearing is not required. If you have not obtained this information already, call the court clerk and find it out before you complete this item.

If a hearing is not required, check the box before the words "will not attend the hearing." Below that, fill in the words "Petition submitted ex parte." Obviously, in this situation, the minor does not need to go to court for a hearing—and neither do you.

If a hearing is required, check the box next to the word "will," to indicate the minor will attend the hearing. The minor's attendance at the temporary guardianship hearing is required in many counties, and is always advisable when a temporary guardianship petition is heard.

Item 7: If you are not attaching any additional pages, fill in the number "0." Otherwise, count up and enter the number of total pages to be attached.

Date and Signature: Skip the first space for the date and the first line for a signature (under which it says signature of attorney). Fill in today's date in the next space provided.

Directly underneath, to the left of the second signature line (under which it says signature of petitioner), type or clearly print your name in capital letters. Then sign your name on the line provided (under which it says signature of petitioner). If there is more than one person petitioning to be the guardian, each of you must sign here.

(Proposed) Order Appointing Temporary Guardian

You will need to prepare a proposed order for the judge to sign, appointing you as the minor's temporary guardian pending the hearing.

How to Complete the Form

CAPTION: Order Appointing Temporary Guardian

Fill in the caption following the general instructions in Chapter 3.

Check the box next to the word "person" to indicate you are seeking temporary guardianship of the minor's person, and "estate" if you are also seeking temporary guardianship of the estate. Fill in the minor's name and check the box before the word "minor."

Where you seek guardianship of more than one minor, use one form for each child, listing the name of each minor on a separate form.

Leave the case number blank, unless a case number has been assigned because you already filed regular guardianship documents with the court.

Item 1a: If you are submitting your temporary guardianship papers to a judge without a required hearing, fill in the words "Submitted ex parte" in Item 1a after the space for the judge's name, and skip to Item 2.

If a hearing is required and you know the name of the judge who will preside, or if you have been appointed temporary guardian following a court hearing for a regular guardianship, fill in the judge's name. If you don't know the judge's name, leave item 1a blank.

Item 1b: Fill in the date, time, and location of the temporary guardianship hearing.

Item 1c: Check the first box and fill in your full first, middle, and last names.

Item 1d: Put the words "appearing In Pro Per."

Item 1e: Check the first box and in the blank provided, fill in the minor's full first, middle, and last names.

Item 1f: Ordinarily this item is left blank, except for the rare situation where the minor for whom you are seeking the guardianship has an attorney. If so, fill in the attorney's name. (If the minor is being represented separately by an attorney, there's a good likelihood that the guardianship will be contested, and you'll need the help of a lawyer yourself. See Chapter 13.)

Item 1g: Put the names of both of the minor's parents here.

Item 1h: If the minor's parents have an attorney, there's a good likelihood that the guardianship is contested, and you will need the help of an attorney. Assuming there is no attorney for the parents, leave this item blank.

Item 1i: If there is someone who has visitation rights with the minor, put that person's name here.

Item 1j: Again, if the person who has visitation rights is represented by a lawyer, you probably need to be as well.

Item 1k-l: It's very unlikely that the Public Guardian will be involved in your guardianship case unless the case is contested. If you need to fill in the names of the Public Guardian or that person's attorney, you probably need to consult a lawyer about the guardianship.

Item 2a: Check this box only if you skipped Item 1d of the Petition for Appointment of Temporary Guardian.

Item 2b: If you checked Item 1d of the Petition for Appointment of Temporary Guardian, check the first box next to the words "Notice of time and place of hearing" and the third box next to the words "should be." Then fill in the names of the people for whom notice should be dispensed with.

Item 3: Check a total of two or three boxes in this item. Check the box before the words "provide for temporary care, maintenance, and support." If you're petitioning for temporary guardianship of the minor's estate, check the box before the words "protect property from loss or injury."

Check the next boxes before the words "pending the hearing on the petition for appointment of a general guardian." Leave the rest of the item blank. (The other two boxes apply only for temporary guardianships pending appeal or suspension of some other guardian's powers—situations in which an attorney should be consulted.)

Item 4a: If you're applying for temporary guardianship of the minor's person, fill in your name, address, and telephone number in the spaces provided. After the words "of *(name)*" fill in the minor's full first, middle, and last names.

Item 4b: If you're petitioning for temporary guardianship of the minor's estate, fill in your name, address, and telephone number in the spaces provided. After the words "of *(name)*," fill in the minor's full first, middle, and last names.

CAPTION: Page Two of the Order Appointing Temporary Guardian

Fill in the minor's full first, middle, and last names. Leave the case number blank, unless a case number has been assigned because you already filed regular guardianship documents with the court.

Item 5: If you checked the second box in Item 2b, check this box to indicate that you will not

Sample Order Appointing Temporary Guardian, page 1

GC-140

ATTORNEY OR PARTY WITHOUT ATTORNEY *(Name, State Bar number, and address):*	FOR COURT USE ONLY

ATTORNEY OR PARTY WITHOUT ATTORNEY *(Name, State Bar number, and address):*

Patrica Ann Lee
2 West Street
Santa Ana, CA 92702

TELEPHONE NO.: 714-555-1212   FAX NO. *(Optional):*

E-MAIL ADDRESS *(Optional):*

ATTORNEY FOR *(Name):* In Pro Per

SUPERIOR COURT OF CALIFORNIA, COUNTY OF Orange
STREET ADDRESS: 700 Civic Center Drive West
MAILING ADDRESS: P.O. Box 838
CITY AND ZIP CODE: Santa Ana, CA 92702
BRANCH NAME:

TEMPORARY GUARDIANSHIP OF THE ☑ PERSON ☐ ESTATE OF
(Name): Daniel Frank Lee

MINOR

ORDER APPOINTING TEMPORARY GUARDIAN	CASE NUMBER:

WARNING: THIS APPOINTMENT IS NOT EFFECTIVE UNTIL LETTERS HAVE ISSUED.

1. The petition for appointment of a temporary guardian came on for hearing as follows *(check boxes c–l to indicate personal presence):*

   a. Judicial officer *(name):* submitted ex parte

   b. Hearing date: Time: ☐ Dept.:   ☐ Room:

   c. ☐ Petitioner *(name):*

   d. ☐ Attorney for petitioner *(name):*

   e. ☐ Minor *(name):*

   f. ☐ Attorney for minor *(name):*

   g. ☐ Minor's parents *(names):*

   h. ☐ Attorney for minor's parents *(names):*

   i. ☐ Person with valid visitation order *(name):*

   j. ☐ Attorney for person with valid visitation order *(name):*

   k. ☐ Public Guardian *(name):*

   l. ☐ Attorney for Public Guardian *(name):*

THE COURT FINDS

2. a. ☑ Notice of the time and place of hearing has been given as required by law.

   b. ☐ Notice of the time and place of hearing ☐ has been ☐ should be   dispensed with for *(names):*

3. It is necessary that a temporary guardian be appointed to ☑ provide for temporary care, maintenance, and support ☐ protect property from loss or injury ☑ pending the hearing on the petition for appointment of a general guardian. ☐ pending an appeal under Probate Code section 1301. ☐ during the suspension of powers of the guardian.

THE COURT ORDERS

4. a. ☑ *(Name):* Patricia Ann Lee

     (Address): 2 West Street, Santa Ana, CA 92702   *(Telephone):* 714-555-1212

     is appointed temporary guardian of the PERSON of *(name):* Daniel Frank Lee
     and Letters shall issue upon qualification.

   b. ☐ *(Name):*

     (Address):   *(Telephone):*

     is appointed temporary guardian of the ESTATE of *(name):*
     and Letters shall issue upon qualification.

Page 1 of 2

Form Adopted for Mandatory Use Judicial Council of California GC-140 [Rev. January 1, 2009]	**ORDER APPOINTING TEMPORARY GUARDIAN** **(Probate—Guardianships and Conservatorships)**	Probate Code, §§ 2250–2254

Sample Order Appointing Temporary Guardian, page 2

GC-140

TEMPORARY GUARDIANSHIP OF (Name): Daniel Frank Lee	CASE NUMBER:
MINOR	

5. ☐ Notice of hearing to the persons named in item 2b is dispensed with.

6. a. ☑ Bond is not required.

    b. ☐ Bond is fixed at: $ _____ to be furnished by an authorized surety company or as otherwise provided by law.

    c. ☐ Deposits of: $ _____ are ordered to be placed in a blocked account at (specify institution and location):

        and receipts shall be filed. No withdrawals shall be made without a court order. ☐ Additional orders in attachment 6c.

    d. ☐ The temporary guardian is not authorized to take possession of money or any other property without a specific court order.

7. ☐ In addition to the powers granted by law, the temporary guardian is granted other powers. These powers are specified
    ☐ in attachment 7. ☐ below (specify):

8. ☐ Other orders as specified in attachment 8 are granted.

9. ☑ Unless modified by further order of the court, this order expires on (date):

10. Number of boxes checked in items 4–9: __3__

11. Number of pages attached: __0__

Date:

_____
JUDICIAL OFFICER

☐ SIGNATURE FOLLOWS LAST ATTACHMENT

ORDER APPOINTING TEMPORARY GUARDIAN
(Probate—Guardianships and Conservatorships)

need to have anyone served with notice of the hearing.

Item 6a: Check the first box only, before the words, "Bond is not required," if you're only petitioning for guardianship of the minor's person. If you're seeking temporary guardianship of the minor's estate, put the same figures here that you put in your petition for temporary guardianship in Item 5.

It's possible that the judge may want to use different figures, in which case the judge will probably ask you to prepare a new order. You could also come to the hearing prepared with another version of the Order—which you don't submit in advance—on which you've left these items blank, but have completed the rest of the form. If the judge wants to use different figures than the ones you put in, you could offer the form with the blanks for the judge to fill in.

Item 6d: Check this box if you are only seeking guardianship of the person.

Items 7 and 8: Leave these items blank. You are not asking for any orders other than to have the temporary guardianship granted.

Item 9: Check the box, but leave this item blank, because you don't necessarily know the date the temporary guardianship will expire. The judge will fill in the date at the hearing, and if all goes well, the temporary guardianship should be replaced by the permanent guardianship before the date the temporary order expires.

Item 10: Count the number of boxes you checked in Items 4–9, and fill in that number.

Item 11: Check the box. If you are not attaching any additional pages, fill in the word "None." Otherwise, count up and enter the number of total pages to be attached.

The form is now complete. The date and signature will be filled in by the judge who signs the order.

(Proposed) Letters of Temporary Guardianship

The Letters of Temporary Guardianship is the document that says you have permission to serve as the minor's temporary guardian.

How to Complete the Form

CAPTION: Letters of Temporary Guardianship

Fill in the caption, following the general instructions in Chapter 3. You only need to check the box at the top of the caption that says "After recording return to" if you are seeking guardianship of the minor's estate and the minor owns real property.

Where you seek guardianship of more than one minor, use one form for each child, listing the name of each minor on a separate form.

Check the box next to the word "Guardianship," and in capital letters fill in the minor's full first, middle, and last names. Check the box next to the word "Minor."

Check the box entitled "Guardianship," then check the box next to the word "person" to indicate you are seeking temporary guardianship of the minor's person.

Leave the case number blank, unless a case number has been assigned because you already filed regular guardianship documents with the court.

Item 1: In the blank after the word "(*Name*)," fill in your full first, middle, and last names. Then check the box before the word "guardian." Check the box before the word "person." Finally, fill in the minor's full first, middle, and last names following the words "estate of (*name*)," even though you do not check the "estate" box to the left of them—the blank for the minor's name applies to all types of guardianships.

Item 2: Leave this entire item blank. It applies only if you have been granted powers beyond those ordinarily granted for temporary guardianships (such as subjecting the minor to involuntary nonemergency medical treatment), for which you need an attorney's assistance.

Item 3: Leave this item blank. The judge will fill it in at the hearing.

Item 4: Check this box if you are seeking only guardianship of the person. Then check the box before the word "guardian."

Item 5: If you are not attaching any additional pages, fill in the word "None." Otherwise, count up and enter the number of pages to be attached.

Leave the rest of the form blank, including the date.

CAPTION: Page Two of the Letters of Temporary Guardianship

Check the box next to the word "Guardianship" and type the minor's name in the box, then check the box next the word "Minor." Leave the case number blank unless you already have one.

Affirmation: Check the box before the word "Guardianship" and then before the word "guardian." Fill in the date and place you are completing the form. Then sign your name on the signature line. In this item, you promise to fulfill the duties of a temporary guardian.

Certification: Leave this item blank. The clerk will fill out this item, which simply says that it is a certified copy of the original Letters of Temporary Guardianship in the court's file.

Notice of Hearing (If Service Is Required)

If you do not need to have the minor or the minor's parents served, you may skip this step. However, if they must be served, prepare a Notice of Hearing following the instructions in Chapter 5, with these exceptions:

Item 1: After the words "(representative capacity, if any)," enter the words "proposed temporary guardian of the person." Just below this, after the words "has filed (specify)," enter the words "Petition for Appointment of Temporary Guardian."

Item 4: Fill in the information in the box about the date, time, and place of the hearing.

Filing Documents, Serving Papers, and Obtaining Letters of Temporary Guardianship

If the minor's parents are available and agree with the temporary guardianship, prepare and have them sign an Attachment 1d to the Petition for Appointment of Temporary Guardian. Obtaining these signatures can be helpful in getting the temporary guardianship petition approved. You're now ready to file your papers with the court.

Filing Temporary Guardianship Papers With the Court

If you are filing your temporary guardianship documents at the same time as the regular guardianship petition, go back to Chapter 6 for filing instructions.

If you have already filed regular guardianship documents, make at least two or three copies of all documents (depending on whether the court requires an extra copy, and whether you are sending the documents to court by mail), plus one for the minor and the minor's parents, if service is required on them.

Before you file your papers, make sure you know when and where to take the temporary guardianship documents, according to the information you gathered in the section of this chapter entitled "Call the Court."

Sample Letters of Temporary Guardianship or Conservatorship, page 1

GC-150

ATTORNEY OR PARTY WITHOUT ATTORNEY *(Name, State Bar number, and address):*

☐ After recording return to:

Patricia Ann Lee
2 West Street
Santa Ana, CA 92702

TELEPHONE NO.: 714-555-1212
FAX NO. *(Optional):*
E-MAIL ADDRESS *(Optional):*
ATTORNEY FOR *(Name):* In Pro Per

SUPERIOR COURT OF CALIFORNIA, COUNTY OF Orange
STREET ADDRESS: 700 Civic Center Drive West
MAILING ADDRESS: P.O. Box 838
CITY AND ZIP CODE: Santa Ana, CA 92702
BRANCH NAME:

TEMPORARY ☑ GUARDIANSHIP ☐ CONSERVATORSHIP
OF *(Name):* Daniel Frank Lee

☑ MINOR ☐ CONSERVATEE

LETTERS OF TEMPORARY ☑ **GUARDIANSHIP** ☐ **CONSERVATORSHIP**
☑ **Person** ☐ **Estate**

FOR RECORDER'S USE ONLY

CASE NUMBER:

FOR COURT USE ONLY

LETTERS

1. *(Name):* Patricia Ann Lee
   is appointed temporary ☑ guardian ☐ conservator of the ☑ person
   ☐ estate of *(name):*
   Daniel Frank Lee
2. ☐ Other powers that have been granted or restrictions imposed on the temporary
   ☐ guardian ☐ conservator are ☐ specified in Attachment 2.
   ☐ specified below.

3. These Letters shall expire
   a. ☐ on *(date):*   or upon earlier issuance of Letters to a general guardian or conservator.
   b. ☐ on other date *(specify):*

4. ☑ The temporary ☑ guardian ☐ conservator is not authorized to take possession of money or any other property
   without a specific court order.

5. Number of pages attached: ___0___

WITNESS, clerk of the court, with seal of the court affixed.

(SEAL)

Date:

Clerk, by _____ , Deputy

Page 1 of 2

This form may be recorded as notice of the establishment of a temporary conservatorship of the estate as provided in Probate Code section 1875.

Form Adopted for Mandatory Use
Judicial Council of California
GC-150 [Rev. January 1, 2009]

**LETTERS OF TEMPORARY GUARDIANSHIP OR
CONSERVATORSHIP**
(Probate—Guardianships and Conservatorships)

Probate Code, §§ 2250 et seq., 2890–2893;
Code of Civil Procedure, § 2015.6
www.courtinfo.ca.gov

Sample Letters of Temporary Guardianship or Conservatorship, page 2

	GC-150
TEMPORARY ☑ GUARDIANSHIP ☐ CONSERVATORSHIP OF *(Name):* Daniel Frank Lee ☑ MINOR ☐ CONSERVATEE	CASE NUMBER:

NOTICE TO INSTITUTIONS AND FINANCIAL INSTITUTIONS
(Probate Code sections 2890–2893)

When these *Letters of Temporary Guardianship* or *Letters of Temporary Conservatorship* (Letters) are delivered to you as an employee or other representative of an *institution* or *financial institution* (described below) in order for the temporary guardian or temporary conservator of the estate (1) to take possession or control of an asset of the minor or conservatee named above held by your institution (including changing title, withdrawing all or any portion of the asset, or transferring all or any portion of the asset) or (2) to open or change the name of an account or a safe-deposit box in your financial institution to reflect the guardianship or conservatorship, you must fill out Judicial Council form GC-050 (for an institution) or form GC-051 (for a financial institution). An officer authorized by your institution or financial institution must date and sign the form, and you must file the completed form with the court.

There is no filing fee for filing the form. You may either arrange for personal delivery of the form or mail it to the court for filing at the address given for the court on page 1 of these Letters.

The temporary guardian or temporary conservator should deliver a blank copy of the appropriate form to you with these Letters, but it is your institution's or financial institution's responsibility to complete the correct form, have an authorized officer sign it, and file the completed form with the court. If the correct form is not delivered with these Letters or is unavailable for any other reason, blank copies of the forms may be obtained from the court. The forms may also be accessed from the judicial branch's public Web site free of charge. The Internet address (URL) is *www.courtinfo.ca.gov/forms/.* Select the form group *Probate—Guardianships and Conservatorships* and scroll down to form GC-050 for an institution or form GC-051 for a financial institution. The forms may be printed out as blank forms and filled in by typewriter (nonfillable form), or may be filled out online and printed out ready for signature and filing (fillable form).

An *institution* under California Probate Code section 2890(c) is an insurance company, insurance broker, insurance agent, investment company, investment bank, securities broker-dealer, investment advisor, financial planner, financial advisor, or any other person who takes, holds, or controls an asset subject to a conservatorship or guardianship other than a financial institution. Institutions must file a *Notice of Taking Possession or Control of an Asset of Minor or Conservatee* (form GC-050) for an asset of the minor or conservatee held by the institution. A single form may be filed for all affected assets held by the institution.

A *financial institution* under California Probate Code section 2892(b) is a bank, trust (including a Totten trust account but excluding other trust arrangements described in Probate Code section 82(b)), savings and loan association, savings bank, industrial bank, or credit union. Financial institutions must file a *Notice of Opening or Changing a Guardianship or Conservatorship Account or Safe-Deposit Box* (form GC-051) for an account or a safe deposit box held by the financial institution. A single form may be filed for all affected accounts or safe deposit boxes held by the financial institution.

LETTERS OF TEMPORARY ☐ GUARDIANSHIP ☐ CONSERVATORSHIP
AFFIRMATION

I solemnly affirm that I will perform according to law the duties of temporary ☑ guardian. ☐ conservator.

Executed on *(date):* 2/1/20xx , at *(place):* Santa Ana, CA

▶

Patricia Ann Lee
_____
(TYPE OR PRINT NAME)

_____
(SIGNATURE OF APPOINTEE)

CERTIFICATION

I certify that this document, including any attachments, is a correct copy of the original on file in my office and that the Letters issued to the person appointed above have not been revoked, annulled, or set aside and are still in full force and effect.

(SEAL)	Date:
	Clerk, by _____, Deputy

GC-150 [Rev. January 1, 2009]	**LETTERS OF TEMPORARY GUARDIANSHIP OR CONSERVATORSHIP** **(Probate—Guardianships and Conservatorships)**	Page 2 of 2

If you are submitting your temporary guardianship documents ex parte, let the clerk know it's an urgent matter. Clerks can and do submit papers to judges more quickly if they feel the case needs immediate attention. Ask the clerk when you can expect the judge to sign the Order Appointing Temporary Guardian. Generally this takes one to five days, depending on the court's size and local procedures.

Serve Temporary Guardianship Papers and Complete Proofs of Service (If Required)

If your court requires service on anyone— generally the minor if 12 or over, the minor's parents, and anyone with visitation rights— have them served with copies of the Notice of Hearing and Petition for Appointment of Temporary Guardian (including any attachments). Usually, personal service will be required, but some courts may allow notification of the parents or other relatives by telephone. If you have documents served, complete a proof of service for each person and immediately file it with the court. (Chapter 6 gives instructions on how to have documents served and how to complete proofs of service.)

Attend Hearing (If Required)

If a hearing is required, you and the minor must attend. At the hearing, the judge will decide whether to grant the temporary guardianship, and if it's granted, will sign the Order Appointing Temporary Guardian. (General information about court hearings is contained in Chapter 9.)

If the judge asks how long you want the temporary guardianship to last, say that you would like it to run until the date the regular guardianship is scheduled to be heard. If this is more than 30 days away, the judge should grant the temporary guardianship for 30 days, and you will need to have it extended before the regular guardianship is heard. (See "How to Extend the Temporary Guardianship," below.)

Obtain Issued Letters of Temporary Guardianship

If you attended a hearing, the judge at the hearing usually signs and gives you copies of the Order Appointing Temporary Guardian. In larger courts, the judge may sign the order after the hearing, so you may need to return to court to pick it up later.

If the temporary guardianship papers were submitted ex parte, call the clerk on the date the clerk told you the judge would sign the order to find out whether it's been signed. If the judge hasn't signed the order, ask politely whether the clerk knows why. It may just be a technical error. If not, and the judge refuses to sign it, you may either have to wait until your scheduled hearing date to get a regular guardianship or get help from a lawyer.

Once your Order Appointing Temporary Guardian has been signed by a judge, you still need to have the court clerk issue Letters of Temporary Guardianship. The letters will be your proof for any agencies, health care providers, and others, that you can act as temporary guardian. You obtain Letters of Temporary Guardianship in the same way as regular Letters of Guardianship, by submitting the signed Order Appointing Temporary Guardian to the clerk. (See Chapter 9.)

How to Extend the Temporary Guardianship

A temporary guardianship lasts up to 30 days (PC § 2257). However, you may need the temporary guardianship to extend for a longer period of time, generally because the hearing on the regular guardianship is set for more than

30 days away. If so, you can submit an ex parte request for an order extending the temporary guardianship.

Call the court and find out how to submit an ex parte motion for an order extending a temporary guardianship pending the regular guardianship hearing. The procedure may be similar to the procedure for obtaining a temporary guardianship. Usually you submit your documents to the judge or the clerk, and then either wait for the signature or return in a day or two to pick up the signed order. The court may require that the minor's parents and others be notified about the motion, possibly by telephone. If advance notice is necessary, find out the method of notice required, and how far in advance of the hearing it must be done.

Ex Parte Motion, Declaration, and Order Extending Temporary Guardianship

In this document you state why an extension of the temporary guardianship is needed, and leave room for the judge to sign an order extending the guardianship. Use the accompanying sample as a guide.

Filing Documents, Serving Papers, and Obtaining Order and Letters

Following the guidelines in Chapter 3, make copies of the Ex Parte Motion, Declaration, and Order Extending Temporary Guardianship, and file them with the court at least five days before the Letters of Temporary Guardianship expire. If your court requires notification or service, follow those requirements. (How to serve documents and prepare proofs of service is covered in Chapter 6.)

To obtain new Letters of Temporary Guardianship, follow the instructions above, by submitting the signed order to the clerk. If you need to have the Letters of Temporary Guardianship extended again, do the same thing again.

Ex Parte Motion, Declaration, and Order Extending Temporary Guardianship

PARTY WITHOUT AN ATTORNEY *(Name and Address)*: RUTH MARCI NORTON 100 Any Street Nevada City, CA 95959 *In Pro Per*	TELEPHONE NO: 916-555-1212	FOR COURT USE ONLY

NAME OF COURT: NEVADA COUNTY SUPERIOR COURT
STREET ADDRESS: Courthouse
MAILING ADDRESS: 201 Church Street
CITY AND ZIP CODE: Nevada City, CA 95959
BRANCH NAME:

GUARDIANSHIP OF THE PERSON OF (NAME):

JANICE LYNN NORTON   MINOR

EX PARTE MOTION, DECLARATION, AND ORDER EXTENDING TEMPORARY GUARDIANSHIP	CASE NUMBER 1000

MOTION

Petitioner moves the court for an order extending the duration of the temporary guardianship of the person of _____
JANICE LYNN NORTON

This motion is made on the grounds that the temporary guardianship is due to expire before a regular guardian is appointed, and it would be in the best interests of the minor for the temporary guardianship to be extended for reasons set out in the declaration of the temporary guardian.

DECLARATION OF TEMPORARY GUARDIAN

1. Petitioner (name): __RUTH MARCI NORTON__ is the duly appointed, qualified, and
acting temporary guardian of the person of __JANICE LYNN NORTON__.
2. Petitioner has been acting as temporary guardian since __February 19__, __20xx__.
3. The temporary guardianship is due to expire on __March 21__, __20xx__.
4. The hearing on the regular guardianship is set for __April 1__, __20xx__.
5. The best interests of the ward require the extension of the temporary guardianship until __April 1, 20xx__,
_____, or for thirty days, whichever is sooner because:

As temporary guardian, I am responsible for making decisions about Janice's educational and personal needs. There is no one else to make these decisions for her. Janice is 12 years old and needs an adult to care for her. I have been nominated guardian by Janice's mother. Extending the temporary guardianship will allow the smooth supervision of Janice's needs until a regular guardianship is established.

I declare under penalty of perjury under the laws of the State of California that the foregoing is true and correct. Executed this __15th__ day of __March__, __20xx__ at __Nevada City__, California.

RUTH MARCI NORTON   *Ruth Marci Norton*
....
(TYPE OR PRINT NAME)   (SIGNATURE OF DECLARANT)

ORDER

The court having considered the motion and good cause appearing, IT IS ORDERED that the temporary guardianship of the person of _____ is extended until

_____, _____, or for thirty days, whichever is sooner.

Dated:...   _____
(JUDGE OF THE SUPERIOR COURT)

      **EX PARTE MOTION DECLARATION, AND ORDER
EXTENDING TEMPORARY GUARDIANSHIP**

The Guardianship Investigation

A legal guardianship is set up to take care of the best interests of the minor, and every county has an agency that is designated to investigate guardianships to make sure that they are in the child's best interest. At a minimum, the county agency is required to check for reports of child abuse or neglect by the proposed guardian, and report their findings to the court (PC § 1516). Some counties conduct a more detailed investigation than this for all proposed guardianships; some only conduct a detailed investigation if the proposed guardian isn't related to the minor; and some don't require any investigation at all. Each county sets its own policy about investigations.

In order to alert the county that an investigation is required, you must serve the proper agency with a copy of your guardianship petition. Usually, the local social services agency is responsible for investigating guardianships, but sometimes there is an investigator associated with the probate court.

The word "investigation" might sound scary, but the process really isn't. Usually, somebody from either the court or a county agency contacts the proposed guardian and arranges a convenient time to come to the house for an interview. At the arranged time, the investigator talks to the guardian and to the minor—unless the minor is too young to talk.

For guardianship of a minor's person, whoever conducts the investigation would want to see where the minor would be living, and to know whether the proposed guardian is in a position to adequately care for the minor. Some investigators meet with the proposed guardian and minor more than once. Often investigators speak with the minor's natural parents as well. After the interviews, the investigator provides a written report to the court, and makes a recommendation about whether the guardianship should be granted.

Each Court Has Its Own Policies for Investigations

If you haven't done so already, check with your court to find out whether an investigation is required for your guardianship case. Call the court and say you are seeking a guardianship, and specify whether it is for the minor's person, estate, or both. Let the clerk know whether you are related to the minor (by blood), and ask whether an investigation is required. If so, find out what agency or court investigator will conduct the investigation. Make sure a copy of the guardianship papers are sent to that investigator, if they haven't been mailed already. Some local courts require service on the investigating agency at least 30 days before the scheduled hearing date. If you haven't had the agency served by then, check your court's service requirements. (If you need to continue the case, see Chapter 6.) You can serve the county agency by mail.

Guardianship of a Minor's Person

In every proposed guardianship of a minor's person, screenings by the local social service agency for reports of abuse or neglect are required. Additionally, an investigation is often required when the proposed guardian is not a close relative of the minor. Many counties require investigations no matter how close the relationship between the proposed guardian and minor. Courts have different rules about who is considered a close relative. For example, one court might consider a stepparent a relative, while another might not. All courts will consider blood-related grandparents, aunts, and uncles to be relatives, but courts will vary on how closely related a cousin must be (for example, first, second, or third cousin).

Investigations are not meant to resolve custody disputes, so investigators do not decide who will be the best guardian in a contested situation. When guardianships are contested, the matter should be referred to the court's family services division for resolution.

Guardianship of a Minor's Estate

Most courts waive investigations for guardianship of a minor's estate. However, depending on the circumstances of the guardianship and the assets involved, the court could require an investigation even if you are only seeking guardianship of a minor's estate. For example, an investigation might be required if the court has questions about your ability to handle the minor's assets, or if there is a dispute about the ownership of the minor's property.

Investigation Procedure

Because investigations vary from one county to another, we cannot tell you exactly what will happen in your county. This section provides an overview of how investigations generally are handled.

Who Conducts the Investigation?

If the proposed guardian is related to the minor, the investigation may be conducted by a special probate court investigator, a probation officer, or a domestic relations investigator. Proposed guardians who are not related to the minor are generally investigated by a local social services agency (PC § 1513).

Investigator May Check Background Sources

The investigator may choose to look at the minor's school records, medical and psychological records and written summaries, probation records, and public and private social service records (PC § 1513(e)).

Depending on local policies, the investigator may also check into your background. For example, the investigator may obtain information by:

- discussing the guardianship with the minor's living parents, if they are available to be interviewed
- contacting relatives entitled to notice of the guardianship, and interviewing them about how they feel about your being appointed guardian
- talking with the minor's day care or school teachers and counselors to get information about the minor's academic performance and behavior
- talking with neighbors
- checking your background for instances of child abuse and neglect, and
- requiring that you be fingerprinted and checking into your record for prior offenses.

Some Courts Use Questionnaires

To help assess whether to grant a guardianship, many courts require prospective guardians to fill out extensive questionnaires. These typically ask for personal information about your education, employment, marital history, health, criminal record, housing, and who lives with you. Generally, you will also need to answer questions about why you are seeking the guardianship, and how you plan to care for the minor. These questionnaires may seem long and intimidating, but they usually are not really difficult to complete.

Home Interviews

Before the hearing date, the investigator may want to conduct at least one interview at your home. Some investigators will meet with you more than once, while others just schedule one interview. The investigator will talk with you, probably your spouse (if you have one living with you), and the minor—unless the minor is too young to talk. The investigator may want to talk with you and the minor separately.

At the interview, you may be asked to provide some personal information about things like your marital status, your own children, employment, education, health, how you plan to take care of the minor or the minor's assets, and your means of financial support. The investigator may want to discuss why a guardianship is needed, and why you want to be the guardian. You may be asked how long you've known the minor, and how long the minor has been living with you. In addition, the investigator may want the names of several references.

If you are seeking guardianship of a minor's person, the investigator may want to see where the minor will be staying, whether you have adequate space and a comfortable place for the minor to live, and if the minor has enough age-appropriate clothing, toys, and room to play. The investigator should discuss any special educational, emotional, psychological, or physical needs the minor may have. Investigators often want to look at the minor's report cards and other school reports, so it's a good idea to have these handy.

If you are seeking guardianship of a minor's estate, the investigator may want information about your experience managing finances. The investigator may also want some information about your own financial situation.

Tips on Dealing With the Investigator

When you meet with the investigator, bear in mind that the goal of the investigation isn't to trick you. The best approach is to be honest and relaxed, and to do your best to answer all questions. Remember, both you and the investigator want what's best for the minor.

If the minor is old enough to understand, give a heads-up that someone will be talking to both of you about the guardianship. Explain that it's not because the minor has done anything wrong, and that the investigator simply wants to make sure you'll be a good caretaker. Say that the investigator wants to make sure you're the one the minor wants as a guardian, and it's okay for the minor to tell the investigator the truth about the minor's feelings.

What if there is something in your background that you're not proud of? It's quite possible that an unfortunate event from your past may not even come up, especially if it happened a long time ago and no one is likely to contest the guardianship. But if the investigator asks about something that you're worried about, be honest in your answer. If the investigator later finds out you haven't been honest, it may throw into question other information you've given, and the investigator may not give a favorable recommendation to the court.

It's unlikely that an investigator will hold your past against you if your situation has changed, and past events don't have a bearing on your ability to care for the minor. For example, if you were convicted of shoplifting when you were a teenager and haven't been arrested or convicted since then, it's unlikely that an investigator would hold the shoplifting conviction against you. But if you're still having frequent run-ins with the law, an investigator may be hesitant to recommend you as guardian.

The Investigator's Report

After the investigation is completed, and before the hearing date, the investigator writes a report to the court with a recommendation about whether the guardianship should be granted.

The report briefly discusses the circumstances that made the guardianship necessary, and your relationship with the minor. If the minor has any special emotional, psychological, educational, or developmental needs, the investigator will assess whether you can meet them.

The investigator's report will discuss the type of relationship you and the minor have. For example, the report would include the length of time you and the minor have known one another, or have been close. If the minor is already living with you, the investigator would discuss what led to that arrangement, and how it seems to be working out.

Generally, the report includes a summary of your attitudes about the guardianship and how you plan to care for the minor or the minor's estate. For guardianships of a minor's person, the report might discuss whether you can support the minor, or if you've made other arrangements. The report also should include the minor's natural parents' future plans. Finally, the investigator makes a recommendation to the court about whether the guardianship should be granted. Judges almost always follow the investigator's recommendation.

Depending on local policies, the report may be sent to the court in advance of the hearing date, or it may not be filed until that very day. Some investigators also send copies of the report to the proposed guardian. If you haven't received a copy several days before the hearing date, call the court and find out whether it is in the file, and how you can get a copy. If it's not available in the court file until the day of the hearing, make sure you arrive a little early so you can look at the report before the hearing begins.

Note: The investigator's report is confidential, meaning that not everyone can get a copy of it. However, it may be read by anyone who has been served with notice of the guardianship proceeding (PC § 1513(d)).

Fees for the Investigation

Investigation costs vary from county to county, and run from $200 to about $1,000. Costs of the investigation may be charged to:

- either or both of the minor's parents
- whoever has physical custody and care of the minor
- the proposed guardian or court-appointed guardian
- the minor's estate (if you're seeking guardianship of the minor's estate or person and estate), or
- some other person, depending on the financial situation (PC § 1513.1).

If you are the only one caring for the minor, and the minor does not have an estate, it's likely that you will be required to pay the investigator's fees. However, part or all of the investigation fees may be waived on the basis of hardship. For example, if you applied for and were granted a waiver of court fees and costs, this waiver would include the costs of an investigation. (See Chapter 3.)

Important: In cases where an investigation is conducted, you generally cannot obtain Letters of Guardianship until the investigation has been paid for. The clerk may require a copy of the paid receipt for the investigation before issuing Letters of Guardianship.

If the Investigator Recommends Against Granting Guardianship

In all probability, the investigator will recommend that you be appointed guardian. But in the rare instance when she recommends against it, but you believe you are qualified, you will need assistance from a lawyer. (See Chapter 13.)

If the Investigator Recommends Granting Temporary Guardianship

Occasionally, investigators are hesitant to recommend a permanent guardianship because they feel the situation may not be best for the minor unless it changes somewhat. For example, the minor may have special educational needs that aren't being met, and a change in school programs is recommended. Or the minor may need to see a therapist or social worker to help with psychological problems. Perhaps a proposed guardian may be required to see a counselor to deal with an alcohol problem.

In such instances, investigators may recommend a temporary guardianship, and a review of both the guardian and minor—often in about six months—to see whether the conditions have been met. (Information on temporary guardianships is in Chapter 7.)

The Hearing: Preparing, Attending, and What to Do Afterward

This chapter discusses the court hearing, at which a judge decides whether to appoint you as the minor's guardian. Going to a hearing in a courtroom may sound scary to you. But it can be quite easy, as long as you and the minor are prepared.

Getting Ready for the Hearing

It's a good idea for you to read or reread this chapter at least two weeks before the hearing date. That way, you won't be scrambling around just before the hearing, trying to figure out forms and procedures. If you follow the guidelines and instructions here, you shouldn't have problems handling the hearing yourself. Following are instructions about how to prepare for the court hearing. Remember that you should see a lawyer well before the hearing date if you have any reason to believe the guardianship will be contested. (Chapter 13 discusses how to find a lawyer.)

Prepare Yourself

Several days before the hearing, review all the documents you've filed with the court—especially the Petition for Appointment of Guardian of Minor. You may want to make a few notes about the specific information you've filled out in the petition, and make sure you're familiar with any facts on which you based your statements. For example, if the minor is on probation in a juvenile court case, know the facts and status of the case and have copies of any documents that have been filed in court.

If an investigation was conducted and you haven't received a copy of any report by the investigator, you may want to go to the courthouse and ask to see it, which you have a right to do. (More information on the investigation is contained in Chapter 8.)

Be ready to answer the judge's questions about why the guardianship is necessary, as well as about your relationship with the minor, your ability to care for the minor or the minor's assets, and how the minor's parents and other relatives feel about your being guardian. You may want to make notes about what you plan to say on the stand. (It's not advisable to read from this book when you're in front of the judge.) (See "Attend the Hearing," below, for more about what to say in front of the judge.)

Gather Documents

You'll need copies of all of the papers you've sent to the court, as well as any supporting documents and notes you've prepared. You might not be asked to show the judge any of these papers. However, if you don't have them with you, it easily could mean a delay. You may want to put these documents into labeled file folders or an accordion file. Organize the documents so that you can quickly find any one of them. The documents you'll need are listed below.

What to Bring to the Hearing

- Any notes you've made to prepare for the guardianship proceeding
- copies of all guardianship papers you filed with the court (see checklist in Chapter 6)
- the minor's birth certificate
- death certificates of the minor's parents or other relatives entitled to notice of the guardianship proceeding
- copies of any court documents affecting the minor, such as adoption, juvenile court, and divorce or custody orders
- copies of all proofs of service (Chapter 6)
- extra copy of the unsigned Letters of Guardianship (Chapter 5)
- extra copy of the proposed Order Appointing Guardian of Minor (Chapter 5), if the minor is age 12 or over, and
- this book.

Double-Check What You've Done

Before you go in for the guardianship hearing, make sure you have:

- completed all documents discussed in Chapters 4, 5, and 6 and filed them with the court
- filled in and submitted a proposed Order Appointing Guardian form to the court clerk following the instructions in Chapter 6, so that it will already be in the file for the judge to sign
- served everyone entitled to notice as instructed in Chapter 6
- completed and filed proofs of service with the court as discussed in Chapter 6
- made arrangements to bring the minor to the guardianship hearing, and

- filled in a Proof of Service by Mail of Order Appointing Guardian—if the minor is at least 12 years old—if necessary, following the instructions in "Getting the Letters of Guardianship Issued by the Clerk," below.

Many courts require that you submit a proposed Order Appointing Guardian to the court when you file your petition, or several days before the hearing date. Some courts will refuse to hear your case if they don't have a proposed Order Appointing Guardian in the file several days before the hearing date. So if you haven't already sent the proposed order to the court, call the clerk and find out whether you can bring it to the hearing with you. (If you must continue the case, see Chapter 6, which tells you how.)

If for some reason you have not filed the proofs of service with the court in advance of the hearing date, bring the originals—along with copies for your files—to the hearing.

Prepare the Minor

It's important that you take time to talk to the minor about what's going to happen in court. Say that you will be going to court to get legal documents saying that you're responsible for the minor's care. Reassure the minor that although the two of you are going to court, you're not having a trial, and your court appearance probably will last only a few minutes in front of a judge. Say that the minor hasn't done anything wrong, and that you're glad to be taking over this responsibility.

If the minor has questions or fears, you can state confidently that no one will be asking hard questions like in TV shows or movies. Most likely, the judge will be kind, speak gently, and ask a few questions like: "Do you understand that Ms. Guardian here is asking me to allow her to take care of you just like a mother?" or something similar. Let the minor know that it's important always to tell the truth to the judge.

Make a Trip to the Courthouse (Optional)

If you have time, an extra trip to the courthouse can make the hearing go much more easily. Several days before the hearing, we suggest you and the minor go to the very courtroom where the hearing will be held. You might find it helpful to go a week or so before your case will be heard, at a time when the courtroom is empty, or when other guardianship cases are scheduled. Call the probate court to find out when guardianships are normally heard. If the minor is frightened about appearing before a judge, visiting the courtroom and getting a preview of what will happen there can make the whole experience less intimidating.

Make Sure Your Hearing Is on the Court Calendar

In Chapter 6, we discuss how to request a hearing date from the court clerk. You listed this date on the Notice of Hearing, and served it along with other necessary papers on the minor's relatives and agencies entitled to notice of the guardianship.

Call the court clerk a few days before the hearing and ask to confirm that the case is still "on calendar," meaning it is scheduled to take place as planned. If you don't know in which courtroom the judge would hear the case, ask the clerk for this information. Make sure you know exactly where and when you should arrive for the hearing. Find out as much information as possible over the phone, so you won't be harried on the day of the hearing.

> **TIP**
>
> **Some courts make court calendars available on the Internet.** To check whether your local court posts its calendar on the Internet, check the court's website. You can find a list of court websites at www.courtinfor.ca.gov/courts/find.htm.

If the clerk says your case isn't on calendar, give the case number and name of the case, and ask the clerk to locate the file. If the Petition for Appointment of Guardian of Minor, Notice of Hearing, filled-out Proof(s) of Service, and other necessary papers all are in the file, the case should be set for hearing. If all your paperwork is in order, ask the clerk to add the matter to the court's list of cases to be heard. You may need to be persistent with the clerk, and ask to speak to a supervisor if you're not getting the cooperation you need.

If all your papers aren't in the file or aren't filled out correctly, find out what went wrong. It's possible that you made a mistake in completing or serving the papers. Or maybe you forgot to send in some required document. Make sure you understand exactly what you need to fix. If necessary, go to the clerk's office to look at the case file and see what's missing or incorrect. In the rare situation where you took or sent documents to the court and they never made it to the file, you may be able to get your case put on calendar by showing the court clerk your file-stamped copies of documents, or by providing duplicates.

Unless your guardianship case is on calendar, you can't go into court and have it heard by a judge. If for any reason your case is not scheduled to be heard when you thought it should have been, you must contact the court clerk about getting a new hearing date, following the instructions in Chapter 6. Then you'll need to prepare a new Notice of Hearing, and have copies of it, the Petition for

Appointment of Guardian of Minor, and any other necessary documents served again on *everyone* entitled to notice of the guardianship. (Chapter 6 discusses how to have guardianship papers served.)

The Day of the Hearing

At last you're ready to attend the hearing. Remember that going through a court hearing is easier than you might expect. Make sure you have followed the instructions for preparing yourself and the minor for the hearing.

Before You Leave Home

Appearances might count, so dress cleanly and neatly. If you own any, wear business-type clothing. Whatever you choose, make sure you and the minor are dressed neatly and comfortably. Give yourself enough time to get to the courthouse well before your case is scheduled so you can find the right place. Arrive at least half an hour before the scheduled hearing time if you know where you're going, and give yourself even more time if you're not familiar with the building.

Before you leave home, double-check that you have ready everything listed in "Getting Ready for the Hearing," above. Also remember to bring along a checkbook or cash to obtain certified Letters of Guardianship. The cost for five certified Letters of Guardianship could be anywhere from $25 to $75—unless your court costs and fees were waived.

CAUTION

Do you need a bond? If you are seeking guardianship of a minor's estate, you cannot obtain Letters of Guardianship from the clerk until you've first obtained a bond in an amount the judge will order at the hearing, unless bond is waived. (See "Obtaining Bond" in Chapter 10.)

Find the Courtroom

Most counties have more than one Superior Court judge. Each judge has an individual courtroom, called a "department," which is identified by a number or letter such as Department 1 or Department A. In some counties, you go straight to the assigned courtroom for your hearing. In some of the larger counties, you may need to go to a special department (often called a "master calendar department") to find out to which courtroom your case has been assigned.

Usually you'll find a list of cases to be heard that day posted outside the assigned courtroom. If you can't find one, go to the clerk's office and ask to see a copy of the calendar for guardianship or probate cases scheduled to be heard in that department. Look at this listing to see when your case will be called.

Guardianship Investigation

In some courts, where a formal investigation is not required, an investigator comes to the courtroom and meets with the proposed guardian and minor before the hearing. If this happens, the investigator will talk to you briefly about the guardianship.

If a formal investigation was conducted and you were not sent a copy of the report, you may be able to see it before the hearing. Sometimes the investigator's report is not filed until the day of the hearing. Check with the clerk or bailiff before the hearing begins to see whether a copy of the report is in the case file. (For a detailed discussion of guardianship investigations, see Chapter 8.)

Videotape of Guardian's Responsibilities

Some counties require proposed guardians to watch a video that explains the guardian's duties. If that's required by the county where you're filing, you must attend.

Attend the Hearing

When you get to the proper courtroom for your hearing, tell the clerk or bailiff you are there. You may be required to sign in, or to fill out an additional form listing your name and the name of the guardianship case. If the minor cannot keep quiet while you're waiting for your turn, it's fine for you and the minor to wait outside the courtroom. Some courthouses have a special waiting room for children, complete with toys and books. Check with the clerk or bailiff to find out whether your courtroom has such a facility. If you will be outside the courtroom, tell the clerk or bailiff your situation and where you will be, and ask them to get you when your case is called.

Appearing Before the Judge

If you're waiting in the courtroom, you may get to watch the judge hear other cases. In some counties, other types of cases will be heard first, but you might have an opportunity to see a guardianship case take place before yours.

When your case is called, stand up and answer: "Ready, Your Honor." You and the minor should go right on up to the table in front of the judge's bench. The clerk or bailiff will swear you in, asking you to promise to tell the truth. You can take time to arrange yourself and your papers, so relax. Always call the judge "Your Honor."

First, identify yourself by giving your name and saying that you are the petitioner and proposed guardian. Then, identify the minor as the one for whom you're seeking the guardianship. Speak slowly and clearly, and loud enough for the courtroom reporter to hear so that the information can be typed into the court records. You will probably need to spell out your name and the minor's.

Many judges will ask you questions to get the information they want, but some will just tell you to begin. If the judge simply wants you to start, explain why the guardianship is needed, how long you've known the minor, and how you plan to handle your duties as guardian. If you're seeking guardianship of a minor's estate, briefly summarize the minor's assets, why it is necessary to manage them, and that you are able and willing to do so. The judge may have some questions about service of the guardianship papers, or want more information about why notice should be dispensed with if you claim that certain relatives can't be located.

When the judge asks questions, it is only to become better informed and satisfied that the best legal solution is reached. Try to stay relaxed—and just answer briefly and exactly what is asked. There's no need to volunteer information that is not asked for.

After you are finished, the judge may ask the minor a few simple questions like: "Do you understand that _____ wants me to allow her to take care of you just like a parent? Is this okay with you?" The judge may ask the minor about school or sports to make the minor feel more at ease.

When you and the minor are finished talking and the judge has no more questions, the judge will recite the orders being made in your case. The judge will probably complete and sign the original Order Appointing Guardian right there. If you submitted an Order Dispensing Notice, the judge should also sign that, unless it appears to the judge that you didn't try hard enough to locate the minor's relatives. If that's the situation, the judge would probably continue the case. See "Handling Problems at the Hearing," below.

It's possible that even if the judge approves the guardianship, you may not get a signed Order Appointing Guardian right away. This is especially common in large counties. Also, it may take some time—a few minutes to a few hours—for the judge to give the court file back to the clerk. You may be able to get the Order Appointing Guardian signed by the judge, and get file-stamped copies from the clerk on the same day as your hearing. But if you're less lucky, you may have to come back to court a day or so later for that step, or leave the clerk a large stamped, self-addressed envelope to mail the order to you.

If the judge signed any orders, the clerk should hand you stamped copies. If the minor is at least 12 years old, the clerk should also give the minor a copy of the Order Appointing Guardian of Minor.

Before you leave the courtroom, make sure you take with you:

- a copy of the signed Order Appointing Guardian (or be sure you have a clear understanding of how you'll get the order)

- a copy of the signed Order Dispensing Notice, if you want notice of the guardianship waived for any relatives who either signed a Waiver of Notice and Consent or could not be located, and

- unissued Letters of Guardianship and copies.

You should have sent all of these documents to the court when you initially filed your papers with the court. If the judge signs the Order Appointing Guardian but neglects to give any of the listed documents back to you, check with the bailiff or clerk before you leave the courtroom. The clerk should be able to locate them in your file.

Handling Problems at the Hearing

Usually you will not have trouble with the guardianship hearing. However, it will probably make you feel better to have a little information about what to do if something does go wrong.

Before the Hearing

Before you leave your house, write down the phone number of the department you're going to if you know it, and of the main court clerk if you don't. That way, if you get delayed you can call to let the court know when you expect to arrive.

Occasionally court personnel are less than helpful to people who are representing themselves in court. If a clerk or even the judge is rude or refuses to help you, do your best to keep your composure. Start by calmly trying to get to the root of the problem. It may be a simple issue you can correct.

If the person you're dealing with can't help you, seek assistance from someone else, such as another clerk or a supervisor. Keep in mind that the judge, court clerks, and bailiff aren't allowed to give you legal advice—but they will try to help you with procedures. Your goal should be simply to correct the problem. Double-check everything with the help of this book.

After the Hearing

If the judge won't grant the guardianship yet, it may be because you left out something important in your paperwork. Politely ask the judge to explain; it's quite likely that you can provide additional information that will resolve the matter.

If you can't figure out what the problem is, or you feel you can't handle the situation, you can ask for a continuance. A continuance simply postpones the hearing to a later date. Pause for a moment to collect your thoughts.

Then politely tell the judge: "Your Honor, I request that this matter be continued two weeks [*or longer if you need additional time*], to give me time to seek legal advice." During the next recess (when the court is not in session), see whether the clerk or bailiff can help you. If you are able to figure out what went wrong and how to correct it, you'll need to arrange to appear at another hearing to be held on a new "continued" date.

If the judge is very difficult, it's possible that you might not get a continuance, which means that you'll have to start the process all over again. If that happens, seek the help of a lawyer so you don't end up in the same situation. (See Chapter 13.)

If the judge continues the case, you will not have to serve new notices of hearing unless the problem is that not everyone was properly served. If everyone was correctly served, they either will be there to hear the judge set the new court date or, by not appearing, they have given up the right to be told about it.

If There's a Dispute Over Custody or Visitation Rights

In very rare circumstances, you may arrive at the hearing thinking everything will go smoothly, and find yourself face-to-face with a parent, relative, or other adult who either wants custody of the minor or wants visitation rights. If you're in this unfortunate situation, it's unlikely that the judge will hear the guardianship that day. In larger counties, the case will probably be transferred to the family law department. You will need to consult a lawyer to help work out a contested guardianship or dispute over custody or visitation. (See Chapter 13.)

If the Judge Won't Sign the Order Appointing Guardian

If the judge grants your petition but refuses to sign the Order Appointing Guardian, this means the judge thinks there is something wrong with your proposed order. Listen carefully to what the judge says is wrong. At the recess, if you still don't understand, ask the clerk what is wrong (or look at the clerk's docket sheet, a public record). Occasionally, a judge will make an order that is different from the proposed order you prepared and submitted prior to the hearing. If so, you will have to prepare a new proposed order after the hearing and submit it to the court clerk for the judge to sign. Do it as soon as possible, and mail or bring it to the court for the judge's signature.

If the Judge Will Only Sign a Temporary Order

Occasionally, a judge will not sign an Order Appointing Guardian because of questions or hesitations about allowing the guardianship. This could be because the guardianship investigation raised some issues that the judge believes should be taken care of—such as counseling for the minor, or a change in living situation. It's possible, however, that the judge will sign an order appointing you temporary guardian, and set another hearing to decide on the permanent guardianship. If this happens, you will need to fill in documents for a temporary guardianship and submit them to the judge to sign. Instructions on how to file for a temporary guardianship are in Chapter 7.

Getting the Letters of Guardianship Issued by the Clerk

Before you leave the courthouse, you may be able to obtain issued Letters of Guardianship—the court document that confirms your authority to act as guardian. Until you obtain issued Letters of Guardianship, you are not officially considered the minor's guardian, even if the judge signed an order appointing you guardian. After the hearing, if you need to send the Order Appointing Guardian to the court to be signed and returned to you, follow the instructions below only after you receive the signed order. You can either obtain signed Letters of Guardianship by going to the clerk's office in person, or by sending your request to the court, following the instructions in Chapter 3.

Write In the Judge's Changes on Copies of Order Appointing Guardian

Before the clerk will issue Letters of Guardianship, there should be a signed Order Appointing Guardian from the judge in the file. If the judge made any changes to the proposed order, make sure these changes are made on all the copies. If they haven't been made by the judge or the clerk, write in the same changes on the copies before you file them with the court clerk.

If you send the Order Appointing Guardian to the court after the hearing to be signed and returned to you, follow these instructions after you receive the signed order back. You can either obtain signed Letters of Guardianship by going to the clerk's office in person, or sending your request to the court following the instructions in Chapter 3.

Take Letters of Guardianship to Clerk

As indicated earlier, if the judge signs the order at the hearing, you should have the Letters of Guardianship issued and certified while you're at the court for the hearing if possible, instead of mailing the forms to the court. That will save you from having to make an extra trip to court if there is a problem with the orders.

The clerk will file any orders and proofs of service, and return file-stamped copies to you. The clerk will then issue the original Letters of Guardianship. The clerk also will provide you with as many certified copies as you request. You'll pay for each of them, unless your court costs and fees were waived by the court.

To obtain issued Letters of Guardianship, take or send to the filing clerk:

- unissued Letters of Guardianship and copies
- a copy of the signed Order Appointing Guardian of Minor
- the original and copies of a completed and signed Proof of Service by Mail of Order Appointing Guardian of Minor and copies, if you completed this form after reading and following the instructions in "Special Procedure If the Minor Is 12 or Older," below.
- a copy of the signed Order Dispensing Notice if there is one, and
- check or cash to pay for issued Letters of Guardianship. Call the clerk to find out how much it will cost—certified copies have become much more expensive in recent years as courts try to generate revenue any way they can. It's a good idea to get five copies—you may have to give some of them away to agencies that need proof that you are the court-appointed guardian.

Proof of Payment of Investigation May Be Required

If an investigation was conducted, the clerk may require proof that the costs of the investigation were paid in full before issuing Letters of Guardianship. You may either need to show a receipt, or wait to obtain Letters of Guardianship until after the clerk has reviewed the file.

Special Procedures for Guardianship of a Minor's Estate

Skip this section if you were only appointed guardian of a minor's person. If you were appointed guardian of a minor's estate or person and estate, read this section. Also read Chapter 10, which gives important information and identifies forms you'll need in order to complete the process of becoming guardian and obtaining Letters of Guardianship.

You May Need to Obtain Bond or Establish a Blocked Account

If you are required to obtain bond or set up a blocked account (see Item 9d in the Order Appointing Guardian of Minor), you will have to do so before you can obtain issued Letters of Guardianship from the clerk. (Instructions for Letters of Guardianship when an estate is involved are in Chapter 10.)

You May Need to Sign Instructions About Managing the Estate

In some counties, before the court clerk will issue Letters of Guardianship, you may need to sign a document with general instructions from the court as to how you must manage the minor's estate. The instruction document should either have been given to you by the judge or clerk at the hearing, or should be available to you from the clerk. If the clerk doesn't ask for a signed copy of these instructions, you don't need one.

Special Procedure If the Minor Is 12 or Older

You may skip this section if the minor is under 12 years of age. However, if the minor is 12 or older, you might need to prepare one new document, depending on whether or not you carefully followed instructions in this book so far.

The law requires that the minor be notified in writing before Letters of Guardianship are issued. Naturally, if the minor attended the guardianship hearing, it doesn't make sense for you to go home and have documents mailed to the minor. The minor already knows about it and should have been given a copy of the Order Appointing Guardian at the hearing.

Fortunately, you probably have already solved this problem, if you completed Item 14 in the Order Appointing Guardian of Minor. (See Chapter 5.) If the judge signed the Order Appointing Guardian—including Item 14—you may skip the rest of this section.

If the minor is at least 12 years old and a judge does not grant Item 14 of the Order Appointing Guardian of Minor, you cannot get Letters of Guardianship until you prepare a Proof of Service by Mail of Order Appointing Guardian of Minor, and have that order served on the minor.

First, have a friend or relative over the age of 18 mail a copy of the Order Appointing Guardian to the minor. Instructions for having documents served are in Chapter 6. Then complete the Proof of Service by Mail of Order Appointing Guardian of Minor.

The Order Appointing Guardian of Minor may be served personally instead of mailed to the minor. If documents are served personally, instead complete a Proof of Service for Personal Service following the instructions in Chapter 6.

Proof of Service by Mail of Order Appointing Guardian of Minor

This document states that the Order Appointing Guardian was served on the minor.

How to Complete the Form

CAPTION: Proof of Service by Mail of Order Appointing Guardian of Minor

Fill in the caption following the general instructions in Chapter 3.

Check the box entitled "Guardianship," as well as boxes next to the words "Person," "Estate," or both. Check the box next to the word "Minor."

After the words "Proof of Service by Mail of Order Appointing," check the box before the word "Guardian."

After the words "My residence or business address is," fill in the business or residence address of the person who served the Order Appointing Guardian of Minor.

Check the box between the words "I served the Order Appointing" and "Guardian."

Item 1: Fill in the date the Order Appointing Guardian of Minor was mailed to the minor.

Item 2: Fill in the city and state where the Order Appointing Guardian of Minor was mailed to the minor.

Fill in the date and place the document will be signed. In the spaces provided, fill in the name of the person who mailed the documents and have them sign.

Item a: Check this box, and fill in the name and address of each minor who is at least 14 years of age.

Sample Proof of Service by Mail of Order Appointing Guardian

ATTORNEY OR PARTY WITHOUT ATTORNEY (NAME AND ADDRESS):	TELEPHONE NO.:	FOR COURT USE ONLY
Jennifer Beth Padilla 5000 Any Way Santa Cruz, CA 95060	408-555-1212	

ATTORNEY FOR (NAME): In Pro Per

SUPERIOR COURT OF CALIFORNIA, COUNTY OF Santa Cruz

STREET ADDRESS: 701 Ocean Street

MAILING ADDRESS: Courthouse, Room 110

CITY AND ZIP CODE: Santa Cruz, CA 95060

BRANCH NAME:

[X] GUARDIANSHIP [ ] CONSERVATORSHIP OF THE [X] PERSON [X] ESTATE
OF (NAME):

Eliza Victoria Wilson   [X] Minor [ ] Conservatee

PROOF OF SERVICE BY MAIL OF ORDER APPOINTING [X] GUARDIAN [ ] CONSERVATOR	CASE NUMBER: 2000

PROOF OF SERVICE BY MAIL
(Personal delivery also permitted. Probate Code, § 1466)

I am over the age of 18 and not a party to this cause. I am a resident of or employed in the county where the mailing occurred. My residence or business address is:

25 Some Street, Santa Cruz, CA 95060

I served the Order Appointing [X] Guardian [ ] Conservator by enclosing a true copy in a sealed envelope addressed to each person whose name and address is given below and depositing the envelope in the United States mail with the postage fully prepaid.

(1) **Date of deposit:** 9/22/xx   (2) **Place of deposit (city and state):** Santa Cruz, CA

I declare under penalty of perjury under the laws of the State of California that the foregoing is true and correct and that this declaration is executed on (date): . . 9/22/xx . . . . at (place): . . . . Santa Cruz, CA . . .

Emma Frand
....
(Type or print name)

Emma Frand
_____
(Signature of declarant)

NAME AND ADDRESS OF EACH PERSON TO WHOM NOTICE WAS MAILED

a. [X] **Ward 14 years of age or older:** Eliza Victoria Wilson
5000 Any Way
Santa Cruz, CA 95060

b. [ ] **Conservatee:**

c.

[ ] List of names and addresses continued in attachment.

**PROOF OF SERVICE BY MAIL
OF ORDER APPOINTING
GUARDIAN OR CONSERVATOR**

Guardianship of a Minor's Estate

A guardian of a minor's estate handles assets and property belonging to the minor. A guardianship of the estate often is not needed if the minor only owns a small amount of money or assets (usually $5,000 or less). If you haven't already read Chapter 1, please do so now, as that will help you determine what type of guardianship you need. This chapter only applies if you are seeking an "estate" guardianship, meaning a guardianship of a minor's estate or both person and estate.

This chapter shows you how to complete the forms necessary to obtain a guardianship of a minor's estate. To become guardian of a minor's estate, you follow almost the same procedures as for a guardianship of a minor's person. This is straightforward and you should have little difficulty doing it on your own. This chapter tells you how to fill out the estate items in the petition and provides an overview of what's involved in guardianship of a minor's estate after you are appointed, but it doesn't explain the postappointment procedures in detail. You will need to consult other resources or seek the help of a legal professional once you obtain the estate guardianship. (See Chapter 13.)

How to Use This Chapter

Here are some suggestions about how to use this chapter. This advice applies whether you are seeking guardianship of a minor's person and estate, or only guardianship of the estate:

Step 1: Follow the instructions and complete the forms in Chapters 4 and 5. You will be referred to the next section of this chapter to complete specific items pertaining to the minor's estate in the Petition for Appointment of Guardian of Minor form.

Step 2: Follow the instructions in Chapter 6 for filing guardianship papers with the court and having relatives and agencies served.

Step 3: Follow the instructions in Chapter 9 for appearing in court and being appointed guardian. Chapter 9 also explains what to do after the hearing.

Step 4: After the hearing, read "After the Guardianship Hearing" in this chapter. If you need to post bond, make deposits, or set up blocked accounts before Letters of Guardianship will be issued, follow the instructions for doing so. Once you obtain Letters of Guardianship, read "Arranging to Have Assets Transferred," below, and arrange for the transfer of assets, if applicable.

Step 5: Do your own legal research or arrange to hire a legal professional to help you handle the minor's estate and fulfill the legal reporting requirements. To help you understand and evaluate how a legal professional can help you, an overview of the court's requirements is set out below.

Step 6: If you want to use funds from the minor's estate to support the minor, read "Using Funds From the Estate for Support of the Minor," below.

Step 7: Carefully read the section in this chapter on ongoing responsibilities. There you will find an overview of your duties as guardian of a minor's estate, and your ongoing reporting responsibilities to the court. You will also need to read Chapter 11, which gives you a general overview of a guardian's responsibilities.

Completing Estate Items in the Petition

Most instructions for the Petition for Appointment of Guardian of Minor are covered in Chapter 5. However, Items 1c, 1e, 7, and 9, which pertain only to the guardianship of a minor's estate, are covered in this section.

How to Complete the Form

CAPTION: Petition for Appointment of Guardian of Minor

Remember to check the boxes to indicate whether you are seeking guardianship of the estate only, or of both the person and estate.

Item 1c: This item deals with the requirement that the guardian of a minor's estate post a "bond" (PC § 2320). A bond is basically a financial guarantee that the estate will be reimbursed if the guardian takes improper actions, such as stealing or mishandling estate funds.

If you want to be appointed guardian of the minor's estate, you will not have to post a bond if:

- both living parents nominate you as guardian and agree to waive bond and the court doesn't require otherwise (PC §§ 1500(a), 2324), or

- the estate consists of property given by another person (either while alive or through a will), and that person has requested waiver of the bond, either in a written nomination of guardian or in a will (PC §§ 1501, 2324).

If either of the above applies, check only 1c (1) "bond not be required for the reasons stated in Attachment 1c." Then prepare an "Attachment 1c" following the instructions in Chapter 3, and label it "Attachment 1c to Petition for Appointment of Guardian of Minor: Information on Bond Requirements" at the top. On Attachment 1c, state in plain and concise language why you think bond is not required, and document your reasons. For example, if a donor of property nominates you and waives bond, you might type, "Dennis Manning left real estate to the minor in his will and requested that no bond be required. A copy of the will follows this attachment." Or if both parents have waived bond and nominated

you as guardian, you might type, "Petitioner was nominated guardian by both parents, who requested that no bond be required. A copy of the nomination follows this attachment."

If the parents nominated you by signing a Nomination of Guardian as set out in Chapter 4, you will also need a document stating that the parents waive bond. On a blank piece of paper, type the words "I, *[parent's name]*, am a parent of *[minor's name]*, the subject of this guardianship. I nominate *[your name]* as guardian of the *[estate or person and estate]* of *[minor's name]*, and request that no bond be required." Have the parents sign and date the document, and make it the next page of this attachment.

If you don't qualify to have bond waived, your task becomes a little more complicated. Here's why. When attorneys handle guardianships, bond is usually acquired from surety companies—companies willing to guarantee the guardian's actions in exchange for the payment of an annual premium (usually ranging anywhere from $50 to several hundred dollars). If the minor and/or the estate are harmed, sureties generally may be sued for compensation within four years after the guardian stops serving. It's likely the sureties would then sue the guardian for reimbursement.

Unfortunately, most surety companies will not bond guardians who represent themselves in court without an attorney. A guardian who needs bond and cannot obtain it from a surety company may:

- obtain bond from personal sureties—such as friends or relatives (the bond amount must be twice as much as the amount required were a surety company used)

- deposit nonestate money, certificates of deposit, or certain bonds with the court clerk or assign an interest in financial accounts to the court clerk, or

• place funds from the minor's estate in a "blocked account"—an account that requires written permission from the court before the guardian can withdraw funds or remove assets. The amount of bond required is reduced by the sum held in blocked accounts.

If you don't qualify to have bond waived, check Box 1c(2) "$____ bond be fixed." You'll then have to calculate the amount of bond needed. If the surety is a personal one, the bond equals twice the amount required for a surety company (PC § 2320). If you need to use a surety company, you might have to ask a lawyer to help you get bond. However, the information below will help you calculate what the bond might be, and assess the assets of the estate, so that a lawyer can help you more efficiently and you'll be ready to get the bond issued.

For a surety bond or deposit with the court clerk, the amount of bond equals the estimated value of the minor's personal property, plus the estimated yearly gross income from real estate, personal property, and public benefits, plus a reasonable amount for the cost of recovery to collect on the bond, including attorneys' fees and costs. California Rule of Court 7.207 defines the cost of recovery by first separating the estates into categories—estates valued at less than $500,000 and those valued at more. If the minor's estate in your guardianship is worth more than $500,000, you should have an attorney rather than using this book.

If the estate is worth less than $500,000, the costs of recovery are ten percent (10%) of the value of the following:

• the appraised value of personal property of the estate

• the appraised value, less encumbrances, of real property of the estate that the guardian or conservator has the independent power to sell without approval or confirmation of the court (PC §§ 2590 and 2591(c)(1))

• the probable annual income from all assets of the estate, and

• the probable annual gross payments described in PC § 2320(c)(3).

To figure out the amount of bond, fill in the figures on the small worksheet that follows, using our instructions and checking the example provided. (You'll need these figures again in Item 12, so write them in on the worksheet, or on a separate piece of paper.)

Worksheet for Calculating Bond

Personal property:	$_____
Annual gross income from	
Real property:	$_____
Personal property:	$_____
Costs of recovery:	$_____
TOTAL:	
(if using surety company or making deposits with clerk)*	
	$_____

* If personal sureties are used, this amount must be doubled.

Personal property: In this blank, list the total estimated value of the minor's assets other than real estate: all bank accounts, vehicles, stocks, jewelry, antiques, and all other property. Do not have these assets appraised, because someone called a "probate referee" will be appointed by the court to appraise them (regardless of any appraisal you've had done already), so you will end up paying to have the property appraised twice.

With court permission, you can hire an independent appraiser, rather than a probate referee, to appraise a "unique, artistic, unusual or special item of tangible personal property." The procedure for doing this is beyond the scope of this book.

Important: If, aside from cash or money in bank or similar accounts, the minor does not own anything of value except to her—such as clothes and old toys—just list the total of cash and bank accounts owned in the space provided for the value of personal property. If you list a dollar amount for any personal property other than cash or money in bank accounts, that property will have to be appraised, and the estate must pay for the appraisal. Naturally this would be an unnecessary expense for old clothes and toys.

Annual gross income from real property: If the minor receives any income from real estate (for example, rent), list the amount of the annual gross income (total yearly amount received before taxes).

Annual gross income from personal property: If the minor receives any income from personal property (for example, interest on savings accounts), or public benefits, such as Social Security, indicate the amount of the annual gross income from that (total yearly amount received before taxes).

Total: Add the amounts of the personal property, the real property income, and the personal property income. Enter the total in the space provided.

EXAMPLE:

Mindy Minor has belongings worth approximately $11,000 (that do not bring in any income), a $10,000 bank account that pays 5% interest per year, and a house that rents out for $600 a month. The amount of bond, if issued by a surety company, is calculated as follows:

Personal Property		
Personal possessions ($11,000)	+	
Cash in bank account ($10,000)	=	$21,000
Annual gross income from rental property ($600 per month rental income × 12 months)	=	7,200
Annual income from bank account (5% of $10,000)	=	500
Subtotal	=	$28,700
Recovery costs (10% of subtotal)	=	$2,870
TOTAL BOND REQUIRED	=	$31,570

Next, fill in the amount of bond needed. If you plan to deposit some funds or assets in a blocked account, deduct that sum from the amount of bond required.

EXAMPLE:

Let's use the example of Mindy Minor mentioned above. Recall that $31,570 total bond is required. Mindy Minor has $10,000 cash in a bank account. If the $10,000 stays in a blocked account, the amount of bond would be reduced to $21,570 ($10,000 lower than the original $31,570).

If you're planning to use personal sureties, fill in double the amount required when a surety company is used and prepare an Attachment 1c following the instructions in Chapter 3. In Attachment 1c, specify that "Bond will be furnished by personal sureties. As provided in

Probate Code Section 2320(b), the amount of bond is for twice the amount required for a bond given by a surety company."

If you are petitioning for guardianship of the estate of more than one minor (they must be full or half brothers or sisters, or you must petition for each separately), add the figures for each minor's property to get the total amount of the bond.

Item 1c(3) applies if the minor's estate includes money or assets that you plan to keep in a blocked account during the guardianship. You can enter into a special agreement with a bank, trust company, or other financial institution to "block" an account. Blocked accounts require written permission from the court before the guardian can withdraw funds or remove assets. Some guardians prefer to establish blocked accounts because the amount of bond required is reduced by the sum in the blocked account—and annual premiums the estate would have to pay a surety company also decrease.

Assets in a blocked account typically are money or securities, but they could also include personal property such as jewelry to be held in a bank's safety deposit box. If you want to set up a blocked account as an alternative to bond, you will need to specify the name and location of the financial institution in which you expect to have the blocked account. Generally this will be the place where the account or asset is located already—otherwise, you may not be able to transfer assets without court approval. Call the financial institution and explain that you are seeking guardianship of a minor's estate and want to set up a blocked account. Then find out the procedures and fees—if any—for doing this. (Instructions on how to set up a blocked account after the judge signs an order appointing you guardian are contained in "Establishing a Blocked Account," below.)

If any money will be deposited in a blocked account, check 1c(3) and fill in the amount in the space provided in the sentence "$_____ in deposits in a blocked account be allowed." In the blank that follows, fill in the name and address of the financial institution where the blocked account will be.

Item 1e: Do not check this box. This item is checked only when you wish the court to allow you to undertake certain unusual or speculative actions in handling the minor's estate. As a guardian of the minor's estate, you normally cannot legally enter into any but the simplest investments. For example, money usually must be invested in a savings account, and real estate must be rented out for reasonable market value. If, however, you wish to operate a farm, sell off and purchase other investment property, borrow money against the minor's property for investment, lend money, exercise stock options, or hire employees on the minor's behalf, you must first apply to the court for special authority to do so, and explain why it is necessary (PC §§ 2590, 2591). This authority is known as "independent powers." This book does not cover such situations. If you think that you, as guardian of the minor's estate, will require authority to do any sophisticated investing, consult an attorney. (See Chapter 13.)

Item 7: List the total estimated value of what the minor owns. The instructions given above for Item 1c show you how to calculate the amount of bond needed; you now can use that same information in this item. If you did not calculate bond in Item 1c, follow the instructions above for completing the Worksheet for Calculating Bond printed in this book.

Then simply total the income from all sources and enter it into the space after "Annual gross income from all sources…"

Item 9: Usually, this box is not checked. The instructions to Item 1e above discuss the need for court permission to undertake certain unusual or speculative investments when handling the minor's property. If you wish to seek this sort of permission, see a lawyer.

After the Guardianship Hearing

At the guardianship hearing, the judge may name you as the minor's guardian, but require that you obtain bond or set up a blocked account before Letters of Guardianship will be issued. This section tells you how to go about fulfilling those requirements, and what to do once you've completed them.

Obtaining Bond

If you are required to post a bond, the bond amount will be reflected in the order the judge signed at the hearing. Don't obtain bond before the hearing, because the judge might raise or lower it from the amount you requested in the petition.

Surety Company

Remember that most surety companies will not bond guardians unless they are represented by an attorney. Surety companies are listed in the yellow pages under "Bond" or "Surety." If you successfully obtain bond through a surety company, get a completed Bond on Qualifying and Order document from the surety company. You may reimburse yourself from the estate for money you spend out of your own pocket for guardianship bond premiums. Keep copies of all receipts and documents pertaining to the bond. (Chapter 11 gives information on reimbursement for such expenses.)

Personal Sureties

To use personal sureties, you must find at least two friends, relatives, or business associates willing to serve. You cannot be one of the sureties. Everyone willing to serve should understand that they may be held personally liable for any damages caused by your improper actions—regardless of whether your mistakes were intentional or accidental. Although sureties may later seek reimbursement from you, they stand to lose the full amount of bond if you mismanage the estate.

All those you select must meet these requirements (Code of Civil Procedure § 995.510):

- They must be California residents who own their homes or live in California.
- They cannot be lawyers or officers of a California court.
- For bonds of $10,000 or less, each personal surety's net worth must be at least the amount of required bond in personal property, real estate, or both. Their net worth is calculated over and above all debts and liabilities and excludes property exempt from enforcement of a money judgment.
- For bonds over $10,000, three or more personal sureties may be used. Each personal surety's net worth may be less than the amount of bond as long as the total worth of all sureties is twice the amount of bond. Again, net worth is calculated over and above all debts and liabilities and excludes property exempt from enforcement of a money judgment.

Many courts have these two local forms, which you must prepare, photocopy, and file with the court:

- Bond (Personal) on Qualifying and Order: This sets out the surety's willingness to provide bond. It must be signed by a judge before being effective.

• Declaration of Personal Surety: A separate declaration must be prepared for each surety. The document gives information about the surety's assets and helps a judge decide if the surety is qualified.

Establishing a Blocked Account

The judge may have reduced the amount of bond required by allowing some assets to be placed in a blocked account. You must obtain written permission from the court before you can withdraw funds from such an account.

If you asked for a blocked account as an alternative to the bond, the name and location of the financial institution in which you expect to have the blocked account should have been specified in Item 9c of the Order Appointing Guardian of Minor.

To establish the blocked account, take a copy of the order to the financial institution, which will need to complete some paperwork to designate the account as blocked. Ask for a signed receipt showing the balance in the account and indicating that it is a blocked account. You must provide this document to the court to prove that the account is blocked. Make several copies of the blocked account receipt before you file it with the court. You may take it to the court for filing at the same time you file any bond.

Making Deposits With the Court

If you plan to make deposits with the court, contact the court and find out its procedures. The court should have its own agreement form for authorizing deposits. If the court does not have a deposit agreement for you, use the one in Appendix C.

Getting Letters of Guardianship

Once you have obtained any bond or set up blocked accounts that were required, follow the instructions in Chapter 9 for obtaining issued Letters of Guardianship. Remember to also take or send to the court the original receipts showing you have obtained bond or set up blocked accounts. Make sure you keep copies of those receipts.

Arranging to Have Assets Transferred

If a guardianship of the estate was necessary so the minor could inherit or receive assets, they may be obtained once Letters of Guardianship are issued. The institution or agency holding the assets will require certified Letters of Guardianship. Contact them to find out their procedures.

Assets with title will need to be transferred either to your name, as guardian of the estate, or to the minor's estate itself. Such assets include real estate, vehicles, stocks, bonds, securities, businesses, money market accounts, and mutual funds. Contact the title company, business, or financial institution that is holding the assets and arrange to have them transferred. If you need help having assets with title transferred, see a lawyer or do your own legal research. (See Chapter 13.)

Consult Other Resources to Meet Court Reporting Requirements

You will be required to file at least one document with the court within 90 days after the date Letters of Guardianship are issued. In this section we give you a brief overview of the court's reporting requirements. To comply

---

Timeline of Reporting Requirements for Guardianship of a Minor's Estate

- **Within three weeks from date Letters of Guardianship are issued:** Suggested date for filing Application and Order Appointing Probate Referee form with the court, if required. (Some courts appoint the referee at the hearing appointing the guardian.)
- **90 days after Letters of Guardianship are issued:** Inventory and Appraisal due.
- **After 90 days from date Letters of Guardianship are issued:** May petition court for compensation for yourself or to pay for the help of a lawyer; the court's local rules may require that you wait one year.
- **One year after Letters of Guardianship are issued:** First Accounting due.
- **Every one to two years after Letters of Guardianship are issued (or as directed by the court):** Accountings due.
- **When Guardianship is no longer needed:** Final Accounting and termination documents due; a hearing may be required. The court must give permission for the guardianship to end.

---

with these requirements on an ongoing basis, though, you should hire a legal professional. Paralegals specializing in the probate area may be your best bet, because they should know the court's special rules for financial reporting requirements. Or you can seek the help of a probate attorney. (See Chapter 13 for information on legal professionals.)

Although a bookkeeper or accountant may be useful in helping you establish a financial record-keeping system, you should inquire about the accountant's experience with court accountings. The accountant needs to know the legal requirements for reporting on estate

guardianships, which do not conform to standard accounting methods.

Most courts have probate policy manuals that govern that court's specific accounting requirements for guardianships. You will generally have to complete documents setting a hearing at which you must appear, unless the court grants otherwise. There's an overview of these procedures below.

If the minor is living with someone else, you may need that person's help in preparing the accounting records if money was spent for the minor's support. Arrange this in advance, and make sure that adult keeps track of receipts and expenditures following the guidelines in "Ongoing Responsibilities for the Guardian of a Minor's Estate," below.

Probate Referee Appraises Noncash Property

If the minor owns any real estate or personal property other than cash or accounts in financial institutions, the court will require that such property be appraised. You must use an independent court-appointed appraiser, called a "probate referee" or an "inheritance tax referee" in some counties. The court must give specific approval for written appraisals from someone other than the probate referee, before the appraisals will be accepted. Otherwise, the court-appointed probate referee must appraise the minor's noncash property. For the appraisal, the minor's estate will be charged a fee of one-tenth of 1% of the total value of the assets appraised with a minimum of $75 and generally a maximum of $10,000 (PC §§ 8961, 8963, 8964). The referee may also receive actual and necessary expenses, such as mileage for driving to inspect real estate.

The probate referee does not need to appraise money (including bank accounts, savings and loan and credit union accounts, certificates of deposit, U.S. savings bonds, and money market funds held in a brokerage house). However, the probate referee will need to appraise all other personal property, including stocks and bonds (even if its value is listed in the open stock exchange), jewelry, annuity policies, real estate, vehicles, promissory notes, business interests, coin collections, antiques, and other personal possessions.

To obtain the services of a probate referee, you will need to file an Application and Order Appointing Probate Referee form with the court. We suggest you do this within three weeks of the date Letters of Guardianship are issued.

Inventory and Appraisal

Within 90 days of the date the clerk issues Letters of Guardianship of the minor's estate, you must prepare and file with the court a Judicial Council form entitled "Inventory and Appraisal" (GC-040). In this form you give the court an inventory of all money, goods, or other property coming into your hands as guardian. In the context of this chapter, the term "money" includes bank accounts, savings and loan and credit union accounts, certificates of deposit, U.S. savings bonds, and money market funds held in a brokerage house. If the only property you're holding for the minor is money—including bank accounts—or U.S. savings bonds with a fixed redemption value, you don't need to have it appraised, but you still need to file an inventory. If there is property in the estate other than money and U.S. savings bonds, you will need to obtain a court-appointed referee to determine the value of the property.

Petitioning the Court for Compensation

You may petition the court for compensation for your services any time after the Inventory and Appraisal is filed, but it must be no sooner than 90 days of the date Letters of Guardianship were issued. If you use an attorney, you may also petition the court to compensate him for his services. Many courts require that you wait an entire year before you can be compensated, so you may make this request when you file your First Accounting as described just below. (Compensation is covered in more detail in Chapter 11.)

First Accounting

One year after the Letters of Guardianship are issued, you must file a First Accounting with the court and possibly attend a hearing. The First Accounting shows what income was received and spent during the year, what money and property you are currently handling for the minor, and any reimbursements or compensation you have received as a guardian. (See "Petitioning the Court for Compensation," just above, and Chapter 11.)

Local court accounting requirements vary, but all courts insist that you keep extremely accurate records. Some courts require a receipt for each expenditure, or only for expenditures exceeding a certain amount (often $20 or more). Original bank and brokerage house statements must be filed for the first and last months of the accounting period.

Note: If the guardianship estate has not had any activity for the entire year—for example, because all the money is in a blocked account—you can advise the court and generally obtain a waiver of accounting for one year.

Periodic Accountings

Beginning with the two-year anniversary of the date that Letters of Guardianship were issued (one year after the First Accounting is due), you must file an accounting with the court. You may also need to appear in court for a hearing on the accounting. Some courts require accountings every year, while other courts require them every two years. Depending on the court's local rules as well as the amount and nature of the estate, accountings may be required more or less frequently.

Each accounting will contain the same information described in "First Accounting," just above, but it will be entitled "Second Accounting" (and so on for each year), and will provide current information about the minor's assets. If the guardianship estate has been inactive for the entire year, you can advise the court and generally obtain a waiver of accounting for that year.

Filing Documents to End Guardianship

A guardianship of a minor's estate can be terminated when it's no longer needed, such as when:

- the minor reaches age 18 or dies
- the assets of the estate are used up, or
- the guardianship is no longer in the minor's best interests.

To end a guardianship of a minor's estate, you must file documents requesting that the guardianship be terminated with the court, along with a final accounting and documents signed by the minor confirming that the minor has received the assets that belong to her. The court may also require that you attend a hearing. Termination of guardianships is discussed in more detail in Chapter 12.

Using Funds From the Estate for Support of the Minor

If you become guardian of a minor's estate, you may be able to get court permission to use estate funds to support the minor. This varies greatly according to the situation, but here is a broad outline of how it usually works.

Guardians Who Are Parents

The law requires that parents support their minor children, regardless of whether their children are living with them (FC §§ 3550(b), 3900, 4000). Parents must typically support an unmarried child who is over 18 years of age, is a full-time high school student, and is not self-supporting (FC § 13901(a)). If you are a parent of a minor and also guardian of the minor's estate, you usually cannot use funds from the estate for the support of your child unless you have received specific permission from the court to do this. The authorization would have to be in the form of a court order. This book does not cover the procedure for obtaining an order. If this is your situation, you will need to do your own research or hire an attorney. (See Chapter 13.)

Guardians Who Are Not Parents

If you are guardian of the person and estate of a minor whose parents have died or cannot support her, you usually can use funds from the minor's estate to support and take care of her and to provide her with an education. However, you must first go to court and obtain an order allowing you to use the estate's funds either on an ongoing basis or for a given purpose (PC § 2422). We do not cover the procedure for obtaining an order in this book. If this is your situation, you will need the help of an attorney.

(See Chapter 13 for information on finding and dealing with lawyers.)

Dawn is named guardian of her nephews, Hal and Homer. The boys' parents die in an automobile crash, and Dawn obtains legal guardianships of her nephews' persons and estates. Dawn is a single mother of three children and cannot possibly support her nephews. Fortunately, Hal's and Homer's parents left them substantial assets. With the help of a lawyer, Dawn asks the court for permission to use a reasonable amount of the money from the boys' estate on an ongoing basis for their support and education. Her motion is granted. As required for a guardianship of the estate, Dawn is responsible to the court for periodic accountings.

Gerry's mother and father are divorced, and his father has left the area and remarried. For the first few years after he remarries, Gerry's father sends child support payments, but then Gerry's mother and father informally agree that the child support payments aren't needed anymore. Gerry's mother dies suddenly, and her assets pass to Gerry. Gerry's grandparents obtain guardianship of his person and estate, notifying Gerry's father of the guardianship proceeding as required by law. Gerry's father contacts the grandparents and says that he'd be willing to resume paying child support. However, Gerry's grandparents don't like Gerry's father, and they tell him they don't want his child support money. Because Gerry's grandparents both are retired and on a limited income, they seek permission from the court to use the estate's assets to support Gerry. A judge denies their request on the basis that Gerry's father can and should be paying child support. Gerry's grandparents then make arrangements to receive child support payments from his father.

Ongoing Responsibilities for the Guardian of a Minor's Estate

A guardian of an estate must keep in contact with the court until the guardianship ends. A guardian's responsibilities are covered in general in Chapter 11, which you should read and follow. In addition, you may want to use the services of a legal professional to help set up and maintain the minor's estate. (See Chapter 13.)

This section provides a brief overview of your legal responsibilities as guardian of a minor's estate. It does not give you investment advice or other suggestions about how to manage the minor's property. As an estate guardian, you must manage and protect the assets of the estate honestly and for the best interests of the minor. And just to make sure you do, the court requires you to keep it updated about the minor's property and how you've been managing it.

If you are authorized to spend money from the minor's estate to support him (see "Using Funds From the Estate for Support of the Minor," above), you must use it to provide for the "comfortable and suitable support, maintenance and education" of the minor (PC § 2420). You also are required to manage the minor's assets prudently, and not take any risks, such as speculative investing. In addition, you may not combine your money with the minor's, and you may not mismanage or do anything illegal with the minor's assets, including borrowing money for your personal use, even if you intend to pay it back. It is illegal to "borrow" money from the estate without a court order, and is considered embezzlement, regardless of your intentions to pay it back.

Minor's Assets and Accounts Must Be Kept Separate

It is absolutely fundamental to your role as a guardian that all of the minor's money, assets, and accounts are always kept separate from yours and everyone else's.

All assets belonging to the minor, including those with title (such as real estate), must either be in the name of the estate or in your name and specifying your role as guardian of the estate. Even if an asset is listed in your name as guardian of the minor's estate, remember that you are handling it for the minor—it does not belong to you.

All of the minor's accounts must be kept in the name of the minor's estate, and may not be mixed with your own. As guardian, you have authority to make deposits and withdrawals. Whenever you set up an account as estate guardian, you must provide the financial institution with a certified copy of the Letters of Guardianship. The account must be in the name of the minor's estate, with you being authorized to sign as guardian of the minor. For example, the name on the account for the minor, Mary Jones, is "Estate of Mary Jones," and the authorized signer on the account is "Joe Evans, Guardian of the Estate of Mary Jones."

 TIP

Shop around for the best banking deal. Some banks charge special fees to process guardianship bank accounts. These fees typically run about one-tenth of 1% of the amount in the account simply to open it (commonly called an "acceptance fee"), and the same percentage to close the account. It's worth checking around with different banks for one with a policy of charging little or nothing extra for guardianship accounts.

Carefully Manage the Minor's Assets

At the beginning of this section, we said that you must manage the minor's finances prudently, and not take any risks. Here are some general guidelines for taking care of the estate.

Save Receipts

You must account to the court for all expenditures you make on behalf of the minor or his estate, so keep all receipts, no matter how small the amount. You will need information on the breakdown of these expenditures for periodic accountings required by the court that tell how you managed the estate's assets. Depending on the court's policies, you may also need copies of the actual receipts. Keep the receipts in a safe, organized place such as in an envelope or file folder. Even though the court may never ask to see the original receipts, you're better off safe than sorry.

If you are authorized to spend the estate's money to support the minor, it's even more important that you keep copies of receipts for any funds you spent on that support. Depending on what the court authorized, this might include costs of the minor's food, housing, education, clothing, or medical care.

If you are not authorized to spend the estate's money to support the minor, expenditures can only pertain to your management of the estate. For example, this might include insurance premiums on the minor's assets, accountants' fees, or payments made to settle a claim.

Keep Original Documents From Financial Institutions

Keep all statements, correspondence, and other documents you get from financial institutions. You are required to attach *original* bank statements to your financial accountings.

Keep Accurate Accounting Records

You must record every transaction you make on behalf of the minor's estate, no matter how small, down to the penny. Make sure you have an accurate means of record keeping. You might want to consult with an accountant or bookkeeper about establishing a good system, and then have it reviewed periodically. Generally, reasonable accountant's fees can be paid directly by the estate. Keep copies of all receipts—you will need to give the court a breakdown and proof of these expenditures.

If possible, hire someone who is familiar with accounting requirements for guardianships. The probate court does not follow standard accounting principles in its reporting requirements. You might also want to hire a legal assistant or attorney. (See Chapter 13.)

Maintain Adequate Insurance for the Minor's Assets

You must maintain adequate insurance against fire, theft, or other possible hazards on any valuable estate property that might require it. For example, if the minor's estate includes a house and a vehicle, you would need to insure both of them. Federally insured banking facilities always should be used to deposit the minor's funds because they are considered stable. See a lawyer if you have any questions about whether to insure property the minor owns. (See Chapter 13.)

Avoid Conflict of Interest

Never get into transactions in which your own financial interests and those of the estate could conflict. Make sure that you never personally profit from the financial transactions of the estate. For example, do not purchase assets from the estate without paying a fair price. If you have any doubt about a transaction, seek court approval before undertaking it. (See "Getting Court Approval," below.)

Filing Tax Returns

As guardian of the minor's estate, you have full authority to prepare, sign, and file tax returns on behalf of the minor and the minor's estate. You may claim exemptions for the minor under applicable tax laws (PC § 2461). You can hire an accountant if you don't want to complete the tax returns yourself, and pay for these services directly out of the minor's estate. Keep copies of all receipts; you will need to give the court information about these expenditures.

Maintain Adequate Bond

When you petition to be guardian of a minor's estate, you are almost always required to post bond unless both parents waive it. This is a sort of financial guarantee that would reimburse the estate if you stole or misappropriated estate assets. (How to apply for a bond is discussed above. Information on seeking reimbursement by the estate for bond premiums is covered in Chapter 11.)

During the entire time of the guardianship, you must have the appropriate bond amount. If the assets of the estate increase or decrease substantially, you must adjust the amount of bond by going to court for an order allowing the change in the amount of bond.

Getting Court Approval

As guardian of a minor's estate, you are not given freedom to do whatever you think is appropriate with the estate's assets. It is common for a guardian of a minor's estate to be a little uncertain about the legal or ethical propriety of a transaction. A guardian can sometimes be held personally liable for mismanaging a minor's estate, so it pays to be cautious. Fortunately, if you are concerned about a questionable transaction, you can always ask the court beforehand for legal permission to undertake that action (PC § 2403). You must follow certain procedures and give notice to people entitled to it before you can undertake any substantial financial transactions such as:

- selling, purchasing, or undertaking any action that involves the estate's real property (PC § 2501, PC §§ 2463–2464)

- compromising or settling a claim against the estate for more than $25,000 (PC § 2502)

- becoming personally involved in a trans-action, such as settling a claim by the minor against you or changing the terms of a debt you owe to the minor or her estate (PC § 2503)

- settling a wrongful death or personal injury claim (PC § 2504)

- borrowing or lending money on behalf of the estate (PC § 2550), or

- purchasing an automobile for the minor. That might require proof of car insurance and court approval.

Court approval is not mandatory if a lease is being extended, renewed, or modified, as long as its unexpired term is two years or less and the monthly rental amount is less than $750, or the lease is month-to-month. A guardian also does not need a court order to maintain or make repairs on the house where the minor lives (PC § 2457) if the minor owns the house.

This book does not cover the procedures for obtaining court approval of estate transactions. See Chapter 13 for information on how to find and deal with lawyers.

Receiving Benefits and Reporting to Agencies

Sometimes a guardianship of a minor's estate includes receiving and expending money or benefits from an agency that requires periodic accountings to show how the money has been spent. In such a situation, you must comply with the organization's requirements.

For example, the Veterans Administration is almost certain to require accountings. Social Security and other agencies may also require them. These reports do not get filed with the court. However, you may want to attach them as exhibits to your accountings.

Reimbursements and Compensation of the Guardian

With court approval, a guardian may be reimbursed or compensated for expenses incurred personally in taking care of a minor's estate, or for time spent taking care of a minor's estate. (See Chapter 11.)

Minors Cannot Sign Contracts

Minors are normally not permitted to make contracts on their own (CC § 1556). If they do, these contracts are not usually legally valid. As guardian, you are not responsible for any contracts the minor might sign, unless you enter into the contract as a cosigner. In certain situations the minor may obtain counseling or medical treatment without a guardian's consent, and the guardian is not liable for the cost of such services (FC §§ 6920–6929). ●

Now That You're a Guardian: Rights and Responsibilities

Y ou probably turned to this chapter because you have obtained a court-ordered legal guardianship. Congratulations! You have put in time and effort to accomplish this task. Now that you're a guardian, you have certain rights and responsibilities. These will vary, depending upon whether you are guardian of a minor's person, estate, or both.

Note: You may notice that the minor for whom you're a guardian is referred to as a "ward" in legal documents or by the court. This is simply the legal terminology for a minor who has a legal guardian.

What to Do With Letters of Guardianship

Letters of Guardianship are legal proof that you are the guardian of a minor. Any time you need to show anyone that you are the minor's legal guardian, simply provide a copy of the Letters of Guardianship. Naturally, if you obtained a guardianship because an agency or institution insisted on one, you should now take or send to the organization a copy of the Letters of Guardianship.

Many organizations will ask for the court order instead of, or in addition to, the Letters of Guardianship. Even though that's not technically correct under the law, it's generally easier to give over copies of both the order and the Letters of Guardianship if that's what's requested.

It's possible to make photocopies of the Letters of Guardianship, but you may have problems getting others to accept them as legal proof of your status, because photocopies could be altered and are not considered official copies of court documents. It's better to get certified copies stamped with the court's seal by following the instructions in Chapter 9. Certified copies are free if you cannot afford to pay court fees and had fees waived by the court. Keep extra certified copies in a convenient, safe place.

Responsibilities of Guardians of a Minor's Estate

If you are guardian of a minor's estate only, you may skip the next section of this chapter, but you will need to read all of Chapter 10. If you are guardian of both a minor's person and estate you will need to read both this entire chapter and Chapter 10.

Responsibilities of Guardians of a Minor's Person

The discussion in this section only covers responsibilities of a guardian of a minor's person.

Taking Care of the Minor

As guardian of a minor's person, you have legal custody of the minor. You now have a legal duty to take care of the minor, something you were probably doing even before being appointed guardian. As guardian, you are responsible for the basic needs of the minor, which includes providing the minor with food, shelter, and health care, as well as taking charge of the minor's educational and emotional development. And, no doubt, you will also be giving the minor a lot of loving care. If you are guardian of the minor's person and estate, the minor's funds cannot be used to support the minor without prior court approval. This subject is covered in more detail in Chapter 10.

Residence for the Minor

As legal guardian, you must have an established residence for the minor in California, usually at your home, but possibly at a boarding school.

You must obtain court permission before you can move the minor to a residence outside of California. That requires filing papers with the court, serving the people who are entitled to notice, attending a hearing, and getting an order signed by the court. If you don't obtain an order from the court, it may, at its discretion, require the minor to be returned to California. A legal action could also be brought against you for breaking the law. The court can require guardianship proceedings to be conducted in any other place a minor is living for four or more months (PC § 2352). If you plan to move the minor out of California, you'll need to hire a lawyer or do your own legal research to make sure you comply with the law. (See Chapter 13.)

Medical Treatment

In general, you have the same right as a parent to consent to and require medical treatment for the minor. For example, you can take the minor to the doctor or dentist for routine examinations and medical treatment. And you usually have the right to add the minor to your health insurance plan.

There are several exceptions to your right to give consent for the minor's medical treatment. Except in emergencies, surgical procedures usually require the consent of both you and the minor, if the minor is 14 years of age or older (PC § 2353(b)). As guardian, you cannot involuntarily place the minor in a mental health treatment facility unless she is a danger to herself or others or is gravely disabled (PC § 2356(a), W&I § 5150). There are also laws that prevent a guardian from allowing a minor to be treated with experimental drugs, given convulsive treatment, or sterilized. If the minor needs medical or psychological treatment that falls into any of these categories, you will need to obtain an order from the court and will require the help of an attorney. (See Chapter 13.)

Receiving Benefits

As guardian of the minor's person, you may receive public assistance, Social Security, or other benefits for the minor. Any funds received are to be used for the minor's benefit, and some of these agencies require accountings in which you show how you spent the money. You may also be required to account to the court for these funds.

Liabilities

Along with a legal guardianship comes some liability. Like parents, legal guardians may have to pay for a minor's actions. For example:

- If the minor intentionally does something wrong (called "willful misconduct" in legal lingo) that results in injury or death to another person, or damage to property (such as spray painting or defacing property), you could be held liable for damages in an amount up to $25,000 (CC § 1714.1).

- If the minor shoplifts or steals library materials, you could be held liable for between $50 and $1,000 plus the actual value of the merchandise or books (Penal Code § 490.5). Some courts will allow you to perform public service instead of paying a fine. Your liabilities are not limited to a $50 to $500 fine if the law allows for other remedies.

- If you sign the minor's driver's license application or give the minor permission—either express or implied—to drive a vehicle and the minor is involved in an accident, you could be liable to pay for injuries or death as a result of the accident. The amount of damages for one accident could be up to $15,000 for the injury or death of one person and up to $30,000 for the injury or death of everyone involved in the accident. Additionally, you could be liable for property damages up to $5,000 as a result of the accident (Vehicle Code §§ 17707–17709).

- If the minor injures or kills someone by discharging a firearm, you could be held liable for damages in an amount up to $30,000 for the injury or death of one person, or up to $60,000 for injury or death to more than one person (CC § 1714.3). If you were negligent—for example, by leaving a gun where the minor would have access to it—you could have additional liability.

Visitation Rights

This book is not intended to resolve disputes over child custody or visitation rights. The minor's parents' visitation rights are not taken away simply because someone else is the minor's guardian. In addition, where only a temporary guardianship is ordered, anyone with court-ordered visitation rights keeps those rights unless the court orders otherwise (PC § 2250(e)).

Even after a guardian has been named, an adult may seek visitation rights by filing papers in the guardianship court case. If this situation arises in any guardianship in which you are involved, you will need to see a lawyer. (See Chapter 13.)

Minors Cannot Sign Contracts

Minors are normally not permitted to make contracts on their own (CC § 1556). If they do, these contracts are not usually legally valid. As guardian, you are not responsible for any contracts the minor might sign, unless you

enter into the contract as a cosigner. In certain situations the minor may obtain counseling or medical treatment without a guardian's consent, and the guardian is not liable for the cost of such services (FC §§ 6920–6929).

Responsibilities to the Court

Notify Court About Address Changes

As legal guardian, you must notify the court if either you or the minor move. As long as you're moving within California, this simply involves filling out two forms, having copies served, and filing the forms with the court.

CAUTION

There are special procedures you must follow if you plan to move the minor out of California. (See "Residence for the Minor," above.) However, if you are moving the minor to another California county, the guardianship case can be transferred following the procedures in the next section of this chapter.

Pre-Move Notice of Proposed Change of Personal Residence of Ward

You must notify the court both before and after you change the minor's residence within California. Before you move, use this form, a blank copy of which is in Appendix C and a sample of which is below.

How to Complete the Form

CAPTION: Pre-Move Notice of Proposed Change of Personal Residence of Ward

Fill in the caption following the general instructions in Chapter 3. In the title section, check the box before the word "Ward (name)," and type the name of the minor.

Sample Pre-Move Notice of Proposed Change of Personal Residence of Ward, page 1

GC-079

ATTORNEY OR PARTY WITHOUT ATTORNEY *(Name, State Bar number, and address):*	FOR COURT USE ONLY
Patricia Ann Lee 2 West Street Santa Ana, CA 92702 TELEPHONE NO.: 714-555-1212 FAX NO. *(Optional):* E-MAIL ADDRESS *(Optional):* ATTORNEY FOR *(Name):* In Pro Per	

SUPERIOR COURT OF CALIFORNIA, COUNTY OF Orange
STREET ADDRESS: 700 Civic Center Drive West
MAILING ADDRESS: Santa Ana, CA 92702
CITY AND ZIP CODE:
BRANCH NAME:

☐ CONSERVATORSHIP ☑ GUARDIANSHIP OF THE PERSON ☐ AND ESTATE OF

(Name): Daniel Frank Lee

☐ CONSERVATEE ☑ MINOR

PRE-MOVE NOTICE OF PROPOSED CHANGE OF PERSONAL RESIDENCE OF ☐ CONSERVATEE ☑ WARD *(Name):* Daniel Frank Lee	CASE NUMBER: 12357

INFORMATION FOR CONSERVATOR OR GUARDIAN OF THE PERSON:

(1) You must mail, **at least 15 days before the date of the proposed move** (unless you can show that an emergency requires a shorter time), a notice of your intention to change your conservatee's or ward's **personal residence** (his or her residence as defined in rules 7.1063(b) or 7.1013(b) of the Cal. Rules of Court) to the conservatee, the ward if 12 years of age or older, the conservatee's or ward's attorney; and **(a) in a conservatorship,** the conservatee's spouse or registered domestic partner; and the conservatee's relatives named in the petition for appointment of a conservator in your case (the conservatee's second-degree relatives, or if there are no spouse, registered domestic partner, and second-degree relatives, the persons named in Probate Code section 1821(b)(1)–(4) as the conservatee's "deemed relatives"); or **(b) in a guardianship,** the ward's parents; any person who had legal custody of the ward when the first petition for appointment of a guardian was filed in your case, the guardian of the ward's estate, and any person nominated as a guardian for the ward who was not appointed. **Use copies of this form for the notice described above. File the original of the notice form with the court and show proof of mailing. See page 2 of this form for proof of mailing. If there is more than one ward in your case, file and mail copies of a separate form for each ward moved.** (See rules 7.1013(a) and (b), or 7.1063(a) and (b) of the Cal. Rules of Court.)

(2) You must also give notice to the court and others, **after the move,** of any change in the conservatee's or ward's residence within the State of California. **Do not use this form for that notice.** Use form GC-080, *Post-Move Notice of Change of Residence of Conservatee or Ward,* for that notice. (See rules 7.1013(c)–(e), and 7.1063(c)–(e) of the Cal. Rules of Court.)

(3) You must obtain court permission **before** the conservatee or ward can move to a new residence outside California.

NOTICE IS GIVEN as follows:

1. I intend to change the above-named conservatee's or ward's personal residence on *(date):* September 1, 2009

2. The conservatee's or ward's residence address after the move will be *(street address, including residence or facility name and room or apartment number, if any, and city, county, and zip code):*

   2349 Brown Avenue
   Santa Ana, CA 94702

3. The new residence will be a *(describe type of residence or facility, for example, single family residence; apartment or condominium; board and care, intermediate care, or skilled nursing):*

4. ☐ I cannot give at least 15 days' notice of this intended change because of the emergency described below *(specify):*

   ☐ Continued on Attachment 4. *(State name of this case, case number, and title of this form on the top of attached page.)*

Date: August 3, 20xx

I declare under penalty of perjury under the laws of the State of California that the foregoing is true and correct.

Patricia Ann Lee ▶

(TYPE OR PRINT NAME OF CONSERVATOR OR GUARDIAN)   (SIGNATURE OF CONSERVATOR OR GUARDIAN)   Page 1 of 2

Form Adopted for Mandatory Use Judicial Council of California GC-079 [New January 1, 2008]	**PRE-MOVE NOTICE OF PROPOSED CHANGE OF PERSONAL RESIDENCE OF CONSERVATEE OR WARD** (Probate—Guardianships and Conservatorships)	Probate Code, § 2352 Cal. Rules of Court, rules 7.1013, 7.1063 *www.courtinfo.ca.gov*

Sample Pre-Move Notice of Proposed Change of Personal Residence of Ward, page 2

GC-079

☐ CONSERVATORSHIP ☑ GUARDIANSHIP OF THE PERSON ☐ AND ESTATE OF	CASE NUMBER:
(Name): Daniel Frank Lee	12357
☐ CONSERVATEE ☑ MINOR	

PROOF OF MAILING

1. I am over the age of 18. I am the appointed conservator or guardian of the above-named conservatee or ward, the conservator's or guardian's attorney, or an employee of the attorney. I am a resident of or employed in the county where the mailing occurred.

2. My residence or business address is (specify):

3. I mailed the foregoing *Pre-Move Notice of Proposed Change of Personal Residence of Conservatee or Ward* to each person named below by enclosing a copy in an envelope addressed as shown below AND

   a. ☑ **depositing** the sealed envelope on the date and at the place shown in item 4 with the United States Postal Service with the postage fully prepaid.

   b. ☐ **placing** the envelope for collection and mailing on the date and at the place shown in item 4 following our ordinary business practices. I am readily familiar with this business's practice for collecting and processing correspondence for mailing. On the same day that correspondence is placed for collection and mailing, it is deposited in the ordinary course of business with the United States Postal Service in a sealed envelope with postage fully prepaid.

4. a. Date mailed: August 3, 20xx   b. Place mailed (city, state): Santa Ana, CA

I declare under penalty of perjury under the laws of the State of California that the foregoing is true and correct.

Date: August 3, 20xx

Patricia Ann Lee   ▶

_____   _____
(TYPE OR PRINT NAME OF PERSON COMPLETING THIS FORM)   (SIGNATURE OF PERSON COMPLETING THIS FORM)

NAME AND ADDRESS OF EACH PERSON TO WHOM NOTICE WAS MAILED

Name and relationship to conservatee or ward	Address (number, street, city, state, and zip code)
1. Daniel Frank Lee Conservatee or ward at least 12 years of age	2 West Street, Santa Ana, CA 92702
2. Attorney for conservatee or ward	
3. Spouse or domestic partner of conservatee	
4. Martin Lee Parent of ward	2501 Hyde Street, San Francisco, CA 94109
5. Parent of ward	

☐ Continued on an attachment. *(You may use form GC-079 (MA) to show additional addressees.)*

GC-079 [New January 1, 2008]	**PRE-MOVE NOTICE OF PROPOSED CHANGE OF PERSONAL RESIDENCE OF CONSERVATEE OR WARD** (Probate—Guardianships and Conservatorships)	Page 2 of 2

Item 1: Fill in the date you expect to move.

Item 2: Fill in the address where you intend to move with the minor.

Item 3: Fill in the type of place the minor will be living—usually either a house or apartment.

Item 4: If you're moving sooner than 15 days from the date you're filling in the form, check this box and either fill in your reasons in the small space provided, or check the box in front of the words "Continued on Attachment 4," and prepare an Attachment 4. Your reasons might be that your job required you to move with no warning, or that your apartment has become uninhabitable.

Fill in the date the form was completed, type or print your name, and sign your name in the spaces provided.

Page 2: Pre-Move Notice of Proposed Change of Personal Residence of Ward

CAPTION: At the top of page two, check the box before the word "Guardianship," and, if your guardianship is of the estate as well as the person, check the box in front of the word "Estate." Fill in the minor's full name and check the box before the word "Minor."

Proof of Mailing: The second page of this form is a proof of service form on which you will indicate that you served the appropriate people with the notice of your intention to move. The people you have to serve are listed in the information box on the first page of the form, and the list is much more limited than the list of people you had to serve with the guardianship petition. For this document, you need only serve the minor's parents, any person who had legal custody of the minor at the time you filed your original petition, and any person who was nominated as guardian but not appointed (in other words, someone you beat out for the position).

Item 1: There's nothing to fill out for this item.

Item 2: Fill in your home or work address.

Item 3: Check the appropriate box depending on whether you sent copies of the notice by putting them directly into a mailbox (Item 3a), or put them in the outgoing mail at your work (Item 3b).

Item 4: Fill in the date mailed and the city and state where you mailed the notice.

Name and Address: Under the heading "Name and Address of Each Person to Whom Notice Was Mailed," fill in the required information. Each of the boxes numbers 1 through 5 calls for the name and relationship to the minor of each person you're serving, and lists the persons who must get notice.

Item 1: If the minor is 12 or older, list the minor's name under this item, and put in the address where you mailed the notice to the minor—probably your current address rather than the address to which you're moving.

Item 2: Leave this item blank.

Item 3: Leave this item blank.

Items 4 and 5: If both of the minor's parents are living, include their names and addresses here.

If you do have to serve someone else who had legal custody of the minor at the time you filed your petition, or another person who sought guardianship, you'll have to check the box at the bottom of the form that says "Continued on an attachment," and prepare an attachment using Form GC-079(MA), a copy of which is in Appendix C.

Make enough copies of the form to mail a copy to each person you have listed; put those copies in the mail and then sign the Proof of Mailing. Then make copies of the form and file them with the court following the instructions in Chapter 3.

Post-Move Notice of Change of Personal Residence of Ward

Once you have moved, you must notify the court and the people entitled to notice that the move actually occurred and that you and the minor are settled in at the new address. This form is very similar to the pre-move notice, but not exactly the same.

How to Complete the Form

CAPTION: Post-Move Notice of Change of Personal Residence of Ward

Fill in the caption following the general instructions in Chapter 3. In the title section, check the box before the word "Ward (name)," and type the name of the minor.

Item 1: Fill in the date you and the minor moved in to your new home.

Item 2: Fill in the new address.

Item 3: Leave this box blank, as it is only for conservatorships.

Fill in the date the form was completed, type or print your name, and sign your name in the spaces provided.

Page 2: Post-Move Notice of Change of Personal Residence of Ward

CAPTION: At the top of page two, check the box before the word "Guardianship," and, if your guardianship is of the estate as well as the person, check the box in front of the word "Estate." Fill in the minor's full name and check the box before the word "Minor."

Proof of Mailing: The second page of this form is a proof of service form on which you will indicate that you served the appropriate people with the notice of your intention to move. You must serve the same people you served with the pre-move notice (if you didn't fill out a pre-move notice, see the instructions above).

Item 1: There's nothing to fill out for this item.

Item 2: Fill in your home or work address.

Item 3: Check the appropriate box depending on whether you sent copies of the notice by putting them directly into a mailbox (Item 3a), or put them in the outgoing mail at your work (Item 3b).

Item 4: Fill in the date mailed and the city and state where you mailed the notice.

Name and Address: Under the heading "Name and Address of Each Person to Whom Notice Was Mailed," fill in the required information. Each of the boxes numbers 1 through 5 calls for the name and relationship to the minor of each person you're serving, and lists the persons who must get notice.

Item 1: If the minor is 12 or older, list the minor's name under this item, and put in the address where you mailed the notice to the minor—probably your current address rather than the address to which you're moving.

Item 2: Leave this item blank.

Item 3: Leave this item blank.

Items 4 and 5: If both of the minor's parents are living, include their names and addresses here.

If you do have to serve someone else who had legal custody of the minor at the time you filed your petition, or another person who sought guardianship, you'll have to check the box at the bottom of the form that says "Continued on an attachment," and prepare an attachment using Form GC-080(MA), a copy of which is in Appendix C.

Make enough copies of the form to mail a copy to each person you have listed; put those copies in the mail and then sign the Proof of Mailing. Then make copies of the form and file them with the court following the instructions in Chapter 3.

Sample Post-Move Notice of Change of Personal Residence of Ward, page 1

GC-080

ATTORNEY OR PARTY WITHOUT ATTORNEY *(Name, State Bar number, and address):*

Patricia Ann Lee
2349 Brown Avenue
Santa Ana, CA 92702
TELEPHONE NO.: 714-555-1212   FAX NO. *(Optional):*
E-MAIL ADDRESS *(Optional):*
ATTORNEY FOR *(Name):* In Pro Per

FOR COURT USE ONLY

SUPERIOR COURT OF CALIFORNIA, COUNTY OF Orange
STREET ADDRESS: 700 Civic Center Drive West
MAILING ADDRESS:
CITY AND ZIP CODE: Santa Ana, CA 92702
BRANCH NAME:

☐ CONSERVATORSHIP ☑ GUARDIANSHIP OF THE PERSON ☐ AND ESTATE OF
(Name): Daniel Frank Lee

☐ CONSERVATEE ☑ MINOR

POST-MOVE NOTICE OF CHANGE OF RESIDENCE OF ☐ **CONSERVATEE**

☑ **WARD** *(Name):* Daniel Frank Lee

CASE NUMBER:
12357

INFORMATION FOR CONSERVATOR OR GUARDIAN OF THE PERSON:

(1) Every time your conservatee or ward moves to a new residence in California, you must, **within 30 days of the date of the move**, give written notice of the change to the court and, unless the court excuses you for good cause to prevent harm to the conservatee or ward, mail a copy of the notice to the attorney for the conservatee or ward; and **(a) in a conservatorship**, mail copies of the notice to the conservatee's spouse or registered domestic partner and the conservatee's relatives named in the petition for appointment of a conservator in your case (the conservatee's second-degree relatives, or if there is no spouse, registered domestic partner, and second-degree relatives, the persons named in Probate Code section 1821(b)(1)–(4) as the conservatee's "deemed relatives"); or **(b) in a guardianship**, mail copies of the notice to the ward's parents, any person who had legal custody of the ward when the first petition for appointment of a guardian was filed in your case, the guardian of the ward's estate, and any person nominated as a guardian for the ward who was not appointed.

(2) **Use this form for the notice described above.** Do not mail a copy to the conservatee or ward. To give notice to the court, file the original of this form after filling out the proof of mailing on the second page. (See rules 7.1013(c) and (d), or 7.1063(c) and (d) of the Cal. Rules of Court.) If there is more than one ward in your case, file and mail copies of a separate form for each ward moved.

(3) You must also give notice, **before the move**, of an intent to move the conservatee or ward from his or her personal residence (as defined in rules 7.1063(b) and 7.1013(b) of the Cal. Rules of Court). **Do not use this form for that notice.** Use form GC-079, *Pre-Move Notice of Proposed Change of Personal Residence of Conservatee or Ward*, for that notice.

(4) You must obtain court permission **before** the conservatee or ward can move to a new residence outside California.

NOTICE IS GIVEN as follows:

1. On *(date):* September 1, 20xx the conservatee or ward named above moved to the residence described in item 2.

2. New address *(street address, city, county, and zip code):*
   2349 Brown Avenue, Santa Ana, CA 92702
   Telephone number: 714-555-1212   Other contact telephone number, if any *(if none, write "None"):* 714-201-0101

3. ☐ *(Check this box if this case is a conservatorship.)* The conservatee's new residence identified in 2 is the least restrictive appropriate residence that is available to meet his or her needs and is in the conservatee's best interest.

Date: September 5, 20xx

I declare under penalty of perjury under the laws of the State of California that the foregoing is true and correct.

Patricia Ann Lee
_____   ▶   _____
(TYPE OR PRINT NAME OF CONSERVATOR OR GUARDIAN)   (SIGNATURE OF CONSERVATOR OR GUARDIAN)

Page 1 of 2

Form Adopted for Mandatory Use
Judicial Council of California
GC-080 [Rev. January 1, 2008]

**POST-MOVE NOTICE OF CHANGE OF RESIDENCE
OF CONSERVATEE OR WARD**
(Probate—Guardianships and Conservatorships)

Probate Code, § 2352
Cal. Rules of Court, rules 7.1013, 7.1063
www.courtinfo.ca.gov

Sample Post-Move Notice of Change of Personal Residence of Ward, page 2

GC-080

☐ CONSERVATORSHIP ☑ GUARDIANSHIP OF THE PERSON ☐ AND ESTATE OF	CASE NUMBER:
(Name): Daniel Frank Lee	12357
☐ CONSERVATEE ☑ MINOR	

PROOF OF MAILING

1. I am over the age of 18. I am the appointed conservator or guardian of the above-named conservatee or ward, the conservator's or guardian's attorney, or an employee of the attorney. I am a resident of or employed in the county where the mailing occurred.

2. My residence or business address is *(specify)*:
   2349 Brown Avenue, Santa Ana, CA 92702

3. I mailed the foregoing *Post-Move Notice of Change of Residence of Conservatee or Ward* to each person named below by enclosing a copy in an envelope addressed as shown below AND

   a. ☑ **depositing** the sealed envelope on the date and at the place shown in item 4 with the United States Postal Service with the postage fully prepaid.

   b. ☐ **placing** the envelope for collection and mailing on the date and at the place shown in item 4 following our ordinary business practices. I am readily familiar with this business's practice for collecting and processing correspondence for mailing. On the same day that correspondence is placed for collection and mailing, it is deposited in the ordinary course of business with the United States Postal Service in a sealed envelope with postage fully prepaid.

4. a. Date mailed: September 5, 20xx   b. Place mailed *(city, state):* Santa Ana, California

I declare under penalty of perjury under the laws of the State of California that the foregoing is true and correct.

Date: September 5, 20xx

Patricia Ann Lee

▶

(TYPE OR PRINT NAME OF PERSON COMPLETING THIS FORM)	(SIGNATURE OF PERSON COMPLETING THIS FORM)

NAME AND ADDRESS OF EACH PERSON TO WHOM NOTICE WAS MAILED

Name and relationship to conservatee or ward	Address *(number, street, city, state, and zip code)*
1. Attorney for conservatee or ward	
2. Spouse or registered domestic partner of conservatee	
3. Martin Lee Parent of ward	2501 Hyde Street, San Francisco, CA 94109
4. Parent of ward	
5. Person with legal custody of ward at beginning of this proceeding	

☐ Continued on an attachment. *(You may use form GC-080(MA) to show additional addressees.)*

GC-080 [Rev. January 1, 2008]

POST-MOVE NOTICE OF CHANGE OF RESIDENCE OF CONSERVATEE OR WARD
(Probate—Guardianships and Conservatorships)

Page 2 of 2

Court Proceedings and Special Notice

During the guardianship, you might need to go to court to obtain permission to do something. This typically applies only to guardianships of the estate (see Chapter 10), but occasionally it may be needed for guardianships of the person if you want to:

- have the guardianship case transferred to a different California court
- move the minor outside of California
- place the minor in a mental health treatment facility, or
- insist the minor receive involuntary medical treatment.

All of these situations are covered in "Responsibilities of Guardians of a Minor's Person," above.

If you go to court to obtain permission to do anything listed above, you must serve all the relatives listed on the Guardianship Notification Worksheet as well as anyone who filed a document requesting special notice of these hearings (PC § 2700). This request should have been mailed to you by the person filing such a Request for Special Notice. You will also need to follow specific procedures for filing papers, attending a hearing, and obtaining an order. We do not give instructions for most of those types of court proceedings in this book. (See Chapter 13 for information about doing your own legal research and hiring a lawyer.)

Transferring the Guardianship to Another California Court

If you and the minor move to another county, you may need to obtain a guardianship in a court in that county. Certain agencies (for example, public assistance agencies in some counties) may require a guardianship in their own county before they will give benefits. This process for transferring the guardianship to another court may be followed either before or after the guardian has been appointed by the court.

As petitioner or guardian, you are entitled by law to have the guardianship transferred to another court, as long as it is in the best interests of the minor and the minor's estate. You will need to complete and have several forms served, appear at a court hearing, and pay court fees to have the case transferred. Here's how to have your guardianship case transferred.

Call the Court

Call the court from which you are transferring the case—*not* the new court to which you want the case moved. Say you're filing a petition to have the guardianship proceeding transferred, and ask whether you can obtain a hearing date over the phone. If you can get a hearing date, obtain one at least 25 days away—you'll need to have papers served at least 20 days before the hearing takes place. If you can't get the hearing date now, you will get one when you file your papers with the court. Next, ask the court clerk what fees the old court charges for transferring your case, and whether the fees must be paid when you file your papers. If you are guardian of a minor's estate, the fees for transferring the case will be paid out of the minor's estate.

Note: You must also pay a fee to the new court when your papers are transferred.

You're now ready to complete the forms required to have the case transferred.

Complete Petition for Transfer of Guardianship Proceeding

In this petition, you tell the court why the guardianship case should be transferred to another court.

How to Complete the Form

CAPTION: Petition for Transfer of Guardianship Proceeding

Fill in the caption following the general instructions in Chapter 3.

Item 1: In the blanks, fill in your name and the county to which you want the case transferred. If the new court has a district or branch name, put it after the name of the county (for example, "Santa Clara, North County Branch"). Then in your own words state why the case should be transferred. For example, this might be "Andrew Smith and I moved to Santa Clara County in January 2011. I applied for TANF, and was informed that I cannot obtain benefits unless the guardianship is transferred to this county. It would be in the minor's best interests for me to obtain TANF benefits to help support him."

Item 2: Check the first box before the word "guardian" if you have already been appointed guardian by the court and have obtained issued Letters of Guardianship. Check the second box before the words "proposed guardian" if you have petitioned to be guardian but have not yet been appointed. Then check the box next to the words "person," "estate," or both, depending on the type of guardianship you have or are seeking. In the blank space, fill in the minor's name exactly as it appears on the other guardianship papers.

Item 3: Skip this entire item (3, 3a, and 3b) if you are the guardian or proposed guardian of the minor's person only. Otherwise, check the first box before the word "guardian" if you have already been appointed guardian of the minor's estate by the court and have obtained issued Letters of Guardianship. Check the second box before the words "proposed guardian" if you have petitioned to be guardian of the minor's estate but have not yet been appointed.

Item 3a: Check this box only if the space provided gives enough room for you to list the estate's property. Then list and briefly describe each piece of property, tell its approximate value, and where it is located.

Item 3b: Check this box if you need additional space to list the minor's property. Prepare and label an Attachment 3b to this petition, following the instructions in Chapter 3. Then list and briefly describe each piece of property, and tell its approximate value and where it is located.

Item 4: In the space provided, fill in your name and current residence address.

Item 5: In the space provided, fill in the minor's name and current residence address.

Item 6: In this item, list the names and addresses of the minor's close relatives. Follow the instructions for listing these relatives covered in Item 18 of the Petition for Appointment of Guardian of Minor in Chapter 5.

Item 7: In addition to the relatives listed in Item 6, just above, anyone who has filed a document with the court requesting special notice of further hearings must get a copy of this petition. If you aren't sure whether someone filed a request for special notice, call the court. Give the clerk the case name and file number, and ask the clerk to pull the file and see whether special notice was requested. If it was, get the names and addresses of anyone who filed a request for special notice.

Sample Petition for Transfer of Guardianship Proceeding

PARTY WITHOUT AN ATTORNEY *(Name and Address):* TELEPHONE NO:	FOR COURT USE ONLY
ANGELO MARTIN FREDERICKS 916-555-1212 222 Any Street Yreka, CA 96097 *In Pro Per*	

NAME OF COURT: SISKIYOU SUPERIOR COURT
STREET ADDRESS: 311 4th Street
MAILING ADDRESS: P.O. Box 338
CITY AND ZIP CODE: Yreka, CA 96097
BRANCH NAME:

GUARDIANSHIP OF THE ☒ PERSON ☐ ESTATE OF (NAME):

JOE GEORGE FREDERICKS

MINOR

PETITION FOR TRANSFER OF GUARDIANSHIP PROCEEDING	CASE NUMBER: 2001

1. Petitioner (name): ____ANGELO MARTIN FREDERICKS____ requests that this guardianship proceeding be transferred to the Superior Court of the State of California, County of ____SHASTA____.

Such transfer would be in the best interests of the ward for the following reason(s):
The minor and I are moving to Redding, California, on 9/1/09. In order to register him in school and obtain welfare benefits, I need a guardianship in Shasta County, the county in which we'll be living.

2. Petitioner is the ☒ guardian or ☐ proposed guardian of the:
☒ person ☐ estate of JOE GEORGE FREDERICKS____.

3. ☐ Petitioner is the ☐ guardian or ☐ proposed guardian of the estate in this proceeding. The character, value, and location of the estate's property:

   a. ☐ is as follows:

   b. ☐ is described in Attachment 3a.

4. The guardian's name and address are: ____ANGELO MARTIN FREDERICKS, 222 Any Street,____ Yreka, CA 96097

5. The ward's name and address are: ____JOE GEORGE FREDERICKS, 222 Any Street,____ Yreka, CA 96097

6. The names, residence addresses, and relationships of the ward's father, mother, spouse, and all relatives within the second degree of the ward so far as known to petitioner are as follows:

   a. Father: ____Gene Fredericks, 440 Another Street, Yreka, CA 96097____

   b. Mother: ____Ann Fredericks, Deceased____

   c. Spouse: ____None____

   d. ____Brother: Andrew Fredericks, 111 City Street, Los Angeles, CA 90012____

   e. ☒ List of names and addresses continued as Attachment 6.

7. A request for special notice:

   a. ☒ has not been filed.

   b. ☐ has been filed, and notice of hearing on this petition will be given by law to: _____

8. Petitioner requests an order transferring this proceeding to the Superior Court of the State of California, County of ____Shasta____.

   I declare under penalty of perjury under the laws of the State of California that the foregoing is true and correct.

Date: 3/3/xx

ANGELO MARTIN FREDERICKS	*Angelo Martin Fredericks*
(TYPE OR PRINT NAME)	(SIGNATURE OF PETITIONER)

NP   **PETITION FOR TRANSFER OF GUARDIANSHIP PROCEEDING**

Item 7a: If no request for special notice was filed, check this box.

Item 7b: If a request for special notice was filed any time after you filed your initial guardianship papers, check this box and in the space provided, fill in the name and address of each person who requested the special notice.

Item 8: In the blank after the words "County of," again fill in the name of the county where you want the case transferred. If the new court has a district or branch name, put it after the name of the county.

Sign and date the form in the spaces indicated, and print or type your name.

Complete (Proposed) Order for Transfer of Guardianship Proceeding

Before the guardianship proceeding can be transferred to another court, a judge must sign an order.

How to Complete the Form

CAPTION: Order for Transfer of Guardianship Proceeding

Fill in the caption following the general instructions in Chapter 3.

Item 1: In this item, state when the hearing will be held and who will attend. If there are any changes or additions, they may be filled in at the hearing by the judge or clerk.

Item 1a: This item is left blank, unless you know the name of the judge or commissioner who will be hearing the guardianship case. If you do, fill in the name.

Item 1b: If you obtained the hearing date and location from the court clerk, fill in this information in the spaces provided.

Item 1c: Check this box. Fill in your full first, middle, and last names.

Item 1d: Check this box. Then after the words "Attorney for petitioner (name)," fill in your full first, middle, and last names, followed by the words "appearing In Pro Per."

Item 1e: Ordinarily this item is left blank, except for the rare situation where the minor is independently represented by an attorney. If that's the case, check the box and fill in the attorney's name, address, and phone number.

Item 2a: Check the first box before the words "all notices required by law have been given." This means you will be having all of the people listed in Items 6 and 7 of the Petition for Transfer of Guardianship Proceeding served with notice of the hearing.

Item 2b: In the first space fill in the minor's name exactly as it appears on the other documents already filed with the court. In the second space fill in the case number of the guardianship case in the court from which it is being transferred. In the last blank after the words "County of," fill in the name of the county where you want the case transferred. If the new court has a district or branch name, put it after the name of the county.

Item 3: In the blank provided, again fill in the name of the county where you want the case transferred. If the new court has a district or branch name, put it after the name of the county.

Leave the date and judge's signature line blank. These will be filled in at the hearing.

Complete Notice of Hearing

Complete a Notice of Hearing following the instructions in Chapter 5, with these exceptions:

Item 1: If you have been appointed guardian or temporary guardian by the court, after the words "(representative capacity, if any)," enter the words "guardian of the person," "guardian

Sample Order for Transfer of Guardianship Proceeding

PARTY WITHOUT AN ATTORNEY *(Name and Address):*   **TELEPHONE NO:**
      ANGELO MARTIN FREDERICKS   916-555-1212
      222 Any Street
      Yreka, CA 96097
 In Pro Per
	FOR COURT USE ONLY

NAME OF COURT: SISKIYOU SUPERIOR COURT **STREET ADDRESS:** 311 4th Street **MAILING ADDRESS:** P.O. Box 338 **CITY AND ZIP CODE:** Yreka, CA 96097 **BRANCH NAME:**	

GUARDIANSHIP OF THE   ☒ **PERSON**   ☐ **ESTATE OF (NAME):**
 	
     JOE GEORGE FREDERICKS
 	
                                   MINOR	

ORDER FOR TRANSFER OF GUARDIANSHIP PROCEEDING	**CASE NUMBER:** 2001

1. The Petition for Transfer of Guardianship Proceeding came on for hearing as follows (check boxes c, d, and e to indicate personal presence):

   a. Judge (name):

   b. Hearing Date: 4/1/xx   Time: 9:00 a.m.   ☒ Dept: 1   ☒ Div.: 1   ☒ Room: 1

   c. ☒ Petitioner (name):   ANGELO MARTIN FREDERICKS

   d. ☒ Attorney for petitioner (name):   ANGELO MARTIN FREDERICKS, appearing In Pro Per

   e. ☐ Attorney for ward (name, address, and telephone):

2. THE COURT FINDS

   a. ☒ all notices required by law have been given.

   b. Transfer of the Guardianship of   JOE GEORGE FREDERICKS ,

       Case Number   2001 , from this court to the Superior Court of the State of California,

       County of   SHASTA is in the best interests of the ward.

3. THE COURT ORDERS that this proceeding be transferred to the Superior Court of the State of California, County of

       SHASTA .

   Dated: ....   _____

                                                    (JUDGE OF THE SUPERIOR COURT)

of the estate," or "guardian of the person and estate," or the word "temporary," before each of these types of guardianships if that applies. If you have not been appointed guardian, indicate that you are "proposed guardian of the person," "proposed guardian of the estate," or "proposed guardian of the person and estate."

Just below this, after the words "has filed (specify)," enter the words "Petition for Transfer of Guardianship Proceeding."

Item 4: Fill in the information in the box about the date, time, and place of the hearing if you obtained these over the phone. Otherwise, have the clerk fill in this information when you file your papers with the court.

Copy and File Documents With the Court

You are now ready to copy the documents. Make at least two to three photocopies of each document, depending on whether the court requires an additional copy. In addition, make one copy each of the Notice of Hearing and Petition for Transfer of Guardianship Proceeding for each person listed in Items 6 and 7 of the Petition for Transfer of Guardianship Proceeding.

File the documents following the instructions in Chapter 3. If you have not already obtained a hearing date, get one from the clerk. The date should be at least 25 days away to give you enough time to get the papers served as required. Make sure all copies of the Notice of Hearing have the date, time, and place listed on them. If the clerk gives you the original signed Notice of Hearing, keep it in a safe place; you will need to file it with the court after everyone entitled to notice has been served.

Have Papers Served and Complete and File Proof of Service

Have copies of the Notice of Hearing and Petition for Transfer of Guardianship Proceeding served by mail on each person listed in Items 6 and 7 of the Petition for Transfer of Guardianship Proceeding at least 20 days before the scheduled hearing date. Instructions for having documents served by mail are contained in Chapter 6. If you don't have papers served in time, you will need to have the hearing continued.

Finally, complete a proof of service by mail following the instructions in Chapter 6. Have the person who served the papers sign the proof of service. Make two or three copies, and take or send them to the court at least one week before the hearing date. If you have the original signed Notice of Hearing, also file it with the court.

Call the Court to Find Out the Tentative Decision

In most courts, several days before the scheduled hearing date, your petition is sent to the office of the judge or commissioner. First, a clerk reviews your papers to make sure everything is in order. Then, the judge makes a tentative ruling on your petition—called a "pre-grant decision"—based solely on the papers you've submitted.

Call the court two days before the hearing is scheduled to find out whether the judge has made a tentative decision on your petition. In some counties this information is given on a recorded tape or on the court's website either one or two days before the hearing. In other counties you talk to a clerk. If there is a problem with the petition, the clerk can probably tell you what's wrong and what you need to do to fix it.

If the judge tentatively grants your petition, find out from the clerk whether you need to attend the hearing. In some counties, petitions that are granted by the judge ahead of time are not called at the hearing unless someone shows up to contest them. If you do not have any reason to believe the petition would be contested, you may not need to appear at the hearing. Find out from the clerk how you may get copies of the proposed order you submitted, once the judge signs it.

Attend the Hearing

We advise that you go to court even if the pre-grant decision was in your favor, just in case someone shows up to contest your petition at the last minute. Bring copies of all your documents, including the proofs of service, to the hearing. Let the clerk or bailiff know you are present—especially if the petition was tentatively granted by the judge ahead of time.

At the hearing, the judge will decide whether to allow the case to be transferred. In almost all instances, this is a formality because there are good reasons to have the case transferred. The judge may simply grant and sign the Order for Transfer of Guardianship Proceeding without asking you any questions. However, the judge may want additional information from you. For example, the judge may want to make sure you and the minor have moved to the new residence permanently, rather than just staying there for a few months.

Make sure you get a signed copy of the Order for Transfer of Guardianship Proceeding before you leave the court. If an agency requires proof that the case will be transferred to a different court, you may need to show a copy of the signed order.

Old Court Transfers Case and Charges Estate Transfer Fees

After the Order for Transfer of Guardianship Proceeding is granted, the court from which the case is being transferred will arrange to have the file transferred to the new court, and transferring fees (probaby around $50) will be charged to the minor's estate (PC § 2216(b)). A few days after the order is granted, call the clerk of the old court to find out when the transfer will be completed.

Contact the New Court and Pay Transfer Fees

After the date the transfer should have taken place, call the clerk of the new court and find out whether the case was transferred. You will have to pay the new court the same filing fee that would be required if you had filed an original petition there. These fees may be reimbursed by the estate.

If you seek waiver of those fees on the basis that you and the estate can't afford them, you'll have to fill out documents and file them with the new court. (See Chapter 3 and Chapter 6.) Ask whether you will be sent a document in the mail giving you the new case number, or whether you can simply get it over the phone. You will need the new case number for any further contact you may have with the new court.

Reimbursements and Compensation of the Guardian

With court approval, a guardian of the minor's estate or person and estate may be reimbursed or paid for:

- expenses incurred personally in taking care of a minor or the minor's estate, and

- time spent taking care of a minor or the minor's estate.

It is not common for a court to grant a guardian compensation for taking care of a minor, unless there are extraordinary circumstances. Usually, courts only grant guardianship of a minor's person if the proposed guardian is willing to take on the responsibilities and demands of acting as the minor's parent, so they will not allow compensation for that responsibility.

Guardianship Expenses

A guardian of a minor's estate is not personally responsible for paying the estate's expenses. The guardian normally is permitted to hire competent professional help—an accountant and perhaps an investment advisor as needed, as long as the expense is reasonably related to the size of the estate. A guardian may also hire an attorney to represent either the minor or the estate, but approval from the court should be obtained before the estate hires a lawyer.

Typically, the guardian of a minor's estate—or person and estate—may be reimbursed for the following:

- money paid for the benefit of the minor's estate. With court approval, the guardian may be allowed interest on the amount paid out, at the legal rate payable on judgments (PC § 2466). You will need to see a lawyer if you wish to seek this type of reimbursement.

- expenses incurred for the support, maintenance, and education of the ward, if the guardianship is for the estate and person—this includes maintaining and repairing the place where the minor lives (PC § 2457)

- paying the minor's or estate's debts, if proven to the court to be legitimate and correct, and

- the collection, care, and administration of the minor's estate (PC § 2430(a)(4)).

You should consult an attorney if you have incurred such expenses, or anticipate doing so. (See Chapter 13.)

Reimbursement of Court Costs and Bond Premiums

You do not need court approval to reimburse yourself for official court costs paid to the county clerk to obtain the guardianship of the minor's estate. You can simply pay yourself back out of the assets of the estate, and then indicate these expenditures on the accountings you file with the court. You may also reimburse yourself for amounts paid as premiums on your bond. Remember to keep receipts and records of all expenditures and reimbursements for filing with the court in an accounting.

Compensation for a Guardian's Time

You may be eligible for reasonable compensation from the estate for your services, if you have spent a lot of time tending to the affairs of the estate. To receive compensation, you must petition the court. The amount of compensation is typically fixed by local court rule or practice, and usually amounts to a certain percentage of the overall estate. The court may also authorize periodic payments to the guardian for services (PC § 2643). The guardian would need to document reasons why compensation should be granted.

You may petition the court for compensation any time after the Inventory and Appraisal is filed (see Chapter 10), but it must be no sooner than 90 days after the date Letters of

Guardianship were issued (PC § 2640). Some courts have local rules that require simultaneous filings of a petition for compensation and the Inventory and Appraisal. Unless you have prior court approval, you cannot compensate yourself for your services. If you plan to petition the court for compensation for your services, arrange to hire an attorney. (See Chapter 13.) Although you must petition the court for compensation no sooner than 90 days after the date Letters of Guardianship were issued, some courts will not allow the money to be disbursed until one year after Letters of Guardianship were issued, after accounting documents have been filed with the court.

If the Guardianship Is Contested After You Are Appointed

At many times in this book, we have advised you to see a lawyer if the guardianship is contested before you are appointed guardian. Although unusual, a guardianship could be contested even after the court appoints a guardian. A guardianship could be contested for many reasons, and in a number of ways. For example, an absent parent could simply show up at your doorstep and say she wants her children back. Or a parent or relative could claim you're not doing your job right, and hire an attorney to take the matter to court to end the guardianship. If someone tries to have you removed or suspended as guardian, there are likely to be many legal complications, so you will need to see a lawyer to help sort them out. (See Chapter 13.) ●

Ending the Guardianship

As you know, a guardian has a number of responsibilities and possible liabilities. A guardian of a minor's person must care for the minor by providing a home, taking care of the minor's physical needs, overseeing the minor's education, and perhaps managing agency benefits. A guardian of a minor's estate must handle the minor's assets prudently, maintain bond if required, keep accurate accounting records, and make periodic reports to the court.

Perhaps you turned to this chapter because you're serving as a minor's legal guardian, and no longer want the responsibility. It could be that your personal situation has changed and you're no longer in a position to take care of the minor, the estate, or both. Or maybe you turned to this chapter because a guardianship is no longer needed. Possibly the minor's parents are able to resume care, and you want to step down from the guardian position.

A guardianship—unlike the adult-child relationship between a natural or adoptive parent and child—does not last forever. Because a guardianship is set up to take care of a minor, it generally ends when the minor reaches age 18. (Guardianship of a minor's estate does not end automatically when the minor reaches age 18. See below.) Additionally, with permission of the court, a guardian may step down, which generally means that a different adult will take over the position of guardian. If there is no appropriate adult willing to take over the guardianship and the guardian can no longer serve, the juvenile court or a public guardian can be appointed to take over. Or with permission of the court, the guardianship itself may be ended ("terminated"). When a guardianship terminates, it no longer exists. This can happen when it isn't needed anymore, usually because one or both of the minor's parents can take care of their child or the estate again.

EXAMPLE 1:

Barbara is guardian of the person of her niece, Cathy. Barbara obtained the guardianship when Cathy's widowed mother—a single parent—went into the army, and needed someone else to have legal guardianship. Cathy's mother finishes her time in the service, and returns to California. She wants to regain custody of her daughter, and is a fine parent. Cathy's natural mother will resume caring for her, so a guardianship is no longer necessary. Barbara goes to court and obtains a termination of the guardianship using the forms in this book.

EXAMPLE 2:

Andrew is guardian of the person of his granddaughter, Patty. Andrew is in his 70s, and is beginning to have serious health problems. He realizes that taking care of Patty is too much work for him, and discusses the problem with other family members. Patty's aunt is able to take over as guardian and she is glad to help out. With the help of a lawyer, Andrew resigns as guardian, and Patty's aunt is appointed successor guardian.

EXAMPLE 3:

Herman is guardian of the person and estate of his cousin, Johnny. When Herman obtained the guardianship, Johnny's estate consisted of approximately $25,000 cash. With the court's permission, he has used money from the estate to support Johnny, and there is approximately $18,000 left. Herman wants to put the money into a blocked account—meaning that he would need a court order to withdraw it. He wants to end the guardianship of the estate so that he doesn't have to make periodic reports to the court or continue to pay bond premiums. With the help of an attorney, Herman terminates the guardianship of Johnny's estate. He continues acting as the guardian of Johnny's person.

Note: If the guardian dies, the guardianship itself does not end. Instead, a successor guardian must be appointed. If you are concerned about what will happen to the minor if you die before the minor reaches age 18, you may want to do some estate planning. (See Chapter 1.)

Termination of the Guardianship

Guardianships of the person may terminate automatically, or they may be ended earlier if the guardian or another interested person files papers with the court and obtains a judge's permission. Guardianships of a minor's estate can only be terminated by filing special forms with the court and appearing in court.

Automatic Termination of a Guardianship of a Minor's Person

A guardianship of the minor's person terminates automatically when the minor:

- is legally adopted
- reaches age 18 or is emancipated
- marries, or
- dies.

If any of these occur, the guardianship relationship legally terminates automatically. There is no need to go to court to obtain an order.

Termination of a Guardianship of a Minor's Estate

A guardianship of the minor's estate terminates when:

- the estate is used up
- the minor reaches age 18 or is emancipated, or
- the minor dies.

A guardianship of the minor's estate does not terminate if the minor marries or is adopted, even though guardianship of the minor's person terminates automatically when either of those happens.

When the estate is used up, or the minor reaches age 18 or dies, the former guardian is required to file a "final account" with the court, itemizing how money was spent and received on the minor's behalf, and what property remains in the estate. After the court approves the final account, the remaining property in the estate must be turned over to the minor or the legal representative of the deceased minor's estate. This procedure is beyond the scope of this book. (See Chapter 13 for information on finding lawyers and doing your own research.)

How to Terminate Guardianship of a Minor's Person

The guardian, minor, parent, or other interested person may request that a court order put an end to a guardianship. The forms in this section should be used if one or both of the minor's parents can resume parental duties, making a legal guardian unnecessary.

Call the Court

Call the court and tell the clerk you want to file a Petition for Termination of Guardianship. Find out whether you can obtain a hearing date over the phone. If you can get a hearing date, obtain one at least 25 days away, because you'll need to have papers served at least 20 days before that date. If you can't get the hearing date now, you will get one when you file your papers with the court. You're now ready to complete the required forms.

Complete Petition for Termination of Guardianship

In this petition, you tell the court why the guardianship case should be terminated.

How to Complete the Form

CAPTION: Petition for Termination of Guardianship

Fill in the caption following the general instructions in Chapter 3.

Item 1: In the blanks, fill in your name and the minor's name exactly as they appear on the original issued Letters of Guardianship. Check the appropriate boxes to indicate a termination of a guardianship of the person or the estate, and, if of an estate, a box indicating the reason for the termination.

Item 2: Check the box next to "minor's guardian."

Items 3 and 4: Check the applicable box(es) and fill in your name and the date you were appointed guardian. This is on the original issued Letters of Guardianship.

Item 5: Check the appropriate "person" or "estate" box and the "stated below" box. Then, explain in your own words why a guardianship is no longer necessary. For example: "The minor's mother has recovered fully from her illness and is now able to resume caring for her daughter. Copies of written statements by her doctor and psychologist are attached to this petition." Or "The minor's mother was honorably discharged from the U.S. Army on

November 1, 20xx, has returned to California, and wishes to resume caring for her son."

Item 6: Check box a or b to indicate whether a request for special notice has or has not been filed in the court proceeding by anyone. If someone has filed such a request, check box b and list the names of any persons who have requested special notice. If you aren't sure whether someone filed a request for special notice, call the court. Give the clerk the case name and file number, and ask that the clerk pull the file and see whether special notice was requested. (See Chapter 11.) The names of anyone requesting special notice should be listed here, and a copy of this petition and the notice of hearing should be sent to them.

Item 7: Check this box only if any of the minor's relatives or anyone else entitled to notice of the proceeding cannot be located, or if you believe for some other reason that notice should not be given. You will have to prepare an "Attachment 7 to Petition for Termination of Guardianship," where you list each such person's name and explain why you could not locate these individuals. See Chapter 4 for more on this subject.

Item 8: You should use this item if you're concerned that the minor's parents might not support you in continuing to see and visit with the minor after the guardianship is terminated. You can check this box to ask the court to make a determination about visitation as part of the termination order. If you do check it, you'll need to prepare an Attachment 8 stating the reasons for the request. For example, "I would like to continue to take the minor bowling each Wednesday after school, as we have been doing during the time I have served as guardian. The minor is attached to me and to this regular weekly time we spend together, and it is in her best interests that the visits continue." If you check this box, you'll also need to attach

Sample Petition for Termination of Guardianship, page 1

GC-255

ATTORNEY OR PARTY WITHOUT ATTORNEY *(Name, State Bar number, and address):*	FOR COURT USE ONLY
Murray Arthur Bart 5 Sidewalk Street Los Angeles, CA 90053 TELEPHONE NO.: 213-555-1212　　FAX NO. *(Optional):* E-MAIL ADDRESS *(Optional):* ATTORNEY FOR *(Name):* In Pro Per	

SUPERIOR COURT OF CALIFORNIA, COUNTY OF Los Angeles
STREET ADDRESS: 111 N. Hill Street
MAILING ADDRESS: P.O. Box 151
CITY AND ZIP CODE: Los Angeles, CA 90053
BRANCH NAME:

GUARDIANSHIP OF THE [X] PERSON [ ] ESTATE OF *(Name):* Suzanna Ginger Gerard　　　　　　　　　MINOR	CASE NUMBER: 2020
PETITION FOR TERMINATION OF GUARDIANSHIP	HEARING DATE AND TIME:　　　DEPT.:

1. Petitioner *(name):* **requests that**
   a. [X] the guardianship of the PERSON of *(minor):* Suzanna Ginger Gerard　be terminated.
   b. [ ] the guardianship of the ESTATE of *(minor):*　be terminated.
   　　(1) [ ] The estate has been entirely exhausted through expenditures or disbursements (Probate Code, § 2626).
   　　(2) [ ] The estate falls within the provisions of Probate Code section 2628(b) (small estate), and no accounts have been required.
   　　(3) [ ] Other *(specify):*

2. Petitioner is the [ ] minor [X] minor's guardian [ ] minor's parent.
3. [X] *(Name):* Murray Arthur Bart　　　　　　　　was appointed guardian of the PERSON of the minor named in item 1a on *(date):* April 12, 20xx
4. [ ] *(Name):*　　　　　　　　was appointed guardian of the ESTATE of the minor named in item 1b on *(date):*
5. It is in the best interest of the minor that the guardianship of the [X] person [ ] estate be terminated for the reasons [ ] stated in Attachment 5 [X] stated below *(specify):*
   Suzanna's mother, Elsa Gerard, received an honorable discharge from the U.S. Army on August 22, 20xx. Suzanna has been living with her since September 15, 20xx. She is happy living with her mother, who is able to provide her with the care she needs, and there is no more need for her to have a guardian other than her mother.
6. A request for special notice
   a. [X] has not been filed.
   b. [ ] has been filed and notice will be given to *(names):*

7. [ ] Notice to the persons identified in Attachment 7 should be dispensed with because
   a. [ ] they cannot with reasonable diligence be given notice *(specify names and efforts to locate in Attachment 7).*
   b. [ ] other good cause exists to dispense with notice *(specify names and reasons in Attachment 7).*

8. [ ] Petitioner is the minor's guardian. Petitioner requests reasonable visitation with the minor after termination of the guardianship as specified in Attachment 8. A completed *Declaration Under Uniform Child Custody Jurisdiction and Enforcement Act (UCCJEA)* (form FL-105/GC-120) is also attached.

NOTICE:	This guardianship will terminate automatically when the child reaches age 18. No petition or court order is necessary to terminate the guardianship at that time. Nevertheless, if this is a guardianship of the estate, termination of the guardianship does not eliminate the requirement that a final report or account must be filed. (See Prob. Code, § 1600.)

Page 1 of 2

Form Adopted for Mandatory Use Judicial Council of California GC-255 [Rev. January 1, 2006]	**PETITION FOR TERMINATION OF GUARDIANSHIP** **(Probate—Guardianships and Conservatorships)**	Probate Code §§ 1460, 1601, 2626, 2627, 2636 www.courtinfo.ca.gov

Sample Petition for Termination of Guardianship, page 2

		GC-255

GUARDIANSHIP OF THE [X] PERSON [ ] ESTATE OF *(Name):* Suzanna Ginger Gerard	MINOR	CASE NUMBER: 2020

9. The names and residence addresses of the guardian, minor, and minor's parents, brothers, sisters, and grandparents are *(specify):*

a. Guardian: Murray Arthur Bart
   5 Sidewalk Street
   Los Angeles, CA 95003

b. Minor: Suzanna Ginger Gerard
   8 Skateboard Lane
   Los Angeles, CA 90053

c. Father: Unknown
   2 Scarborough Drive
   Cleveland, OH 44118

d. Mother: Elsa Gerard
   8 Skateboard Lane
   Los Angeles, CA 90053

e. Brother or sister: n/a

f. Brother or sister: n/a

g. Brother or sister: n/a

h. Maternal grandfather: Deceased

i. Maternal grandmother: Rose Bart

j. Paternal grandfather: Deceased

k. Paternal grandmother: Deceased

l. [ ] Additional names and addresses continued on Attachment 9.

10. Number of pages attached: 0

Date:

▶ _____
(SIGNATURE OF ATTORNEY OR PETITIONER WITHOUT AN ATTORNEY *)

* (Signature of all petitioners also required (Prob. Code, § 1020).)

I declare under penalty of perjury under the laws of the State of California that the foregoing is true and correct.

Date: September 30, 20xx

Murray A. Bart
_____
(TYPE OR PRINT NAME)

▶ _____
(SIGNATURE OF PETITIONER)

_____
(TYPE OR PRINT NAME)

▶ _____
(SIGNATURE OF PETITIONER)

CONSENT TO TERMINATION AND WAIVER OF SERVICE AND NOTICE OF HEARING

11. [X] I consent to the termination of the guardianship of the [X] person [ ] estate of the minor and waive service of a copy of, and notice of the hearing on, this petition.

Date: 9/20/20xx   Rose Bart
_____
(TYPE OR PRINT NAME)

▶ (SIGNATURE OF [ ] MINOR * [ ] GUARDIAN [ ] PARENT [ ] OTHER)

Date: _____
(TYPE OR PRINT NAME)

▶ (SIGNATURE OF [ ] MINOR * [ ] GUARDIAN [ ] PARENT [ ] OTHER)

Date: _____
(TYPE OR PRINT NAME)

▶ (SIGNATURE OF [ ] MINOR * [ ] GUARDIAN [ ] PARENT [ ] OTHER)

Date: _____
(TYPE OR PRINT NAME)

▶ (SIGNATURE OF [ ] MINOR * [ ] GUARDIAN [ ] PARENT [ ] OTHER)

[ ] Additional signatures on Attachment 11.

* Minor over 12 years of age.

GC-255 [Rev. January 1, 2006]

PETITION FOR TERMINATION OF GUARDIANSHIP
(Probate—Guardianships and Conservatorships)

Page 2 of 2

a Declaration Under Uniform Child Custody Jurisdiction and Enforcement Act (UCCJEA), Form GC-120. This is the same form you prepared and filed along with your original petition for guardianship, but you'll need to prepare an updated one for this purpose.

Item 9: In this item, list the names and addresses of the minor's closest relatives. Follow the instructions for listing these relatives that are explained in the instructions for Item 18 of the Petition for Appointment of Guardian of Minor in Chapter 5.

Item 10: Fill in the number of pages attached (if none, put in a zero).

Sign and date the form in the spaces indicated, and print or type your name.

On the bottom of the back page form, there is a box labeled "Consent to Termination and Waiver of Notice." Fill in the names of anyone you listed in Item 9 who is entitled to notice of the court hearing and who is willing to agree to the termination of the guardianship. This includes a minor who is 12 years old or older. For each person willing to agree to the termination of the guardianship, type the date and that person's name, check the box indicating the person is either the minor (12 or over), parent, or other person, and have him or her sign it. You will not have to serve anyone who's signed the form.

Complete (Proposed) Order Terminating Guardianship

Before the guardianship proceeding can be terminated, a judge must sign an order.

How to Complete the Form

CAPTION: Order Terminating Guardianship

Fill in the caption following the general instructions in Chapter 3.

Item 1: In this item, give information about when the hearing will be held and who will attend. If there are any changes or additions, they may be filled in at the hearing by the judge or clerk.

Item 1a: This item is left blank, unless you know the name of the judge or commissioner who will be hearing the guardianship case. If so, fill in the name.

Item 1b: If you obtained information from the clerk about the hearing date and location, fill this in in the spaces provided.

Item 1c: Check this box. Fill in your full first, middle, and last names.

Item 1d: Leave this item blank.

Item 1e: Check this box if the minor will be present at the hearing, and fill in the minor's first, middle, and last names.

Item 1f: Ordinarily this item is left blank, except for the rare situation where the minor has an independent attorney. If that's the case, check the box and fill in the attorney's name, address, and phone number.

Item 1g: If you are the guardian of the minor's person, check this box and fill in your first, middle, and last names. If someone else is the guardian of the minor's person and you're petitioning to have that guardianship terminated, check the box and fill in their name. If neither of these is the case, leave the item blank.

Item 1h: If you're guardian of the person and you have an attorney, check this box and fill in the attorney's name. Otherwise leave the item blank.

Item 1i: If you're the guardian of the estate, check this box and fill in your first, middle, and last names. If someone else is the guardian of the minor's estate and you're petitioning to have that guardianship terminated, check the box and fill in their name. If neither of these is the case, leave the item blank.

Item 1j: If you're guardian of the estate and you have an attorney, check this box and fill in the attorney's name. Otherwise, leave the item blank.

Item 1k: If either of the minor's parents are going to attend the hearing, check this box and fill in the name(s) here. Otherwise, leave the item blank.

Item 1l: If either of the minor's parents has an attorney who will attend the hearing, check this box and fill in the attorney's name here. Otherwise, leave the item blank.

Item 2a: If you've served everyone you were required to serve, check this box.

Item 2b: Check this box only if you checked Item 7 in the Petition for Termination (and attached an Attachment 7), requesting that certain persons not be given notice. If so, check box 2b here and check the box next to the words "should be." Then list the names of those persons.

Item 2c: Check this box if you're terminating the guardianship of the person.

Item 2d: Check this box if you're terminating a guardianship of the estate, and check the boxes corresponding to the reasons for termination that you listed in Item 1b of the Petition for Termination.

Items 3 and 4: Check the applicable box or boxes for termination of guardianship of the person and/or estate, and list the minor's first, middle, and last name.

Item 5: Check this box only if you checked Item 2b.

Item 6: Leave this item blank unless you have requested visitation with the minor following termination of the guardianship under Item 8 of the Petition for Termination of Guardianship. If that's the case, prepare an Attachment 6 that follows the same format as your request for visitation.

Item 7: Leave this item blank.

Leave the date and judge's signature line blank. These will be filled in at the hearing.

Complete Notice of Hearing

Complete a Notice of Hearing following the instructions in Chapter 5 with these exceptions:

Item 1: After the words "(representative capacity, if any)," enter the words "guardian of the person." Just below this, after the words "has filed (specify)," enter the words "Petition for Termination of Guardianship."

Item 4: Fill in the information in the box about the date, time, and place of the hearing, if you obtained these over the phone. Otherwise, have the clerk fill in this information when you file your papers with the court.

Copy and File Documents With the Court

You are now ready to copy the documents. Following the instructions in Chapter 3, make at least two or three photocopies of each document, depending on whether the court requires an additional copy. In addition, make one copy of the Notice of Hearing and Petition for Termination of Guardianship for each person listed in Items 6 and 7 of the Petition for Termination of Guardianship.

File the documents following the instructions in Chapter 3. There should not be a filing fee for the petition. If you have not already obtained a hearing date, get one from the court clerk. You may either request one in person (if you take in your papers), or in a letter to the court. Remember that the hearing date should be at least 25 days away to give you enough time to get the papers served as required. Make sure all copies of the Notice of Hearing have the date, time, and place listed. If the clerk gives you the original signed Notice of Hearing, keep it in a safe place. You will need to file it with the court after everyone entitled to notice has been served.

Have Papers Served at Least 20 Days Before Hearing Date, and Complete and File Proof of Service

Have copies of the Notice of Hearing and Petition for Termination of Guardianship served by mail on each person listed in Items 6 and 7 of the Petition for Termination of Guardianship at least 20 days before the scheduled hearing date. Instructions for having documents served by mail are contained in Chapter 6. If you don't have papers served in time, you must have the hearing continued. (See Chapter 6.)

Finally, complete a proof of service by mail following the instructions in Chapter 6. Have the person who served the papers sign the proof of service. Make two or three copies, and take or send them to the court at least one week before the hearing date. If you have the original signed Notice of Hearing, also file it with the court then.

Call the Court to Find Out the Tentative Decision

In most courts, several days before the scheduled hearing date your petition is sent to the office of the judge or commissioner. First, a clerk reviews your papers to make sure everything is in order. Then the judge makes a tentative ruling on your petition—called a "pregrant decision"—based solely on the papers you've submitted.

Call the court two days before the hearing is scheduled to find out whether the judge has made a tentative decision on your petition. In some counties this information is given on a recorded tape either one or two days before the hearing, and some counties might even have pregrants listed on their website. (See Chapter 9 for how to look up court information on the Internet.) In other counties you talk to a clerk. If there is a problem with the petition, the clerk can probably tell you what's wrong and what you need to do to fix it.

If the judge tentatively granted your petition, find out from the clerk whether you need to attend the hearing. In some counties, petitions that are granted by the judge ahead of time are not called at the hearing unless someone shows up to contest them. If you do not have any reason to believe the petition would be contested, you may not need to appear at the hearing. Find out from the clerk how to get copies of the order you submitted once the judge signs it.

Attend the Hearing

Even if the pregrant decision was in your favor, you might still want to go to court if there's any chance someone might show up to contest your petition at the last minute. Bring copies of all your documents, including the proofs of service, to the hearing. Let the clerk or bailiff know you are present—especially if the petition was tentatively granted by the judge ahead of time, because it may not then be called automatically in court.

The minor should attend the hearing with you. If the minor's parent will resume caring for the minor, the parent should attend the hearing as well.

At the hearing, the judge will decide whether to allow the guardianship to be terminated. The judge may simply grant and sign the Order for Termination of Guardianship without asking any questions. However, the judge may ask you for additional information, questioning you or the minor's parent about why the guardianship is no longer needed. The judge may ask the minor's opinion about returning to live with a parent or remaining with you. The judge may question you, the minor, and the parent about how the parent's situation has changed. The judge will want to make sure the parent is now able to care for the child.

Sample Order Terminating Guardianship

GC-260

ATTORNEY OR PARTY WITHOUT ATTORNEY *(Name, State Bar number, and address):*	FOR COURT USE ONLY

ATTORNEY OR PARTY WITHOUT ATTORNEY *(Name, State Bar number, and address):*
Murray Arthur Bart
5 Sidewalk Street
Los Angeles, CA 95003
TELEPHONE NO.: 213-555-1212   FAX NO. *(Optional):*
E-MAIL ADDRESS *(Optional):*
ATTORNEY FOR *(Name):*   In Pro Per

SUPERIOR COURT OF CALIFORNIA, COUNTY OF Los Angeles
STREET ADDRESS: 111 N. Hill Street
MAILING ADDRESS: P.O. Box 151
CITY AND ZIP CODE: Los Angeles, CA 90053
BRANCH NAME:

GUARDIANSHIP OF THE [X] PERSON [ ] ESTATE OF

(Name): Suzanna Ginger Gerard   MINOR

ORDER TERMINATING GUARDIANSHIP	CASE NUMBER:

1. The petition to terminate the guardianship came on for hearing as follows *(check boxes c–l to indicate personal presence):*
   a. Judicial Officer *(name):*
   b. Hearing date: 11/1/20xx   Time: 1:30 p.m. [X] Dept. 13   [ ] Rm.:
   c. [X] Petitioner *(name)* Murray Arthur Bart
   d. [ ] Attorney for petitioner *(name):*
   e. [X] Minor *(name):* Suzanna Ginger Gerard
   f. [ ] Attorney for minor *(name):*
   g. [ ] Guardian of the person *(name):*
   h. [ ] Attorney for guardian of the person *(name):*
   i. [ ] Guardian of the estate *(name):*
   j. [ ] Attorney for guardian of the estate *(name):*
   k. [X] Parent of minor *(name):* Elsa Gerard
   l. [ ] Attorney for parent *(name):*

THE COURT FINDS

2. a. [X] All notices required by law have been given.
   b. [ ] Notice of hearing [ ] has been [ ] should be dispensed with to the following persons *(specify):*

   c. [X] It is in the minor's best interest to terminate the guardianship of the PERSON.
   d. [ ] It is in the minor's best interest to terminate the guardianship of the ESTATE.
      (1) [ ] The estate has been entirely exhausted through expenditures or disbursements (Prob. Code, § 2626).
      (2) [ ] The estate falls within the provisions of Probate Code section 2628(b) (small estate), and no accounts have been required.
      (3) [ ] Other reasons *(specify):*

THE COURT ORDERS

3. [X] The guardianship of the PERSON of *(minor):* Suzanna Ginger Gerard   is terminated.
4. [ ] The guardianship of the ESTATE of *(minor):*   is terminated.
5. [ ] Notice of hearing to the persons named in item 2b is dispensed with.
6. [ ] Visitation between the minor and the guardian [ ] of the person [ ] of the estate is ordered as provided in Attachment 6.
7. [ ] Other *(specify):*

[ ] Continued on Attachment 7.

Date:
_____
JUDICIAL OFFICER
[ ] Signature follows last attachment.

Page 1 of 1

Form Adopted for Mandatory Use Judicial Council of California GC-260 [Rev. January 1, 2006]	**ORDER TERMINATING GUARDIANSHIP** **(Probate—Guardianships and Conservatorships)**	Probate Code §§ 1601–1602, 2626–2628 *www.courtinfo.ca.gov*

It's possible that the judge could require an investigation before allowing the guardianship to end. If so, the judge will instruct you on whether and when you must return to court. (Investigations are covered in Chapter 8.) If the judge will not allow you to terminate the guardianship, you will need the help of a lawyer. (See Chapter 13.)

Resignation of the Guardian

A guardian cannot simply decide to stop serving in that role without first getting an order from the court. A guardian who stops acting as guardian without a court's approval is still responsible for all the duties and liabilities of a guardian. However, when a guardian resigns with court approval, the guardianship continues and the court names a new person to step in and take over the guardian's duties. Some common reasons a guardian would seek permission from the court to resign are:

- The guardian will be moving out of California and cannot take the minor along, perhaps because work requires moving overseas to a place that is not safe for children.

- The guardian can't handle the job any longer for personal reasons, perhaps because of very poor health or an inability to handle a difficult minor, and another nonparent is better suited and willing to take on the responsibility. (If a natural parent wants to resume caring for a child, a guardianship may not be needed any longer. See above.)

Judges do not generally let guardians resign without good reason, and will be reluctant to let you resign unless someone else is available to take over. In situations where a guardian must resign quickly, a temporary guardian is sometimes named to take over the responsibilities before the next regular guardian can be appointed. In very rare, extreme cases where no one can take over and it would be detrimental for the minor to stay with the present guardian, the court might order the juvenile court or a public guardian to take over.

The process of resigning as guardian is beyond the scope of this book and will require the help of an attorney. (See Chapter 13.)

Contested Situations: Removal or Suspension of the Guardian

A guardian may be "removed," meaning the court orders the guardian to stop serving. When a guardian is removed, the guardianship itself may continue if the court names a successor guardian. Pending a hearing on whether the guardian is to be removed, a guardian's powers can be "suspended," temporarily taking away the right to act as the minor's legal guardian.

A proceeding to remove a guardian can be initiated by the ward, a parent, or any interested person. This is done by filing and serving the guardian with a copy of a petition for removal of guardian. The procedures for defending against this are beyond the scope of this book. If you are ever served with a petition for removal, see a lawyer right away. (See Chapter 13.)

Removal of the Guardian of a Minor's Person

A guardian of a minor's person can be removed for any of the following reasons:

- failing to perform duties—namely, failing to adequately care for the minor

- involuntarily placing the minor in a mental health facility, subjecting the minor to involuntary medical treatment, allowing the prescription for or administration of unauthorized experimental drugs or convulsive treatment, or sterilizing the minor, without obtaining prior court approval

- being convicted of a felony
- gross immorality—the definition of "gross immorality" would be up to a judge— however, this might include being involved in serious drug use or child abuse, or
- any other reason that the court determines is detrimental to the minor.

Removal of the Guardian of a Minor's Estate

A guardian of a minor's estate can be removed for any of the following reasons:

- being negligent in handling the minor's funds
- failing to file the appropriate court documents when required, including the "Inventory and Appraisal" and periodic financial accountings (see Chapter 10)
- failing to perform duties, including keeping track of the minor's receipts and expenditures of funds
- having a financial interest adverse to the minor, such as buying a company the minor owns for less than it's worth
- bankruptcy or insolvency
- "gross immorality," such as embezzling the minor's money, or
- being convicted of a felony.

Lawyers and Legal Research

This chapter provides useful information if you need to hire a lawyer or other legal professional, or if you need to do legal research beyond the scope of this book. You should consult an attorney if the guardianship is contested at any point.

Although seeking a lawyer's help isn't essential, a lawyer who has experience in what to say and how to say it may be more skillful than you are in arguing why you should be appointed or retained as guardian.

If your guardianship is not contested, and you just want someone to prepare legal forms or check your work—but not provide legal advice—you may be able to save considerable money by using a legal document preparer instead of a lawyer. (See "What a Legal Document Preparer Can Do," below.)

Finding Free or Low-Cost Legal Help

Programs offering free legal help have dwindled in the past few years. But if you have a low income, you may be able to find free legal help with your guardianship. Although the qualifications for "low income" vary from county to county, you may be eligible for free legal help if you qualify for public assistance, or your income is in the range set out in the court fee waiver chart in Chapter 3.

Legal Aid Offices

Most counties have a legal aid office (often called legal services or legal assistance) that provides free or low-cost advice, consultation, and sometimes representation to low-income people. As a result of funding cutbacks, not all legal aid offices handle guardianship cases, but you may get a referral from them for free legal assistance, or to attorneys who offer reasonably priced services. To find a local legal aid office, check in the telephone book's white pages under "Legal Aid" or "Legal Services," in the yellow pages under "Attorneys," ask the clerk at your court, or contact the county bar association.

County Bar Associations (Volunteer Legal Service Programs)

Some county bar associations have established their own legal service programs or corporations to help low-income people with legal problems by providing free or low-cost legal services.

Increasingly, county bar associations are becoming aware of the need for assistance in obtaining guardianships. For example, the Volunteer Legal Services Corporation, run by the Alameda County Bar Association, holds a guardianship clinic once a month for low-income people. The clinic provides an overview of guardianships of the person, assists in completing the necessary forms, and helps people prepare to represent themselves in court.

Check with your local bar association for information on available legal services and to find out whether your income level qualifies you for assistance. To find a listing for the bar association in your county, check in the phone book or with directory assistance.

Resources for Minors

An organization that gives legal information referrals both within and outside the Bay Area, as well as represents minors, is Legal Services for Children, 1254 Market Street, 3rd Floor, San Francisco, CA 94102; telephone 415-863-3762, Web address www.lsc-sf.org.

What a Legal Document Preparer Can Do

An increasing number of paralegals are striking out on their own—as "legal document assistants" (LDAs)—who offer direct assistance in completing paperwork to people who are undertaking their own legal tasks. Simple procedures such as uncontested divorces, name changes, bankruptcies, and child support modifications are all routinely handled by LDAs at a much lower cost than a lawyer would charge. LDAs cannot give you legal advice, and they cannot represent you in court. Only lawyers can do that. They can, however, assist you in preparing your own guardianship documents. If you work with an LDA, you will get your forms typed, and can probably obtain some important tips on local court rules and procedures. But you must go to court on your own and represent yourself.

To find LDAs in your area, check in the yellow pages of the telephone book under "Legal Document Assistant," "Paralegal," or "Typing Services," or check the website of the California Association of Legal Document Assistants at www.calda.org.

Finding and Hiring a Lawyer

Lawyers—also called attorneys—are the only people allowed to give legal advice in California. Lawyers must be licensed by passing the California bar examination, which tests their knowledge of different areas of law. Almost all lawyers have gone to law school, but a few have followed special self-study courses and passed the bar without attending law school.

Lawyers who work on their own are called "sole practitioners." But lawyers often set up businesses or partnerships in which they work together, which are called "law firms" or "law offices." Law firms often handle a variety of legal matters, and individual lawyers in the firms tend to specialize in one or a few fields. When you hire a lawyer, it is important that you find someone who specializes in the type of law in which you need help. For example, a corporate or criminal defense lawyer, although backed by many years of legal experience, may well know nothing at all about how to set up a guardianship.

What a Lawyer Can Do

It may come as a surprise to realize that lawyers are simply people you hire to work for you. So you're best off hiring someone you trust will work competently for you. There are a variety of ways you can choose to use a lawyer's services, depending on your needs.

Consultation and Advice

You can often arrange to meet with a lawyer to discuss a problem and whether the lawyer can help with it. Frequently these initial consultations are free or relatively reasonably priced. For example, a fee of about $75 to $150 for a half-hour consultation is probably common. Find out the consultation fee before you go in. If the fee seems too high, you and the lawyer may be able to agree on a lower price, or you can shop around until you find an attorney you can afford. Lawyers who give free legal consultations naturally hope to get new clients from the meetings.

At the consultation, a lawyer should listen to the details of your situation, analyze it for you, and advise you on your best plan of action. Bring a list of questions you want answered, and make sure the lawyer answers them in a way you understand. Ideally, the lawyer will give you more than just conclusions, and will educate you about your whole situation and the alternatives from which you can make your own choices. If you are willing to put in some time and work of your own, using a lawyer as a consultant may be the most worthwhile for you. Talk is relatively cheap and may allow you to avoid more serious—and more expensive—problems later.

Contested Guardianships

Occasionally, guardianships end up being contested in court. Having a lawyer handle a court case is very expensive. Unfortunately, archaic language, forms, and courtroom procedures make it difficult for nonlawyers to represent themselves except in small claims court. If you hire a lawyer to represent you in court, you can help make the courtroom procedures less baffling by learning what happens there and why. Some lawyers encourage willing clients to help out with some of the legwork of a case, such as gathering and organizing documents, which can keep legal fees down.

Checking Your Work

Some people are comfortable preparing all their own guardianship papers following the instructions in this book, but want the security that comes with having someone experienced check the work. You may be able to find a lawyer to do this, but that will probably require shopping around a bit. If you do find a lawyer who is experienced in guardianships, and is willing to check your work, make sure you agree on an hourly rate or flat fee in advance.

Finding a Lawyer

Finding a lawyer you trust and who also charges reasonable prices is not always an easy task. There is always the realistic fear that if you just pick a name out of the telephone book you may get an attorney who is unsympathetic, or perhaps will charge too much.

Here are some suggestions for how to find lawyers. Check around until you find someone you feel comfortable hiring.

Group Legal Practices

A new but rapidly growing aspect of California law practice is the group legal practice program. Some groups, including unions, employers, and consumer action groups, offer plans to their members for legal work at rates substantially lower than those available through most private practitioners. If you are a member of such a plan, check with it first if you need a lawyer. However, beware of plans that do no more than refer you to a local attorney who will supposedly give you a good price. Make sure, instead, that the referral is to someone who is experienced with guardianships.

Legal Insurance

Legal insurance plans are marketed by companies such as Hyatt Legal Plans, Pre-Paid Legal Services, Bank of America, Montgomery Ward, and others. These plans often are offered by mail to credit card customers, and in some cases are sold door-to-door. Many of these plans offer several free legal consultations, a simple will, and some letter writing for a small monthly charge. But when it comes to more complicated matters, including guardianships, you often get a list of local lawyers who will handle the problem at a supposedly discounted fee. The danger is that the free services become a sort of feeder mechanism to produce paying clients. As with any other consumer transaction, you should take the responsibility to carefully check out legal insurance by finding out exactly what you get for your money.

Private Attorneys

If you have hired a lawyer who served you well for some other purpose (estate planning, divorce, or personal injury), that lawyer may be a good person to contact. If that lawyer does not handle guardianships, ask for a referral to another good attorney who specializes in them. Or a trustworthy friend, relative, or coworker may know a reliable attorney you can contact.

If you seek help from a lawyer, make sure you find one who has handled guardianships before. This might be a probate attorney or an attorney specializing in family law. You might find a probate lawyer who has handled a number of conservatorships. The forms for guardianships and conservatorships are almost identical, so a lawyer with conservatorship experience should be appropriate. These suggestions should make your search a little easier:

- Check Nolo's Lawyer Directory at www. nolo.com/lawyers. The directory contains advertising profiles of attorneys in your area who practice probate and family law, and you can search for one who is experienced in doing guardianships. The comprehensive profiles give you information about the lawyer's education, experience, and specialties, as well as fee policies and whether the lawyer is willing to review documents prepared by clients.

- Call referral panels set up by local bar associations. There is often a small fee if you meet with the lawyer for an initial consultation. You may get a good referral from these panels, but be sure to question the lawyer about past experience in handling guardianship cases. Be aware that some lawyers list their names on referral panels because they don't have enough business, or are new and inexperienced. Referral panels claim to screen the people they list—but many do not.

- Consult the ads in the classified section of the newspaper or phone book under "Attorneys." This often gives you a good idea as to price and range of services offered.

- Shop around by calling different law offices and briefly explaining your situation and the kind of help you want. Try to talk to a lawyer personally to get an idea of how friendly and sympathetic the lawyer is to your concerns. Ask how much it would cost for a visit, or whether an initial consultation would be free.

- Bear in mind that a lawyer does not have to work downtown or in a fancy office to do good legal work. As a general rule, lawyers in big cities and those working in large firms are pricier than lawyers who work in small towns or smaller firms.

Agreeing on Legal Fees

Unless attorneys offer free initial consultations, their hourly rates generally range from $150 to $300, with some lawyers charging up to $450 per hour or more. However, guardianships are not a difficult area of the law and there is seldom any reason to pay a high-end fee. It is common for people to negotiate and agree on fees before they hire a lawyer—and many lawyers are willing to adjust their fees. More and more lawyers are using flat-fee billing, too, so you might want to ask whether that is an option. With a flat fee, you agree to the fee in advance and pay the full amount regardless of how long the work actually takes.

Whether you hire an attorney just to check your paperwork, or to handle the case from beginning to end, you and the lawyer should agree on the fee to be charged before any work begins.

Regardless of the fee arrangement, you must pay for court fees, service of process, and other fees such as costs of an investigation. Either the attorney will ask you to pay these costs up front, or will advance the costs and bill you later for reimbursement. Most guardianships will require well over $750 in costs—the court filing fees for the guardianship are at least $355, and fees for a court investigation or service of process are additional.

Make sure you understand what law office costs you will be expected to pay. For example, some lawyers charge clients for the costs of each photocopy made for a case, as well as postage and long distance telephone calls, while other lawyers include these office costs in their hourly fees.

Lawyers sometimes require a "retainer" before they'll start working on your case—usually at least several hundred dollars. When costs and lawyers' fees are billed, they are deducted from this retainer. If fees exceed the retainer, you are billed for the excess. But if the retainer is more money than the legal fees and costs, you are given a refund. You should be sent bills regularly, regardless of whether or not you give the lawyer a retainer. If you have any questions about fees, you can ask the attorney for copies of all bills and records of time spent on your case.

Get the Fee Agreement in Writing

In California, an attorney should give you an agreement in writing if the total amount you pay, including all attorneys' fees, is likely to be more than $1,000. Regardless of the expected or agreed amount of the fee, it is always a good idea to get the fee arrangement in writing. The law also requires that the written contract clearly explain all charges and services, and that it set out both the lawyer's and client's responsibilities.

Fees tend to be the biggest cause for misunderstanding between a lawyer and client, and a written agreement can go a long way in preventing problems. Make sure you understand the fee agreement before you sign it. In addition to the lawyers' fees, get a clear picture of what costs you will be paying.

Doing Your Own Legal Research

You may have questions about your guardianship that this book does not answer. If you need additional legal information, can't get the answer from a court clerk, and don't wish to consult a lawyer, you will need to do some research on your own.

If you decide to delve into the world of legal research, we recommend that you start by getting a copy of *Legal Research: How to Find & Understand the Law,* by Steve Elias and Susan Levinkind (Nolo). This hands-on guide to the law library addresses the research methods discussed here in much more detail and will answer most of the questions that are likely to arise in the course of your research.

Citations in This Book

Throughout this book you will encounter numbered references to California law. These are called "citations," and most refer to a set of statutes called the California Probate Code, which is abbreviated as PC. Thus, PC § 2551(b) means Probate Code Section 2551, Subsection (b). Another group of references is to probate policy manuals or memoranda, which set out local rules for specific courts. (See below.) Citations are included in this book so that you can look up the reference in the law library if you want. The box that follows explains most of the citations used in this book.

Legal Citations	
Abbreviation	**Legal Reference**
CC	Civil Code
CCP	Code of Civil Procedure
CRC	California Rules of Court
EC	Education Code
FC	Family Code
PC	Probate Code
W&I	Welfare & Institutions Code
USC	United States Code

Right now these references may seem like gobbledygook to you. But once you've visited the local law library, you'll quickly become familiar with them.

How to Do Legal Research

Here is an overview of the steps you'll take to do legal research:

1. Find a law library.

2. If you want to find a general discussion of your issue, you will need to check in an encyclopedia, form book, or practice manual (sometimes called background resources). Use the background resource to find references to relevant statutes. (**Note:** If you want to look up specific statutes and already have the citations, you can skip this step.)

3. Locate and read the statutes.

4. Locate and read cases that interpret the statutes.

Now that you have a general idea of the steps involved in legal research, let's take a more detailed look at each of them.

Find a Law Library

Each California county has a law library that is open to the public without charge. In larger counties, the law library is fully staffed and maintains a relatively complete collection of books. In smaller counties, the law library may be a small room off the court clerk's office that is only open during certain hours.

Regardless of the size of the library, you will find most law librarians willing and even pleased to give you a hand, as long as you don't ask them to answer legal questions or interpret what you find in the books. This might be considered practicing law, and they are prohibited from that and tend to be very cautious. If you encounter any difficulty getting access or help because you are not a lawyer, you may need to give a gentle reminder that the law library is paid for out of court filing fees, and that the California constitution requires public access.

 TIP

Check your local public library for legal resources. Some local public libraries also have quite extensive collections of law and legal research books. Before making a special trip to the law library, you may first want to check with the public library.

Consult Background Resources

If you do not have a particular legal citation, or you need help with documents or procedures not covered in this book, look in background resource materials that provide general information about the law. These include encyclopedias, form books, and practice manuals.

Here are several background resources that you can consult when you begin researching the law and procedures of guardianships:

- *California Guardianship Practice*, by California Continuing Education of the Bar (CEB). This guide is specifically dedicated to dealing with guardianships, and provides information and sample forms.
- *California Family Law Practice and Procedure*, 2nd edition, by Kathryn Kirkland, Ira Lurvey, Diana Richmond, and Stephen James Wagner, Editorial Consultants (Matthew Bender). This book provides information and samples of guardianship forms and procedures.
- *California Forms of Pleading and Practice* (Matthew Bender). If you want guidance on a particular procedure not covered in this book, turn to this attorneys' form book. Look in the "G" or "Guardianship" volume of this multivolume set to find the information you need.
- *California Probate Procedure*, 6th edition, by Hon. Arthur K. Marshall and Andrew S. Garb (Michie). This three-volume set gives a wide variety of information and forms. Volume One provides an overview of guardianship law, and provides citations to statutes and case law. It is somewhat dense, but still quite readable. Volume Two contains probate policy manuals for many counties. If you use this resource, make sure they are the most up-to-date policy manuals. Volume Three provides checklists and local forms for use in many counties. Again, make sure these forms are the most current.

Read the Law

Background resources, including this book, are only discussions about law and procedure—they are not the law itself. That's why background resources provide you with citations to relevant statutes (laws passed by the California legislature) and court interpretations of these laws. Reading these statutes is a crucial step in doing legal research.

In California, guardianships are primarily governed by a group of statutes called the Probate Code. The Probate Code governs the processes described in this book.

You may find statutes in a single volume of the California Probate Code, or as part of a book that collects the California Probate Code and other related codes (generally these books also have the Civil Code, Evidence Code, Family Code, Code of Civil Procedure, some Rules of Court, and portions of the Government Code). You usually can find these books in a public library.

There also are multivolume annotated book sets that give the statutes and annotations—information about each statute. They explain when a law was first passed, when different sections were amended, and give citations to and very short summaries of cases in which courts interpreted the statute. The case law summaries are by no means complete, and it's hard to tell from them whether they're related to the particular issue you're researching. Read the case yourself rather than relying on the annotation.

You may find that reading statutes leaves you less than fully enlightened. They can be difficult to understand or ambiguous. It can help to read what courts have said about them, and that's the next step.

Read Cases

The term "case law" refers to judges' published opinions about a dispute that was resolved in court. These decisions give important information about how a law has been interpreted. If you can find a case decision in which the facts were similar to your situation, you can get some guidance on how a court might decide your case. A law librarian can explain to you how to find a case that is cited in the annotations to a statute.

Probate Policy Manuals or Memoranda

Although all probate courts follow the basic procedures outlined in the Probate Code, most counties have a few special rules of their own. Many counties have printed pamphlets called probate policy manuals or memoranda. These pamphlets tell you things such as when particular forms must be presented to the court, what must be included in court documents, and where to call for information.

Call the court clerk and find out how to get the probate policy manual for that county. You may need to go to the library to look at it, or it may be available from the court clerk or online. Some libraries have books that include probate policy manuals for counties throughout California. Make sure that you look at the probate policy manual for the specific county in which you are filing the guardianship. You don't need to be concerned with other counties' rules.

Resources for Additional Copies of Judicial Council Forms

Most of the forms needed for a guardianship are Judicial Council forms. (See Chapter 3.) If you need additional or updated copies of these forms, you can obtain them either free or for a small fee from the superior court clerk. You can also download the official Judicial Council forms—or complete them in a PDF format— by visiting the California courts' self-help website at www.courtinfo.ca.gov. You can fill out forms online, print them out, and even save the forms to your own computer.

If you're going to the law library, ask the librarian where they keep copies of Judicial Council forms. Some law libraries keep copies in a special binder, which may be kept behind the librarian's desk. You can probably also photocopy the forms you need from these resources:

- *California Forms of Pleading and Practice— Judicial Council Forms* (Matthew Bender). This book contains the official forms published by the California Judicial Council.

- *West's California Judicial Council Forms* (West Publishing Company). This softcover book contains official forms published by the California Judicial Council. Check supplements to make sure you're copying the current forms. If the supplement shows an updated form, you'll need to get it from another source, because the supplements are printed on pages much smaller than regular Judicial Council forms. ●

Glossary of Guardianship Terms

To handle your own guardianship, you'll have to make an effort to understand some of the common legal terms you'll run into along the way. The legal profession uses language that is specialized and sometimes difficult to understand. The plain-English definitions in this book are geared toward guardianships. If you find yourself branching out in another area of law, these terms might be used slightly differently.

If you come across a confusing term that isn't defined in this glossary or elsewhere in the book, check in Nolo's *Plain-English Law Dictionary*, which is available as a book or online at www.nolo.com. You could also try a regular dictionary, but be sure to read the entire definition, as specialized legal meanings often are listed last. You also can check *Black's Law Dictionary*, available in all law libraries. Don't be intimidated if the definitions there are hard to understand; that book is notoriously confusing to everyone. A law librarian might be helpful if you can't find a satisfactory definition, as long as you don't ask for legal advice or interpretation.

Adult: A person who has attained the age of majority. In California, this is someone who is 18 years of age or older.

Appoint: When a court gives someone legal authority and responsibility to fulfill particular duties. For example, a judge appoints a guardian.

Benefits: Money or other rights to which someone is entitled, such as welfare, Social Security, or insurance.

Bond: A document guaranteeing that a certain amount of money will be paid if a guardian of an estate does not perform the required legal duties. A bond usually is issued by a surety company.

Calendar: Master list kept by a court that shows when cases are scheduled to be heard in court. To "calendar" (verb) means to schedule a hearing.

Case: A legal action that is taken to court. When you file your guardianship papers, a new case with its own case number is opened.

Child: The natural born or legally adopted daughter or son of a parent. Sometimes the term "child" may refer to a minor.

Commissioner: A lawyer appointed by the county's judges to assist in finding facts, hearing testimony, and resolving issues. Court commissioners frequently hear guardianship cases and have the same authority as judges to issue opinions in those cases.

Contested: A hearing or case is contested when someone objects, either in person or in writing.

Continuance: The postponement of a hearing, trial, or other scheduled court appearance. A continuance may be granted for many reasons, including when someone in the case is not prepared, or needs time to seek the advice of an attorney.

Court: The place where cases are filed and heard. This term might also refer to a judge. For example, you might say that the guardianship was granted by "the court," even though a judge actually made the decision.

Custody (Legal): The court-ordered right to make decisions on behalf of a minor about matters such as medical and educational needs.

Custody (Physical): Having physical charge and control over a minor, usually when the minor is living with someone. This traditionally is a court-ordered right, but the term is sometimes used to refer to informal custody arrangements.

Discharge: To relieve someone of offered duties in a given capacity (for example, to relieve someone of responsibility as a guardian). This typically occurs when a minor reaches the age of majority, or when a judge allows a guardian to resign.

Dismiss: To stop a legal action before it reaches a legal conclusion (for example, to stop a guardianship case before a guardian is appointed).

Estate: The possessions, property, and liabilities belonging to a minor.

Estate (Guardianship of): See **Guardianship (of Estate)**.

Estate Planning: The method of designating how and to whom property is to be transferred after death.

Ex parte: (Pronounced "ex-partay.") Without notice. Ex parte papers that are filed with a court are not served on anyone.

Foster Parents: Specially licensed adults who take a minor into their home after the minor is removed from biological parents' home by a court.

Guardian: An adult who has been given the legal right by a court to control and care for a minor or the minor's property.

Guardian ad litem: An adult, usually a close relative or attorney, who is appointed solely for the purpose of appearing on behalf of a minor in a civil lawsuit for money. (This book does not cover guardians ad litem.)

Guardianship (of Estate): Legal recognition by a court that an adult has legal responsibility for taking care of a minor's property.

Guardianship (generally): Legal recognition by a court that an adult has legal custody of and is responsible for taking care of a minor or the minor's property.

Guardianship (of Person): Legal recognition by a court that an adult has legal custody of and is responsible for taking care of a minor, including responsibility for the minor's physical, medical, educational, and health needs.

Guardianship (Temporary): Legal recognition by a court that an adult has responsibility for a minor or the minor's estate for a specified, limited time.

Hearing: A legal proceeding (other than a trial) held before a judge or court commissioner.

In Pro Per: Someone who is representing herself in a legal proceeding.

Investigator (court): Someone who is appointed by the court to look into a case. Depending on the court's policies, this would probably be a probation officer, domestic relations investigator, or other court-appointed official.

Judge: A public official who has legal authority to hear and decide cases in a court.

Letters (of Guardianship): A document issued by the court that designates legal authority.

Majority (Age of): The age at which a minor legally becomes an adult. In California this is the age of 18.

Maternal: Related through blood ties to someone's mother. For example, a maternal uncle would be the brother of one's mother, and a maternal grandmother would be the mother of one's mother.

Minor: A person who has not attained the age of majority. In California, this is someone under age 18.

Nominate: To name someone for an appointment (for example, a parent may nominate a proposed guardian). Someone who has been nominated is called a nominee.

Notice (of Hearing): Written notification of a legal event (such as a trial or a hearing). By law this notification must be given to any person involved or interested in a legal action.

Order: Decision rendered by a judge. This may be after a hearing or after you present papers for the judge to consider.

Papers: Legal documents.

Paternal: Related through blood ties to someone's father. For example, a paternal uncle would be the brother of one's father, and a paternal grandmother would be the mother of one's father.

Person (Guardianship of): See **Guardianship (of Person)**.

Petition: In the context of this book, an application or request that a guardianship be established, or authority to undertake a procedure be given.

Petitioner: In the context of this book, the person who files a petition, generally someone who is seeking a guardianship.

Probate Court (or Probate Division of the Superior Court): A division of the court that handles guardianship cases. The probate court also handles other matters, such as conservatorships, distribution of deceased people's assets, and administration of trusts.

Process (Service of): See **Service of Process**.

Property: Assets someone owns—including real estate, personal belongings (furniture, jewelry, clothing), bank accounts, stocks, bonds, interest in a business, the right to receive benefits, and a variety of other tangible and nontangible things.

Remove: To take someone out of an appointed position.

Resign: To voluntarily give up an appointed position.

Service of Process: Delivering court papers to a person or organization entitled to know what is happening in a case. There are detailed laws that specify how and by whom papers must be delivered.

Surety or Surety Company: A person or entity that is liable for another's debts. A surety company usually provides insurance for guardianship of an estate in the form of a bond.

Suspend: To temporarily stop someone or something, such as a guardian from performing her duties.

Temporary Guardianship: See **Guardianship (Temporary)**.

Terminate: To end something, such as a guardianship.

Ward: A minor who is in a court-appointed guardianship.

Forms for Informal Guardianship Situations

Caregiver's Authorization Affidavit

Use of this affidavit is authorized by Part 1.5 (commencing with Section 6550) of Division 11 of the California Family Code.

Instructions: Completion of items 1-4 and the signing of the affidavit is sufficient to authorize enrollment of a minor in school and authorize school-related medical care. Completion of items 5-8 is additionally required to authorize any other medical care. Print clearly.

The minor named below lives in my home and I am 18 years of age or older.

1. Name of minor: _____.

2. Minor's birth date: _____.

3. My name (adult giving authorization): _____.

4. My home address: _____

   _____.

_____

5. [ ] I am a grandparent, aunt, uncle, or other qualified relative of the minor (see back of this form for a definition of "qualified relative").

6. Check one or both (for example, if one parent was advised and the other cannot be located):
   [ ] I have advised the parent(s) or other person(s) having legal custody of the minor of my intent to authorize medical care, and have received no objection.

   [ ] I am unable to contact the parent(s) or other person(s) having legal custody of the minor at this time, to notify them of my intended authorization.

7. My date of birth: _____.

8. My California driver's license or identification card number: _____.

Warning: Do not sign this form if any of the statements above are incorrect, or you will be committing a crime punishable by a fine, imprisonment, or both.

I declare under penalty of perjury under the laws of the State of California that the foregoing is true and correct.

Dated: _____ Signed: _____

Notices:

1. This declaration does not affect the rights of the minor's parents or legal guardian regarding the care, custody, and control of the minor, and does not mean that the caregiver has legal custody of the minor.

2. A person who relies on this affidavit has no obligation to make any further inquiry or investigation.

Additional Information:

TO CAREGIVERS:

1. "Qualified relative," for purposes of item 5, means a spouse, parent, stepparent, brother, sister, stepbrother, stepsister, half brother, half sister, uncle, aunt, niece, nephew, first cousin, or any person denoted by the prefix "grand" or "great," or the spouse of any of the persons specified in this definition, even after the marriage has been terminated by death or dissolution.

2. The law may require you, if you are not a relative or a currently licensed foster parent, to obtain a foster home license in order to care for a minor. If you have any questions, please contact your local department of social services.

3. If the minor stops living with you, you are required to notify any school, health care provider, or health care service plan to which you have given this affidavit. The affidavit is invalid after the school, health care provider, or health care service plan receives notice that the minor no longer lives with you.

4. If you do not have the information requested in item 8 (California driver's license or I.D.), provide another form of identification such as your Social Security number or Medi-Cal number.

TO SCHOOL OFFICIALS:

1. Section 48204 of the Education Code provides that this affidavit constitutes a sufficient basis for a determination of residency of the minor, without the requirement of a guardianship or other custody order, unless the school district determines from actual facts that the minor is not living with the caregiver.

2. The school district may require additional reasonable evidence

that the caregiver lives at the address provided in item 4.

TO HEALTH CARE PROVIDERS AND HEALTH CARE SERVICE PLANS:

1. A person who acts in good faith reliance upon a caregiver's authorization affidavit to provide medical or dental care, without actual knowledge of facts contrary to those stated on the affidavit, is not subject to criminal liability or to civil liability to any person, and is not subject to professional disciplinary action, for that reliance if the applicable portions of the form are completed.

2. This affidavit does not confer dependency for health care coverage purposes.

JURAT FORM – CAREGIVER'S AUTHORIZATION AFFIDAVIT

STATE OF CALIFORNIA   )
)
)
COUNTY OF _____)

On _____, before me, _____,
a notary public, personally appeared _____,
personally known to me (or proved to me on the basis of
satisfactory evidence) to be the person whose name is
subscribed to the within instrument, and acknowledged to
me that he or she executed the same in his or her
authorized capacity and that by his or her signature on the
instrument, the person, or the entity upon behalf of which
the person acted, executed the instrument.

    I certify under PENALTY OF PERJURY under the laws of
the State of California that the foregoing paragraph is true
and correct.

_____
Signature of Notary Public

                                         NOTARY SEAL
                                         (Stamp seal above)

_____
Print Name of Notary Public

Guardianship Authorization

Minor

Name: _____

Birthdate: _____ Age: _____ Year in School: _____

Parent 1

Name: _____

Street Address: _____

City: _____ State: _____ Zip Code: _____

Home Phone: _____ Work Phone: _____

Cell Phone: _____

Parent 2

Name: _____

Street Address: _____

City: _____ State: _____ Zip Code: _____

Home Phone: _____ Work Phone: _____

Cell Phone: _____

Proposed Guardian

Name: _____

Street Address: _____

City: _____ State: _____ Zip Code: _____

Home Phone: _____ Work Phone: _____

Cell Phone: _____

Relationship to Minor: _____

In case of emergency, if proposed guardian cannot be reached, please contact: _____

Name: _____ Phone: _____

Cell Phone: _____

Authorization & Consent of Parent(s)

1. I affirm that the minor indicated above is my child and that I have legal custody of her/him. I give my full authorization and consent for my child to live with the proposed guardian, or for the proposed guardian to set a place of residence for my child.

2. I give the proposed guardian permission to act in my place and make decisions pertaining to my child's educational and religious activities including but not limited to enrollment, permission to participate in activities, and consent for medical treatment at school.

3. I give the proposed guardian permission to authorize medical and dental care for my child, including but not limited to medical examinations, X-rays, tests, anesthetic, surgical operations, hospital care, or other treatments that in the proposed guardian's sole opinion are needed or useful for my child. Such medical treatment shall only be provided upon the advice of and supervision by a physician, surgeon, dentist, or other medical practitioner licensed to practice in the United States.

4. I give the proposed guardian permission to apply for benefits on my child's behalf including but not limited to Social Security, public assistance, health insurance, and Veterans Administration benefits.

5. I give the proposed guardian permission to apply and obtain for my child any or all of the following: Social Security number, Social Security card, and U.S. passport.

6. This authorization shall cover the period from _____, 20_____, to _____, 20_____.

7. During the period when the proposed guardian cares for my child, the costs of my child's upkeep, living expenses, medical and dental expenses shall be paid as follows: _____
    _____

I declare under penalty of perjury under the laws of the State of California that the foregoing is true and correct.

Parent's Signature: _____   Date: _____, 20_____

Parent's Signature: _____   Date: _____, 20_____

Notarization

State of California

County of _____

On this _____ day of _____, 20_____, before me, a notary public of the State of California, personally appeared _____, personally known to me (or proved to me on the basis of satisfactory evidence) to be the person(s) whose name(s) is/are subscribed to this instrument, and acknowledged that she/he/they executed the same, in his/her/their authorized capacity(ies) and that by his/her/their signature(s) on the instrument the person(s), or the entity upon behalf of which the person(s) acted, executed the instrument.

I certify under PENALTY OF PERJURY under the laws of the State of California that the foregoing paragraph is true and correct.

WITNESS my hand and official seal.

Notary Public: _____   [Seal]

Consent of Proposed Guardian

I solemnly affirm that I will assume full responsibility for the minor who will live with me during the period designated above. I agree to make necessary decisions and to provide consent for the minor as set forth in the above Authorization & Consent by Parent(s). I also agree to the terms of the costs of the minor's upkeep, living expenses, medical and/or dental expenses set forth in the above Authorization & Consent of Parent(s).

I declare under penalty of perjury under the laws of the State of California that the foregoing is true and correct.

Proposed Guardian's Signature: _____   Date: _____, 20_____

Notarization

State of California

County of _____

On this _____ day of _____, 20___, before me, a notary public of the State of California, personally appeared _____, personally known to me (or proved to me on the basis of satisfactory evidence) to be the person(s) whose name(s) is/are subscribed to this instrument, and acknowledged that she/he/they executed the same, in his/her/their authorized capacity(ies) and that by his/her/their signature(s) on the instrument the person(s), or the entity upon behalf of which the person(s) acted, executed the instrument.

I certify under PENALTY OF PERJURY under the laws of the State of California that the foregoing paragraph is true and correct.

WITNESS my hand and official seal.

Notary Public: _____   [Seal]

Forms for Obtaining a Court-Ordered Guardianship

Form Name	Judicial Council Form Number	Chapter
Declaration	MC-030	3
Additional Page: Attach to Judicial Council Form or Other Court Paper	MC-020	3
Request for Dismissal	CIV-110	3
Request to Waive Court Fees	FW-001	3
Order on Court Fee Waiver (Superior Court)	FW-003	3
Guardianship Notification Worksheet	N/A	4
Attachment 10 to Petition for Appointment of Guardian of Minor	N/A	4
Consent of Proposed Guardian, Nomination of Guardian, and Consent to Appointment of Guardian and Waiver of Notice	GC-211	4
Petition for Appointment of Guardian of Minor	GC-210	5
Guardianship Petition—Child Information Attachment	GC-210(CA)	5
Declaration Under Uniform Child Custody Jurisdiction and Enforcement Act (UCCJEA)	FL-105/GC-120	5
Notice of Hearing—Guardianship or Conservatorship	GC-020	5
Order Dispensing With Notice—Guardianship or Conservatorship	GC-021	5
Order Appointing Guardian of Minor	GC-240	5
Letters of Guardianship	GC-250	5
Confidential Guardian Screening Form	GC-212	5
Duties of Guardian and Acknowledgment of Receipt	GC-248	5
Request for Hearing About Court Fee Waiver Order (Superior Court)	FW-006	6
Order on Court Fee Waiver After Hearing (Superior Court)	FW-008	6
Notice and Acknowledgment of Receipt—Civil	POS-015	6
Proof of Service of Summons	POS-010	6
Proof of Service by First-Class Mail—Civil	POS-030	6

ATTORNEY OR PARTY WITHOUT ATTORNEY *(Name, State Bar number, and address):*

FOR COURT USE ONLY

TELEPHONE NO.:   FAX NO. *(Optional):*

E-MAIL ADDRESS *(Optional):*

ATTORNEY FOR *(Name):*

SUPERIOR COURT OF CALIFORNIA, COUNTY OF

STREET ADDRESS:

MAILING ADDRESS:

CITY AND ZIP CODE:

BRANCH NAME:

PLAINTIFF/PETITIONER:

DEFENDANT/RESPONDENT:

DECLARATION	CASE NUMBER:

I declare under penalty of perjury under the laws of the State of California that the foregoing is true and correct.

Date:

_____
(TYPE OR PRINT NAME)

_____
(SIGNATURE OF DECLARANT)

☐ Attorney for ☐ Plaintiff ☐ Petitioner ☐ Defendant
☐ Respondent ☐ Other *(Specify):*

GUARDIANSHIP OF (Name):	CASE NUMBER:
Minor	

This form must be attached to another form or court paper before it can be filed in court.

I declare under penalty of perjury under the laws of the State of California that the foregoing is true and correct.

Date:

. . . .
(TYPE OR PRINT NAME)   ▶ _____
                                                                          (SIGNATURE OF DECLARANT)

☐ Petitioner/Plaintiff ☐ Respondent/Defendant ☐ Attorney
☐ Other *(specify)*:

(See reverse for a form to be used if this declaration is not to be attached to another court paper before filing)

Form Approved by the
Judicial Council of California
MC-031 [New January 1, 1987]

ATTACHED DECLARATION

1

2

3

4

5

6

7

8

9

10

11

12

13

14

15

16

17

18

19

20

21

22

23

24

25

26 (Required for verified pleading) The items on this page stated on information and belief are (specify item numbers, **not** line numbers):

27

This page may be used with any Judicial Council form or any other paper filed with the court.

Page _____

Form Approved by the
Judicial Council of California
MC-020 [New January 1, 1987]

ADDITIONAL PAGE
Attach to Judicial Council Form or Other Court Paper

CRC 201, 501

ATTORNEY OR PARTY WITHOUT ATTORNEY (Name, State Bar number, and address):	FOR COURT USE ONLY

TELEPHONE NO.:   FAX NO. (Optional):

E-MAIL ADDRESS (Optional):

ATTORNEY FOR (Name):

SUPERIOR COURT OF CALIFORNIA, COUNTY OF

STREET ADDRESS:

MAILING ADDRESS:

CITY AND ZIP CODE:

BRANCH NAME:

PLAINTIFF/PETITIONER:

DEFENDANT/RESPONDENT:

REQUEST FOR DISMISSAL	CASE NUMBER:
☐ **Personal Injury, Property Damage, or Wrongful Death** ☐ **Motor Vehicle** ☐ **Other** ☐ **Family Law** ☐ **Eminent Domain** ☐ **Other** (specify) :	

- A conformed copy will not be returned by the clerk unless a method of return is provided with the document. -

1. TO THE CLERK: Please **dismiss** this action as follows:

    a. (1) ☐ With prejudice   (2) ☐ Without prejudice

    b. (1) ☐ Complaint   (2) ☐ Petition

       (3) ☐ Cross-complaint filed by (name):   on (date):

       (4) ☐ Cross-complaint filed by (name):   on (date):

       (5) ☐ Entire action of all parties and all causes of action

       (6) ☐ Other (specify):*

2. (Complete in all cases except family law cases.)

    ☐ Court fees and costs were waived for a party in this case. (This information may be obtained from the clerk. If this box is checked, the declaration on the back of this form must be completed).

Date:

 . . . .   ▶

(TYPE OR PRINT NAME OF ☐ ATTORNEY ☐ PARTY WITHOUT ATTORNEY)   (SIGNATURE)

*If dismissal requested is of specified parties only of specified causes of action only, or of specified cross-complaints only, so state and identify the parties, causes of action, or cross-complaints to be dismissed.

Attorney or party without attorney for:

    ☐ Plaintiff/Petitioner   ☐ Defendant/Respondent

    ☐ Cross–Complainant

3. **TO THE CLERK:** Consent to the above dismissal is hereby given.**

    Date:

                                      ▶

(TYPE OR PRINT NAME OF ☐ ATTORNEY ☐ PARTY WITHOUT ATTORNEY)   (SIGNATURE)

** If a cross-complaint – or Response (Family Law) seeking affirmative relief – is on file, the attorney for cross-complainant (respondent) must sign this consent if required by Code of Civil Procedure section 581 (i) or (j).

Attorney or party without attorney for:

    ☐ Plaintiff/Petitioner   ☐ Defendant/Respondent

    ☐ Cross–Complainant

(To be completed by clerk)

4. ☐ Dismissal entered as requested on (date):

5. ☐ Dismissal entered on (date):   as to only (name):

6. ☐ Dismissal **not entered** as requested for the following reasons (specify):

7. a. ☐ Attorney or party without attorney notified on (date):

   b. ☐ Attorney or party without attorney not notified. Filing party failed to provide

      ☐ a copy to be conformed   ☐ means to return conformed copy

Date: Clerk, by _____ , Deputy

Form Adopted for Mandatory Use
 Judicial Council of California
 CIV-110 [Rev. July 1, 2009]

REQUEST FOR DISMISSAL

Code of Civil Procedure, § 581 et seq.;
 Gov. Code, § 68637(c); Cal. Rules of Court, rule 3.1390 <br> www.courtinfo.ca.gov

PLAINTIFF/PETITIONER:	CASE NUMBER:
DEFENDANT/RESPONDENT:	

Declaration Concerning Waived Court Fees

The court has a statutory lien for waived fees and costs on any recovery of $10,000 or more in value by settlement, compromise, arbitration award, mediation settlement, or other recovery. The court's lien must be paid before the court will dismiss the case.

1. The court waived fees and costs in this action for *(name):*

2. The person in item 1 *(check one):*
   a. ☐ is not recovering anything of value by this action.
   b. ☐ is recovering less than $10,000 in value by this action.
   c. ☐ is recovering $10,000 or more in value by this action. *(If item 2c is checked, item 3 must be completed.)*

3. ☐ All court fees and costs that were waived in this action have been paid to the court *(check one):* ☐ Yes ☐ No

I declare under penalty of perjury under the laws of the State of California that the information above is true and correct.

Date: _____

_____   ▶ _____
(TYPE OR PRINT NAME OF ☐ ATTORNEY ☐ PARTY MAKING DECLARATION)   (SIGNATURE)

FW-001 Request to Waive Court Fees

CONFIDENTIAL

If you are getting public benefits, are a low-income person, or do not have enough income to pay for household's basic needs and your court fees, you may use this form to ask the court to waive all or part of your court fees. The court may order you to answer questions about your finances. If the court waives the fees, you may still have to pay later if:

- You cannot give the court proof of your eligibility,
- Your financial situation improves during this case, or
- You settle your civil case for **$10,000** or more. The trial court that waives your fees will have a lien on any such settlement in the amount of the waived fees and costs. The court may also charge you any collection costs.

Clerk stamps date here when form is filed.

Fill in court name and street address:

(1) Your Information *(person asking the court to waive the fees):*

Name: _____

Street or mailing address: _____

City: _____ State: _____ Zip: _____

Fill in case number and name:

Case Number:

Case Name:

Phone number: _____

(2) Your Job, if you have one *(job title):* _____

Name of employer: _____

Employer's address: _____

(3) Your lawyer, if you have one *(name, firm or affiliation, address, phone number, and State Bar number):*

_____

_____

a. The lawyer has agreed to advance all or a portion of your fees or costs *(check one):* Yes ☐ No ☐

b. *(If yes, your lawyer must sign here)* Lawyer's signature: _____

If your lawyer is not providing legal-aid type services based on your low income, you may have to go to a hearing to explain why you are asking the court to waive the fees.

(4) What court's fees or costs are you asking to be waived?

☑ Superior Court (See *Information Sheet on Waiver of Superior Court Fees and Costs* (form FW-001-INFO).)

☐ Supreme Court, Court of Appeal, or Appellate Division of Superior Court (See *Information Sheet on Waiver of Appellate Court Fees and Costs* (form APP-015/FW-015-INFO).)

(5) Why are you asking the court to waive your court fees?

a. ☐ I receive *(check all that apply):* ☐ Medi-Cal ☐ Food Stamps ☐ SSI ☐ SSP ☐ County Relief/General Assistance ☐ IHSS (In-Home Supportive Services) ☐ CalWORKS or Tribal TANF (Tribal Temporary Assistance for Needy Families) ☐ CAPI (Cash Assistance Program for Aged, Blind and Disabled)

b. ☐ My gross monthly household income (before deductions for taxes) is less than the amount listed below. *(If you check 5b you must fill out 7, 8 and 9 on page 2 of this form.)*

Family Size	Family Income	Family Size	Family Income	Family Size	Family Income	*If more than 6 people at home, add $389.59 for each extra person.*
1	$1,128.13	3	$1,907.30	5	$2,686.46	
2	$1,517.71	4	$2,296.88	6	$3,076.05	

c. ☐ I do not have enough income to pay for my household's basic needs *and* the court fees. I ask the court to *(check one):* ☐ waive all court fees ☐ waive some of the court fees ☐ let me make payments over time *(Explain):* _____ *(If you check 5c, you must fill out page 2.)*

(6) ☐ Check here if you asked the court to waive your court fees for this case in the last six months.

(If your previous request is reasonably available, please attach it to this form and check here: ☐ *)*

I declare under penalty of perjury under the laws of the State of California that the information I have provided on this form and all attachments is true and correct.

Date: _____

_____ ▶ _____
Print your name here   *Sign here*

Judicial Council of California, *www.courtinfo.ca.gov*
Revised July 2, 2009, Mandatory Form
Government Code, § 68633
Cal. Rules of Court, rules 3.51, 8.26, and 8.818

Request to Waive Court Fees

FW-001, Page 1 of 2

*If you checked 5a on page 1, do not fill out below. If you checked 5b, fill out questions 7, 8, and 9 only. If you checked 5c, you **must** fill out this entire page. If you need more space, attach form MC-025 or attach a sheet of paper and write Financial Information and your name and case number at the top.*

⑦ ☐ Check here if your income changes a lot from month to month. Fill out below based on your average income for the past 12 months.

⑧ **Your Monthly Income**

a. Gross monthly income *(before deductions):* $ _____
   List each payroll deduction and amount below:
   (1) _____ $ _____
   (2) _____ $ _____
   (3) _____ $ _____
   (4) _____ $ _____

b. Total deductions *(add 8a (1)-(4) above):* $ _____

c. Total monthly take-home pay *(8a minus 8b):* $ _____

d. List the source and amount of *any* other income you get each month, including: spousal/child support, retirement, social security, disability, unemployment, military basic allowance for quarters (BAQ), veterans payments, dividends, interest, trust income, annuities, net business or rental income, reimbursement for job-related expenses, gambling or lottery winnings, etc.
   (1) _____ $ _____
   (2) _____ $ _____
   (3) _____ $ _____
   (4) _____ $ _____

e. **Your total monthly income is** *(8c plus 8d):* $ _____

⑨ **Household Income**

a. List all other persons living in your home and their income; include only your spouse and all individuals who depend in whole or in part on you for support, or on whom you depend in whole or in part for support.

	Name	Age	Relationship	Gross Monthly Income
(1)	_____	____	_____	$ _____
(2)	_____	____	_____	$ _____
(3)	_____	____	_____	$ _____
(4)	_____	____	_____	$ _____

b. **Total monthly income of persons above:** $ _____

Total monthly income *and* household income *(8e plus 9b):* $ _____

To list any other facts you want the court to know, such as unusual medical expenses, family emergencies, etc., attach form MC-025. Or attach a sheet of paper, and write Financial Information and your name and case number at the top. Check here if you attach another page. ☐

***Important!* If your financial situation or ability to pay court fees improves, you must notify the court within five days on form FW-010.**

⑩ **Your Money and Property**

a. Cash ----------------------------- $ _____

b. All financial accounts *(List bank name and amount):*
   (1) _____ $ _____
   (2) _____ $ _____
   (3) _____ $ _____
   (4) _____ $ _____

c. Cars, boats, and other vehicles

Make / Year	Fair Market Value	How Much You Still Owe
(1) _____	$ _____	$ _____
(2) _____	$ _____	$ _____
(3) _____	$ _____	$ _____

d. Real estate

Address	Fair Market Value	How Much You Still Owe
(1) _____	$ _____	$ _____
(2) _____	$ _____	$ _____
(3) _____	$ _____	$ _____

e. Other personal property (jewelry, furniture, furs, stocks, bonds, etc.):

Describe	Fair Market Value	How Much You Still Owe
(1) _____	$ _____	$ _____
(2) _____	$ _____	$ _____
(3) _____	$ _____	$ _____

⑪ **Your Monthly Expenses**
(Do not include payroll deductions you already listed in 8b.)

a. Rent or house payment & maintenance $ _____
b. Food and household supplies $ _____
c. Utilities and telephone $ _____
d. Clothing $ _____
e. Laundry and cleaning $ _____
f. Medical and dental expenses $ _____
g. Insurance (life, health, accident, etc.) $ _____
h. School, child care $ _____
i. Child, spousal support (another marriage) $ _____
j. Transportation, gas, auto repair and insurance $ _____
k. Installment payments (list each below):
   Paid to:
   (1) _____ $ _____
   (2) _____ $ _____
   (3) _____ $ _____
l. Wages/earnings withheld by court order $ _____
m. Any other monthly expenses *(list each below):*
   Paid to: How Much?
   (1) _____ $ _____
   (2) _____ $ _____
   (3) _____ $ _____

Total monthly expenses *(add 11a –11m above):* $ _____

FW-003 — Order on Court Fee Waiver (Superior Court)

① Person who asked the court to waive court fees:

Name: _____

Street or mailing address: _____

City: _____ State: _____ Zip: _____

② Lawyer, if person in ① has one *(name, address, phone number, e-mail, and State Bar number):* _____

_____

_____

③ A request to waive court fees was filed
on *(date):* _____

☐ The court made a previous fee waiver order in this case
on *(date):* _____

Read this form carefully. All checked boxes ☑ are court orders.

Clerk stamps date here when form is filed.

Fill in court name and street address:

Superior Court of California, County of

Fill in case number and case name:

Case Number:

Case Name:

Notice: The court may order you to answer questions about your finances and later order you to pay back the waived fees. If this happens and you do not pay, the court can make you pay the fees and also charge you collection fees. If there is a change in your financial circumstances during this case that increases your ability to pay fees and costs, you must notify the trial court within five days. (Use form FW-010.) If you win your case, the trial court may order the other side to pay the fees. If you settle your civil case for **$10,000** or more, the trial court will have a lien on the settlement in the amount of the waived fees. The trial court may not dismiss the case until the lien is paid.

---

④ After reviewing your *(check one):*   ☐ *Request to Waive Court Fees*   ☐ *Request to Waive Additional Court Fees*
the court makes the following orders:

a. ☐ The court **grants** your request, as follows:

(1) ☐ **Fee Waiver.** The court grants your request and waives your court fees and costs listed below. *(Cal. Rules of Court, rule 3.55.)* You do not have to pay the court fees for the following:

- Filing papers in Superior Court
- Making copies and certifying copies
- Sheriff's fee to give notice
- Reporter's daily fee *(for up to 60 days following the fee waiver order at the court-approved daily rate)*
- Preparing and certifying the clerk's transcript on appeal
- Giving notice and certificates
- Sending papers to another court department
- Court-appointed interpreter in small claims court
- Court fees for phone hearings

(2) ☐ **Additional Fee Waiver.** The court grants your request and waives your additional superior court fees and costs that are checked below. *(Cal. Rules of Court, rule 3.56.)* You do not have to pay for the checked items.

☐ Jury fees and expenses
☐ Fees for court-appointed experts
☐ Reporter's daily fees *(beyond the 60-day period following the fee waiver order)*
☐ Other *(specify):* _____

☐ Fees for a peace officer to testify in court
☐ Court-appointed interpreter fees for a witness

(3) ☐ **Fee Waiver for Appeal.** The court grants your request and waives the fees and costs checked below, for your appeal. *(Cal. Rules of Court, rules 3.55, 3.56, 8.26, and 8.818.)* You do not have to pay for the checked items.

☐ Preparing and certifying clerk's transcript for appeal
☐ Other *(specify):* _____

Judicial Council of California, *www.courtinfo.ca.gov*
Revised July 1, 2009, Mandatory Form
Government Code, § 68634(e)
California Rules of Court, rule 3.52

Order on Court Fee Waiver (Superior Court)

FW-003, Page 1 of 2

b. ☐ The court **denies** your request, as follows:

> **Warning!** If you miss the deadline below, the court cannot process your request for hearing or the court papers you filed with your original request. If the papers were a notice of appeal, the appeal may be dismissed.

(1) ☐ The court **denies** your request because it is incomplete. You have **10 days** after the clerk gives notice of this order (see date below) to:
- Pay your fees and costs, or
- File a new revised request that includes the items listed below *(specify incomplete items):*

_____

(2) ☐ The court **denies** your request because the information you provided on the request shows that you are not eligible for the fee waiver you requested *(specify reasons):* _____

_____

The court has enclosed a blank *Request for Hearing About Court Fee Waiver Order (Superior Court)*, form FW-006. You have **10 days** after the clerk gives notice of this order (see date below) to:
- Pay your fees and costs, or
- Ask for a hearing in order to show the court more information. *(Use form FW-006 to request hearing.)*

c. ☐ The court needs more information to decide whether to grant your request. You must go to court on the date below. The hearing will be about *(specify questions regarding eligibility):* _____

_____

☐ Bring the following proof to support your request if reasonably available:_____

_____

| Hearing Date → | Date: _____ Dept.: _____ | Time: _____ Rm.: _____ | Name and address of court if different from page 1: _____ _____ |

> **Warning!** If item c is checked, and you do not go to court on your hearing date, the judge will deny your request to waive court fees, and you will have 10 days to pay your fees. If you miss that deadline, the court cannot process the court papers you filed with your request. If the papers were a notice of appeal, the appeal may be dismissed.

Date: _____

_____
Signature of (check one): ☐ *Judicial Officer* ☐ *Clerk, Deputy*

Request for Accommodations. Assistive listening systems, computer-assisted real-time captioning, or sign language interpreter services are available if you ask at least 5 days before your hearing. Contact the clerk's office for *Request for Accommodation,* Form MC-410. (Civil Code, § 54.8.)

Clerk's Certificate of Service

I certify that I am not involved in this case and *(check one):*   ☐ A certificate of mailing is attached.

☐ I handed a copy of this order to the party and attorney, if any, listed in ① and ②, at the court, on the date below.

☐ This order was mailed first class, postage paid, to the party and attorney, if any, at the addresses listed in ① and ②, from *(city):* _____ , California on the date below.

Date: _____   Clerk, by _____ , Deputy

Order on Court Fee Waiver (Superior Court)

Guardianship Notification Worksheet
Part 1. Relatives

(1) Names and addresses of minor's relatives and other people entitled to notice	(2) Need to locate?	(3) Date located	(4) Will sign Waiver of Notice & Consent?	(5) Need to have served?	(6) Service type, if need to have served (see Chapter 6 for instructions)	(7) Date served or Order Dispensing Notice	(8) Date file Proof of Service
Minor			Cannot sign since under 18	Only if 12 or over, or if minor has a child	Personal		
Minor's mother					Personal or Notice and Acknowledgment of Receipt		
Minor's father					Personal or Notice and Acknowledgment of Receipt		
Minor's maternal grandparents (mother's parents)					Mail		
Minor's paternal grandparents (father's parents)					Mail		
Minor's spouse—can only petition for guardianship of the estate				Can sign only if 18 or over	Mail		

Guardianship Notification Worksheet

Part 1. Relatives (continued)

(1) Names and addresses of minor's relatives and other people entitled to notice	(2) Need to locate?	(3) Date located	(4) Will sign Waiver of Notice & Consent?	(5) Need to have served?	(6) Service type, if need to have served (see Chapter 6 for instructions)	(7) Date served or Order Dispensing Notice	(8) Date file Proof of Service
Minor's sisters and brothers (include their ages; if parents not listed elsewhere on worksheet, list their names and addresses)			Cannot sign since under 18	Only if 12 or over, or if minor has a child	Mail, if over 12. Serve parents, if under 18		
Minor's children (if child's other parent not listed elsewhere on worksheet, list name and address)			Cannot sign since under 18		Not required, but must serve both of child's parents		
Anyone presently having legal custody of minor (not including you)					Personal or Notice and Acknowledgment of Receipt		
Anyone nominated minor's legal guardian (not including you)					Personal or Notice and Acknowledgment of Receipt		
Anyone who has physical custody of minor (not including you)					Mail		

Guardianship Notification Worksheet
Part 2. Agencies

(1) Name and address of agencies entitled to notice (see Chapter 6)	(2) Need to have served?	(3) Service type, if need to have served	(4) Date Served	(5) Date file Proof of Service
Local Social Service Agency		Mail		
Court investigator		Mail		
State Director of Social Services		Mail		
Director of Mental Health		Mail		
Director of Developmental Services		Mail		
Veterans Administration		Mail		

GUARDIANSHIP OF (Name):	Case Number:

ATTACHMENT 10
to Petition for Appointment of Guardian of Minor

I_____, declare that I am _____ in this

guardianship case, that I have made the following attempts to locate _____, who is

related to the minor in this action as _____. To date my efforts have been

unsuccessful.

1. ☐ I checked in telephone directories for listings. The details of my attempts are:

2. ☐ I checked with directory assistance. The details of my attempts are:

3. ☐ I checked with friends and relatives. The details of my attempts are:

4. ☐ I checked with former employers. The details of my attempts are:

5. ☐ I checked the last known residence address. The details of my attempts are:

6. ☐ I checked with voter registration records. The details of my attempts are:

7. ☐ I checked with the motor vehicles department. The details of my attempts are:

8. ☐ Other (specify):

I declare under penalty of perjury under the laws of the state of California that the foregoing is true and correct.

Date:

....
(TYPE OR PRINT NAME)

_____
(SIGNATURE)

ATTORNEY OR PARTY WITHOUT ATTORNEY (Name, State Bar number, and address):

TELEPHONE NO.:   FAX NO. (Optional):

E-MAIL ADDRESS (Optional):

ATTORNEY FOR (Name):

SUPERIOR COURT OF CALIFORNIA, COUNTY OF

STREET ADDRESS:

MAILING ADDRESS:

CITY AND ZIP CODE:

BRANCH NAME:

GUARDIANSHIP OF THE ☐ PERSON ☐ ESTATE OF (Name):

☐ **CONSENT OF PROPOSED GUARDIAN**
☐ **NOMINATION OF GUARDIAN**
☐ **CONSENT TO APPOINTMENT OF GUARDIAN AND WAIVER OF NOTICE**

CASE NUMBER:

CONSENT OF PROPOSED GUARDIAN

1. I consent to serve as guardian of the ☐ person ☐ estate of the minor.

Date:

▶

_____
(TYPE OR PRINT NAME)

_____
(SIGNATURE OF PROPOSED GUARDIAN)

NOMINATION OF GUARDIAN

2. I am ☐ a parent of the minor ☐ a donor of a gift to the minor. I nominate (name and address):

as guardian of the ☐ person ☐ estate of the minor.

3. I am ☐ a parent of the minor ☐ a donor of a gift to the minor. I nominate (name and address):

as guardian of the ☐ person ☐ estate of the minor.

Date:

▶

_____
(TYPE OR PRINT NAME)

_____
(SIGNATURE)

> **NOTICE: The guardian of the person of a minor child has full legal and physical custody until the child becomes an adult or is adopted, the court changes guardians, or the court terminates the guardianship. Parents or other interested persons must petition the court to terminate the guardianship. The court will not do so unless the judge decides that termination would be in the child's best interest.**

CONSENT TO APPOINTMENT OF GUARDIAN AND WAIVER OF NOTICE

4. I consent to appointment of the guardian as requested in the *Petition for Appointment of Guardian of Minor*, filed on
(date): _____. I am entitled to notice in this proceeding, but I waive notice of hearing of the petition, including notice of any request for independent powers contained in it. I waive timely receipt of a copy of the petition.

▶

DATE	(TYPE OR PRINT NAME)	(SIGNATURE)	RELATIONSHIP TO MINOR

▶

DATE	(TYPE OR PRINT NAME)	(SIGNATURE)	RELATIONSHIP TO MINOR

▶

DATE	(TYPE OR PRINT NAME)	(SIGNATURE)	RELATIONSHIP TO MINOR

☐ Continued on Attachment 4.

Page 1 of 1

Form Adopted for Mandatory Use
Judicial Council of California
GC-211 [Rev. January 1, 2004]

CONSENT OF PROPOSED GUARDIAN, NOMINATION OF GUARDIAN, AND CONSENT TO APPOINTMENT OF GUARDIAN AND WAIVER OF NOTICE

Probate Code, §§ 1204, 1500–1502

ATTORNEY OR PARTY WITHOUT ATTORNEY *(Name, State Bar number, and address):*	FOR COURT USE ONLY
TELEPHONE NO.: FAX NO. *(Optional):* E-MAIL ADDRESS *(Optional):* ATTORNEY FOR *(Name):*	

SUPERIOR COURT OF CALIFORNIA, COUNTY OF
STREET ADDRESS:
MAILING ADDRESS:
CITY AND ZIP CODE:
BRANCH NAME:

GUARDIANSHIP OF *(Name):*	CASE NUMBER:
MINOR	

PETITION FOR APPOINTMENT OF GUARDIAN OF ☐ MINOR ☐ MINORS ☐ Person* ☐ Estate*	HEARING DATE AND TIME:	DEPT.:

1. **Petitioner** *(name each):*

requests that

    a. ☐ *(Name):*
       (Address
       and telephone):

       be appointed guardian of the PERSON of the minor or minors named in item 2 and Letters issue upon qualification.

    b. ☐ *(Name):*
       (Address
       and telephone):

       be appointed guardian of the ESTATE of the minor or minors named in item 2 and Letters issue upon qualification.

    c. (1) ☐ bond not be required ☐ because the petition is for guardian of the person only ☐ because the proposed guardian is a corporate fiduciary or an exempt government agency ☐ for the reasons stated in Attachment 1c.

       (2) ☐ $ bond be fixed. It will be furnished by an authorized surety company or as otherwise provided by law. *(Specify reasons in Attachment 1c if the amount is different from the minimum required by Prob. Code, § 8482.)*

       (3) ☐ $ in deposits in a blocked account be allowed. Receipts will be filed. *(Specify institution and location):*

    d. ☐ authorization be granted under Probate Code section 2590 to exercise the powers specified in Attachment 9.
    e. ☐ orders relating to the powers and duties of the proposed guardian of the person under Probate Code sections 2351–2358 be granted *(specify orders, facts, and reasons in Attachment 1e).*
    f. ☐ an order dispensing with notice to the persons named in Attachment 10 be granted.
    g. ☐ other orders be granted *(specify in Attachment 1g).*

2. Attached is a copy of *Guardianship Petition—Child Information Attachment* (form GC-210(CA)) for **each** minor for whom this petition requests the appointment of a guardian. The full legal name and date of birth of each minor is :

    a. Name: Date of Birth *(month/day/year):*

    b. Name: Date of Birth *(month/day/year):*

    c. Name: Date of Birth *(month/day/year):*

    d. Name: Date of Birth *(month/day/year):*

    ☐ The names and dates of birth of additional minors are specified on Attachment 2 to this petition.

* You MAY use this form or form GC-210(P) for a guardianship of the person. You MUST use this form for a guardianship of the estate or the person and estate. Do NOT use this form for a temporary guardianship.

Page 1 of 3

Form Adopted for Mandatory and Alternative Mandatory Use Instead of Form GC-210(P) Judicial Council of California GC-210 [Rev. July 1, 2009]

PETITION FOR APPOINTMENT OF GUARDIAN OF MINOR
(Probate—Guardianships and Conservatorships)

Probate Code, § 1510; Cal. Rules of Court, rule 7.101 www.courtinfo.ca.gov

GUARDIANSHIP OF *(Name):*	CASE NUMBER:
MINOR	

3. Petitioner is
   a. ☐ related to the minor or minors named in item 2, as shown in item 7 of each minor's attached form GC-210(CA).
   b. ☐ the minor named in item 2, who is 12 years of age or older.
   c. ☐ other person on behalf of minor or minors named in item 2, as shown in item 7 of each minor's attached form GC-210(CA).

4. The proposed guardian is *(check all that apply):*
   a. ☐ a nominee *(affix a copy of nomination as Attachment 4a or file* Nomination of Guardian (form GC-211, items 2 and 3) with this petition.
   b. ☐ related to the minor or minors named in item 2, as shown in item 3 of each minor's attached form GC-210(CA).
   c. ☐ other, as shown in item 3 of each minor's attached form GC-210(CA).
   d. ☐ a professional fiduciary within the meaning of the Professional Fiduciaries Act. The proposed guardian's license status is shown in item 1 on page 1 of the attached Professional Fiduciary Attachment. *(Use form GC-210(A-PF)/GC-310(A-PF) for this attachment.)*

5. ☐ Petitioner, with intent to adopt, has accepted or intends to accept physical care or custody of the minor.

6. ☐ A person other than the proposed guardian has been nominated as the guardian of the minor by ☐ will ☐ other writing. A copy of the nomination is affixed as Attachment 6. *(Specify name and address of nominee in item 2 of minor's attached form GC-210(CA).)*

7. ☐ **Character and estimated value of property of the estate** *(complete if petition requests appointment of a guardian of the estate or the person and estate):*
   a. Personal property: $
   b. Annual gross income from all sources, including real and personal property, wages, pensions, and public benefits: $ _____
   c. **Total:** $ _____
   d. Real property: $

8. Appointment of a guardian of the ☐ person ☐ estate of the minor or minors named in item 2 is necessary or convenient for the following reasons:

☐ Continued in Attachment 8.   ☐ Parental custody would be detrimental to the minor or minors named in item 2.

9. ☐ Granting the proposed guardian of the estate powers to be exercised independently under Probate Code section 2590 would be to the advantage and benefit and in the best interest of the guardianship estate. Reasons for this request and the powers requested are specified in Attachment 9.

10. ☐ Notice to the persons named in Attachment 10 should be dispensed with under Probate Code section 1511 because
    ☐ they cannot with reasonable diligence be given notice *(specify names and efforts to locate in Attachment 10).*
    ☐ giving notice to them would be contrary to the interest of justice *(specify names and reasons in Attachment 10).*

PETITION FOR APPOINTMENT OF GUARDIAN OF MINOR
(Probate—Guardianships and Conservatorships)

GUARDIANSHIP OF (Name):	CASE NUMBER:
┌─ MINOR	

11. ☐ (Complete this item if this petition is filed by a person who is not related to a minor named in item 2 and is not a petition for appointment of a guardian of the estate only.)

   a. ☐ Petitioner is the proposed guardian and will promptly furnish all information requested by any agency referred to in Probate Code section 1543.

   b. ☐ Petitioner is not the proposed guardian. A statement by the proposed guardian that he or she will promptly furnish all information requested by any agency referred to in Probate Code section 1543 is affixed as Attachment 11b.

   c. The proposed guardian's home ☐ is ☐ is not a licensed foster family home.

   d. ☐ The proposed guardian has never filed a petition for adoption of the minor ☐ except as specified in Attachment 11d.

12. ☐ Attached to this petition is a *Declaration Under Uniform Child Custody Jurisdiction and Enforcement Act (UCCJEA)* (form FL-105/GC-120) concerning all children listed in item 2. *(Guardianship of the person or the person and estate.)*

13. Filed with this petition are the following *(check all that apply):*

   ☐ *Consent of Proposed Guardian* (form GC-211, item 1)
   ☐ *Nomination of Guardian* (form GC-211, items 2 and 3)
   ☐ *Consent to Appointment of Guardian and Waiver* of Notice (form GC-211, item 4)
   ☐ *Petition for Appointment of Temporary Guardian* (form GC-110)
   ☐ *Petition for Appointment of Temporary Guardian of the Person* (form GC-110(P))
   ☐ *Confidential Guardianship Screening Form* (form GC-212)

   Other (*specify*):

14. All attachments to this form are incorporated by this reference as though placed here in this form. There are _____ pages attached to this form.

Date: _____

▶ _____
(SIGNATURE OF ATTORNEY*)

* (All petitioners must also sign (Prob. Code, § 1020).)

I declare under penalty of perjury under the laws of the State of California that the foregoing is true and correct.

Date: _____

_____   ▶ _____
(TYPE OR PRINT NAME)   (SIGNATURE OF PETITIONER)

_____   ▶ _____
(TYPE OR PRINT NAME)   (SIGNATURE OF PETITIONER)

_____   ▶ _____
(TYPE OR PRINT NAME)   (SIGNATURE OF PETITIONER)

PETITION FOR APPOINTMENT OF GUARDIAN OF MINOR
(Probate—Guardianships and Conservatorships)

Guardianship of *(all children's names):*

This child's name:

Fill out a separate copy of this form for **each** child for whom you want the court to appoint a guardian.

This form is attached to the Petition, ☐ **item 2 of form GC-210,** or ☐ **item 8 of form GC-210(P).**

The Petition asks for the appointment of a guardian of this child's *(specify):* ☐ person ☐ estate ☐ person and estate

① Tell the court about this child

a. Child's full legal name: _____ Date of birth: _____

                    First   *Middle*   *Last*   *Month/Day/Year*

b. Child's current address: _____

c. *(Answer the questions in item c only if the Petition to which this form is attached asks for the appointment of a guardian of this child's person or this child's person and estate.)*

  (1) Is this child a member of, or eligible for membership in, an Indian tribe recognized by the federal government? ☐ No ☐ Not sure ☐ Yes, *(specify tribe):* _____
      (If you checked "Yes" to item (1), this guardianship case is subject to the Indian Child Welfare Act *("ICWA") (25 U.S.C. § 1901, et seq.). If you checked "Not sure" or "No" to item 1, answer item (2)).*

  (2) Do you know or have reason to know (within the meaning of Prob. Code, § 1460.2, Welf. & Inst. Code, § 224.3, and rule 7.1015 of the Cal. Rules of Court), that this child may be an Indian child?
      ☐ No ☐ Yes *(If you checked "Yes" to either item (1) or item (2), you must fill out a* Notice of Child Custody Proceeding for Indian Child *(Form ICWA-030) ("Notice"). Your attorney must serve copies of the* Notice, *together with copies of your petition and all attachments, including this form, on the child's parents; any Indian custodian (as defined in ICWA, at 25 U.S.C. § 1903, and Probate Code section 1449); any Indian tribe that may have a connection to the child; the Bureau of Indian Affairs; and possibly the U. S. Secretary of the Interior, by certified or registered U. S. Mail, return receipt requested. If you are not represented by an attorney in this case, the court will serve copies of these papers, but you must first fill out the original* Notice *and deliver it to the court. After service, the original* Notice *and all return receipts must be filed with the court. Service of the* Notice *is in addition to service of any other notices required in this case.)*

d. Is this child married? ☐ Yes ☐ No ☐ Never married   If you checked "No," was this child formerly married but the marriage was dissolved or ended in divorce? ☐ Yes ☐ No
   (The court cannot appoint a guardian of the person for a minor child who is married or whose marriage was dissolved or ended in divorce.)

e. Is this child receiving public assistance? ☐ Yes ☐ No ☐ Unknown *(If you checked "Yes," fill out below.)*

Type of Aid	Monthly Benefit	Type of Aid	Monthly Benefit
☐ TANF (Temporary Asst. for Needy Families)	$	☐ Other *(explain):*	$
☐ Social Security	$	☐ Other *(explain):*	$
☐ Dept. Veterans Affairs Benefits	$		

f. Name and address of the person with *legal* custody of this child: _____

Judicial Council of California
www.courtinfo.ca.gov
Revised January 1, 2008, Mandatory Form
Probate Code, §§ 1449, 1459.5, 1510,
Cal Rules of Court, rule 7.1015

Guardianship Petition—Child Information Attachment
(Probate—Guardianships and Conservatorships)

GC-210(CA), Page 1 of 4

→

Guardianship of *(all children's names):* _____

This child's name: _____

Case Number:

---

(1) Tell the court about this child (continued)

g. ☐ *(Check this box and fill out below if the person the child lives with is not the person with legal custody.)*
Name and address of the person this child lives with (has the care of the child): _____
_____
_____

h. ☐ *(Check this box if this child has been involved in an adoption, juvenile court, marriage dissolution (divorce), domestic relations, custody, or other similar court case.)* Describe the court case below:

Type of Case	Court District or County and State	Case Number (if known)

i. ☐ *(Check this box if this child is in or on leave from an institution supervised by the California Department of Developmental Services or the California Department of Mental Health.)* Write the name of the institution here: _____

(2) List the names and addresses of this child's relatives and other persons shown below:

Relationship	Name	Home Address (Street, City, State, Zip)
Father	_____	_____
Mother	_____	_____
Grandfather (Father's father)	_____	_____
Grandmother (Father's mother)	_____	_____
Grandfather (Mother's father)	_____	_____
Grandmother (Mother's mother)	_____	_____
Brother/Sister	_____	_____
Brother/Sister	_____	_____
Brother/Sister	_____	_____

Guardianship of *(all children's names):* _____

This child's name: _____

2 **Names and addresses of this child's relatives and other persons (continued):**

Relationship	Name	Home Address (Street, City, State, Zip)
Brother/Sister	_____	_____
		_____
Brother/Sister	_____	_____
		_____

☐ *Check here if this child has additional brothers or sisters, including half-brothers and half-sisters, and list their names and addresses on a separate sheet of paper. Write "Form GC-210(CA)," the name of this child, and "Item 2:—Other Siblings" at the top of the paper and attach it to this form.*

Spouse
(Guardianship of the estate only) _____ _____

Person nominated as guardian of this child
(Other than a proposed guardian listed in **3** *)* _____ _____

3 **Information about the proposed guardian:**

a. Name *(name all proposed guardians if more than one):* _____
_____
_____

b. Relationship(s) to the child named in **1** *(check all that apply):*
☐ Relative *(specify relationships of all proposed guardians to the child):* _____
_____

☐ Not a relative *(explain interest in or connection to this child):* _____
_____
_____

4 *Explain why appointing the person in* **3** *guardian would be best for this child:* _____
_____
_____
_____
_____

☐ *Check here if you need more space. Continue your explanation on a separate sheet of paper. Write "Form GC-210(CA)," the name of this child, and "Attachment 4:—Best Interest of Child" at the top of the paper and attach it to this form.*

---

5   Do one or both of this child's parents agree that the person in ③ can be the child's guardian?

     a. Father: ☐ Yes   ☐ No   ☐ Not known at this time.

     b. Mother: ☐ Yes   ☐ No   ☐ Not known at this time.

     (You may file a filled-out Consent to Appointment of Guardian and Waiver of Notice *(form GC-211, item 4) signed by the child's parent or parents (or any adult relative listed in* ② *) who agree. The court may excuse you from having to give notice of the court hearing on your request for appointment of a guardian to a parent or other relative who signs that form.)*

6   **Suitability for guardianship of this child**

     a.   Does this child live with the person in ③ now?   ☐ Yes   ☐ No

     b.   If the court approves the guardianship, will this child live with the person in ③ ?   ☐ Yes   ☐ No

     c.   Does the person in ③ plan to adopt this child now?   ☐ Yes   ☐ No

7   ☐ **Check this box if you (the petitioner) are *not* the person in ③ , and fill in below.**

     Your relationship to this child:

     ☐ Relative *(specify):* _____

     ☐ Not a relative *(explain your interest in or connection to this child):* _____

     _____

     _____

     _____

8   Except as otherwise stated in this form, the statements made in the Petition to which this form is attached fully apply to this child.

ATTORNEY OR PARTY WITHOUT ATTORNEY *(Name, State Bar number, and address):*	FOR COURT USE ONLY

TELEPHONE NO.:   FAX NO. *(Optional):*

E-MAIL ADDRESS *(Optional):*

ATTORNEY FOR *(Name):*

SUPERIOR COURT OF CALIFORNIA, COUNTY OF

STREET ADDRESS:

MAILING ADDRESS:

CITY AND ZIP CODE:

BRANCH NAME:

(This section applies only to family law cases.)

PETITIONER:

RESPONDENT:

OTHER PARTY:

(This section apples only to guardianship cases.)

GUARDIANSHIP OF *(Name):*   Minor

CASE NUMBER:

DECLARATION UNDER UNIFORM CHILD CUSTODY JURISDICTION AND ENFORCEMENT ACT (UCCJEA)

1. **I am a party** to this proceeding to determine custody of a child.

2. ☐ My present address and the present address of each child residing with me is confidential under Family Code section 3429 as I have indicated in item 3.

3. There are *(specify number):*   minor children who are subject to this proceeding, as follows:
   (Insert the information requested below. The residence information must be given for the last FIVE years.)

a. Child's name		Place of birth	Date of birth	Sex
Period of residence	Address	Person child lived with *(name and complete current address)*		Relationship
to present	☐ Confidential	☐ Confidential		
to	Child's residence *(City, State)*	Person child lived with *(name and complete current address)*		
to	Child's residence *(City, State)*	Person child lived with *(name and complete current address)*		
to	Child's residence *(City, State)*	Person child lived with *(name and complete current address)*		

b. Child's name		Place of birth	Date of birth	Sex
☐ Residence information is the same as given above for child a. *(If NOT the same, provide the information below.)*				
Period of residence	Address	Person child lived with *(name and complete current address)*		Relationship
to present	☐ Confidential	☐ Confidential		
to	Child's residence *(City, State)*	Person child lived with *(name and complete current address)*		
to	Child's residence *(City, State)*	Person child lived with *(name and complete current address)*		
to	Child's residence *(City, State)*	Person child lived with *(name and complete current address)*		

c. ☐ Additional residence information for a child listed in item a or b is continued on attachment 3c.

d. ☐ Additional children are listed on form *FL-105(A)/GC-120(A)*. *(Provide all requested information for additional children.)*

Form Adopted for Mandatory Use
Judicial Council of California
FL-105/GC-120 [Rev. January 1, 2009]

**DECLARATION UNDER UNIFORM CHILD CUSTODY
JURISDICTION AND ENFORCEMENT ACT (UCCJEA)**

Family Code, § 3400 et seq.;
Probate Code, §§ 1510(f), 1512
www.courtinfo.ca.gov

SHORT TITLE:	CASE NUMBER:

4. Do you have information about, or have you participated as a party or as a witness or in some other capacity in, another court case or custody or visitation proceeding, in California or elsewhere, concerning a child subject to this proceeding?

☐ Yes ☐ No *(If yes, attach a copy of the orders (if you have one) and provide the following information):*

Proceeding	Case number	Court *(name, state, location)*	Court order or judgment *(date)*	Name of each child	Your connection to the case	Case status
a. ☐ Family						
b. ☐ Guardianship						
c. ☐ Other						

Proceeding	Case Number	Court *(name, state, location)*
d. ☐ Juvenile Delinquency/ Juvenile Dependency		
e. ☐ Adoption		

5. ☐ One or more domestic violence restraining/protective orders are now in effect. *(Attach a copy of the orders if you have one and provide the following information):*

Court	County	State	Case number *(if known)*	Orders expire *(date)*
a. ☐ Criminal				
b. ☐ Family				
c. ☐ Juvenile Delinquency/ Juvenile Dependency				
d. ☐ Other				

6. Do you know of any person who is not a party to this proceeding who has physical custody or claims to have custody of or visitation rights with any child in this case? ☐ Yes ☐ No *(If yes, provide the following information):*

a. Name and address of person	b. Name and address of person	c. Name and address of person
☐ Has physical custody ☐ Claims custody rights ☐ Claims visitation rights	☐ Has physical custody ☐ Claims custody rights ☐ Claims visitation rights	☐ Has physical custody ☐ Claims custody rights ☐ Claims visitation rights
Name of each child	Name of each child	Name of each child

I declare under penalty of perjury under the laws of the State of California that the foregoing is true and correct.

Date:

▶

_____
(TYPE OR PRINT NAME)

_____
(SIGNATURE OF DECLARANT)

7. ☐ Number of pages attached:_____

NOTICE TO DECLARANT: You have a continuing duty to inform this court if you obtain any information about a custody proceeding in a California court or any other court concerning a child subject to this proceeding.

DECLARATION UNDER UNIFORM CHILD CUSTODY JURISDICTION AND ENFORCEMENT ACT (UCCJEA)

ATTORNEY OR PARTY WITHOUT ATTORNEY *(Name, State Bar number, and address):*

FOR COURT USE ONLY

TELEPHONE NO.:   FAX NO. *(Optional):*

E-MAIL ADDRESS *(Optional):*

ATTORNEY FOR *(Name):*

SUPERIOR COURT OF CALIFORNIA, COUNTY OF

STREET ADDRESS:

MAILING ADDRESS:

CITY AND ZIP CODE:

BRANCH NAME:

☐ GUARDIANSHIP   ☐ CONSERVATORSHIP   OF THE   ☐ PERSON   ☐ ESTATE

OF *(Name):*

☐ MINOR   ☐ (PROPOSED) CONSERVATEE

NOTICE OF HEARING—GUARDIANSHIP OR CONSERVATORSHIP

CASE NUMBER:

This notice is required by law.
This notice does not require you to appear in court, but you may attend the hearing if you wish.

---

1. NOTICE is given that *(name):*
   (representative capacity, if any):
   has filed *(specify):*

2. You may refer to documents on file in this proceeding for more information. *(Some documents filed with the court are confidential. Under some circumstances you or your attorney may be able to see or receive copies of confidential documents if you file papers in the proceeding or apply to the court.)*

3. ☐ The petition includes an application for the independent exercise of powers by a guardian or conservator under
   ☐ Probate Code section 2108   ☐ Probate Code section 2590.
   Powers requested are   ☐ specified below   ☐ specified in Attachment 3.

4. A HEARING on the matter will be held as follows:

   a. Date: Time: ☐ Dept.:   ☐ Room:

   b. Address of court   ☐ same as noted above   ☐ is *(specify):*

Assistive listening systems, computer-assisted real-time captioning, or sign language interpreter services are available upon request if at least 5 days notice is provided. Contact the clerk's office for *Request for Accommodations by Persons with Disabilities and Order* (form MC-410). (Civil Code section 54.8.)

Page 1 of 2

NOTICE OF HEARING—GUARDIANSHIP OR CONSERVATORSHIP
(Probate—Guardianships and Conservatorships)

<table>
<tr>
<td>☐ GUARDIANSHIP ☐ CONSERVATORSHIP OF THE ☐ PERSON ☐ ESTATE
OF (Name):

☐ MINOR ☐ (PROPOSED) CONSERVATEE</td>
<td>CASE NUMBER:</td>
</tr>
</table>

NOTE: *

A copy of this *Notice of Hearing—Guardianship or Conservatorship* ("Notice") must be "served" on—delivered to—each person who has the right under the law to be notified of the date, time, place, and purpose of a court hearing in a guardianship or conservatorship. Copies of this Notice may be served by mail in most situations. In a guardianship, however, copies of this Notice must sometimes be personally served on certain persons; and copies of this Notice may be personally served instead of served by mail in both guardianships and conservatorships. The petitioner (the person who requested the court hearing) **may not personally perform either service by mail or personal service**, but must show the court that copies of this Notice have been served in a way the law allows. The petitioner does this by arranging for someone else to perform the service and complete and sign a proof of service, which the petitioner then files with the original Notice.

This page contains a proof of service that may be used only to show service by mail. To show personal service, each person who performs the service must complete and sign a proof of personal service, and each signed copy of that proof of service must be attached to this Notice when it is filed with the court.. You may use form GC-020(P) to show personal service of this Notice.

* *(This Note replaces the clerk's certificate of posting on prior versions of this form. If notice by posting is desired, attach a copy of form GC-020(C), Clerk's Certificate of Posting Notice of Hearing—Guardianship or Conservatorship. (See Prob. Code, § 2543(c).)*

PROOF OF SERVICE BY MAIL

1. I am over the age of 18 and not a party to this cause. I am a resident of or employed in the county where the mailing occurred.

2. My residence or business address is *(specify):*

3. I served the foregoing *Notice of Hearing—Guardianship or Conservatorship* on each person named below by enclosing a copy in an envelope addressed as shown below AND

    a. ☐ **depositing** the sealed envelope with the United States Postal Service on the date and at the place shown in item 4 with the postage fully prepaid.

    b. ☐ **placing** the envelope for collection and mailing on the date and at the place shown in item 4 following our ordinary business practices. I am readily familiar with this business's practice for collecting and processing correspondence for mailing. On the same day that correspondence is placed for collection and mailing, it is deposited in the ordinary course of business with the United States Postal Service in a sealed envelope with postage fully prepaid.

4. a. Date mailed: b. Place mailed *(city, state):*

5. ☐ I served with the *Notice of Hearing—Guardianship or Conservatorship* a copy of the petition or other document referred to in the Notice.

I declare under penalty of perjury under the laws of the State of California that the foregoing is true and correct.

Date:

▶

_____   _____
(TYPE OR PRINT NAME OF PERSON COMPLETING THIS FORM)   (SIGNATURE OF PERSON COMPLETING THIS FORM)

NAME AND ADDRESS OF EACH PERSON TO WHOM NOTICE WAS MAILED

	Name of person served	Address *(number, street, city, state, and zip code)*
1.		
2.		
3.		
4.		

☐ Continued on an attachment. *(You may use form DE-120(MA)/GC-020(MA) to show additional persons served.)*

NOTICE OF HEARING—GUARDIANSHIP OR CONSERVATORSHIP
(Probate—Guardianships and Conservatorships)

ATTORNEY OR PARTY WITHOUT ATTORNEY *(Name, state bar number, and address)*:

TELEPHONE AND FAX NOS.:

FOR COURT USE ONLY

ATTORNEY FOR *(Name)*:

SUPERIOR COURT OF CALIFORNIA, COUNTY OF

STREET ADDRESS:

MAILING ADDRESS:

CITY AND ZIP CODE:

BRANCH NAME:

☐ GUARDIANSHIP ☐ CONSERVATORSHIP OF *(Name)*:

☐ MINOR ☐ CONSERVATEE

ORDER DISPENSING WITH NOTICE

CASE NUMBER:

1. **THE COURT FINDS** that a petition for *(specify)*:
   has been filed and

   a. ☐ *(for guardianship only)* the following persons cannot with reasonable diligence be given notice *(names)*:

   b. ☐ *(for guardianship only)* the giving of notice to the following persons is contrary to the interest of justice *(names)*:

   c. ☐ good cause exists for dispensing with notice to the following persons referred to in Probate Code section 1460(b) *(names)*:

   d. ☐ other *(specify)*:

2. **THE COURT ORDERS** that notice of hearing on the petition for *(specify)*:

   a. ☐ is not required except to persons requesting special notice under Probate Code section 2700.
   b. ☐ is dispensed with to the following persons *(names)*:

Date: _____

_____
JUDGE OF THE SUPERIOR COURT

Form Approved by the
Judicial Council of California
GC-021 [Rev. January 1, 1998]
Mandatory Form [1/1/2000]

**ORDER DISPENSING WITH NOTICE
GUARDIANSHIP OR CONSERVATORSHIP**

WEST GROUP
Official Publisher

Probate Code, § 1460

ATTORNEY OR PARTY WITHOUT ATTORNEY *(Name, state bar number, and address)*:

TELEPHONE AND FAX NOS.:

FOR COURT USE ONLY

ATTORNEY FOR *(Name)*:

SUPERIOR COURT OF CALIFORNIA, COUNTY OF

STREET ADDRESS:

MAILING ADDRESS:

CITY AND ZIP CODE:

BRANCH NAME:

GUARDIANSHIP OF THE ☐ PERSON ☐ ESTATE OF *(Name)*:

MINOR

ORDER APPOINTING GUARDIAN OF ☐ MINOR ☐ MINORS

CASE NUMBER:

WARNING: THIS APPOINTMENT IS NOT EFFECTIVE UNTIL LETTERS HAVE ISSUED.

1. The petition for appointment of guardian came on for hearing as follows *(check boxes c, d, and e to indicate personal presence)*:

   a. Judge *(name)*:
   b. Hearing date: Time: ☐ Dept.:   ☐ Room:

   c. ☐ Petitioner *(name)*:
   d. ☐ Attorney for Petitioner *(name)*:
   e. ☐ Attorney for minor *(name, address, and telephone)*:

THE COURT FINDS

2. a. ☐ All notices required by law have been given.
   b. ☐ Notice of hearing to the following persons ☐ has been ☐ should be   dispensed with *(names)*:

3. ☐ Appointment of a guardian of the ☐ person ☐ estate   of the minor is necessary and convenient.

4. ☐ Granting the guardian powers to be exercised independently under Probate Code section 2590 is to the advantage and benefit and is in the best interest of the guardianship estate.

5. ☐ Attorney *(name)*:   has been appointed by the court as legal counsel to represent the minor in these proceedings. The cost for representation is: $

6. ☐ The appointed court investigator, probation officer, or domestic relations investigator is *(name, title, address, and telephone)*:

THE COURT ORDERS

7. a. *(Name)*:
   (Address):   *(Telephone)*:

   is appointed guardian of the PERSON of *(name)*:
   and *Letters* shall issue upon qualification.

Do NOT use this form for a temporary guardianship.   (Continued on reverse)

Form Approved by the
Judicial Council of California
GC-240 [Rev. January 1, 1998]
Mandatory Form [1/1/2000]

ORDER APPOINTING GUARDIAN OF MINOR

WEST GROUP
Official Publisher

Probate Code, §§ 1514, 2310

7. b. *(Name)*:

   (Address):   *(Telephone)*:

   is appointed guardian of the ESTATE of *(name)*:
   and *Letters* shall issue upon qualification.

8. ☐ Notice of hearing to the persons named in item 2b is dispensed with.

9. a. ☐ Bond is not required.
   b. ☐ Bond is fixed at: $ to be furnished by an authorized surety company or as otherwise
           provided by law.
   c. ☐ Deposits of: $ are ordered to be placed in a blocked account at *(specify institution and
           location)*:

           and receipts shall be filed. No withdrawals shall be made without a court order. ☐ Additional orders in Attachment 9c.
   d. ☐ The guardian is not authorized to take possession of money or any other property without a specific court order.

10. ☐ For legal services rendered on behalf of the minor, ☐ parents of the minor ☐ minor's estate   shall pay to
        (name):   the sum of: $
        ☐ forthwith ☐ as follows *(specify terms, including any combination of payors)*:

11. ☐ The guardian of the estate is granted authorization under Probate Code section 2590 to exercise independently the powers
        specified in Attachment 11 ☐ subject to the conditions provided.

12. ☐ Orders are granted relating to the powers and duties of the guardian of the person under Probate Code sections 2351-2358
        as specified in Attachment 12.

13. ☐ Orders are granted relating to the conditions imposed under Probate Code section 2402 upon the guardian of the estate as
        specified in Attachment 13.

14. ☐ Other orders as specified in Attachment 14 are granted.

15. ☐ The probate referee appointed is *(name and address)*:

16. Number of boxes checked in items 8-15: _____

17. Number of pages attached: _____

Date:

_____
                                                        JUDGE OF THE SUPERIOR COURT
                                          ☐ SIGNATURE FOLLOWS LAST ATTACHMENT

GC-240 [Rev. January, 1 1998]   **ORDER APPOINTING GUARDIAN OF MINOR**   WEST GROUP   Page two
                                                                                       Official Publisher

ATTORNEY OR PARTY WITHOUT ATTORNEY *(Name, State Bar number, and address):*	FOR COURT USE ONLY
TELEPHONE NO.: FAX NO. *(Optional):* E-MAIL ADDRESS *(Optional):* ATTORNEY FOR *(Name):*	

SUPERIOR COURT OF CALIFORNIA, COUNTY OF
STREET ADDRESS:
MAILING ADDRESS:
CITY AND ZIP CODE:
BRANCH NAME:

GUARDIANSHIP OF
(Name):

                                             MINOR

LETTERS OF GUARDIANSHIP ☐ Person ☐ Estate	CASE NUMBER:

LETTERS

1. *(Name):*   is appointed guardian of the ☐ person ☐ estate
   of *(name):*

2. ☐ Other powers have been granted and conditions have been imposed as follows:

    a. ☐ Powers to be exercised independently under Probate Code section 2590 are specified in attachment 2a *(specify powers, restrictions, conditions, and limitations).*

    b. ☐ Conditions relating to the care and custody of the property under Probate Code section 2402 are specified in attachment 2b.

    c. ☐ Conditions relating to the care, treatment, education, and welfare of the minor under Probate Code section 2358 are specified in attachment 2c.

    d. ☐ Other powers granted or conditions imposed are ☐ specified on attachment 2d. ☐ specified below.

3. ☐ The guardian is not authorized to take possession of money or any other property without a specific court order.

4. Number of pages attached: _____

WITNESS, clerk of the court, with seal of the court affixed.

(SEAL)	Date: Clerk, by _____ , Deputy

                                                          Page 1 of 2

Form Adopted for Mandatory Use
 Judicial Council of California
 GC-250 [Rev. January 1, 2009]

LETTERS OF GUARDIANSHIP
(Probate—Guardianships and Conservatorships)

Probate Code, §§ 2310, 2311, 2890–2893 <br> www.courtinfo.ca.gov

GUARDIANSHIP OF	CASE NUMBER:
__ *(Name):*	
MINOR	

NOTICE TO INSTITUTIONS AND FINANCIAL INSTITUTIONS
(Probate Code sections 2890–2893)

When these *Letters of Guardianship* (Letters) are delivered to you as an employee or other representative of an *institution* or *financial institution* (described below) in order for the guardian of the estate (1) to take possession or control of an asset of the minor named above held by your institution (including changing title, withdrawing all or any portion of the asset, or transferring all or any portion of the asset) or (2) to open or change the name of an account or a safe-deposit box in your financial institution to reflect the guardianship, you must fill out Judicial Council form GC-050 (for an institution) or form GC-051 (for a financial institution). An officer authorized by your institution or financial institution must date and sign the form, and you must file the completed form with the court.

There is no filing fee for filing the form. You may either arrange for personal delivery of the form or mail it to the court for filing at the address given for the court on page 1 of these Letters.

The guardian should deliver a blank copy of the appropriate form to you with these Letters, but it is your institution's or financial institution's responsibility to complete the correct form, have an authorized officer sign it, and file the completed form with the court. If the correct form is not delivered with these Letters or is unavailable for any other reason, blank copies of the forms may be obtained from the court. The forms may also be accessed from the judicial branch's public Web site free of charge. The Internet address (URL) is *www.courtinfo.ca.gov/forms/.* Select the form group *Probate—Guardianships and Conservatorships* and scroll down to form GC-050 for an institution or form GC-051 for a financial institution. The forms may be printed out as blank forms and filled in by typewriter (nonfillable form) or may be filled out online and printed out ready for signature and filing (fillable form).

An *institution* under California Probate Code section 2890(c) is an insurance company, insurance broker, insurance agent, investment company, investment bank, securities broker-dealer, investment advisor, financial planner, financial advisor, or any other person who takes, holds, or controls an asset subject to a conservatorship or guardianship other than a financial institution. Institutions must file a *Notice of Taking Possession or Control of an Asset of Minor or Conservatee* (form GC-050) for an asset of the minor or conservatee held by the institution. A single form may be filed for all affected assets held by the institution.

A *financial institution* under California Probate Code section 2892(b) is a bank, trust (including a Totten trust account but excluding other trust arrangements described in Probate Code section 82(b)), savings and loan association, savings bank, industrial bank, or credit union. Financial institutions must file a *Notice of Opening or Changing a Guardianship or Conservatorship Account or Safe-Deposit Box* (form GC-051) for an account or a safe-deposit box held by the financial institution. A single form may be filed for all affected accounts or safe-deposit boxes held by the financial institution.

LETTERS OF GUARDIANSHIP
AFFIRMATION

I solemnly affirm that I will perform according to law the duties of guardian.

Executed on *(date):*   , at *(place):*

▶

_____
(TYPE OR PRINT NAME)

_____
(SIGNATURE OF APPOINTEE)

CERTIFICATION

I certify that this document, including any attachments, is a correct copy of the original on file in my office, and that the Letters issued to the person appointed above have not been revoked, annulled, or set aside, and are still in full force and effect.

(SEAL)	
	Date:
	Clerk, by _____ , Deputy

LETTERS OF GUARDIANSHIP
(Probate—Guardianships and Conservatorships)

CONFIDENTIAL (DO NOT ATTACH TO PETITION)

GC-212

ATTORNEY OR PARTY WITHOUT ATTORNEY *(Name, State Bar number, and address)*:	FOR COURT USE ONLY
TELEPHONE NO.: FAX NO. *(Optional)*: E-MAIL ADDRESS *(Optional)*: ATTORNEY FOR *(Name)*:	

SUPERIOR COURT OF CALIFORNIA, COUNTY OF

STREET ADDRESS:

MAILING ADDRESS:

CITY AND ZIP CODE:

BRANCH NAME:

GUARDIANSHIP OF *(Name)*: MINOR	CASE NUMBER:
CONFIDENTIAL GUARDIAN SCREENING FORM Guardianship of ☐ Person ☐ Estate	HEARING DATE AND TIME: DEPT.:

The proposed guardian must complete and sign this form. The person requesting appointment of a guardian must submit the completed and signed form to the court with the guardianship petition.
This form must remain confidential.

How This Form Will Be Used

This form is **confidential** and will not be a part of the public file in this case. Each proposed guardian must complete and sign a separate copy of this form under rule 7.1001 of the California Rules of Court. The information provided will be used by the court and by persons and agencies designated by the court to assist the court in determining whether to appoint the proposed guardian as guardian. The proposed guardian **must** respond to each item.

1. a. **Proposed guardian** *(name)*:
   b. Date of birth:
   c. Social security number: d. Driver's license number: State:
   e. Telephone numbers: Home: Work: Other:

2. ☐ I am ☐ I am not   required to register as a sex offender under California Penal Code section 290. *(If you checked "I am," explain in Attachment 2.)*

3. ☐ I have ☐ I have not   been charged with, arrested for, or convicted of a crime deemed to be a felony or a misdemeanor. *(If you checked "I have," explain in Attachment 3.)*
   ☐ *(Check here if you have been arrested for drug or alcohol-related offenses.)*

4. ☐ I have ☐ I have not   had a restraining order or protective order filed against me in the last 10 years. *(If you checked "I have," explain in Attachment 4.)*

5. ☐ I am ☐ I am not   receiving services from a psychiatrist, psychologist, or therapist for a mental health–related issue. *(If you checked "I am," explain in Attachment 5.)*

6. Do you, or does any other person living in your home, have a social worker or parole or probation officer assigned to him or her?
   ☐ Yes ☐ No   *(If you checked "Yes," explain in Attachment 6 and provide the name and address of each social worker, parole officer, or probation officer.)*

7. Have you, or has any other person living in your home, been charged with, arrested for, or convicted of any form of child abuse, neglect, or molestation? ☐ Yes ☐ No *(If you checked "Yes," explain in Attachment 7.)*

8. ☐ I am ☐ I am not   aware of any reports alleging any form of child abuse, neglect, or molestation made to any
   ☐   agency charged with protecting children (e.g., Child Protective Services) or any other law enforcement agency regarding me or any other person living in my home. *(If you checked "I am," explain in Attachment 8 and provide the name and address of each agency.)*

9. Have you, or has any other person living in your home, habitually used any illegal substances or abused alcohol?
   ☐ Yes ☐ No   *(If you checked "Yes," explain in Attachment 9.)*

Page 1 of 2

Form Adopted for Mandatory Use
Judicial Council of California
GC-212 [Rev. July 1, 2009]

CONFIDENTIAL GUARDIAN SCREENING FORM
(Probate—Guardianships and Conservatorships)

Probate Code, § 1516;
Family Code, § 3011;
Cal. Rules of Court, rule 7.1001
www.courtinfo.ca.gov

GUARDIANSHIP OF *(Name):*	CASE NUMBER:
MINOR	

10. Have you, or has any other person living in your home, been charged with, arrested for, or convicted of a crime involving illegal substances or alcohol?

    [ ] Yes [ ] No *(If you checked "Yes," explain in Attachment 10.)*

11. Do you or does any other person living in your home suffer from mental illness?

    [ ] Yes [ ] No *(If you checked "Yes," explain in Attachment 11.)*

12. Do you suffer from any physical disability that would impair your ability to perform the duties of guardian?

    [ ] Yes [ ] No *(If you checked 'Yes," explain in Attachment 12.)*

13. [ ] I have or may have [ ] I do not have an adverse interest that the court may consider to be a risk to, or to have an effect on, my ability to faithfully perform the duties of guardian.

    (If you checked "I have or may have," explain in Attachment 13.)

14. [ ] I have [ ] I have not previously been appointed guardian, conservator, executor, or fiduciary in another proceeding.

    (If you checked "I have," explain in Attachment 14.)

15. [ ] I have [ ] I have not been removed as guardian, conservator, executor, or fiduciary in any other proceeding.

    (If you checked "I have," explain in Attachment 15.)

16. [ ] I am [ ] I am not a private professional fiduciary, as defined in Business and Professions Code section 6501(f).

    (If you checked "I am," respond to item 17. If you checked "I am not," go to item 18.)

17. [ ] I am [ ] I am not currently licensed by the Professional Fiduciaries Bureau of the Department of Consumer Affairs. My license status and information is stated in item 1 on page 1 of the Professional Fiduciary Attachment signed by me and attached to the petition that proposes my appointment as guardian in this matter. *(Complete and sign the Professional Fiduciary Attachment and attach it to the petition, or deliver it to the petitioner for attachment, before the petition is filed. See item 4d of the petition. Use form GC-210(A-PF)/GC-310(A-PF) for this attachment.)*

18. [ ] I am [ ] I am not a responsible corporate officer authorized to act for *(name of corporation):*

    a California nonprofit charitable corporation that meets the requirements for appointment as guardian of the proposed ward under Probate Code section 2104. I certify that the corporation's articles of incorporation specifically authorize it to accept appointments as guardian. *(If you checked "I am," explain the circumstances of the corporation's care of, counseling of, or financial assistance to the proposed ward in Attachment 18.)*

19. [ ] I have [ ] I have not filed for bankruptcy protection within the last 10 years.

    (If you checked "I have," explain in Attachment 19.)

MINORS' CONTACT INFORMATION

20. Minor's name: _____ School *(name):* _____
    Home telephone: _____ School telephone: _____ Other telephone: _____

21. Minor's name: _____ School *(name):* _____
    Home telephone: _____ School telephone: _____ Other telephone: _____

22. Minor's name: _____ School *(name):* _____
    Home telephone: _____ School telephone: _____ Other telephone: _____
    [ ] Information on additional minors is attached.

DECLARATION

I declare under penalty of perjury under the laws of the State of California that the foregoing is true and correct.

Date: _____

▶

_____   _____
(TYPE OR PRINT NAME OF PROPOSED GUARDIAN)   (SIGNATURE OF PROPOSED GUARDIAN)*

* Each proposed guardian must fill out and file a separate screening form.

ATTORNEY OR PARTY WITHOUT ATTORNEY *(Name, state bar number, and address)*:	FOR COURT USE ONLY
TELEPHONE NO.: FAX NO. *(Optional)*: E–MAIL ADDRESS *(Optional)*: ATTORNEY FOR *(Name)*:	

SUPERIOR COURT OF CALIFORNIA, COUNTY OF
STREET ADDRESS:
MAILING ADDRESS:
CITY AND ZIP CODE:
BRANCH NAME:

GUARDIANSHIP OF THE ☐ PERSON ☐ ESTATE

OF *(Name)*: MINOR

DUTIES OF GUARDIAN and Acknowledgment of Receipt	CASE NUMBER:

DUTIES OF GUARDIAN

When you are appointed by the court as a guardian of a minor, you become an officer of the court and assume certain duties and obligations. An attorney is best qualified to advise you about these matters. You should clearly understand the information on this form. You will find additional information in the *Guardianship Pamphlet (for Guardianships of Children in the Probate Court)* (Form GC-205), which is available from the court.

1. GUARDIANSHIP OF THE PERSON

If the probate court appoints you as a *guardian of the person* for a child, you will be required to assume important duties and obligations.

a. **Fundamental responsibilities** - The guardian of the person of a child has the care, custody, and control of the child. As guardian, you are responsible for providing for food, clothing, shelter, education, and all the medical and dental needs of the child. You must provide for the safety, protection, and physical and emotional growth of the child.

b. **Custody** - As guardian of the person of the child, you have full legal and physical custody of the child and are responsible for **all** decisions relating to the child. The child's parents can no longer make decisions for the child while there is a guardianship. The parents' rights are suspended—not terminated—as long as a guardian is appointed for a minor.

c. **Education** - As guardian of the person of the child, you are responsible for the child's education. You determine where the child should attend school. As the child's advocate within the school system, you should attend conferences and play an active role in the child's education. For younger children, you may want to consider enrolling the child in Head Start or other similar programs. For older children, you should consider their future educational needs such as college or a specialized school. You must assist the child in obtaining services if the child has special educational needs. You should help the child in setting and attaining his or her educational goals.

d. **Residence** - As guardian, you have the right to determine where the child lives. The child will normally live with you, but when it is necessary, you are allowed to make other arrangements if it is in the best interest of the child. You should obtain court approval before placing the child back with his or her parents.

As guardian, you **do not** have the right to change the child's residence to a place outside of California unless you first receive the court's permission. If the court grants permission, California law requires that you establish legal guardianship in the state where the child will be living. Individual states have different rules regarding guardianships. You should seek additional information about guardianships in the state where you want the child to live.

(Continued on reverse)

DUTIES OF GUARDIAN
 (Probate)

GUARDIAN OF (Name):	CASE NUMBER:
MINOR	

e. **Medical treatment** - As guardian, you are responsible for meeting the medical needs of the child. In most cases, you have the authority to consent to the child's medical treatment. However, if the child is 14 years or older, surgery may not be performed on the child unless either (1) both the child and the guardian consent or (2) a court order is obtained that specifically authorizes the surgery. This holds true except in emergencies. A guardian may not place a child involuntarily in a mental health treatment facility under a probate guardianship. A mental health conservatorship proceeding is required for such an involuntary commitment. However, the guardian may secure counseling and other necessary mental health services for the child. The law also allows older and more mature children to consent to their own treatment in certain situations such as outpatient mental health treatment, medical care related to pregnancy or sexually transmitted diseases, and drug and alcohol treatment.

f. **Community resources** - There are agencies in each county that may be helpful in meeting the specific needs of children who come from conflicted, troubled, or deprived environments. If the child has special needs, you must strive to meet those needs or secure appropriate services.

g. **Financial support** - Even when the child has a guardian, the parents are still obligated to financially support the child. The guardian may take action to obtain child support. The child may also be eligible for Temporary Aid for Needy Families, TANF (formerly known as AFDC), social security benefits, Veterans Administration benefits, Indian child welfare benefits, and other public or private funds.

h. **Visitation** - The court may require that you allow visitation or contact between the child and his or her parents. The child's needs often require that the parent-child relationship be maintained, within reason. However, the court may place restrictions on the visits, such as the requirement of supervision. The court may also impose other conditions in the child's best interest.

i. **Driver's license** - As guardian of the person, you have the authority to consent to the minor's application for a driver's license. If you consent, you will become liable for any civil damages that may result if the minor causes an accident. The law requires that anyone signing the DMV application obtain insurance to cover the minor.

j. **Enlistment in the armed services** - The guardian may consent to a minor's enlistment in the armed services. If the minor enters into active duty with the armed forces, the minor becomes emancipated under California law.

k. **Marriage** - For the minor to marry, the guardian **and the court** must give permission. If the minor enters a valid marriage, the minor becomes emancipated under California law.

l. **Change of address** - A guardian must notify the court in writing of any change in the address of either the child or the guardian. This includes any changes that result from the child's leaving the guardian's home or returning to the parent's home. You **must** always obtain **court permission** before you move the child to another state or country.

m. **Court visitors and status reports** - Some counties have a program in which "court visitors" track and review guardianships. If your county has such a program, you will be expected to cooperate with all requests of the court visitor. As guardian, you may also be required to fill out and file status reports. In all counties, you must cooperate with the court and court investigators.

n. **Misconduct of the child** - A guardian, like a parent, is liable for the harm and damages caused by the willful misconduct of a child. There are special rules concerning harm caused by the use of a firearm. If you are concerned about your possible liability, you should consult an attorney.

o. **Additional responsibilities** - The court may place other conditions on the guardianship or additional duties upon you, as guardian. For example, the court may require the guardian to complete counseling or parenting classes, to obtain specific services for the child, or to follow a scheduled visitation plan between the child and the child's parents or relatives. As guardian, you must follow all court orders.

(Continued on page three)

p. Termination of guardianship of the person - A guardianship of the person automatically ends when the child reaches the age of 18, is adopted, marries, is emancipated by court order, enters into active military duty, or dies. If none of these events has occurred, the child, a parent, or the guardian may petition the court for termination of guardianship. But it must be shown that the guardianship is no longer necessary or that termination of the guardianship is in the child's best interest.

2. GUARDIANSHIP OF THE ESTATE

If the court appoints you as *guardian of the child's estate,* you will have additional duties and obligations. The money and other assets of the child are called the child's "estate."' Appointment as guardian of a child's estate is taken very seriously by the court. The guardian of the estate is required to manage the child's funds, collect and make an inventory of the assets, keep accurate financial records, and regularly file financial accountings with the court.

MANAGING THE ESTATE

a. Prudent investments - As guardian of the estate, you must manage the child's assets with the care of a prudent person dealing with someone else's property. This means that you must be cautious and may not make speculative or risky investments.

b. Keeping estate assets separate - As guardian of the estate, you must keep the money and property of the child's estate separate from everyone else's, including your own. When you open a bank account for the estate, the account name must indicate that it is a *guardianship* account and not your personal account. You should use the child's social security number when opening estate accounts. You should never deposit estate funds in your personal account or otherwise mix them with your own funds or anyone else's funds, even for brief periods. Securities in the estate must be held in a name that shows that they are estate property and not your personal property.

c. Interest-bearing accounts and other investments - Except for checking accounts intended for ordinary expenses, you should place estate funds in interest-bearing accounts. You may deposit estate funds in insured accounts in federally insured financial institutions, but you should not put more than $100,000 in any single institution. You should consult with an attorney before making other kinds of investments.

d. Blocked accounts - A *blocked account is* an account with a financial institution in which money is placed. No person may withdraw funds from a blocked account without the court's permission. Depending on the amount and character of the child's property, the guardian may elect **or the court may require** that estate assets be placed in a blocked account. As guardian of the estate, you must follow the directions of the court and the procedures required to deposit funds in this type of account. The use of a blocked account is a safeguard and may save the estate the cost of a bond.

e. Other restrictions - As guardian of the estate, you will have many other restrictions on your authority to deal with estate assets. Without prior court order, you **may not** pay fees to yourself or your attorney. You may not make a gift of estate assets to anyone. You may not borrow money from the estate. As guardian, you may not use estate funds to purchase real property without a prior court order. If you do not obtain the court's permission to spend estate funds, you may be compelled to reimburse the estate from your own personal funds and may be removed as guardian. You should consult with an attorney concerning the legal requirements relating to sales, leases, mortgages, and investment of estate property. If the child of whose estate you are the guardian has a living parent or if that child receives assets or is entitled to support from another source, you must obtain court approval before using guardianship assets for the child's support, maintenance, or education. You must file a petition or include a request for approval in the original petition, and set forth which exceptional circumstances justify any use of guardianship assets for the child's support. The court will ordinarily grant such a petition for only a limited period of time, usually not to exceed one year, and only for specific and limited purposes.

INVENTORY OF ESTATE PROPERTY

f. Locate the estate's property - As guardian of the estate, you must locate, take possession of, and protect the child's income and assets that will be administered in the estate. You must change the ownership of all assets into the guardianship estate's name. For real estate, you should record a copy of your *Letters of Guardianship* with the county recorder in each county where the child owns real property.

(Continued on reverse)

DUTIES OF GUARDIAN
(Probate)

GUARDIAN OF (Name):	CASE NUMBER:
MINOR	

g. **Determine the value of the property** - As guardian of the estate, you must arrange to have a court-appointed referee determine the value of the estate property unless the appointment is waived by the court. You—not the referee—must determine the value of certain "cash items." An attorney can advise you about how to do this.

h. **File an inventory and appraisal** - As guardian of the estate, you must file an inventory and appraisal within 90 days after your appointment. You may be required to return to court 90 days after your appointment as guardian of the estate to ensure that you have properly filed the inventory and appraisal.

INSURANCE

i. **Insurance coverage** - As guardian of the estate, you should make sure that there is appropriate and sufficient insurance covering the assets and risks of the estate. You should maintain the insurance in force throughout the entire period of the guardianship or until the insured asset is sold.

RECORD KEEPING AND ACCOUNTING

j. **Records** - As guardian of the estate, you must keep complete, accurate records of each financial transaction affecting the estate. The checkbook for the guardianship checking account is essential for keeping records of income and expenditures. You should also keep receipts for all purchases. Record keeping is critical because you will have to prepare an accounting of all money and property that you have received, what you have spent, the date of each transaction, and its purpose. You will also have to be able to describe in detail what is left after you have paid the estate's expenses.

k. **Accountings** - As guardian of the estate, you must file a petition requesting that the court review and approve your accounting one year after your appointment and at least every two years after that. The court may ask that you justify some or all expenditures. You should have receipts and other documents available for the court's review, if requested. If you do not file your accounting as required, the court will order you to do so. You may be removed as guardian for failure to file an accounting.

l. **Format** - As guardian of the estate, you must comply with all state and local rules when filing your accounting. A particular format is specified in the Probate Code, which you must follow when you present your account to the court. You should check local rules for any special local requirements.

m. **Legal advice** - An attorney can advise you and help you prepare your inventories, accountings, and petitions to the court. If you have questions, you should consult with an attorney.

3. OTHER GENERAL INFORMATION

a. **Removal of a guardian** - A guardian may be removed for specific reasons or when it is in the child's best interest. A guardian may be removed either on the court's own motion or by a petition filed by the child, a relative of the child, or any other interested person. If necessary, the court may appoint a successor guardian, or the court may return the child to a parent if that is found to be in the child's best interest.

b. **Legal documents** - For your appointment as guardian to be valid, the *Order Appointing Guardian of Minor* must be signed. Once the court signs the order, the guardian **must** go to the clerk's office, where *Letters of Guardianship* will be issued. *Letters of Guardianship* is a legal document that provides proof that you have been appointed and are serving as the guardian of a minor. You should obtain several certified copies of the *Letters* from the clerk. These legal documents will be of assistance to you in the performance of your duties, such as enrolling the child in school, obtaining medical care, and taking care of estate business.

c. **Attorneys and legal resources** - If you have an attorney, the attorney will advise you on your duties and responsibilities, the limits of your authority, the rights of the child, and your dealings with the court. **If you have legal questions, you should consult with your attorney.** Please remember that the court staff cannot give you legal advice.

(Continued on page five)

DUTIES OF GUARDIAN
(Probate)

GUARDIAN OF (Name):	CASE NUMBER:
MINOR	

If you are not represented by an attorney, you may obtain answers to your questions by contacting community resources, private publications, or your local law library.

NOTICE: This statement of duties is a summary and is not a complete statement of the law. Your conduct as a probate guardian is governed by the law itself and not by this summary.

ACKNOWLEDGMENT OF RECEIPT

1. I have petitioned the court to be appointed as a guardian.

2. I acknowledge that I have received a copy of this statement of the duties of the position of guardian.

Date:

_____
(TYPE OR PRINT NAME)

▶ _____
(SIGNATURE OF PETITIONER)

Date:

_____
(TYPE OR PRINT NAME)

▶ _____
(SIGNATURE OF PETITIONER)

Date:

_____
(TYPE OR PRINT NAME)

▶ _____
(SIGNATURE OF PETITIONER)

DUTIES OF GUARDIAN
(Probate)

Request for Hearing About Court Fee Waiver Order (Superior Court)

Clerk stamps date here when form is filed

(1) Your Information *(person who asked the court to waive court fees):*

Name: _____

Street or mailing address: _____

City: _____ State: _____ Zip: _____

Phone number: _____

(2) Your lawyer, if you have one*(name, address, phone number, e-mail, and State Bar number):* _____

_____

_____

_____

Fill in court name and street address:

Superior Court of California, County of

(3) Date of order denying your request to waive court fees *(month/day/year):* _____

☐ *(Check here if you have a copy of the order denying your request, and attach it to this form.)*

Fill in case number and case name:

Case Number:

Case Name:

(4) I ask the court for a hearing on my fee waiver request so that I can bring more information about my financial situation.

(5) ☐ The additional facts that support my request for a fee waiver are *(describe):*
(Use this space if you want to tell the court in advance what facts you want considered at the hearing. If the space below is not enough, attach form MC-025. Or attach a sheet of paper and write Additional Facts and your name and case number at the top. You may also attach copies of documents you want the court to look at.)

_____

_____

_____

_____

_____

_____

_____

Date: _____

▶

_____   _____
Print your name here

Request for Accommodations. Assistive listening systems, computer-assisted real-time captioning, or sign language interpreter services are available if you ask at least five days before your hearing. Contact the clerk's office for *Request for Accommodation,* form MC-410.

Judicial Council of California, *www.courtinfo.ca.gov*
New July 1, 2009, Mandatory Form
Government Code, § 68634(e)(3)

Request for Hearing About Court Fee Waiver Order (Superior Court)

FW-006, Page 1 of 1

American LegalNet, Inc.
www.FormsWorkflow.com

FW-008

Order on Court Fee Waiver
After Hearing (Superior Court)

FW-008

Clerk stamps date here when form is filed.

(1) Person who asked the court to waive court fees:

Name: _____

Street or mailing address: _____

City: _____ State: _____ Zip: _____

(2) Lawyer, if person in ① has one *(name, address, phone number,*

e-mail, and State Bar number): _____

_____

_____

(3) A request to waive court fees was filed *(date):* _____

(4) There was a hearing on *(date):* _____

at *(time):* _____ in *(Department):* _____

The following people were at the hearing *(check all that apply):*

☐ Person in ①   ☐ Lawyer in ②

☐ Others *(names):* _____

_____

Read this form carefully. All checked boxes ☑ are court orders.

Fill in court name and street address:

Superior Court of California, County of

Fill in case number and name:

Case Number:

Case Name:

Notice: The court may order you to answer questions about your finances and later order you to pay back the waived fees. If this happens and you do not pay, the court can make you pay the fees and also charge you collection fees. If there is a change in your financial circumstances during this case that increases your ability to pay fees and costs, you must notify the trial court within five days. (Use form FW-010.) If you win your case, the trial court may order the other side to pay the fees. If you settle your civil case for **$10,000** or more, the trial court will have a lien on the settlement in the amount of the waived fees. The trial court may not dismiss the case until the lien is paid.

(5) After reviewing your *(check one):* ☐ *Request to Waive Court Fees* ☐ *Request to Waive Additional Court Fees*
   the court makes the following order:

a. ☐ The court **grants** your request and waives your court fees and costs as follows:

   (1) ☐ **Fee Waiver.** The court **grants** your request and waives your court fees and costs listed below *(Cal. Rules of Court, rule 3.55.)* You do not have to pay the court fees for the following:
   - Filing papers in superior court
   - Making copies and certifying copies
   - Sheriff's fee to give notice
   - Reporter's daily fee *(for up to 60 days after the grant of the fee waiver, at the court-approved daily rate)*
   - Preparing and certifying the clerk's transcript on appeal
   - Giving notice and certificates
   - Sending papers to another court department
   - Court-appointed interpreter in small claims court
   - Court fees for phone hearing

   (2) ☐ **Additional Fee Waiver.** The court **grants** your request and waives your additional superior court fees and costs that are checked below. *(Cal. Rules of Court, rule 3.56.)* You do not have to pay for the checked items.
   - ☐ Jury fees and expenses
   - ☐ Fees for court-appointed experts
   - ☐ Reporter's daily fees *(beyond the 60-day period after grant of the fee waiver, at court-approved daily rate)*
   - ☐ Other *(specify):* _____
   - ☐ Fees for a peace officer to testify in court
   - ☐ Court-appointed interpreter fees for a witness

   (3) ☐ **Fee Waiver for Appeal.** The court **grants** your request and waives the fees and costs checked below, for your appeal. *(Cal. Rules of Court, rules 8.26 and 8.818.)* You do not have to pay for the checked items.
   - ☐ Preparing and certifying clerk's transcript for appeal
   - ☐ Other *(specify):* _____

Judicial Council of California, *www.courtinfo.ca.gov*
Rev. January 1, 2010, Mandatory Form
Government Code, § 68634(e)
Cal. Rules of Court, rule 3.52

**Order on Court Fee Waiver
After Hearing (Superior Court)**

FW-008, Page 1 of 2

b. ☐ The court **denies** your request and **will not waive or reduce** your fees and costs.

  (1) The reason for this denial is as follows:

    (a) ☐ Your request is incomplete, and you did not provide the information that the court requested *(specify items missing)*:_____

    (b) ☐ You did not go to court on the hearing date to provide the information the court needed to make a decision.

    (c) ☐ The information you provide shows that you are not eligible for the fee waiver you requested because *(check all that apply)*:

        i. ☐ Your income is too high.

        ii. ☐ Other *(explain)*: _____

    (d) ☐ There is not enough evidence to support a fee waiver.

    (e) ☐ Other *(state reasons)*: _____
_____

  (2) ☐ You may pay some court fees and costs over time. You may make monthly payments of $_____ beginning *(date)*: _____ and then payable on the 1st of each month after that, until the fees checked below are paid in full:

    (a) ☐ Filing fees.

    (b) ☐ Other *(describe)*: _____

    You must pay all other court fees and costs as they are due.

c. ☐ The court **partially grants** your request so you can pay court fees without using money you need to pay for your household's basic needs. You are ordered to pay a portion of your fees, **as checked below.** The court only partially grants the request because *(state reasons for partial denial)*:
_____
_____

  (1) ☐ You must pay _____ % of your court fees.

  (2) ☐ The court waives some fees. The fees checked below are waived. You must pay all other court fees.

☐ Filing papers at superior court	☐ Giving notice and certificates
☐ Sheriff's fee to give notice	☐ Sending papers to another court department
☐ Court-appointed interpreter	☐ Court-appointed interpreter fees for a witness
☐ Reporter's daily fee up to 60 days after order	☐ Reporter's daily fees beyond the 60 days
☐ Jury fees and expenses	after initial order
☐ Court-appointed experts' fees	☐ Fees for a peace officer to testify in court
☐ Making certified copies	☐ Court fees for telephone hearings
☐ Other *(describe)*: _____	

  (3) ☐ Other *(specify)*: _____

Warning! If b or c above are checked: You have **10 days** after the clerk gives notice of this order (see date below) to pay your fees as ordered, unless there is a later date for beginning payments in item b(2). If you do not pay, your court papers will not be processed. If the papers are a notice of appeal, your appeal may be dismissed.

Date:_____ ▶ _____
                                         Signature of Judicial Officer

Clerk's Certificate of Service

I certify that I am not involved in this case and *(check one)*:   ☐ A certificate of mailing is attached.

☐ I handed a copy of this order to the party and attorney, if any, listed in ①and ②, at the court, on the date below.

☐ This order was mailed first class, postage paid, to the party and attorney, if any, at the addresses listed in ①and ②, from *(city)*:_____, California on the date below.

Date: _____   Clerk, by _____, Deputy

ATTORNEY OR PARTY WITHOUT ATTORNEY *(Name, State Bar number, and address)*:	*FOR COURT USE ONLY*
TELEPHONE NO.: FAX NO. *(Optional)*: E-MAIL ADDRESS *(Optional)*: ATTORNEY FOR *(Name)*:	

SUPERIOR COURT OF CALIFORNIA, COUNTY OF
STREET ADDRESS:
MAILING ADDRESS:
CITY AND ZIP CODE:
BRANCH NAME:

PLAINTIFF/PETITIONER:

DEFENDANT/RESPONDENT:

NOTICE AND ACKNOWLEDGMENT OF RECEIPT—CIVIL	CASE NUMBER:

TO *(insert name of party being served)*: _____

NOTICE

The summons and other documents identified below are being served pursuant to section 415.30 of the California Code of Civil Procedure. Your failure to complete this form and return it within 20 days from the date of mailing shown below may subject you (or the party on whose behalf you are being served) to liability for the payment of any expenses incurred in serving a summons on you in any other manner permitted by law.

If you are being served on behalf of a corporation, an unincorporated association (including a partnership), or other entity, this form must be signed by you in the name of such entity or by a person authorized to receive service of process on behalf of such entity. In all other cases, this form must be signed by you personally or by a person authorized by you to acknowledge receipt of summons. If you return this form to the sender, service of a summons is deemed complete on the day you sign the acknowledgment of receipt below.

Date of mailing:

_____   ▶   _____
(TYPE OR PRINT NAME)   (SIGNATURE OF SENDER—MUST NOT BE A PARTY IN THIS CASE)

ACKNOWLEDGMENT OF RECEIPT

This acknowledges receipt of *(to be completed by sender before mailing)*:

1. ☐   A copy of the summons and of the complaint.
2. ☐   Other *(specify)*:

(To be completed by recipient):

Date this form is signed:

_____   ▶   _____
(TYPE OR PRINT YOUR NAME AND NAME OF ENTITY, IF ANY,   (SIGNATURE OF PERSON ACKNOWLEDGING RECEIPT, WITH TITLE IF
ON WHOSE BEHALF THIS FORM IS SIGNED)   ACKNOWLEDGMENT IS MADE ON BEHALF OF ANOTHER PERSON OR ENTITY)

Form Adopted for Mandatory Use
Judicial Council of California
POS-015 [Rev. January 1, 2005]

NOTICE AND ACKNOWLEDGMENT OF RECEIPT — CIVIL

Code of Civil Procedure,
§§ 415.30, 417.10
www.courtinfo.ca.gov

ATTORNEY OR PARTY WITHOUT ATTORNEY *(Name, State Bar number, and address):*	*FOR COURT USE ONLY*
TELEPHONE NO.: FAX NO. *(Optional):* E-MAIL ADDRESS *(Optional):* ATTORNEY FOR *(Name):*	

SUPERIOR COURT OF CALIFORNIA, COUNTY OF
  STREET ADDRESS:

  MAILING ADDRESS:

  CITY AND ZIP CODE:

  BRANCH NAME:

PLAINTIFF/PETITIONER:	CASE NUMBER:
DEFENDANT/RESPONDENT:	

PROOF OF SERVICE OF SUMMONS	Ref. No. or File No.:

(Separate proof of service is required for each party served.)

1. At the time of service I was at least 18 years of age and not a party to this action.

2. I served copies of:

  a. ☐ summons

  b. ☐ complaint

  c. ☐ Alternative Dispute Resolution (ADR) package

  d. ☐ Civil Case Cover Sheet *(served in complex cases only)*

  e. ☐ cross-complaint

  f. ☐ other *(specify documents):*

3. a. Party served *(specify name of party as shown on documents served):*

  b. ☐ Person (other than the party in item 3a) served on behalf of an entity or as an authorized agent (and not a person under item 5b on whom substituted service was made) *(specify name and relationship to the party named in item 3a):*

4. Address where the party was served:

5. I served the party *(check proper box)*

  a. ☐ **by personal service.** I personally delivered the documents listed in item 2 to the party or person authorized to receive service of process for the party (1) on *(date):*   (2) at *(time):*

  b. ☐ **by substituted service.** On *(date):*   at *(time):*   I left the documents listed in item 2 with or in the presence of *(name and title or relationship to person indicated in item 3):*

      (1) ☐ **(business)** a person at least 18 years of age apparently in charge at the office or usual place of business of the person to be served. I informed him or her of the general nature of the papers.

      (2) ☐ **(home)** a competent member of the household (at least 18 years of age) at the dwelling house or usual place of abode of the party. I informed him or her of the general nature of the papers.

      (3) ☐ **(physical address unknown)** a person at least 18 years of age apparently in charge at the usual mailing address of the person to be served, other than a United States Postal Service post office box. I informed him or her of the general nature of the papers.

      (4) ☐ I thereafter mailed (by first-class, postage prepaid) copies of the documents to the person to be served at the place where the copies were left (Code Civ. Proc., § 415.20). I mailed the documents on *(date):*   from *(city):*   **or** ☐ a declaration of mailing is attached.

      (5) ☐ I attach a **declaration of diligence** stating actions taken first to attempt personal service.

Page 1 of 2

Form Adopted for Mandatory Use Judicial Council of California POS-010 [Rev. January 1, 2007]	**PROOF OF SERVICE OF SUMMONS**	Code of Civil Procedure, § 417.10

5. c. ☐ **by mail and acknowledgment of receipt of service.** I mailed the documents listed in item 2 to the party, to the address shown in item 4, by first-class mail, postage prepaid,

    (1) on *(date):*   (2) from *(city):*

    (3) ☐ with two copies of the *Notice and Acknowledgment of Receipt* and a postage-paid return envelope addressed to me. *(Attach completed* Notice and Acknowledgement of Receipt.*)* (Code Civ. Proc., § 415.30.)

    (4) ☐ to an address outside California with return receipt requested. (Code Civ. Proc., § 415.40.)

  d. ☐ **by other means** *(specify means of service and authorizing code section):*

    ☐ Additional page describing service is attached.

6. The "Notice to the Person Served" (on the summons) was completed as follows:
  a. ☐ as an individual defendant.
  b. ☐ as the person sued under the fictitious name of *(specify):*
  c. ☐ as occupant.
  d. ☐ On behalf of *(specify):*
    under the following Code of Civil Procedure section:

☐ 416.10 (corporation)	☐ 415.95 (business organization, form unknown)
☐ 416.20 (defunct corporation)	☐ 416.60 (minor)
☐ 416.30 (joint stock company/association)	☐ 416.70 (ward or conservatee)
☐ 416.40 (association or partnership)	☐ 416.90 (authorized person)
☐ 416.50 (public entity)	☐ 415.46 (occupant)
	☐ other:

7. **Person who served papers**
  a. Name:
  b. Address:
  c. Telephone number:
  d. **The fee** for service was: $
  e. I am:
    (1) ☐ not a registered California process server.
    (2) ☐ exempt from registration under Business and Professions Code section 22350(b).
    (3) ☐ a registered California process server:
      (i) ☐ owner ☐ employee ☐ independent contractor.
      (ii) Registration No.:
      (iii) County:

8. ☐ **I declare** under penalty of perjury under the laws of the State of California that the foregoing is true and correct.

    or

9. ☐ **I am a California sheriff or marshal and** I certify that the foregoing is true and correct.

Date:

▶

_____	_____
(NAME OF PERSON WHO SERVED PAPERS/SHERIFF OR MARSHAL)	(SIGNATURE)

ATTORNEY OR PARTY WITHOUT ATTORNEY *(Name, State Bar number, and address):*

FOR COURT USE ONLY

TELEPHONE NO.:

E-MAIL ADDRESS *(Optional):*   FAX NO. *(Optional):*

ATTORNEY FOR *(Name):*

SUPERIOR COURT OF CALIFORNIA, COUNTY OF

STREET ADDRESS:

MAILING ADDRESS:

CITY AND ZIP CODE:

BRANCH NAME:

PETITIONER/PLAINTIFF:

RESPONDENT/DEFENDANT:

| **PROOF OF SERVICE BY FIRST-CLASS MAIL—CIVIL** | CASE NUMBER: |

(Do not use this Proof of Service to show service of a Summons and Complaint.)

1. I am over 18 years of age and **not a party to this action.** I am a resident of or employed in the county where the mailing took place.

2. My residence or business address is:

3. On *(date):*   I mailed from *(city and state):*
   the following **documents** *(specify):*

   [ ] The documents are listed in the *Attachment to Proof of Service by First-Class Mail—Civil (Documents Served)* (form POS-030(D)).

4. I served the documents by enclosing them in an envelope and *(check one):*
   a. [ ] **depositing** the sealed envelope with the United States Postal Service with the postage fully prepaid.
   b. [ ] **placing** the envelope for collection and mailing following our ordinary business practices. I am readily familiar with this business's practice for collecting and processing correspondence for mailing. On the same day that correspondence is placed for collection and mailing, it is deposited in the ordinary course of business with the United States Postal Service in a sealed envelope with postage fully prepaid.

5. The envelope was addressed and mailed as follows:
   a. **Name** of person served:
   b. **Address** of person served:

   [ ] The name and address of each person to whom I mailed the documents is listed in the *Attachment to Proof of Service by First-Class Mail—Civil (Persons Served)* (POS-030(P)).

I declare under penalty of perjury under the laws of the State of California that the foregoing is true and correct.

Date:

▶

_____
(TYPE OR PRINT NAME OF PERSON COMPLETING THIS FORM)

_____
(SIGNATURE OF PERSON COMPLETING THIS FORM)

PROOF OF SERVICE BY FIRST-CLASS MAIL—CIVIL
(Proof of Service)

Code of Civil Procedure, §§ 1013, 1013a
www.courtinfo.ca.gov

SHORT TITLE:	CASE NUMBER:

ATTACHMENT TO PROOF OF SERVICE BY FIRST-CLASS MAIL—CIVIL (PERSONS SERVED)

(This Attachment is for use with form POS-030)

NAME AND ADDRESS OF EACH PERSON SERVED BY MAIL:

Name of Person Served	Address *(number, street, city, and zip code)*

Form Approved for Optional Use
Judicial Council of California
POS-030(P) [New January 1, 2005]

ATTACHMENT TO PROOF OF SERVICE BY FIRST-CLASS MAIL—CIVIL (PERSONS SERVED)
(Proof of Service)

Page ____ of ____

ATTORNEY OR PARTY WITHOUT ATTORNEY *(Name, State Bar number, and address):*	*FOR COURT USE ONLY*
TELEPHONE NO.: FAX NO. *(Optional):* E-MAIL ADDRESS *(Optional):* ATTORNEY FOR *(Name):*	

SUPERIOR COURT OF CALIFORNIA, COUNTY OF

  STREET ADDRESS:

  MAILING ADDRESS:

  CITY AND ZIP CODE:

  BRANCH NAME:

TEMPORARY GUARDIANSHIP OF *(Name):* **MINOR**	CASE NUMBER:
PETITION FOR APPOINTMENT OF TEMPORARY GUARDIAN ☐ **Person*** ☐ **Estate*** ☐ **Person and Estate***	HEARING DATE:
	DEPT.: TIME:

1. **Petitioner** *(name each):*

                                requests that

 a. *(Name):*
   (Address and
   telephone number):

   be appointed temporary guardian of the PERSON of the minor and Letters issue upon qualification.

 b. *(Name):*
   (Address and
   telephone number):

   be appointed temporary guardian of the ESTATE of the minor and Letters issue upon qualification.

 c. (1) ☐ bond not be required because petition is for a temporary guardianship of the person only.

   (2) ☐ bond not be required for the reasons stated in attachment 1c.

   (3) ☐ $ bond be fixed. It will be furnished by an admitted surety insurer or as otherwise provided by law.
      (Specify reasons in Attachment 1c if the amount is different from maximum required by Probate Code section 2320
      and Cal. Rules of Court, rule 7.207(c).)

   (4) ☐ $ in deposits in a blocked account be allowed. Receipts will be filed.
      (Specify institution and location):

 d. ☐ a request for an exception to notice of the hearing on this petition for good cause is filed with this petition.

 e. ☐ the powers specified in attachment 1e be granted in addition to the powers provided by law.

 f. ☐ other orders be granted *(specify in attachment 1f).*

2. **The minor is** *(name):*

  Current address: Current telephone no.:

3. **The minor requires a temporary guardian** to ☐ provide for temporary care, maintenance, and support
 ☐ protect property from loss or injury because *(facts are* ☐ *specified in attachment 3* ☐ *as follows):*

---

*You MAY use this form or form GC-110(P) for a temporary guardianship of the person. You MUST use this form for a temporary guardianship of the estate or the person and estate.

                                 Page 1 of 2

Form Adopted for Mandatory and Alternative
Mandatory Use Instead of Form GC-110(P)
Judicial Council of California
GC-110 [Rev. July 1, 2008]

**PETITION FOR APPOINTMENT OF
TEMPORARY GUARDIAN**
(Probate—Guardianships and Conservatorships)

Probate Code, § 2250;
Cal. Rules of Court, rules 7.101, 7.1012
www.courtinfo.ca.gov

TEMPORARY GUARDIANSHIP OF *(Name):*	CASE NUMBER:
MINOR	

3. ☐ *(Facts supporting appointment of a temporary guardian* (continued))*:*

4. **Temporary guardianship is required**
   a. ☐ pending the hearing on the petition for appointment of a general guardian.
   b. ☐ pending the appeal under Probate Code section 1301.
   c. ☐ during the suspension of powers of the guardian.

5. ☐ **Character and estimated value of the property of the estate** *(complete if a temporary guardianship of the estate or person and estate is requested):*
   a. Personal property: $
   b. Annual gross income from all sources, including real and personal property, wages, pensions, and public benefits: $
   c. Additional amount for cost of recovery on the bond, calculated as required under Cal. Rules of Court, rule 7.207(c): $ _____
   d. **Total:** $ _____

6. Petitioner believes the minor ☐ will ☐ will not attend the hearing.

7. All attachments to this form are incorporated by this reference as though placed here in this form. There are _____ pages attached to this form.

Date: _____

▶ _____
(SIGNATURE OF ATTORNEY*)

* **(Signature of all petitioners also required (Prob. Code, § 1020).)**

I declare under penalty of perjury under the laws of the State of California that the foregoing is true and correct.

Date: _____

_____
(TYPE OR PRINT NAME)

▶ _____
(SIGNATURE OF PETITIONER)

_____
(TYPE OR PRINT NAME)

▶ _____
(SIGNATURE OF PETITIONER)

**PETITION FOR APPOINTMENT OF
TEMPORARY GUARDIAN
(Probate—Guardianships and Conservatorships)**

GC-140

ATTORNEY OR PARTY WITHOUT ATTORNEY *(Name, State Bar number, and address):*	FOR COURT USE ONLY
TELEPHONE NO.: FAX NO. *(Optional):*	
E-MAIL ADDRESS *(Optional):*	
ATTORNEY FOR *(Name):*	

SUPERIOR COURT OF CALIFORNIA, COUNTY OF
STREET ADDRESS:
MAILING ADDRESS:
CITY AND ZIP CODE:
BRANCH NAME:

TEMPORARY GUARDIANSHIP OF THE ☐ PERSON ☐ ESTATE   OF
(Name):

MINOR

ORDER APPOINTING TEMPORARY GUARDIAN	CASE NUMBER:

WARNING: THIS APPOINTMENT IS NOT EFFECTIVE UNTIL LETTERS HAVE ISSUED.

1. The petition for appointment of a temporary guardian came on for hearing as follows *(check boxes c–l to indicate personal presence):*
    a. Judicial officer *(name):*
    b. Hearing date: Time: ☐ Dept.:   ☐ Room:
    c. ☐ Petitioner *(name):*
    d. ☐ Attorney for petitioner *(name):*
    e. ☐ Minor *(name):*
    f. ☐ Attorney for minor *(name):*
    g. ☐ Minor's parents *(names):*
    h. ☐ Attorney for minor's parents *(names):*
    i. ☐ Person with valid visitation order *(name):*
    j. ☐ Attorney for person with valid visitation order *(name):*
    k. ☐ Public Guardian *(name):*
    l. ☐ Attorney for Public Guardian *(name):*

THE COURT FINDS

2. a. ☐ Notice of the time and place of hearing has been given as required by law.
    b. ☐ Notice of the time and place of hearing ☐ has been ☐ should be   dispensed with for *(names):*

3. It is necessary that a temporary guardian be appointed to ☐ provide for temporary care, maintenance, and support
    ☐ protect property from loss or injury ☐ pending the hearing on the petition for appointment of a general guardian.
    ☐ pending an appeal under Probate Code section 1301. ☐ during the suspension of powers of the guardian.

THE COURT ORDERS

4. a. ☐ *(Name):*

      (Address):   *(Telephone):*

      is appointed temporary guardian of the PERSON of *(name):*
      and Letters shall issue upon qualification.

   b. ☐ *(Name):*

      (Address):   *(Telephone):*

      is appointed temporary guardian of the ESTATE of *(name):*
      and Letters shall issue upon qualification.

Page 1 of 2

Form Adopted for Mandatory Use
Judicial Council of California
GC-140 [Rev. January 1, 2009]

ORDER APPOINTING TEMPORARY GUARDIAN
(Probate—Guardianships and Conservatorships)

Probate Code, §§ 2250–2254

TEMPORARY GUARDIANSHIP OF	CASE NUMBER:
(Name):	
MINOR	

5. ☐ Notice of hearing to the persons named in item 2b is dispensed with.

6. a. ☐ Bond is not required.

   b. ☐ Bond is fixed at: $ to be furnished by an authorized surety company or as otherwise
      provided by law.

   c. ☐ Deposits of: $ are ordered to be placed in a blocked account at *(specify institution and
      location):*

      and receipts shall be filed. No withdrawals shall be made without a court order. ☐ Additional orders in attachment 6c.

   d. ☐ The temporary guardian is not authorized to take possession of money or any other property without a specific court
      order.

7. ☐ In addition to the powers granted by law, the temporary guardian is granted other powers. These powers are specified

      ☐ in attachment 7. ☐ below *(specify):*

8. ☐ Other orders as specified in attachment 8 are granted.

9. ☐ Unless modified by further order of the court, this order expires on *(date):*

10. Number of boxes checked in items 4–9: _____

11. Number of pages attached: _____

Date:

_____
JUDICIAL OFFICER

☐ SIGNATURE FOLLOWS LAST ATTACHMENT

ORDER APPOINTING TEMPORARY GUARDIAN
(Probate—Guardianships and Conservatorships)

GC-150

SUPERIOR COURT OF CALIFORNIA, COUNTY OF

STREET ADDRESS:

MAILING ADDRESS:

CITY AND ZIP CODE:

BRANCH NAME:

FOR RECORDER'S USE ONLY

TEMPORARY ☐ GUARDIANSHIP ☐ CONSERVATORSHIP OF *(Name):* ☐ MINOR ☐ CONSERVATEE	CASE NUMBER:
LETTERS OF TEMPORARY ☐ GUARDIANSHIP ☐ CONSERVATORSHIP ☐ **Person** ☐ **Estate**	*FOR COURT USE ONLY*

LETTERS

1. *(Name):*

   is appointed temporary ☐ guardian ☐ conservator of the ☐ person

   ☐ estate of *(name):*

2. ☐ Other powers that have been granted or restrictions imposed on the temporary

   ☐ guardian ☐ conservator are ☐ specified in Attachment 2.

   ☐ specified below.

3. These Letters shall expire

   a. ☐ on *(date):*   or upon earlier issuance of Letters to a general guardian or conservator.

   b. ☐ on other date *(specify):*

4. ☐ The temporary ☐ guardian ☐ conservator is not authorized to take possession of money or any other property
   without a specific court order.

5. Number of pages attached: _____

WITNESS, clerk of the court, with seal of the court affixed.

(SEAL)	Date: Clerk, by _____ , Deputy

Page 1 of 2

This form may be recorded as notice of the establishment of a temporary conservatorship of the estate as provided in Probate Code section 1875.

Form Adopted for Mandatory Use
Judicial Council of California
GC-150 [Rev. January 1, 2009]

**LETTERS OF TEMPORARY GUARDIANSHIP OR
CONSERVATORSHIP**
(Probate—Guardianships and Conservatorships)

Probate Code, §§ 2250 et seq., 2890–2893;
Code of Civil Procedure, § 2015.6
www.courtinfo.ca.gov

TEMPORARY ☐ GUARDIANSHIP ☐ CONSERVATORSHIP OF	CASE NUMBER:
(Name):	
☐ MINOR ☐ CONSERVATEE	

NOTICE TO INSTITUTIONS AND FINANCIAL INSTITUTIONS
(Probate Code sections 2890–2893)

When these *Letters of Temporary Guardianship* or *Letters of Temporary Conservatorship* (Letters) are delivered to you as an employee or other representative of an *institution* or *financial institution* (described below) in order for the temporary guardian or temporary conservator of the estate (1) to take possession or control of an asset of the minor or conservatee named above held by your institution (including changing title, withdrawing all or any portion of the asset, or transferring all or any portion of the asset) or (2) to open or change the name of an account or a safe-deposit box in your financial institution to reflect the guardianship or conservatorship, you must fill out Judicial Council form GC-050 (for an institution) or form GC-051 (for a financial institution). An officer authorized by your institution or financial institution must date and sign the form, and you must file the completed form with the court.

There is no filing fee for filing the form. You may either arrange for personal delivery of the form or mail it to the court for filing at the address given for the court on page 1 of these Letters.

The temporary guardian or temporary conservator should deliver a blank copy of the appropriate form to you with these Letters, but it is your institution's or financial institution's responsibility to complete the correct form, have an authorized officer sign it, and file the completed form with the court. If the correct form is not delivered with these Letters or is unavailable for any other reason, blank copies of the forms may be obtained from the court. The forms may also be accessed from the judicial branch's public Web site free of charge. The Internet address (URL) is *www.courtinfo.ca.gov/forms/.* Select the form group *Probate—Guardianships and Conservatorships* and scroll down to form GC-050 for an institution or form GC-051 for a financial institution. The forms may be printed out as blank forms and filled in by typewriter (nonfillable form), or may be filled out online and printed out ready for signature and filing (fillable form).

An *institution* under California Probate Code section 2890(c) is an insurance company, insurance broker, insurance agent, investment company, investment bank, securities broker-dealer, investment advisor, financial planner, financial advisor, or any other person who takes, holds, or controls an asset subject to a conservatorship or guardianship other than a financial institution. Institutions must file a *Notice of Taking Possession or Control of an Asset of Minor or Conservatee* (form GC-050) for an asset of the minor or conservatee held by the institution. A single form may be filed for all affected assets held by the institution.

A *financial institution* under California Probate Code section 2892(b) is a bank, trust (including a Totten trust account but excluding other trust arrangements described in Probate Code section 82(b)), savings and loan association, savings bank, industrial bank, or credit union. Financial institutions must file a *Notice of Opening or Changing a Guardianship or Conservatorship Account or Safe-Deposit Box* (form GC-051) for an account or a safe deposit box held by the financial institution. A single form may be filed for all affected accounts or safe deposit boxes held by the financial institution.

LETTERS OF TEMPORARY ☐ GUARDIANSHIP ☐ CONSERVATORSHIP
AFFIRMATION

I solemnly affirm that I will perform according to law the duties of temporary ☐ guardian. ☐ conservator.

Executed on *(date):* , at *(place):*

▶

_____
(TYPE OR PRINT NAME)

_____
(SIGNATURE OF APPOINTEE)

CERTIFICATION

I certify that this document, including any attachments, is a correct copy of the original on file in my office and that the Letters issued to the person appointed above have not been revoked, annulled, or set aside and are still in full force and effect.

(SEAL)	Date:
	Clerk, by _____ , Deputy

LETTERS OF TEMPORARY GUARDIANSHIP OR CONSERVATORSHIP
(Probate—Guardianships and Conservatorships)

<table>
<tr>
<td>
PARTY WITHOUT AN ATTORNEY *(Name and Address):*

In Pro Per
</td>
<td>TELEPHONE NO:</td>
<td colspan="2">*FOR COURT USE ONLY*</td>
</tr>
<tr>
<td colspan="2">
NAME OF COURT:

STREET ADDRESS:

MAILING ADDRESS:

CITY AND ZIP CODE:

BRANCH NAME:
</td>
<td colspan="2"></td>
</tr>
<tr>
<td colspan="2">
GUARDIANSHIP OF THE PERSON OF (NAME):

MINOR
</td>
<td colspan="2"></td>
</tr>
<tr>
<td colspan="2">
**EX PARTE MOTION, DECLARATION, AND ORDER
EXTENDING TEMPORARY GUARDIANSHIP**
</td>
<td>CASE NUMBER</td>
<td></td>
</tr>
</table>

MOTION

Petitioner moves the court for an order extending the duration of the temporary guardianship of the person of _____
_____

This motion is made on the grounds that the temporary guardianship is due to expire before a regular guardian is appointed, and it would be in the best interests of the minor for the temporary guardianship to be extended for reasons set out in the declaration of the temporary guardian.

DECLARATION OF TEMPORARY GUARDIAN

1. Petitioner (name): _____ is the duly appointed, qualified, and
   acting temporary guardian of the person of _____.

2. Petitioner has been acting as temporary guardian since _____, _____.

3. The temporary guardianship is due to expire on _____, _____.

4. The hearing on the regular guardianship is set for _____, _____.

5. The best interests of the ward require the extension of the temporary guardianship until _____,
   _____, or for thirty days, whichever is sooner because:

I declare under penalty of perjury under the laws of the State of California that the foregoing is true and correct. Executed this _____ day of _____, _____ at _____, California.

....
(TYPE OR PRINT NAME)

_____
(SIGNATURE OF DECLARANT)

ORDER

The court having considered the motion and good cause appearing, IT IS ORDERED that the temporary guardianship of the person of _____ is extended until _____, _____, or for thirty days, whichever is sooner.

Dated:...

_____
(JUDGE OF THE SUPERIOR COURT)

<table>
<tr>
<td>ATTORNEY OR PARTY WITHOUT ATTORNEY (NAME AND ADDRESS):</td>
<td>TELEPHONE NO.:</td>
<td>FOR COURT USE ONLY</td>
</tr>
</table>

ATTORNEY FOR (NAME):

SUPERIOR COURT OF CALIFORNIA, COUNTY OF

STREET ADDRESS:

MAILING ADDRESS:

CITY AND ZIP CODE:

BRANCH NAME:

☐ GUARDIANSHIP ☐ CONSERVATORSHIP OF THE ☐ PERSON ☐ ESTATE
OF (NAME):

☐ Minor ☐ Conservatee

PROOF OF SERVICE BY MAIL OF
ORDER APPOINTING ☐ GUARDIAN ☐ CONSERVATOR

CASE NUMBER:

PROOF OF SERVICE BY MAIL
(Personal delivery also permitted. Probate Code, § 1466)

I am over the age of 18 and not a party to this cause. I am a resident of or employed in the county where the mailing occurred. My residence or business address is:

I served the Order Appointing ☐ Guardian ☐ Conservator by enclosing a true copy in a sealed envelope addressed to each person whose name and address is given below and depositing the envelope in the United States mail with the postage fully prepaid.

(1) Date of deposit: (2) Place of deposit (city and state):

I declare under penalty of perjury under the laws of the State of California that the foregoing is true and correct and that this declaration is executed on (date): . . . . at (place): . . . .

. . . .
(Type or print name)   (Signature of declarant)

NAME AND ADDRESS OF EACH PERSON TO WHOM NOTICE WAS MAILED

a. ☐ Ward 14 years of age or older:

b. ☐ Conservatee:

c.

☐ List of names and addresses continued in attachment.

PROOF OF SERVICE BY MAIL
OF ORDER APPOINTING
GUARDIAN OR CONSERVATOR

This agreement is made between _____,

conservator of the _____ of _____

and an officer of the Superior Court of California, County of _____. The officer of the Superior Court

of California, County of _____, is authorized to collect, sell, or otherwise apply the deposit to enforce the liability

of _____ on the deposit. The address at which _____ may be

served with notices, papers, and other documents is _____

_____.

_____   County of _____

Officer of the Court

_____   _____

Name and title   Date

_____   _____

Conservator   Date

ATTORNEY OR PARTY WITHOUT ATTORNEY *(Name, State Bar number, and address):*

FOR COURT USE ONLY

TELEPHONE NO.:   FAX NO. *(Optional):*

E-MAIL ADDRESS *(Optional):*

ATTORNEY FOR *(Name):*

SUPERIOR COURT OF CALIFORNIA, COUNTY OF

STREET ADDRESS:

MAILING ADDRESS:

CITY AND ZIP CODE:

BRANCH NAME:

☐ CONSERVATORSHIP ☐ GUARDIANSHIP OF THE PERSON ☐ AND ESTATE OF

(Name):

☐ CONSERVATEE ☐ MINOR

PRE-MOVE NOTICE OF PROPOSED CHANGE OF PERSONAL RESIDENCE OF

☐ **CONSERVATEE** ☐ **WARD** *(Name):*

CASE NUMBER:

INFORMATION FOR CONSERVATOR OR GUARDIAN OF THE PERSON:

(1) You must mail, **at least 15 days before the date of the proposed move** (unless you can show that an emergency requires a shorter time), a notice of your intention to change your conservatee's or ward's **personal residence** (his or her residence as defined in rules 7.1063(b) or 7.1013(b) of the Cal. Rules of Court) to the conservatee, the ward if 12 years of age or older, the conservatee's or ward's attorney; and **(a) in a conservatorship,** the conservatee's spouse or registered domestic partner; and the conservatee's relatives named in the petition for appointment of a conservator in your case (the conservatee's second-degree relatives, or if there are no spouse, registered domestic partner, and second-degree relatives, the persons named in Probate Code section 1821(b)(1)–(4) as the conservatee's "deemed relatives"); or **(b) in a guardianship**, the ward's parents; any person who had legal custody of the ward when the first petition for appointment of a guardian was filed in your case, the guardian of the ward's estate, and any person nominated as a guardian for the ward who was not appointed. **Use copies of this form for the notice described above. File the original of the notice form with the court and show proof of mailing. See page 2 of this form for proof of mailing. If there is more than one ward in your case, file and mail copies of a separate form for each ward moved.** (See rules 7.1013(a) and (b), or 7.1063(a) and (b) of the Cal. Rules of Court.)

(2) You must also give notice to the court and others, **after the move**, of any change in the conservatee's or ward's residence within the State of California. **Do not use this form for that notice.** Use form GC-080, *Post-Move Notice of Change of Residence of Conservatee or Ward,* for that notice. (See rules 7.1013(c)–(e), and 7.1063(c)–(e) of the Cal. Rules of Court.)

(3) You must obtain court permission **before** the conservatee or ward can move to a new residence outside California.

NOTICE IS GIVEN as follows:

1. I intend to change the above-named conservatee's or ward's personal residence on *(date):*

2. The conservatee's or ward's residence address after the move will be *(street address, including residence or facility name and room or apartment number, if any, and city, county, and zip code):*

3. The new residence will be a *(describe type of residence or facility, for example, single family residence; apartment or condominium; board and care, intermediate care, or skilled nursing):*

4. ☐ I cannot give at least 15 days' notice of this intended change because of the emergency described below *(specify):*

☐ Continued on Attachment 4. *(State name of this case, case number, and title of this form on the top of attached page.)*

Date:

I declare under penalty of perjury under the laws of the State of California that the foregoing is true and correct.

▶

_____
(TYPE OR PRINT NAME OF CONSERVATOR OR GUARDIAN)

_____
(SIGNATURE OF CONSERVATOR OR GUARDIAN)

Page 1 of 2

Form Adopted for Mandatory Use
Judicial Council of California
GC-079 [New January 1, 2008]

**PRE-MOVE NOTICE OF PROPOSED CHANGE OF
PERSONAL RESIDENCE OF CONSERVATEE OR WARD**
(Probate—Guardianships and Conservatorships)

Probate Code, § 2352
Cal. Rules of Court, rules 7.1013,
7.1063
www.courtinfo.ca.gov

CONSERVATORSHIP ☐ GUARDIANSHIP OF THE PERSON ☐ AND ESTATE OF	CASE NUMBER:
(Name):	
☐ CONSERVATEE ☐ MINOR	

PROOF OF MAILING

1. I am over the age of 18. I am the appointed conservator or guardian of the above-named conservatee or ward, the conservator's or guardian's attorney, or an employee of the attorney. I am a resident of or employed in the county where the mailing occurred.

2. My residence or business address is *(specify):*

3. I mailed the foregoing *Pre-Move Notice of Proposed Change of Personal Residence of Conservatee or Ward* to each person named below by enclosing a copy in an envelope addressed as shown below AND

   a. ☐ **depositing** the sealed envelope on the date and at the place shown in item 4 with the United States Postal Service with the postage fully prepaid.

   b. ☐ **placing** the envelope for collection and mailing on the date and at the place shown in item 4 following our ordinary business practices. I am readily familiar with this business's practice for collecting and processing correspondence for mailing. On the same day that correspondence is placed for collection and mailing, it is deposited in the ordinary course of business with the United States Postal Service in a sealed envelope with postage fully prepaid.

4. a. Date mailed: b. Place mailed *(city, state):*

I declare under penalty of perjury under the laws of the State of California that the foregoing is true and correct.

Date:

▶

_____
(TYPE OR PRINT NAME OF PERSON COMPLETING THIS FORM)

_____
(SIGNATURE OF PERSON COMPLETING THIS FORM)

NAME AND ADDRESS OF EACH PERSON TO WHOM NOTICE WAS MAILED

	Name and relationship to conservatee or ward	Address *(number, street, city, state, and zip code)*
1.	Conservatee or ward at least 12 years of age	
2.	Attorney for conservatee or ward	
3.	Spouse or domestic partner of conservatee	
4.	Parent of ward	
5.	Parent of ward	

☐ Continued on an attachment. *(You may use form GC-079 (MA) to show additional addressees.)*

GC-079 [New January 1, 2008]

PRE-MOVE NOTICE OF PROPOSED CHANGE OF
PERSONAL RESIDENCE OF CONSERVATEE OR WARD
(Probate—Guardianships and Conservatorships)

Page 2 of 2

| ☐ CONSERVATORSHIP | ☐ GUARDIANSHIP | OF THE PERSON | ☐ AND ESTATE | OF | CASE NUMBER: |

(Name):

☐ CONSERVATEE   ☐ MINOR

ATTACHMENT TO PRE-MOVE NOTICE OF PROPOSED CHANGE OF
PERSONAL RESIDENCE OF CONSERVATEE OR WARD

(This attachment is for use with form GC-079.)

NAME AND ADDRESS OF EACH PERSON TO WHOM NOTICE WAS MAILED

Name and relationship to conservatee or ward	Address *(number, street, city, state, and zip code)*
___ Relationship:	
___ Relationship:	
___ Relationship:	
___ Relationship:	
___ Relationship:	
___ Relationship:	
___ Relationship:	
___ Relationship:	
___ Relationship:	

Page _____ of _____

Form Approved for Optional Use
Judicial Council of California
GC-079(MA) [New January 1, 2008]

ATTACHMENT TO PRE-MOVE NOTICE OF PROPOSED CHANGE OF
PERSONAL RESIDENCE OF CONSERVATEE OR WARD
(Probate—Guardianships and Conservatorships)

ATTORNEY OR PARTY WITHOUT ATTORNEY *(Name, State Bar number, and address):*

FOR COURT USE ONLY

TELEPHONE NO.: FAX NO. *(Optional):*

E-MAIL ADDRESS *(Optional):*

ATTORNEY FOR *(Name):*

SUPERIOR COURT OF CALIFORNIA, COUNTY OF

STREET ADDRESS:

MAILING ADDRESS:

CITY AND ZIP CODE:

BRANCH NAME:

☐ CONSERVATORSHIP ☐ GUARDIANSHIP OF THE PERSON ☐ AND ESTATE OF

(Name):

☐ CONSERVATEE ☐ MINOR

POST-MOVE NOTICE OF CHANGE OF RESIDENCE OF ☐ **CONSERVATEE**

☐ **WARD** *(Name):*

CASE NUMBER:

INFORMATION FOR CONSERVATOR OR GUARDIAN OF THE PERSON:

(1) Every time your conservatee or ward moves to a new residence in California, you must, **within 30 days of the date of the move,** give written notice of the change to the court and, unless the court excuses you for good cause to prevent harm to the conservatee or ward, mail a copy of the notice to the attorney for the conservatee or ward; and **(a) in a conservatorship,** mail copies of the notice to the conservatee's spouse or registered domestic partner and the conservatee's relatives named in the petition for appointment of a conservator in your case (the conservatee's second-degree relatives, or if there is no spouse, registered domestic partner, and second-degree relatives, the persons named in Probate Code section 1821(b)(1)–(4) as the conservatee's "deemed relatives"); or **(b) in a guardianship,** mail copies of the notice to the ward's parents, any person who had legal custody of the ward when the first petition for appointment of a guardian was filed in your case, the guardian of the ward's estate, and any person nominated as a guardian for the ward who was not appointed.

(2) **Use this form for the notice described above.** Do not mail a copy to the conservatee or ward. To give notice to the court, file the original of this form after filling out the proof of mailing on the second page. (See rules 7.1013(c) and (d), or 7.1063(c) and (d) of the Cal. Rules of Court.) If there is more than one ward in your case, file and mail copies of a separate form for each ward moved.

(3) You must also give notice, **before the move,** of an intent to move the conservatee or ward from his or her personal residence (as defined in rules 7.1063(b) and 7.1013(b) of the Cal. Rules of Court). **Do not use this form for that notice.** Use form GC-079, *Pre-Move Notice of Proposed Change of Personal Residence of Conservatee or Ward,* for that notice.

(4) You must obtain court permission **before** the conservatee or ward can move to a new residence outside California.

NOTICE IS GIVEN as follows:

1. On *(date):* the conservatee or ward named above moved to the residence described in item 2.

2. New address *(street address, city, county, and zip code):*

Telephone number: Other contact telephone number, if any *(if none, write "None"):*

3. ☐ *(Check this box if this case is a conservatorship.)* The conservatee's new residence identified in 2 is the least restrictive appropriate residence that is available to meet his or her needs and is in the conservatee's best interest.

Date:

I declare under penalty of perjury under the laws of the State of California that the foregoing is true and correct.

▶

_____
(TYPE OR PRINT NAME OF CONSERVATOR OR GUARDIAN)

_____
(SIGNATURE OF CONSERVATOR OR GUARDIAN)

Page 1 of 2

Form Adopted for Mandatory Use
Judicial Council of California
GC-080 [Rev. January 1, 2008]

**POST-MOVE NOTICE OF CHANGE OF RESIDENCE
OF CONSERVATEE OR WARD**
(Probate—Guardianships and Conservatorships)

Probate Code, § 2352
Cal. Rules of Court, rules 7.1013, 7.1063
www.courtinfo.ca.gov

☐ CONSERVATORSHIP ☐ GUARDIANSHIP OF THE PERSON ☐ AND ESTATE OF	CASE NUMBER:
(Name): ☐ CONSERVATEE ☐ MINOR	

PROOF OF MAILING

1. I am over the age of 18. I am the appointed conservator or guardian of the above-named conservatee or ward, the conservator's or guardian's attorney, or an employee of the attorney. I am a resident of or employed in the county where the mailing occurred.

2. My residence or business address is *(specify):*

3. I mailed the foregoing *Post-Move Notice of Change of Residence of Conservatee or Ward* to each person named below by enclosing a copy in an envelope addressed as shown below AND

   a. ☐ **depositing** the sealed envelope on the date and at the place shown in item 4 with the United States Postal Service with the postage fully prepaid.

   b. ☐ **placing** the envelope for collection and mailing on the date and at the place shown in item 4 following our ordinary business practices. I am readily familiar with this business's practice for collecting and processing correspondence for mailing. On the same day that correspondence is placed for collection and mailing, it is deposited in the ordinary course of business with the United States Postal Service in a sealed envelope with postage fully prepaid.

4. a. Date mailed: b. Place mailed *(city, state):*

I declare under penalty of perjury under the laws of the State of California that the foregoing is true and correct.

Date:

_____   ▶ _____
(TYPE OR PRINT NAME OF PERSON COMPLETING THIS FORM)   (SIGNATURE OF PERSON COMPLETING THIS FORM)

NAME AND ADDRESS OF EACH PERSON TO WHOM NOTICE WAS MAILED

Name and relationship to conservatee or ward	Address *(number, street, city, state, and zip code)*
1. Attorney for conservatee or ward	
2. Spouse or registered domestic partner of conservatee	
3. Parent of ward	
4. Parent of ward	
5. Person with legal custody of ward at beginning of this proceeding	

☐ Continued on an attachment. *(You may use form GC-080(MA) to show additional addressees.)*

GC-080 [Rev. January 1, 2008]

POST-MOVE NOTICE OF CHANGE OF RESIDENCE OF CONSERVATEE OR WARD
(Probate—Guardianships and Conservatorships)

☐ CONSERVATORSHIP ☐ GUARDIANSHIP OF THE PERSON ☐ AND ESTATE OF	CASE NUMBER:
(Name):	
☐ CONSERVATEE ☐ MINOR	

ATTACHMENT TO POST-MOVE NOTICE OF CHANGE OF RESIDENCE OF CONSERVATEE OR WARD

(This attachment is for use with form GC-080.)

NAME AND ADDRESS OF EACH PERSON TO WHOM NOTICE WAS MAILED

Name and relationship to conservatee or ward	Address *(number, street, city, state, and zip code)*
Relationship:	
Relationship:	
Relationship:	
Relationship:	
Relationship:	
Relationship:	
Relationship:	
Relationship:	
Relationship:	

Page _____ of _____

Form Approved for Optional Use
Judicial Council of California
GC-080(MA) [New January 1, 2008]

**ATTACHMENT TO POST-MOVE NOTICE OF
CHANGE OF RESIDENCE OF CONSERVATEE OR WARD
(Probate—Guardianships and Conservatorships)**

NAME OF COURT:

STREET ADDRESS:

MAILING ADDRESS:

CITY AND ZIP CODE:

BRANCH NAME:

GUARDIANSHIP OF THE ☐ PERSON ☐ ESTATE OF (NAME):

MINOR

PETITION FOR TRANSFER OF GUARDIANSHIP PROCEEDING

CASE NUMBER:

1. Petitioner (name): _____ requests that this guardianship proceeding be transferred to the Superior Court of the State of California, County of _____.
   Such transfer would be in the best interests of the ward for the following reason(s):

2. Petitioner is the ☐ guardian or ☐ proposed guardian of the:
   ☐ person ☐ estate of _____.

3. ☐ Petitioner is the ☐ guardian or ☐ proposed guardian of the estate in this proceeding. The character, value, and location of the estate's property:
   a. ☐ is as follows:

   b. ☐ is described in Attachment 3a.

4. The guardian's name and address are: _____
   _____

5. The ward's name and address are: _____
   _____

6. The names, residence addresses, and relationships of the ward's father, mother, spouse, and all relatives within the second degree of the ward so far as known to petitioner are as follows:
   a. Father: _____
   b. Mother: _____
   c. Spouse: _____
   d. _____
   e. ☐ List of names and addresses continued as Attachment 6.

7. A request for special notice:
   a. ☐ has not been filed.
   b. ☐ has been filed, and notice of hearing on this petition will be given by law to: _____
   _____

8. Petitioner requests an order transferring this proceeding to the Superior Court of the State of California, County of
   _____.

I declare under penalty of perjury under the laws of the State of California that the foregoing is true and correct.

Date:

....
(TYPE OR PRINT NAME)

_____
(SIGNATURE OF PETITIONER)

<table>
<tr><td>PARTY WITHOUT AN ATTORNEY (Name and Address):

In Pro Per</td><td>TELEPHONE NO:</td><td>FOR COURT USE ONLY</td></tr>
</table>

NAME OF COURT:
STREET ADDRESS:
MAILING ADDRESS:
CITY AND ZIP CODE:
BRANCH NAME:

GUARDIANSHIP OF THE ☐ PERSON ☐ ESTATE OF (NAME):

MINOR

ORDER FOR TRANSFER OF GUARDIANSHIP PROCEEDING

CASE NUMBER:

1. The Petition for Transfer of Guardianship Proceeding came on for hearing as follows (check boxes c, d, and e to indicate personal presence):

    a. Judge (name):

    b. Hearing Date: Time: ☐ Dept: ☐ Div.:   ☐ Room:

    c. ☐ Petitioner (name):

    d. ☐ Attorney for petitioner (name):

    e. ☐ Attorney for ward (name, address, and telephone):

2. THE COURT FINDS

    a. ☐ all notices required by law have been given.

    b. Transfer of the Guardianship of_____ ,

    Case Number _____, from this court to the Superior Court of the State of California,

    County of _____, is in the best interests of the ward.

3. THE COURT ORDERS that this proceeding be transferred to the Superior Court of the State of California, County of

    _____.

Dated: ....   _____

                                                                        (JUDGE OF THE SUPERIOR COURT)

ATTORNEY OR PARTY WITHOUT ATTORNEY *(Name, State Bar number, and address):*

FOR COURT USE ONLY

TELEPHONE NO.:　　　　　　　　　　FAX NO. *(Optional):*

E-MAIL ADDRESS *(Optional):*

ATTORNEY FOR *(Name):*

SUPERIOR COURT OF CALIFORNIA, COUNTY OF

STREET ADDRESS:

MAILING ADDRESS:

CITY AND ZIP CODE:

BRANCH NAME:

GUARDIANSHIP OF THE ☐ PERSON ☐ ESTATE OF *(Name):*

MINOR

CASE NUMBER:

PETITION FOR TERMINATION OF GUARDIANSHIP

HEARING DATE AND TIME:　　　DEPT.:

1. Petitioner *(name):*　　　　　　　　　　　　　　　　　　　　**requests that**
   a. ☐　the guardianship of the PERSON of *(minor):*　　　　　be terminated.
   b. ☐　the guardianship of the ESTATE of *(minor):*　　　　　be terminated.
      (1) ☐　The estate has been entirely exhausted through expenditures or disbursements (Probate Code, § 2626).
      (2) ☐　The estate falls within the provisions of Probate Code section 2628(b) (small estate), and no accounts have been required.
      (3) ☐　Other *(specify):*

2. Petitioner is the ☐ minor ☐ minor's guardian ☐ minor's parent.

3. ☐ *(Name):*　　　　　　　　　　　　　　　　　　　was appointed guardian of the PERSON
   of the minor named in item 1a on *(date):*　　　　.

4. ☐ *(Name):*　　　　　　　　　　　　　　　　　　　was appointed guardian of the ESTATE
   of the minor named in item 1b on *(date):*　　　　.

5. It is in the best interest of the minor that the guardianship of the ☐ person ☐ estate be terminated for the reasons
   ☐ stated in Attachment 5 ☐ stated below *(specify):*

6. A request for special notice
   a. ☐　has not been filed.
   b. ☐　has been filed and notice will be given to *(names):*

7. ☐　Notice to the persons identified in Attachment 7 should be dispensed with because
   a. ☐　they cannot with reasonable diligence be given notice *(specify names and efforts to locate in Attachment 7).*
   b. ☐　other good cause exists to dispense with notice *(specify names and reasons in Attachment 7).*

8. ☐　Petitioner is the minor's guardian. Petitioner requests reasonable visitation with the minor after termination of the
   guardianship as specified in Attachment 8. A completed *Declaration Under Uniform Child Custody Jurisdiction and
   Enforcement Act (UCCJEA)* (form FL-105/GC-120) is also attached.

NOTICE: **This guardianship will terminate automatically when the child reaches age 18. No petition or court order is necessary to terminate the guardianship at that time. Nevertheless, if this is a guardianship of the estate, termination of the guardianship does not eliminate the requirement that a final report or account must be filed. (See Prob. Code, § 1600.)**

Page 1 of 2

Form Adopted for Mandatory Use
Judicial Council of California
GC-255 [Rev. January 1, 2006]

PETITION FOR TERMINATION OF GUARDIANSHIP
(Probate—Guardianships and Conservatorships)

Probate Code §§ 1460,
1601, 2626, 2627, 2636
www.courtinfo.ca.gov

GUARDIANSHIP OF THE ☐ PERSON ☐ ESTATE OF *(Name):* MINOR	CASE NUMBER:

9. The names and residence addresses of the guardian, minor, and minor's parents, brothers, sisters, and grandparents are *(specify):*

    a. Guardian:

    b. Minor:

    c. Father:

    d. Mother:

    e. Brother or sister:

    f. Brother or sister:

    g. Brother or sister:

    h. Maternal grandfather:

    i. Maternal grandmother:

    j. Paternal grandfather:

    k. Paternal grandmother:

    l. ☐ Additional names and addresses continued on Attachment 9.

10. Number of pages attached: _____

Date:

            ▶
            (SIGNATURE OF ATTORNEY OR PETITIONER WITHOUT AN ATTORNEY *)

* (Signature of all petitioners also required (Prob. Code, § 1020).)

I declare under penalty of perjury under the laws of the State of California that the foregoing is true and correct.
Date:

_____   ▶
      (TYPE OR PRINT NAME)   (SIGNATURE OF PETITIONER)

_____   ▶
      (TYPE OR PRINT NAME)   (SIGNATURE OF PETITIONER)

CONSENT TO TERMINATION AND WAIVER OF SERVICE AND NOTICE OF HEARING

11. ☐ I consent to the termination of the guardianship of the ☐ person ☐ estate of the minor and waive service of a copy of, and notice of the hearing on, this petition.

Date: _____ _____ ▶
                 (TYPE OR PRINT NAME)   (SIGNATURE OF ☐ MINOR * ☐ GUARDIAN ☐ PARENT ☐ OTHER)

Date: _____ _____ ▶
                 (TYPE OR PRINT NAME)   (SIGNATURE OF ☐ MINOR * ☐ GUARDIAN ☐ PARENT ☐ OTHER)

Date: _____ _____ ▶
                 (TYPE OR PRINT NAME)   (SIGNATURE OF ☐ MINOR * ☐ GUARDIAN ☐ PARENT ☐ OTHER)

Date: _____ _____ ▶
                 (TYPE OR PRINT NAME)   (SIGNATURE OF ☐ MINOR * ☐ GUARDIAN ☐ PARENT ☐ OTHER)

☐ Additional signatures on Attachment 11.

                                * Minor over 12 years of age.

ATTORNEY OR PARTY WITHOUT ATTORNEY *(Name, State Bar number, and address)*:

FOR COURT USE ONLY

TELEPHONE NO.:   FAX NO. *(Optional)*:

E-MAIL ADDRESS *(Optional)*:

ATTORNEY FOR *(Name)*:

SUPERIOR COURT OF CALIFORNIA, COUNTY OF

STREET ADDRESS:

MAILING ADDRESS:

CITY AND ZIP CODE:

BRANCH NAME:

GUARDIANSHIP OF THE ☐ PERSON ☐ ESTATE OF

(Name):

MINOR

ORDER TERMINATING GUARDIANSHIP	CASE NUMBER:

1. The petition to terminate the guardianship came on for hearing as follows *(check boxes c–l to indicate personal presence)*:

   a. Judicial Officer *(name)*:

   b. Hearing date: Time: ☐ Dept.   ☐ Rm.:

   c. ☐ Petitioner *(name)*:

   d. ☐ Attorney for petitioner *(name)*:

   e. ☐ Minor *(name)*:

   f. ☐ Attorney for minor *(name)*:

   g. ☐ Guardian of the person *(name)*:

   h. ☐ Attorney for guardian of the person *(name)*:

   i. ☐ Guardian of the estate *(name)*:

   j. ☐ Attorney for guardian of the estate *(name)*:

   k. ☐ Parent of minor *(name)*:

   l. ☐ Attorney for parent *(name)*:

THE COURT FINDS

2. a. ☐ All notices required by law have been given.

   b. ☐ Notice of hearing ☐ has been ☐ should be dispensed with to the following persons *(specify)*:

   c. ☐ It is in the minor's best interest to terminate the guardianship of the PERSON.

   d. ☐ It is in the minor's best interest to terminate the guardianship of the ESTATE.

       (1) ☐ The estate has been entirely exhausted through expenditures or disbursements (Prob. Code, § 2626).

       (2) ☐ The estate falls within the provisions of Probate Code section 2628(b) (small estate), and no accounts have been required.

       (3) ☐ Other reasons *(specify)*:

THE COURT ORDERS

3. ☐ The guardianship of the PERSON of *(minor)*:   is terminated.

4. ☐ The guardianship of the ESTATE of *(minor)*:   is terminated.

5. ☐ Notice of hearing to the persons named in item 2b is dispensed with.

6. ☐ Visitation between the minor and the guardian ☐ of the person ☐ of the estate is ordered as provided in Attachment 6.

7. ☐ Other *(specify)*:

☐ Continued on Attachment 7.

Date:

_____
JUDICIAL OFFICER

☐ Signature follows last attachment.

Page 1 of 1

Form Adopted for Mandatory Use
Judicial Council of California
GC-260 [Rev. January 1, 2006]

ORDER TERMINATING GUARDIANSHIP
(Probate—Guardianships and Conservatorships)

Probate Code §§ 1601–1602,
2626–2628
www.courtinfo.ca.gov

Index

T

 **NOLO** *Keep Up to Date*

 1 Go to Nolo.com/newsletters to sign up for free newsletters and discounts on Nolo products.

- **Nolo Briefs.** Our monthly email newsletter with great deals and free information.

- **Nolo's Special Offer.** A monthly newsletter with the biggest Nolo discounts around.

- **BizBriefs.** Tips and discounts on Nolo products for business owners and managers.

- **Landlord's Quarterly.** Deals and free tips just for landlords and property managers, too.

 2 Don't forget to check for updates at **Nolo.com.** Under "Products," find this book and click "Legal Updates."

Let Us Hear From You

3 Register your Nolo product and give us your feedback at Nolo.com/book-registration.

- Once you've registered, you qualify for technical support if you have any trouble with a download or CD (though most folks don't).

- We'll also drop you an email when a new edition of your book is released—and we'll send you a coupon for 15% off your next Nolo.com order!

GB8

 **NOLO** **Lawyer Directory**

Find a Family Law Attorney

- *Qualified lawyers*
- *In-depth profiles*
- *A pledge of respectful service*

If you have questions about family law, it's important to get the right answers—fast. Whether you're looking for help with divorce, child custody, prenuptial agreements, marriage, living together or adoption, you need a lawyer who will provide expert advice you can rely on.

Nolo's Lawyer Directory is designed to help you search for the right attorney. Lawyers in our program are in good standing with the State Bar Association and have created extensive profiles that feature their professional histories, credentials, legal philosophies, fees and more. Many will review Nolo documents, such as a will or living trust, for a fixed fee. They all pledge to work diligently and respectfully with clients—communicating regularly, providing a written agreement about how legal matters will be handled, sending clear and detailed bills and more.